The Public Relations Strategic Toolkit

The Public Relations Strategic Toolkit presents guidance to instruct and educate students and professionals of public relations and corporate communications. Alison Theaker and Heather Yaxley cover every aspect of critical practice, including definitions of public relations, key theoretical concepts and both original and established methodological approaches. Case studies and interviews are featured to provide real-world context and advice for professional development. The new edition is fully revised with brand new case studies and updated content which reflect significant developments in theory and contemporary practice. It puts particular emphasis on the use of technology (including automation) and social media in current public relations planning, corporate communications and stakeholder engagement.

The book is divided into four parts; covering the profession, corporate communication and stakeholder engagement.

Features include:

- definitions of key terms
- contemporary case studies
- interviews with practitioners
- handy checklists
- practical activities and assignments.

By combining theory and practice, with an invaluable insight from experts in the field, this guide will introduce readers to all the professional skills needed for a career in public relations.

Alison Theaker has over 30 years' experience in public relations as a practitioner, academic and author. She has taught public relations, marketing communications and management in the UK and US. She is the editor of the bestselling textbook, *The Public Relations Handbook*. A Fellow of the Chartered Institute of Public Relations (CIPR), she now runs her own business coaching and training consultancy, The Spark, as well as continuing to teach at undergraduate and postgraduate level for Birmingham City University and Plymouth University, UK.

Heather Yaxley is a rhizomatic academic-educator-consultant-practitioner with a range of interests across public relations, reflective practice and sustainable professional development. She is a CIPR Fellow and Accredited Practitioner, as well as an honorary member and director of the Motor Industry Public Affairs Association Ltd. In 2017, Heather completed her PhD at Bournemouth University, researching career strategies within public relations. She is an experienced university lecturer, a course director for the CIPR qualifications with PR Academy and her academic work has been extensively published. Heather works closely with a number of clients, having established Applause Consultancy in 2000. She blogs at PR Conversations and participates in social media under the name Greenbanana.

The Public Relations Strategic Toolkit

An Essential Guide to Successful Public Relations Practice

Second Edition

Alison Theaker and
Heather Yaxley

Routledge
Taylor & Francis Group

LONDON AND NEW YORK

Second edition published 2018
by Routledge
2 Park Square, Milton Park, Abingdon, Oxon OX14 4RN

and by Routledge
711 Third Avenue, New York, NY 10017

Routledge is an imprint of the Taylor & Francis Group, an informa business

First edition published by Routledge 2013

British Library Cataloguing-in-Publication Data
A catalogue record for this book is available from the British Library

Library of Congress Cataloging-in-Publication Data
Names: Theaker, Alison, author. |
Yaxley, Heather, 1971- author.
Title: The public relations strategic toolkit : an essential guide to successful
public relations practice / Alison Theaker and Heather Yaxley.
Description: Second Edition. |
New York : Routledge, [2017] |
Revised edition of the authors' The public relations strategic toolkit, 2012. |
Includes bibliographical references and index.
Identifiers: LCCN 2017016046|
ISBN 9781138678651 (hardback : alk. paper) |
ISBN 9781138678675 (pbk. : alk. paper) |
ISBN 9781315558790 (ebook) Subjects:
LCSH: Corporations–Public relations. |
Business communication.
Classification: LCC HD59 .T4744 2017 |
DDC 659.2–dc23 LC record available at https://lccn.loc.gov/2017016046

ISBN: 978-1-138-67865-1 (hbk)
ISBN: 978-1-138-67867-5 (pbk)
ISBN: 978-1-315-55879-0 (ebk)

Typeset in Helvetica Neue and Avant Garde
by Sunrise Setting Ltd., Brixham, UK

Contents

Figures

Tables

Acknowledgements

FIGURES

5.1   Heather Yaxley
5.2   Heather Yaxley
6.1   Based on M. Saunders, P. Lewis and A. Thornhill, *Research Methods for Business Students*, 2nd edition. Harlow: FT/Prentice Hall, 2000.
7.1   Adapted from F.W. Anderson, L. Hadley, D. Rockland and M. Weiner, *Guidelines for Setting Measurable Public Relations Objectives: An Update.* Gainesville, FL: Institute for Public Relations, 1999.
7.2   Heather Yaxley
7.3   Heather Yaxley
7.4   Heather Yaxley
8.1   Heather Yaxley
8.2   Heather Yaxley
8.3   Heather Yaxley
8.4   Heather Yaxley
8.5   Heather Yaxley
8.6   Heather Yaxley
9.1   Adapted from S.R. Covey, *The Seven Habits of Highly Effective People: Restoring the Character Ethic.* London: Simon and Schuster, 1989.
9.2   Heather Yaxley
9.3   Heather Yaxley
10.1   Heather Yaxley
11.1   Courtesy of Plymouth University
11.2   Courtesy of Plymouth University
11.3   Courtesy of the Devon Air Ambulance Trust
11.4   Courtesy of the Devon Air Ambulance Trust
11.5   Courtesy of the Devon Air Ambulance Trust
12.1   Courtesy of Beach Schools South West

TABLES

Part I

The profession

Introduction

Alison Theaker

This book is intended to be a kind of 'how to' book with brains for public relations practitioners. So whilst it includes theoretical concepts and discussions about the nature of public relations, it is also full of examples of real-life good practice. When we were discussing how this could be different from its sister book, *The Public Relations Handbook,* we were clear that we wanted it to be of use to those in the field. We both believe that theory improves practice, but it is not the whole story. We are happy to be making changes and updating this second edition.

You will find that each chapter is set out with the same headings. Starting with a Check Point to tell you what is in it, there will be Talking Points to flag up related issues and a Reading Point to direct you to other sources if you want to look at this area in more detail. There will also be several Action Points in each chapter, detailing the experience of practitioners so you can see how these issues might look in practice. The End Point will review what has been covered.

When I started in PR practice in 1982, I was not aware of the range of textbooks available to me that might have helped me perform my job better. Indeed, I was surprised to find a whole shelf of them in the library when I started as the first lecturer on the new BA in Public Relations at the then Leeds Polytechnic (now Leeds Carnegie University). One of the questions that I was asked at interview was, 'What is the difference between education and training?'

Experience and training are good, but by definition they are looking at what has gone before. They are valuable but not the whole story. Education, using theory to try and see why something worked on a deeper level, is vital in enabling us to apply the lessons of experience. It gives us more ways of looking beneath the surface of what happened to us, a variety of lenses through which to view an event. It allows us to use different language when we talk to board members, we can see that we may have been using communication or management theory without being aware of it. We can be critical of our profession and so we can change it. It gives us more tools than just learning on the job. Taking time out to examine our own practice also means we can become objective about what works.

The competence of practitioners was raised in the DTI study in 2003, and is what the many qualifications in PR are trying to address. Any profession will always be judged by the few who don't fulfil the required standards rather than the many who do. However, the willingness of more and more graduates to enter PR, the expansion of both academic and professional courses in the discipline, the ever growing body of knowledge coming from practitioners and academics willing to look at the theory underpinning their practice show the increased willingness of PR to be reflective.

This first Part starts by introducing public relations and looking at some different definitions. Traditionally, this has been a difficult area for practitioners, as everyone seems to have their own idea of what public relations is. By comparing PR to other related professions and business functions such as advertising, marketing and journalism, the picture hopefully gets clearer.

The second chapter investigates exactly what PR practitioners do, looking at the various roles they might play in an organisation, as well as listing the tasks that they perform. This is built on in Chapter 3, which gives an overview of the PR industry in the UK and looks at the various professional bodies who are striving to improve the reputation of public relations.

Finally, Part I is completed with a look at the question of professionalisation and issues affecting the development of public relations. Several prominent academics and practitioners have been asked for their views on the challenges facing the industry in the next five years.

CHAPTER 1

What is public relations?

Alison Theaker

This chapter provides an introduction to public relations and outlines its relationship to journalism, marketing, advertising, promotion and publicity. Practical examples are included to show what PR does and how it works in organisations.

CHECK POINT

After reading this chapter, you should be able to:

- Compare various definitions of public relations
- Assess criticisms of public relations
- Distinguish public relations from journalism, marketing and advertising.

DEFINITIONS

What are your initial impressions of public relations? Perhaps you think it is about organising parties, promoting pop bands, getting press coverage and launching exciting new products. Or maybe you believe it's all about politics – writing speeches, announcing new policies, handling awkward questions or 'spinning' difficult situations. Clearly there are different views of what public relations is – which is why it is important to consider definitions, identify areas of debate and look to establish a common understanding.

Grunig and Hunt (1984) believe Dorman Eaton, a lawyer, was the first to use the term 'public relations' in addressing the Yale Law School on 'The Public Relations and Duties of the Legal Profession' in 1882. The meaning – looking out for the welfare of the public – was reflected by Theodore Vail, president of the American Telephone & Telegraph Co. in the theme of the company's annual report in 1908. How does this use reflect usage of the term today?

In 1976, Rex Harlow gathered 472 definitions of public relations and many hundreds more have been proposed subsequently. Faced with so many opinions, you may feel that John Marston's 1963 view of PR is still true today: 'a brotherhood of some 100,000 whose common bond is its profession and whose common woe is that no two of them can ever quite agree on what that profession is' (cited in Hutton, 1999). Indeed, there is robust debate over whether PR is indeed a profession (L'Etang and Pieczka, 2006a).

Some definitions of public relations are **positivist**; that is, they are based on explaining what is involved in the practice of public relations, or what it achieves within organisations. Others are **normative** and state a vision of what PR should be. Any difference between positivist and normative definitions reveals disagreements about whether the reality of PR lives up to the ideals or aspirations for its practice.

Definitions are also useful in clarifying what public relations is not, distinguishing it from other functions where there may be some confusion. It is important to remember that those who present definitions are putting across their own view of what PR is, should be or is not. They are seeking to persuade, not simply explain or inform. A definition also needs to be put into a social context, since meaning may change over time or be culturally dependent. This can be seen when reviewing different definitions or views of public relations:

- 'Public relations is a distinctive management function which helps establish and maintain mutual lines of communication, understanding, acceptance and cooperation between an organisation and its publics; involves the management of problems or issues; helps management to keep informed on and responsive to public opinion; defines and emphasises the responsibility of management to serve the public interest; helps management keep abreast of and effectively utilise change, serving as an early warning system to help anticipate trends; and uses research and ethical communication techniques as its principal tools.' (Harlow, 1976)
- 'Public Relations is the art and social science of analysing trends, predicting their consequences, counselling organisation's leadership, and implementing

planned programs of action which will serve both the organisation's and the public interest.' (1st World Assembly of Public Relations, Mexico 1978)

- 'Public relations helps our complex, pluralistic society to reach decisions and function more effectively by contributing to mutual understanding among groups and institutions. It serves to bring private and public policies into harmony.' (Public Relations Society of America, first adopted in 1982)

- 'Public Relations is the management of communications between an organization and its publics.' (Grunig and Hunt, 1984)

- 'Public relations is about reputation – the result of what you do, what you say and what others say about you. Public relations is the discipline which looks after reputation, with the aim of earning understanding and support and influencing opinion and behaviour. It is the planned and sustained effort to establish and maintain goodwill and mutual understanding between an organisation and its publics.' (Chartered Institute of Public Relations, first proposed in 1987)

- 'Public relations is the strategic management of relationships between an organization and its diverse publics, through the use of communication, to achieve mutual understanding, realize organizational goals and serve the public interest.' (CPRS, 2008)

- 'Public relations is about building and managing relationships. Our role is to assemble and navigate the complex and ambiguous relationships required to operate either as an organisation or as individuals living and working in our fragmenting environment.' (Catherine Arrow, 2008)

- 'Public relations is the occupation responsible for the management of organisational relationships and reputation. It encompasses issues management, public affairs, corporate communications, stakeholder relations, risk communication and corporate social responsibility. Public relations operates on behalf of many different types of organisation both at the governmental and corporate level, to small business and voluntary sectors. Public relations arises at points of societal change and resistance.' (L'Etang, 2009)

- 'PR practitioners:

  - Participate in defining organisational values, principles, strategies, policies and processes.

  - Apply social networking, research skills and tools to interpret stakeholders' and society's expectations as a basis for decisions.

  - Deliver timely analysis and recommendations for an effective governance of stakeholder relationships by enhancing transparency, trustworthy behaviour, authentic and verifiable representation, thus sustaining the organisation's "licence to operate".

  - Create an internal listening culture, an open system that allows the organisation to anticipate, adapt and respond.' (Stockholm Accords, 2010)

ACTION POINT

What do you think is the purpose of these definitions or views of public relations? Are they positivist and/or normative? Which clarify your understanding? In what way do they distinguish PR from other functions? Do you agree or disagree with the viewpoints expressed?

TALKING POINT

In 2011–12, the Public Relations Society of America (PRSA) invited people to submit their own definitions of public relations. A shortlist was voted upon and the winner was:

'Public relations is a strategic communication process that builds mutually beneficial relationships between organizations and their publics.' (PRSA, 2012)

What do you think of this way of defining a profession? Would other professions do this?

The key elements of PR involve being able to convey information in an appropriate way to a specific public – which may include announcing news, narrating stories or engaging in discussion – in order to build relationships that help achieve relevant aims and objectives.

There are three considerations of the word 'public' that are relevant to understanding public relations:

1   In sociology, 'public' relates to a **community or group of people who have something in common**, for example, an interest or activity. Sometimes the phrase 'general public' is used to indicate everyone, which is so broad that, according to Cutlip *et al.* (2000: 383) 'there simply is no such thing'. This indicates that communications should normally engage with more defined categories of people. PR practice doesn't necessarily mean engaging directly with the public; it often involves indirect methods of communications (such as through the media), although the end goal may be to influence a particular public.

2   The **views of a population** can be determined as 'public opinion'. This is researched using surveys of a sample of people whose individual views, attitudes and beliefs about a particular topic or question are then aggregated. Unless a census of everyone in the population is taken, sampling needs to ensure the results of the survey can be generalised. Such surveys emphasise

a combined opinion; specifically of the majority of respondents, which may hide significant variation of opinion among a public. PR activities are sometimes intended to sway 'public opinion', especially where this is thought to be influential, for example on government policy.

3   The term 'public' can be seen as the **opposite of private**. However, not all PR activities are undertaken in the public domain. Interpersonal communications

READING POINT

The concept of a 'public' and how PR practitioners identify specific groups is considered in Chapter 6.

and building relationships with individuals can be important elements of the PR function. This meaning of public does relate to being well known as in 'public figures', making something public or being 'in the public eye'. It also has a connection to 'news publication' and 'publicity' which are considered below.

CRITICISMS

Course leader Suzanne Fitzgerald at Rowan University in New Jersey, in the US, recently asked her students to find out popular definitions of PR, and one came up with 'Public relations is perfuming manure'. This analogy is not unique. Moloney (2000: 23) quotes a former group editor of *PR Week*, Steven Farish as stating: 'you would be hard pushed to find an industry which is as gleefully vilified as the noble profession of public relations – otherwise known as "the latrine of parasitic misinformation" as it was dubbed by the *Guardian*'.

It is not unusual to see criticism of PR and its practitioners, particularly by the media. Brian Appleyard, a respected journalist wrote in the *Sunday Times* (2003): 'Truth has been destroyed by public relations executives, or "scum" as we like to call them'. PR has been accused of contributing to a decline of journalism into 'churnalism' (Davies, 2008) as media become reliant on press releases and pseudo-events. Suzanne Moore called PR 'that industry made of nothingness' (2011).

Public relations has also been called 'spin', a pejorative term focusing on presenting selective information or lying. An ethics debate organised by *PR Week* in 2007 concluded with practitioners voting against the motion that **PR has a duty to tell the truth.** Others equate public relations to propaganda (see Kill Jill case study below).

The term 'PR disaster' (defined as 'anything that could catalyse embarrassing or negative publicity for any given organization', McCusker, 2006b: 311) implies that practitioners are responsible when issues have not been addressed effectively and dismisses a strategic role for the function in crisis management. Indeed, attempts to explain an organisation's position may be labelled as a 'PR exercise' (defined as 'a situation of communication with no substance within it', Green, 2007: 215).

PR practitioners are accused of being 'invisible persuaders' (Mitchie, 1998) and its use by organisations is exposed by critics such as Stauber and Rampton (2004) and Miller and Dinan (2008) as seeking to subvert society in favour of those with power, and the money to employ skilful PR counsel. L'Etang (1996: 105) sees PR as 'necessarily partisan and intrinsically undemocratic' reflecting that practitioners are employed to represent their paymasters in the best way possible.

Public impressions of those working in public relations are likely to be informed by high-profile publicists and spin-doctors featured in television programmes, movies or in the media. Such fictional and real-life characters are often portrayed in a negative light and consequently serve as poor role models for PR practice.

On the one hand, there's the cliché of PR bunnies (Fröhlich and Peters, 2007): attractive young women working in the fashion, beauty or music industries. Typecast in *The Devil Wears Prada*, *Sex in the City* or *Absolutely Fabulous*, they organise celebrity launches, secure reality television shows for their clients, chat to journalists, enjoy long lunches and drink champagne with handsome men in the best nightclubs.

The other image is the Machiavellian male PR media-manipulator, who will do whatever it takes to promote his clients or protect their reputation. This type of PR practitioner is generally placed at the heart of government or in the boardroom, advising senior executives in crisis situations to adopt clever, but morally dubious strategies or bullying journalists into doing things their way. In the movies, you'll find him in *Wag the Dog* or *Thank you for Smoking* and on television in *Absolute Power* or *West Wing*.

Most public relations work in reality is less glamorous and more ethical. But its key elements can be found in these extreme stereotypes. Generally PR practitioners are involved in communicating and building relationships on behalf of organisations (in the private, public or not-for-profit sectors) or individuals (such as celebrities). To do this, they work with the media and other influencers, produce communications materials, organise events and manage responses to emerging problems.

This explanation presents a benign or neutral perspective of PR, and arguably it is not the function itself which causes issues, but its usage by those with either good or negative ends in mind.

ACTION POINT

In 2008, the Scottish Government and Healthier Scotland ran a high-profile billboard campaign using posters and video, offering viewers the choice to 'Kill Jill: Yes or No'. The 'No' option was connected to the web address for organ donation, with the message, 'If you register online to be a donor you could save a life. If you don't you won't.' The campaign aimed to increase the number of registered organ donors in Scotland. At the time, one person in Scotland died each week through the lack of an organ for transplant.

This campaign was criticised strongly by law professor Hugh McLachlan (2008) in *The Scotsman*. His main issue was that the campaign was funded by the Scottish government. He classified the campaign as propaganda rather than information. 'Information is different from propaganda. Propagandists want us to think feel and act in particular ways. . . . If the Scottish Government and Health Scotland really wanted to give us information rather than propaganda . . . they would tell us what the absolute as well as the relative risks are.' He also pointed out that there was a difference between actually killing someone and 'refraining from doing something that might have postponed his or her death'. Finally he stated, 'Political parties, pressure groups and individual people are entitled to ply the public with propaganda. The state, its agents and agencies are not.'

Unsurprisingly, the article caused a lively debate on *The Scotsman*'s website. Don Smith, who claimed responsibility for creating the advert, felt that he had 'contributed to something positive and worthwhile'. He suggested that such advertising was a 'powerful tool for promoting positive social change', and that lives would be saved as a result of the campaign.

Giles Moffatt (2008) added: 'Brands influence choice, so why should social marketing not? Especially when the majority believe the cause to be good, moral, just and beneficial to society?' He continued, 'There's nothing wrong with social marketing campaigns emphasising a point of view if they are founded in belief and conviction that they are doing the right thing.' This last point caused Hugh McLachlan to respond, 'There certainly is if the state funds and promotes it.'

In 2009, the number of donors on the register rose to a ten-year high. Possibly spurred on by this success, the Scottish Government ran a £500,000 campaign in February 2010, called 'Spare Clare'. Reported in the *Daily Record* (2010), the campaign was backed by liver transplant recipient Claire Riley, who said:

> Being given the gift of life has allowed me to live a full life, free of pain and anxiety. I have been able to go on and have a family of my own. I now have two young sons and no longer lie on the couch unable to move from tiredness – I can play and have fun with my wonderful children like any other healthy, happy mother. This year's campaign encourages Scots to think if they would Spare Clare – Yes or No? As a Claire who has been spared, I can only urge people to give the gift of life. Just ask yourself one question – if your friend, family member or work colleague needed an organ, would you want them spared?

O'Shaughnessy (1996) sought to distinguish social marketing and social propaganda. He felt that the main characteristic of the latter was that it was a deliberate intent to influence or manipulate attitudes for the benefit of the source of the information rather than that of the recipient. It could show explicit bias and be based on lies and deception. 'Propaganda simplifies and exaggerates: it is often propelled by a clear, purposive and coherent ideology' (1996: 54).

Social marketing on the other hand contains an emphasis on customers and should be based on 'some research defined conception of audience wants'. O'Shaughnessy suggested this approach would mean that the message would not be framed in an antagonistic way, but presented more ambivalently and assuming that the audience would therefore make up their own minds. He also recognised that most social marketing agrees with a government agenda, and often sought to change the behaviour of the victim rather than deal with the cause of the problem.

Since then, social marketing has gained in popularity. Weinreich (2006) cites Kotler and Andreasen to suggest that social marketing 'seeks to influence social behaviors not to benefit the marketer, but to benefit the target audience and the general society'. She suggests that 'Rather than dictating the way that information is to be conveyed from the top-down, public health professionals are learning to listen to the needs and desires of the target audience themselves, and building the program from there.' NSMC (2015) state that 'The goal of social marketing is always to change or maintain how people behave', and that an 'intervention' should always benefit people and society.

Given these conflicting viewpoints, and bearing in mind the definitions presented above, do you think that the 'Kill Jill' and 'Spare Clare' campaigns were social propaganda, social marketing or public relations?

DIFFERENCES FROM OTHER MANAGEMENT DISCIPLINES

PR uses a variety of techniques and overlaps with other areas of management. In an effort to further define PR, we will now look at some of these and contrast and compare what each function involves.

Marketing

Public relations and marketing are often seen as adversarial, although it may just be that they pursue similar goals in different ways. Marketeers tend to see PR as a sub-ordinate part of their armoury of tools, and indeed businesses reinforce this by the organisation of their communications functions. Public relations practitioners often see marketing as part of their remit, for they believe it is primarily concerned with selling products to consumers. All organisations have a need for public relations, but not all are

TABLE 1.1 Spheres of responsibility for marketing and PR

Marketing	Marketing Public Relations	Public Relations
Market audit	Image audit	Corporate identity
Market segmentation	Customer response	Community liaison
Product development	Market research	Media relations
Price setting	Paid media strategy	Public affairs
Sales promotions	Employee surveys	Internal communications
Consumer advertising	Corporate advertising	Social media
Product distribution		Exhibitions and events

Adapted from Kotler and Mindak (1978)

involved in marketing. The Fire Service carries out community and media relations, but does not try to convince people to start more fires and so use their services more. They may 'market' safety advice and the availability of the service, however.

The Institute of Marketing defines marketing as: 'The management process responsible for identifying, anticipating and satisfying consumer requirements profitably.' This puts marketing clearly in the arena of creating sales, whilst PR has a broader, reputational remit.

What is clear is that public relations and marketing should ideally be corporate allies, working together for common goals. Kitchen (1997: 227–34) surveyed marketing and PR personnel in the UK. PR was viewed as important for marketing support by the marketeers, while PR executives saw this as a minor area and viewed issues management, employee communications and corporate communications as their priorities. However, there was general agreement that PR was part of integrated marketing communications.

Kitchen suggests that while there is 'a significant relationship between corporate public relations and marketing public relations', the focus of each is different. Marketing aims to create exchanges with consumers and uses PR tools to that end. Public relations on the other hand aims to 'create and maintain mutually beneficial relations with publics who could impact on business success' (Kitchen 1997: 234). So while the marketing team may create special offers and sales promotions, PR people will be seeking media coverage and arranging launch events.

The model in Table 1.1 illustrates the relationship between the three disciplines of marketing, marketing public relations and public relations.

Advertising

The Institute of Practitioners in Advertising's definition of advertising is: 'Advertising presents the most persuasive possible selling message to the right prospects for the product or service at the lowest possible cost.' Whilst advertising is clearly about increasing sales, as we have seen above, PR aims to increase understanding. Whilst advertising buys space or airtime to put across a message which is controlled by the organisation paying for the advert, PR practitioners give newsworthy information to journalists to persuade them to mention products and services in editorial pages or programmes. Once the information is given to the media, they can report it in whatever fashion they like, or choose not to report it at all.

Sometimes, however, an organisation might buy space to put across a general message about its environmental credentials or community involvement. This is known as corporate advertising and is more likely to be written by the PR department. A good clue is whether an advert would aim to get the recipient to buy something or not.

An advertorial or advertising feature is another area of overlap. They often appear in magazines and whilst the space is bought, just like an ad, it is filled with text and images similar to the surrounding editorial. Whilst consumers can differentiate between adverts, advertorial and editorial, the advertorial gives the organisation complete control over the content whilst aiming to make it look more like an independent article.

Advertising works best when it is repeated often, as this reinforces its messages. Ries and Ries (2002) suggested that PR worked best when launching a product, with advertising used to support continued sales.

Journalism

Ivy Ledbetter Lee is credited as being one of the first American pioneers of public relations. An ex-journalist, his Declaration of Principles in 1906 stated that:

> Our plan is, frankly and openly, on behalf of the business concerns and public institutions to supply to the press and public of the United States prompt and accurate information which it is of interest and value to the public to know about
>
> (Grunig, 1984: 33)

At first sight this may not seem dissimilar to the NUJ's Code of Conduct, which declares that a journalist 'Strives to ensure that information disseminated is honestly conveyed, accurate and fair'. Why then is the relationship between journalists and PR practitioners fraught with tension? H. Gregory (2006: 25) suggested that, 'It is the power of public relations that journalists fear, not its weakness. That is one reason why they mock it.'

The *Free Dictionary* defines journalism simply as 'The collecting, writing, editing, and presenting of news or news articles in newspapers and magazines and in radio and television broadcasts' (www.thefreedictionary.com/journalism). However, the institutionalisation of the 'freedom of the press' in Western democracies gives an added weight to journalistic reporting. The implication is that the media report an objective version of the truth, whilst PR practitioners who are employed by organisations or clients can never be impartial. Journalists need PR practitioners to respond to their requests for information and are motivated by getting a good story. The press officer, on the other hand, is invested in presenting their organisation in the most favourable light possible. The PR practitioner may also wish the journalist to report on their organisation to give an added credence or third-party endorsement to its actions.

Before Lee's Principles, the traditional approach to the media by business was to suppress all unfavourable information. The advent of social media and citizen journalism has rendered that approach even more untenable. Journalists will continue to hunt out newsworthy stories and PR practitioners will continue to present the most positive account of their organisation.

END POINT

This chapter has shown that academics and practitioners continue to try and define public relations, but that despite many efforts there is no single accepted definition. This presents a problem as its main ideas are easily adopted by marketing, human resources or other elements in an organisation. However, the main elements of PR are generally agreed to focus on it being a management function, and that it involves communication between an organisation and its publics. Public relations is a growing field and makes a considerable contribution to the economy. This Toolkit aims to explore the elements of public relations and to provide clear guidance on successful techniques and practices used in the industry today.

CHAPTER 2

What do PR practitioners do?

Alison Theaker

This chapter examines the roles of PR practitioners and looks at what they need to be good at.

CHECK POINT

After reading this chapter you should know:

- What the main tasks involved in day to day public relations are
- What research has found PR practitioners actually do
- The differences between working in-house for a specific organisation and in a consultancy.

PUBLIC RELATIONS ROLES

Glen Broom (1982) looked at what public relations practitioners did and formulated them into four dominant roles (Table 2.1). He suggested that there was one technician role and three closely related managerial functions.

Dozier and Broom (1995) later suggested that these roles could be reduced to two more general categories of technician and manager. The technician focused on technical, tactical tasks such as writing, editing, production of materials, maintaining contacts and issuing press releases. The communication manager, on the other hand,

TABLE 2.1 Broom's four practitioner roles (adapted from Cornelissen, 2008)

Role	Characteristics
Communication Technician	Carries out communication programmes. Preparing and producing communication materials. Not part of the management team.
Expert Prescriber	The authority on communication problems and their solutions. While can be part of the management team, is often regarded as the 'expert' so that the other members are generally passive.
Communication Facilitator	A go-between, liaising between the organisation and its stakeholders. A boundary-spanner, conveying organisational views externally and publics' views internally.
Problem-Solving Facilitator	Collaborates with other managers to define and solve communication problems. More likely to play an active part in strategic decision-making for the organisation.

is more likely to participate in management decisions, advise on the implications of policy decisions with regard to public reaction, social responsibility, and evaluate the results of communication programmes. In real life, it is rare to find a practitioner who simply fulfils one or other of these roles exclusively, as all may perform elements of both. It is helpful though to consider whether the work is predominantly one or the other.

Public relations tasks

Public relations practitioners communicate with many different publics or audiences, in many different ways. Table 2.2 provides a guide to the main activities practitioners are involved with.

What does this look like in practice? The following case studies give some accounts of the experiences of people working in the industry.

What do practitioners do? The research perspective

Researchers DeSanto and Moss (2004) recorded what PR managers actually did. They carried out interviews with practitioners in the UK and US and found that managers spent most of their time in meetings, both internal (UK, 16 per cent of time; US, 24 per cent) and external (UK, 31 per cent; US, 15 per cent). One-fifth of managers' time was taken up by administration tasks, while troubleshooting took up 7 per cent of UK managers' time and 15 per cent in the US. Only 10 per cent of PR managers' time was spent in planning. While some of the respondents were members of the top management team and were taken seriously, most had little involvement in policy-making within organisations.

Several surveys have asked practitioners what they do. Despite Genasi's (CEBR, 2005) claim that public relations had 'Developed well beyond traditional media work', 70 per cent of in-house and 48 per cent of consultancy work was then concerned with media

TABLE 2.2 A rough guide to the main activities in public relations

Public relations activity	Explanation	Examples
Internal communications	Communicating with employees	In-house newsletter, suggestion boxes
Corporate PR	Communicating on behalf of whole organisation, not goods or services	Annual reports, conferences, ethical statements, visual identity, images
Media relations	Communicating with journalists; specialists; and editors from local, national, international and trade media, including newspapers, magazines, radio, TV and web-based communication	Press releases, photocalls, video news releases, off-the-record briefings, press events
Business to business	Communicating with other organis-ations, e.g. suppliers, retailers	Exhibitions, trade events, newsletters
Public affairs	Communicating with opinion for-mers (e.g. local/national politicians), monitoring political environment	Presentations, briefings, private meetings, public speeches
Community relations/ corporate social responsibility	Communicating with local com-munity, elected representatives, headteachers, etc.	Exhibitions, presentations, letters, meetings, sports activities and other sponsorship
Investor relations	Communicating with financial organisations/individuals	Newsletters, briefings, events
Strategic communication	ID and analysis of situation, problem and solutions to further organis-ational goals	Researching, planning and executing a campaign to improve ethical reputation of organisation
Issues management	Monitoring political, social, econ-omic and technological environment	Considering effect of US economy on UK organisation
Crisis management	Communicating clear messages in fast-changing situation or emergency	Dealing with media after major rail crash on behalf of police, hospital or local authority
Copywriting	Writing for different audiences to high standards of literacy	Press releases, newsletters, web pages, annual reports
Publications management	Overseeing print/media processes, often using new technology	Leaflets, internal magazines, websites
Events management, exhibitions	Organisation of complex events, exhibitions	Annual conference, press launch, trade shows

Source: Fawkes (2012a)

A DAY IN THE LIFE OF A MARKETING AND PR EXECUTIVE

It is not an easy task to describe the typical day in the life of a PR Account Executive. At the start of every week I try to plan how my week is going to pan out; from ordering tasks in terms of importance to the length of time each task should take. This plan, however, no matter how organised, never seems to work out the way I think. I have found that to be successful in this role you need to be ready for whatever the day has to throw at you. This being said, every morning, I try to look through my emails and keep up to speed with what has happened since the previous evening. Working in an agency means account work is varied, with clients all over the globe. Time difference also means that you're not always at work when your clients are and sometimes tasks need to be actioned as soon as you have got to your desk. Once on top of my emails, I look through the main newspapers, keeping myself and my teams in the loop with everything that has hit the headlines. Working in PR has taught me how important it is to understand your client's markets. If headlines are relevant and in line with client's messaging, the team will have to act quickly to draft comment, have it signed off with the client and contact the relevant journalists with a reactive statement. It is my responsibility, as an Account Executive to know exactly what journalists are the best to contact and then call them with the client's comment. This sort of tactic allows our client to feature as a source of leading industry insight and gives them the opportunity to highlight the company's key messages. I told you PR was full of curveballs!

Throughout the week, my calendar features client and team catch ups. Before any meeting I draft an agenda, so meetings are kept concise and all items that need addressing can be addressed. Then throughout the meeting I note down all actions and deadlines and send them around to team. This is incredibly important for the general organisation of the account and so everybody can know what they are doing.

Probably the most important aspect of my job is promoting any releases to the press and uncovering any editorial opportunities for my clients. Press releases don't often go out every week, but a lot of preparation is needed before the release even goes out, from creating new media lists to tailoring pitches, relevant to the journalist, to increase the chances of coverage. Afterwards, I will follow up with the journalists to ensure they have received the relevant information and to gather feedback I then can report back to the client.

Finding editorial opportunities is probably my favourite aspect of my job. This is an ongoing task that requires a lot of organisation. It is my responsibility to schedule and update any planned opportunities. From here, I approach the relevant journalist to find out any further details and, with the help of the team, pull together a contribution from the client. Throughout the process, I keep the journalist in the loop with any updates and send across the final contribution and ensure the journalist has everything that they need.

Finally, throughout the day I have ongoing admin tasks that ensure the smooth running of client accounts. I regularly update client reports with coverage and any other activity such as features and press releases. This means that we can keep on top of our agreed deliverables and remain organised. At the end of the quarter, I am also responsible for creating an account highlights report to showcase what we have achieved over the last three months.

As you can see, my role is extremely varied and no day is the same. The day in the life of an Account Executive is busy, but at the same time exciting and extremely satisfying.

Aimee Lynn, Spark Communications

Aimee completed a BA in History at the University of Plymouth. She interned at Fireproof PR and gained an insight into the industry. After graduating she moved to London and worked in recruitment for seven months. In March 2015 she started working for Spark Communications as an Account Executive.

A DAY IN THE LIFE OF A CONSULTANCY DIRECTOR

ACTION POINT

I consider myself incredibly fortunate because I love my job and enjoy going to work every day. But running a busy PR agency means that I don't often get to do the things I love most about my job. Today though is not one of those days. Yes, I have a meeting with the accountant (yuk) and yes there's a three-hour meeting in the diary this afternoon to move forward the plans we have to merge with another successful business, but today there's a high-profile incident to manage for one of my big brand clients.

The day started with a large milky coffee and an 8am incident management call, to get everyone up to speed with the incident my client was trying to prevent in London. These operational calls are invaluable for communications professionals, as you get to hear first-hand what is going on on the ground to manage the incident, keep the public safe and prevent the situation escalating.

As a business owner it can be easy to spend your day checking the invoicing, approving holiday requests and networking with potential clients, but for me it is important to be actively involved at times like this. Not only because it protects the company's reputation and reassures the client, but it also allows me to let less experienced members of the team watch what's going on and learn in a risk-free environment.

We all know that incidents like these don't happen in a vacuum and the work for other clients can't take a back seat just because you're working to prevent mass panic in the centre of London. So it's coffee time again while I check the press cuttings for the day, read and approve two news releases and book my children in for an appointment with the dentist (who said PR was glamorous?!).

In advance of the meeting with the accountant, I needed to make sure I had all the latest figures fresh in my head – this really is my idea of hell. I have no real interest in this part of my job. To me it's a necessary evil and something I need to do to ensure my team and business have a secure and stable future. All went well with the figures man – not just because the meeting was a mere 40 minutes, and I was only interrupted twice by calls relating to the morning's incident, but also because he is happy with the pre-work we had done regarding the business merger I mentioned earlier.

We are so very excited about the business merger and this afternoon we will be deciding on the name for new business. So, to set us all up for success I popped out to get biscuits and soft drinks to keep the creativity flowing. I won't share the outputs with you, as I feel the sugar went to people's heads and resulted in some 'off the wall' ideas. I have decided to take everything home and look it over once the children are in bed, with a fresh pair of eyes and a cold glass of sauvignon blanc.

Emma Taynton-Young, MD, Fireproof PR

relations. Bowden-Green (2006) carried out research into how CIPR members in the south-west of England practised PR. He found that two-thirds of them regarded PR as projecting favourable messages through managing relationships with the media.

Whilst the 2006 *PR Week* Survey found that practitioners were working more hours (Johnson, 2007), and the CEBR study in 2005 had found that a quarter of practitioners worked over 48 hours per week, it was questionable whether these long hours were productive. Research by Time Act Solutions with 50 agencies found that they were spending a staggering 45 per cent of their time on account management and reporting back, but less than 20 per cent on media relations – the main task recorded. Strategic counsel took up 0.6 per cent of their time. They seemed to be spending more time getting authorised than actually doing the job. While smaller agencies seemed to be more efficient, spending 42 per cent of time on media relations plus 15 per cent on writing press releases, still only 4 per cent was spent on counselling clients. This does not give a picture of an industry engaged in board-level activity (Gray, 2006b).

Research carried out for *PR Week* UK by Brands2Life also found a disparity between theory and practice. Senior communications people rated customers as their most important stakeholders, then employees and the media. However, media relations was ranked as the most time-consuming task, followed by corporate communications and then internal communications (Bashford, 2006).

The EUPRERA research project, European Communication Monitor (Tench and Yeomans, 2009), sampled 1,524 communications professionals, across 37 different European countries. Three-quarters of them felt they were taken seriously by senior management, with 64 per cent involved in decision-making. Most important disciplines were marketing/brand management, corporate communications, crisis/issue management, investor relations and public affairs/lobbying. However, practitioners were still mainly reliant on media monitoring to assess their effectiveness. The CIPR's 2010 Benchmarking study found that growth was expected in online reputation management, crisis management and internal communications. Sponsorship and events management were expected to decline. Whilst members were broadly comfortable with their knowledge of social media, 23 per cent admitted that their knowledge was limited. Media relations continued to be the most time-consuming task in both in-house (78 per cent) and consultancy (88 per cent). Strategy development and planning were the next main functions in consultancy, with internal communications and strategy development in-house.

Zerfass *et al.* (2010) found that whilst over 70 per cent thought communications were more important since the recession, only 22 per cent had actually gained resources and 37 per cent had lost resources. Media relations with print journalists was expected to decrease by 9.5 per cent but actually increased by 5.2 per cent from 2007 to 2010. The growth of use of online channels was overestimated, as social media had been expected to rise by 41 per cent, but actually only increased by 15 per cent. Less than one-third of organisations had implemented guidelines for social media communications. Evaluation still relied heavily on media response and internet/intranet usage. Only a quarter were tracking the impact of communications on financial strategic targets.

Arrow (2009) complained, 'Even the most professional of practitioners is still implementing regurgitated values, set elsewhere in the organisation.' Despite the high hopes expressed in the industry, the picture painted above still seems to be of an industry which continues to focus on tactical rather than strategic thinking, with media relations still regarded as the core activity.

The PR Census (Gorkana, 2011) commissioned by *PR Week* found that general media relations was still the main function of 21 per cent of practitioners. Whilst online communications was included by 78 per cent of professionals, only 2 per cent regarded it as their main function. Media relations strategy planning, communications strategy development and writing articles and newsletters were the other tasks in the top five. Sha (2011) listed professional competencies as use of information technology; management skills; media relations; research, planning and evaluation of programmes; advanced communication skills and business literacy.

Nayan *et al.* (2012) cited Chong (2011) stating 'Competency is demonstrated in the ability to effectively manage the varying perceptions and expectations of others', suggesting that whether a practitioner is doing a good job is down to the client thinking they are.

Diga and Kelleher (2009) found that practitioners perceived that using social networks increased their influence within organisations and that there was no significant difference between those who were managers or technicians. However, the CIPR's (2015) State of the Profession found that competencies in demand still focused on traditional PR skills, with digital skills appearing in the list of competencies for junior staff but not for senior staff.

Where do they do it?

Again, the lines of demarcation as to the environment in which practitioners operate largely tends to split into two arenas. One is referred to as in-house, where you would be employed by a company to carry out its communications. Most practitioners in the UK, 82 per cent, work in-house (CEBR, 2005). The other would be to work in a public relations consultancy, where you would be employed by the agency but would perform communications tasks for a variety of clients. Some also work as independent consultants or freelancers. Consultancies range from full-service agencies, which might also provide research, advertising and marketing as well as public relations, to specialist agencies which might focus on a particular industry, such as construction or manufacturing, or on PR for particular groups, such as young people or ethnic minorities, or a particular element such as internal communication or financial PR. A freelance practitioner may be employed by either an in-house department or a consultancy to work on specific contracts, whether because of their specialist skills or to cope with peaks in demand or staff absence (see Table 2.3).

READING POINT

Tench and Yeomans (2017) suggest looking at adverts for public relations jobs to see what employers are looking for. This will give an idea of what skills employers are looking for, whether that is technical knowledge or personal qualities, and what experience and qualifications. Relevant publications include the *Guardian* and *Independent* media sections and *PR Week*. It may also be useful to look at the websites of PR consultancies where possible jobs may be included.

TABLE 2.3 Advantages and disadvantages of in-house and consultancy PR functions

	In-house public relations function	Public relations consultancy
Advantages	Dedicated PR professional Intimate knowledge of organisation Usually less expensive Contacts within company Can perform many different tasks	Experience of working for several clients Employed only when needed Objective viewpoint May have specialised contacts
Disadvantages	Have to be paid full time Can get too close to the company view May not be regarded highly by management	May not always be available More expensive to use

Overload

It also seems to be an accepted stereotype that practitioners work long hours and are always on call for their clients. A blog post on *PR Daily* in early 2011 listed '42 more signs you work in PR' (Sebastian, 2011a). The list included the following:

- Your Blackberry sleeps with you every night. Your better half does not.
- You no longer count calories – just your re-tweets.
- You've heard all the lines about sleep: 'Sleep is overrated'.
- Every Friday around 17:00 you think, 'This could be crisis time!'
- You're afraid to go more than 15 minutes without checking Twitter/Facebook/ news feeds to make sure you're not missing anything.

These contributions by PR practitioners themselves seem to indicate that they support the need to be seen to be working longer and harder than anyone else, ready to jump when their clients contact them. Would the same list have been produced by a group of lawyers or accountants?

However, not all who work in PR advise being available 24/7. PR lecturer and consultant Kirk Hazlett (2011b), whilst admitting that he has a full-time job and a part-time one as well as consulting on the side, recommends the need to take 'me time': 'Walk in the sunshine, eat ice cream, and relax.' He mentions this as the solution for 'impending burnout' and suggests that it enables one to return to work recharged with renewed energy and determination.

Zerfass *et al.* (2015) found that the majority of practitioners were working well beyond their contracted hours, with 47.2 per cent stating that they worked 25 per cent more than they were contracted for, and 8.8 per cent working 50 per cent more than they had to. However, two-thirds expressed satisfaction with their job.

TALKING POINT

WHAT SKILLS ARE NEEDED TO WORK IN PR?

Caroline Shepherd (2011) undertook research as part of her undergraduate PR degree at the University of Central Lancashire (UCLAN) to investigate what skills were needed to enable PR graduates to get jobs in the industry. She was inspired by conflicting views on whether a degree in PR was a necessary prerequisite for working in the industry. Many commentators stated that employers valued experience of the work as more important than gaining a degree in PR, although she cited PRCA research (2009) that found that 70 per cent of PR leaders thought a university degree was more important now than 15 years ago.

The majority of her 50 respondents had a PR or media degree, with others having journalism or English degrees and only one not having a degree at all. Two-thirds felt that they had learnt more from their placement year or work experience than from their degree, but nearly half stated that they would not be where they were without their degree. Only one respondent, a mature student, felt that their degree had taught them nothing at all. In education, this was a frustrating perception amongst students that experience taught more than what was learned in the classroom. As Anne Gregory has said, 'Experience is about looking backward at what you have done, whilst education is about looking forward and how you do things.' It is interesting to see that, whilst experience was rated more highly, a significant proportion of respondents recognised that their degree had been instrumental in getting them the job they were in.

An article on *PR Daily* by Becky Johns (2011) reviewed the responses to a question posted on Twitter about whether a high GPA (Grade Point Average) at college was really important. Johns responded that a high grade was not an indication of how someone would perform in the working world, and whilst she advised students to 'Take your classes seriously. Do the work. Show up and learn something,' she concluded that, 'the GPA you achieve in college doesn't matter.' She suggested an alternative list of things that mattered more:

- Knowing how you learn – whether this was by seeing, hearing, writing or practising, this knowledge would be useful in learning things in the workplace.
- Applying theory to real-life situations – taking information and applying it in new situations.
- Time management – managing time to meet deadlines, tackling to-do lists and still have something of a social life.
- Relevant professional experience – using jobs, internships, student organisations and volunteer projects to show that you could do the work.

- A portfolio proving you can produce work – keeping samples of work to show prospective employers.
- The ability to give and receive feedback – learning to accept praise and criticism will help in the workplace as well as being able to collaborate with others.
- Presentation skills – conveying ideas clearly will be important in professional life.
- Writing skills – this will be used in everything from reports to pitches to emails. Many students leave college lacking solid writing ability.
- Your network – who you know is more important than what you know so get into the habit of meeting new people. You are most likely to find jobs through your network.

Cornelissen (2008) reported some comments from practitioners on the qualities needed in communications. Qualities included: personality, lateral thinking, creativity, common sense, being persuasive in writing and verbally, being able to write a press release, sense of humour, interpersonal skills in building relationships. He also included results of a UK survey which found that communication skills (verbal communication, writing, editing) and personal characteristics (integrity, influence, persuasion, diplomacy, critical judgement) were at the top of the list. Other competences were enthusiasm, confidence, reflection and learning from previous experience, intuition and problem-solving.

Jenkin (2016) reported fourteen qualities that he felt were characteristic of a 'kick-ass comms professional'. He questioned whether the traditional press release was still needed in the Twitter era, but stressed that 'seriously good writing' was still important. Interpersonal skills to build trust and relation-ships were the most in-demand for entrants to the profession, although a strategic brain would take longer to develop. An understanding of psycho-logy, business acumen and an entrepreneurial mindset as well as inter-national perspective also made the list. Other skills included creativity, digital communications and the ability to crunch data, whilst qualities such as an 'ethical backbone' and willingness to help others were vital. Being independent and taking responsibility for one's own professional develop-ment and having an awareness of one's personal brand were the final elements.

What other areas of work stress that experience is more important than qualifications? Would you feel happy having surgery from a surgeon who did not have an academic qualification but had just practised for years? What does this preoccupation say about the confidence of public relations practitioners in what they do?

Koch (2016) warned that workplace stress could have serious consequences, from health issues like heart attacks and depression to the loss of talented people who would leave the industry through burnout. He suggested there was a 'culture of silence' in many companies about stress-related illness and recommended that employers needed to train managers in how to deal empathetically with people who were struggling. He cited 2013 research by Mind which found that staff would be 60 per cent more loyal if there was a greater commitment to well-being. As people become more aware of mental health issues through public education campaigns, PR needs to keep its own house in order.

END POINT

Having reviewed some of the research done to try and quantify and codify the work that PR practitioners do, this chapter has suggested that there are four different roles which PR practitioners carry out, with two major categories of technician and manager. PR involves communicating with different audiences in a variety of ways and, despite a desire to be seen as a strategic communicator, most PR practitioners spend most of their time dealing with the media. PR is carried out in-house, in a consultancy or as a freelance, and skills and experience are regarded more highly than academic qualifications.

CHAPTER 3

The PR industry and careers in it

Alison Theaker

This chapter gives an overview of the PR industry, its development and future trends.

CHECK POINT

This chapter includes:

- An overview of the development of the industry
- A review of the main professional bodies
- Information on entry routes
- A discussion on professional development
- Practical guidance and advice from practitioners for those wanting to work in the industry
- Different sectors of the industry.

THE PUBLIC RELATIONS INDUSTRY

The latest estimates are that there about 62,000 people working in public relations in the UK and that PR has a turnover of about £9.62 billion (PRCA, 2016b).

The census (Gorkana, 2011) confirmed that the majority – 64 per cent – of the industry was female and also white British – 84 per cent. However, by 2015 the CIPR (2015) had found that there was a pay inequality gap of £8,483 in favour of men. The average annual salary was £45,633, with consultancy practitioners being the best paid at an average of £51,835. London-based practitioners earned an average of £55,849, while those based in the North earned an average of £38,275. Only 9 per cent identified as being from BME backgrounds, and 6 per cent as having a disability. The census (Gorkana, 2011) had found that only 4 per cent of the UK industry worked in Scotland, Northern Ireland, the Channel Islands, that 6 per cent worked in the North West and another 6 per cent in the North East and Yorkshire (Bussey, 2011).

HISTORY OF PR

So how did public relations begin? American academics James Grunig and Todd Hunt (1984) looked at the origins of the PR industry in the US and classified PR practice into four types. These four models have created much debate, and form a good foundation for discussion of later ideas.

Grunig and Hunt called the first era of PR history the press agentry or publicity model. It relates to the period from 1875 to 1900, when businesses used stunts to promote their products. They cited showman Phineas Barnum as an example of someone who didn't let the truth get in the way of a good story, and who used many tricks to get his events covered for free in the papers. They suggested that this philosophy of faking stories to get coverage is at the root of journalists' antipathy towards present-day PR.

Next came the public information model, which Grunig and Hunt credit to Ivy Ledbetter Lee, originally a journalist who set up a PR agency which prided itself on giving accurate information to the papers. His belief was that providing information to reporters to enable them to do their job was more productive than suppressing news about a company. He is also thought to be one of the first to use the press handout or press release, a staple of today's PR. The major difference in this model was the emphasis on telling the truth. Both these models are essentially one-way methods of communication, where the organisation sends out information it wants the public to know.

With the advent of the First World War, propaganda was used to persuade people to support the war effort. Edward Bernays worked in the Creel Committee on Public Information and experienced how communications were used. He was also a nephew of Sigmund Freud and became interested in his ideas on psychology. Bernays felt that psychological theory could be used to promote commercial interests and worked as a freelance press agent. He claimed to have invented the term 'public relations counsel'. Grunig and Hunt called Bernays' method two-way asymmetrical communication, because it included the use of research to find out what the public thought and took this into account. Often this meant that Bernays used what he found that the public liked about an organisation and emphasised this in its communications. He orchestrated a famous stunt on behalf of Lucky Strike cigarettes based on psychological research into why women did not smoke in public. This showed that cigarettes represented male power which meant that women were less likely to smoke. He organised a group of debutantes to light up cigarettes during the New York Parade, and presented this to the media as lighting 'Torches of Freedom'. Women smoking was thus linked to being more independent. Whilst this model of PR includes two-way communications, even Grunig and Hunt state that the practitioner is merely 'telling management what the public will accept. They do not tell management how to please the public.'

The fourth model is the one that has caused most controversy. Named two-way symmetrical communications and devised by American academics Cutlip and Center, this defined PR as 'the communication and interpretation of ideas and information to the publics of an institution; the communication and interpretation of information, ideas and opinions from those publics to the institution in an effort to bring the two into harmonious adjustment'. Subsequent research by Grunig and others added the notion of 'excellent communications', where this two-way model was presented as an ideal way of practising PR. It implies that the organisation will change its policies not just its communications as a result of learning about public opinion. PR practitioners are then seen as 'boundary-spanners', presenting the views of an organisation and its publics to each other. Several academics such as L'Etang have queried whether this is in fact possible in practice, as the practitioner will surely always work on behalf of the organisation which pays them. The advent of the internet and social media has been heralded by some as the dawning of the age of true two-way communications as it makes organisations' actions more transparent. The rapid spread of opinions through the web and on Facebook and Twitter have meant that organisations now have to pay more attention to them.

Whilst these models were originally put forward after an examination of the historical development of PR in the US, it was not found to be a linear progression. Indeed, Grunig and Hunt suggested that all four models were still practised in a variety of situations. Also, they were only linked to the US profession. Others, such as L'Etang, have studied the history of PR in the UK, where the industry had its beginnings in public sector public relations. PR in the UK has therefore more of an underlying emphasis on public interest.

Are these models of any use to current practitioners, especially as they have been shown to be flawed? Yes and no. It is true that practitioners do practise a variety of methods depending on the situation, and that PR has changed from using mainly one-way communications telling people what an organisation wants them to hear, to being more concerned with developing relationships and having conversations with the publics their organisations are affected by. As more academics and practitioners start to reflect on and examine practice, diverse models of PR can be developed that do not focus on a US-centric view and which take into account practitioners which do not fit into the four models above.

Drawing on her PhD studies into Careers in Public Relations, Heather Yaxley reflects on the occupation's opportunity structure.

TALKING POINT

THINKING ABOUT CAREERS IN PUBLIC RELATIONS

Over the past century, the growth of public relations as an occupation is undisputable. Early career opportunities since the late 1800s distinguished roles as press agents, publicists and public relations counsel in order of prestige and salary. By the mid-20th century, many companies and public sector organisations employed PR practitioners and external agencies. Senior manager roles were increasingly common, with responsibility for large teams in many cases.

Histories tend to present the occupation from a male perspective. However, a broader perspective is emerging thanks in large part to research presented at the International History of Public Relations conference (https://microsites. bournemouth.ac.uk/historyofpr/about/).

Expanding knowledge of the origins of public relations work and its practitioners can be seen in the work of the Museum of Public Relations (www.prmuseum.org/) and a series of books edited by Professor Tom Watson providing an extensive worldwide view on public relations' history.

Careers are commonly presented in literature as involving basic hierarchical progress from technical to managerial work. However, the majority of practitioners are self-employed or work in small organisations where there are few if any opportunities for career progression. Instead, careers are developed predominantly by moves between organisations.

It is also common for non-specialists to enter the field in senior roles (notably former journalists), which challenges the concept of a specific career ladder in PR. Similarly, digital PR developments have offered the chance for many younger practitioners to leapfrog older colleagues who have been less willing or able to take advantage of new opportunities.

There is no defined career development or pathway within public relations as is evident in established professions. Indeed, the openness of the occupation means that it tends to expand and contract quickly, making it responsive to economic and other social changes.

The lack of a formal career framework presents an individualistic perspective of career development. However, this fails to recognise the many barriers that can lead to inequity of career opportunity and may be a contributory factor in the continuing lack of diversity within public relations.

It is difficult to present an organised career system that would accommodate the variety and complexity of the modern field. However, little research has been undertaken concerning careers in public relations. Concepts such as agile career planning and collective support networks have potential to enhance career experiences. They can also help to challenge traditional views of linear progression that are predicated on male 20th-century career experiences and instead recognise the need for adaptability and resilience to overcome barriers concerning equality of opportunity within the occupation.

Professional bodies

The PRCA is the trade body for consultancies in the UK, and members are companies rather than individuals. It opened membership up to in-house teams in late 2009, and freelancers in 2010. It has 350 agency members, and 250 in-house teams, and represents a total of 18,000 practitioners. The CIPR is the association for individual practitioners and has over 10,500 members. The professional bodies together only account for less than 45 per cent of practitioners. Requirements for qualifications and professional and ethical behaviours can only apply to association members.

Other influential professional bodies include the PRSA in the US, which with 22,000 members is the largest association of individual practitioners in the world.

There are also several international bodies. The IPRA (International Public Relations Association) was founded in 1955 with only 15 members in five countries. Small by national association criteria, the organisation has 305 members and 9,252 free members through LinkedIn in 100 countries. The Confédération Européenne de Relations Publiques (CERP) has 48 member organisations including the CIPR. The PRCA is a member of the International Communications Consultants Organisation (ICCO) which has 2,500 member companies in 32 countries. There is also the Global Alliance of Public Relations and Communications Management (GA) and the World Public Relations Forum.

Getting in

The PR industry has had an uneasy relationship with academic qualifications, with many declaring that experience is the best way to gain entry to the profession. With the drive of the Institute towards chartered status, practitioners needed to show that they were qualified to do the work and approving academic and professional courses became a major plank of the case for such status.

The first PR courses were offered in the US. Josef Wright introduced one at the University of Illinois in 1920 and Edward Bernays taught one in the journalism department of the New York University School of Commerce, Accounts and Finance in the 1930s. The 1981 Commission on Public Relations Education recommended that the content of undergraduate and postgraduate courses should include mass communications, PR theories, media relations techniques, research methodology, case studies, work placements and PR management (Cutlip *et al.,* 2000: 150). A further commission in 1987 added ethics, law and evaluation to the list (IPRA, 1990). The Public Relations Education Commission set up by the Public Relations Society of America (PRSA) in 1999, added business context, finance, communication theory and a supervised work placement in practice (Commission of PR Education, 1999). The International Public Relations Association (IPRA) published guidelines for PR education, advising that, 'public relations courses should be taught by individuals with a sound experience and understanding of both the academic and professional aspects of the field' (IPRA, 1990). The suggested curriculum became more and more crowded.

The CIPR approved six courses in 1989, including vocational, undergraduate, postgraduate and Masters programmes in the UK. The number of approved courses has since risen to 35 BA programmes and 20 Masters provided at 30 institutions (a list of approved courses is available on www.cipr.co.uk). In 1998, the CIPR also introduced its own qualifications, the Advanced Certificate and Diploma, which provide a part-time route to qualification for those who are already working in the profession and who are unable to return to full-time education. The PRCA have also introduced their own qualifications, a Foundation, Advanced Certificate and Diploma. Each course is modular in structure and the emphasis is on practical skills.

There are still many in the industry who do not have a relevant qualification, although there are few who do not have any qualifications at all. Some consultancies or in-house departments have a specifically designed graduate training scheme in public relations, but often training tends to be *ad hoc*. Pieczka (2006a) found that public relations expertise, as defined by practitioners, was 'transmitted through practice', and 'concerned with practicality' and the 'ability to apply abstract knowledge to real life problems'.

Academic courses have to tread an uneasy tightrope between developing general graduate skills and satisfying a critical industry which does not always understand the constraints of academic standards. Table 3.1 shows the results of UK research indicating which skills were valued by employers.

PR Week published the results of a survey of 96 in-house PR practitioners in August 2011 which asked what skills were needed now and in the next five years. The top five current skills essentially stayed the same, with the addition of ability to work with social media and technology which shot to the top of the list. The other attributes were essentially personal qualities rather than skills – creative and strategic thinking; charismatic personality and good networker; flexibility to adapt to clients' needs; articulate and persuasive communicator – as well as knowledge of the industry. The supporting article appeared to largely ignore these findings, as apart from digital skills, practitioners were advised that commercial acumen, international experience, work on integrated

TABLE 3.1 Ranking of discipline topics by employers

Subject	%
1. Writing skills	86
2. Media relations	81
3. Public relations practice	80
4. One-year work placements	64
5. Media practice	51
6. Live projects for external clients	40
6. Journalism	40
6. Media analysis	40
7. Internal communications	34
8. Business principles	31
9. Public relations theory	30

Source: Tench and Fawkes (2005) cited in Fawkes in Theaker (2012)

campaign and traditional skills such as building media contacts were key (Magee, 2011b).

An online discussion started by US lecturer Rob Brown in 2011 asked what five things should be taught in a basic PR course. Suggestions included 'Know your audience is the golden rule', and several advised using good and bad examples of PR practice to show what PR involved. Others stressed that PR was not just the use of media relations and social media but encompassed crisis communications, government and investor relations, event planning and speech writing. Pleas for good writing skills were repeated, as was an awareness of cultural differences in a global industry.

Having taught PR at undergraduate and graduate level over 18 years in the UK and US, I would agree with many of these. Writing skills are important whatever industry you are in, and however you communicate. Knowing how to gather information and craft a convincing argument is also important. Convincing students on either side of the Pond that they need help to improve their writing is another matter. Researching this in the US, UK and Australia, I found that teaching writing as an integral part of the subject and setting aside a significant proportion of marks was the only way to motivate students to take the time to redraft their work rather than just submitting their first attempt.

I also feel that teaching the broader spectrum of PR rather than concentrating on media relations is vital. Unfortunately the industry, whilst making noise about wanting strategic thinking, tends to concentrate on whether first job candidates can write a press release or not. Reviewing the training courses on the CIPR website in 2015/16, 14 of the 69 courses on offer were on writing of various types, with the next significant areas covering social media, planning and strategy, and media relations. Other topics included video content for the web, crisis and risk management, stakeholder engagement and change communication.

One US student on a 15-week Introduction to PR Principles said, 'I've never done any PR before. I want to know all about it and whether I should go for a career in the industry.' As courses become more modularised and students can pick and mix from one-semester options, there has become more demand for this kind of instant gratification.

Arik Hanson, principal of ACH Communications in Minnesota, suggested creative ways to get noticed in the application process, including one candidate who compared herself to the many Disney princesses. He felt the most powerful thing was to start a blog to improve visibility in the now commonplace Google search on candidates. It also gives prospective employees the chance to show off those all-important writing skills.

Andrew Cave (2011) looked at the qualities required from corporate communicators. Whilst companies may once have wanted former journalists, he revealed that the most sought after backgrounds were from government and regulators, with higher levels of financial and technological know-how. Organisations were having to deal with a greater range of stakeholders, including NGOs, activists and online networks. There was now more emphasis on integrated communications campaigns and understanding the big picture. Finally, a much more central role for internal communications meant that corporate communications directors had to adopt a more joined-up approach to internal and external messages.

ACTION POINT

Several practitioners were asked if they had any advice for those wishing to enter the industry.

BELIEVE IN YOURSELF!

The first reaction I get from my senior students when they go looking for a job is, 'But I don't know how to *do* anything. How can I even get started?'

My answer is, 'You really *do* know "stuff." You just haven't had to *prove* yourself yet, and you have to believe you *can* do it!'

I've been amazed over the years as I've gotten to know all the things my PR students are doing while maintaining an impressive grade point average.

- They're Resident Assistants, juggling a full load of classes and an internship during the day and then being on duty at night riding herd over a batch of lower classmen and women.

- They're in our Speaking Center helping fellow students hone their public speaking skills in preparation for an upcoming class assignment or job interview.
- They're at the reception desk in our Student Center welcoming guests and providing information to visitors and students.
- They're involved in on-campus clubs and organisations.
- They're already 'working', gaining valuable skills that put them several steps ahead of their competitors from other colleges and universities who are vying for the same entry-level jobs after graduation.

One thing I'm also realising is that these young professionals-in-the-making are capable of:

- Time management.
- Multitasking.
- Communication ability on multiple platforms.
- Commitment with a passion.

I'm not suggesting that they are ready to make a new business presentation to a CEO client. What I am suggesting, though, is that they have the core knowledge and skills to eventually find themselves in that seat. But there's one thing still to be done. It all has to start with the confidence that you *can* do this, that you *do* know that. This holds true not only for college students, but also for anyone wending his or her way through the corporate swamp. Life is a series of learning opportunities, each with its own unique challenges and valuable lessons. Success is going to be realised by overcoming those challenges and fully absorbing those lessons. Most important, though: 'You have to believe in yourself.'

Kirk Kazlett, Assoc Professor, Curry College; PRSA Board of Ethics & Professional Standards; PRSA Educators Academy Board of Directors, Boston USA

WANT A CAREER IN PR?

1   **Pay your dues.** When you are first starting off in a career, you really need to ring-fence a few years just for gaining good, hardworking, unglamorous experience. Get your head down and slog, rather than thinking about the glory. If you get genuine experience early on, you'll have a solid foundation to build on when the bigger, more exciting opportunities come along. Your boss is probably not from Generation Y. So they will expect you to work hard and prove yourself before they give you the keys to the kingdom.

2 **Be nice to people.** It is the right thing to do. And people will remember you later in your career. PR is obviously about managing relationships. Build relationships with journalists – not just for the story you are currently working on but for longer-term benefits. Same goes for clients and colleagues – and not just the marketing director. Where will the most junior member of staff that you deal be in five years' time?

3 **Take a risk!** In this sector, if you risk nothing, you win nothing. Don't be afraid of big ideas, however new you are to the industry. Back your own thoughts and beliefs and you will get noticed. Big, crazy, outlandish ideas often pave the way to killer concepts that are more realistic. Go large knowing that you can scale the idea.

4 **Read … a lot!** Read textbooks and industry publications, read biographies of media and PR people and borrow ideas that you can put in your own words. You are not expected to know everything when you first join the profession but your proactive ideas are what will set you apart. Consider formal studying at undergraduate and postgraduate courses.

5 **Do work you're proud of, at the highest level you are allowed to.** If it is writing a press release, make it your best. As soon as you can, enter industry awards. People who are negative about awards have never won any! Be healthily cynical about them but the process of entering them will help you evaluate what you are proud of and how to communicate this to other people.

6 **Don't be a consumer, be a contributor.** Network including attending industry events, joining industry bodies such as the CIPR. But you will get out of these what you put into them. Find good people and connect them to other good people. Don't worry about what you will get back. When you take the right actions, the results will take care of themselves.

7 **Take your career seriously (but don't take yourself too seriously).** Do build your own brand. Write down your own plan. Be professional online and in real life but remember to be a walking, talking, feeling, loving, laughing person. People hire people they like. Be you. But the best version of you.

8 **Have a personal off-site every 90 days.** In the early years of your career, you will get so busy that you may stop asking yourself the right questions. Become your own PR consultant. 'What am I really trying to achieve? What do I need to do next? How does my boss (or my next boss) think? How do I need to tailor my message to influence them to give me the support I need to progress?'

9 **Become an influencer.** Read books about decision-making and persuasion (anything by Dr Robert Cialdini will do). You will instinctively

understand much of the theory but having a framework for these thoughts will increase your value on a team. The principles of persuasion can be directly applied to your job application and interview too!

10   **Develop a moral compass.** It is so easy to get caught up with the project you are assigned to and to engage your skills rather than your spirit. Eventually, people will respect you more if you figure out how to say *no*. If you don't value your time and beliefs, why should anyone else?

11   **Ask for help but don't be a victim.** You always have a choice. You always have options. Do ask for help but bring your own thoughts and potential solutions to the table.

12   **Understand yourself.** What are your core values? What activities bring your energy? What seems harder for others but comes easy to you? Learn about strengths-based learning. Or you will waste a lot of effort and time in your career.

13   **Be appreciated.** Don't quit when the going gets tough but realise you will spend 80 per cent of your waking hours at work. Life is too short to waste it on negative people or organisations you don't believe in. Only stay if you want to be there. Find the right cause and your work will be better.

14   **Think like a journalist.** Spend time in a newsroom, both broadcast and print. Understand the process. Then critique the content and presentation. When you watch/listen/read the news, ask yourself: *What is the real story? How did this story get here? Practically, how was the story produced?*

15   **Learn to love LinkedIn.** Edit your LinkedIn presence once a month. This will help you stay focused on your career. (Making changes will also put your updates in other people's news streams.) What is your current narrative? What story would you like to tell? Be ruthless. Less but better. Look at other people's entries. Save a copy of yours before you make changes (this will give you confidence to be bolder in cutting things out). Focus on results. Add people to your network but always send them a reason why you would like to connect.

16   **Embrace social media.** Understand it, use it. You're expected to be up-to-date and on trend. Demonstrate how you can apply your personal knowledge of Twitter, Snapchat, Instagram, Pinterest and whatever is coming next to your work. But darned well turn off your smart devices in meetings and whenever you want to concentrate.

Justin McKeown, Founder and Director, Mission Agency Ltd, which provides communications consultancy and training for brands, corporates, public sector bodies and charities.

TEN PIECES OF ADVICE FROM MY INTERNSHIP

1   **Listen carefully and take notes.** You need to know what is expected of you, which is why listening well is a craft that you have to master. You know less than your supervisors, so listen carefully to what they are saying if you want to learn. Always have a pen and a notebook to take notes during briefings or meetings. Observe, follow the discussion and write down important points. You will gain a lot of information about clients, their industries, and your employer.

2   **Ask questions.** Always ask when you don't understand an assignment, when you need clarifications or when you just want to discuss something with your managers such as how to best approach a journalist. You can't do what is asked of you if you don't understand what exactly it is.

3   **Ask for more work.** If you want to get better, take as much responsibility and complete as many tasks as possible and always execute them with enthusiasm. Take the initiative and be proactive to make a real contribution and develop a strong portfolio.

4   **Ask for feedback.** If you want to develop good PR skills you need to know what you are doing well and what your areas of improvement are. Regularly ask your supervisors how you are doing. Be open to criticism, take it as constructive feedback. This will help you acknowledge your weaknesses and turn them into strengths.

5   **Work hard.** I can't stress this one enough. You have to spend enough time to finish your tasks and do it well. You always have to proofread. Never submit unfinished or unchecked work. You can't have spelling and grammar mistakes in your copy. Attention to detail is crucial.

6   **Be flexible.** Public relations is fast-paced and so every day is different. You need to be able to multitask and quickly switch from one task to another. Be prepared to ditch whatever you are working on for new last-minute tasks.

7   **Learn to cope with pressure.** PR work is extremely diverse and always changing. If you can't cope with a lot of pressure, and often, then PR may not be right for you.

8   **Don't be afraid to pick up the phone.** Media relations is a core skill in PR. The sooner you acquire it, the better. Pitch with enthusiasm, have a positive attitude and smile. Journalists prefer to talk to someone in a good mood. Do you like talking to unhappy people? I guess not.

9   **Always speak your mind.** You should be confident and share your ideas. If you don't speak up, you won't find out whether your ideas are

good or not. Your supervisors are there to guide you and give you feedback.

10   **Have fun!** You need to enjoy your work in order to be good at it. If you are more frustrated and exhausted than satisfied and motivated by your job, then PR may not be the career for you.

Iliyana Stareva, Senior Channel Consultant at HubSpot

Professional development

In April 2000 the CIPR introduced Developing Excellence, a continuous professional development (CPD) scheme. This scheme, while voluntary, aims to encourage members to continue their development. The CIPR advises that every member should complete CPD every year and that it is part of being a professional. Practitioners log in to the website and enter their activities. The CIPR provides a list of 600 suggested activities that could contribute to CPD.

With the introduction of Chartered Practitioner status, with an emphasis on preparing a short dissertation and defending this in front of a panel of experts, Accredited Practitioner became a simpler process. Having been involved in the development of the original scheme, this seems to downgrade the requirements needed to a one-off achievement, rather than continual development. The emphasis is still on time spent doing different activities, rather than assessing whether this makes someone better at their job. Like the PRSA model of an exam to gain extra status, this only measures someone's expertise at one moment in time. With the rapid pace of change in the industry this does not really address the issue of needing to take part in life-long learning. The PRCA also launched a programme of skills-focused training in 2008. Like the CIPR scheme, it is voluntary and only affects its members. In 2016, Ingham (2016) announced the introduction of a CPD scheme to raise 'standards and professionalism'.

An online discussion started by Beth Okun, PR spokesperson at the Gwinnett Medical Centre in Georgia, in August 2011 examined the benefits of gaining the PRSA Accreditation. Whilst some practitioners felt undergoing the process demonstrated their commitment to the industry, several responded that it made no difference to their clients. Even though the CIPR promised to educate employers about the need to ask for professional body membership, specific qualifications and Accredited or Chartered status, most advertised jobs in PR do not include it in their job specifications.

Sectors and specialisms

PR is practised in all kinds of organisations, and most use the same tools and techniques. However, as the industry has developed, various areas of expertise have

Would making membership of the one of the professional bodies compulsory improve the quality of PR advice available to clients? Studies in countries where this is the case found that it was very difficult to enforce as there were so many different job titles in the field. In addition, infringement of the law was not actively pursued, with few prosecutions. It also did not tackle the issue of competence.

Would making all members of such bodies at least sign up to the CPD scheme be an improvement? How could the schemes be made more robust? How does PR compare with professions such as law and medicine where CPD is compulsory to practise?

If networking seems to be the most important skill in getting a job, how do your own skills in this area stack up? Have you gained jobs through responding to adverts or by using your own contacts?

emerged. Practitioners working in the same industry have formed special groups, such as MIPAA, which provides support for those working in the motor industry. The CIPR lists various sectoral groups, which members can join to network with those with common interests. Currently these are:

- Construction and Property. In-house and agency professionals in construction, residential and commercial property, architecture, building services, housebuilding, structural and civil engineering.
- Corporate and Financial. Practitioners within the City and industry.
- Education and Skills.
- Not-for-profit.
- Public Affairs. Professionals who interact with Government, the EU and devolved Parliament and Assemblies.
- Health and Medical. Includes NHS, private healthcare, health insurance and the pharmaceutical industry. Also those who deal with patients groups, health charities and medical research.
- CIPR Inside for internal communication professionals.
- Science, Technology, Engineering and Mathematics.
- International. For members working in-house or in a consultancy in an international context, or who want to develop their career in this direction.
- Local Public Services. Members in local government, health, housing and education.
- Marketing Communications.

PR agencies also split their areas of specialism into different sectors. Grayling sets out six divisions of expertise. Some of these relate to categories similar to the CIPR, such as healthcare and pharmaceutical; financial and professional services; consumer; and government and public sector. However, they also add energy, environment and industry, which covers cement and steel manufacturing, mining, oil, gas, electricity and alternative energies. Their clients include government departments, corporates and NGOs globally. Grayling also has a technology, telecoms and media division which offers a full range of media relations and marketing communications to clients in this competitive industry.

There has been academic research into growing areas of PR activity. One such is litigation public relations, investigated by Beke (2011). This is about 'managing the communications process during any legal dispute . . . so as to affect the outcome or its impact on the client's overall reputation' (Haggerty in Beke, 2011). Beke suggests that this area of PR developed in the US, but has changed when it migrated to the UK as a result of the different legal traditions of the two countries. With the growth of litigation and the growth of media interest in prominent disputes, legal teams have increasingly used PR support.

Public affairs has attracted media attention since the 1990s when MPs were found to be offering themselves on a consultancy basis to lobbying firms. Hearings by the Committee on Standards in Public Life unearthed concerns about the ethics of elected representatives being paid to advise those who wished to change or prevent legislation. The CIPR, PRCA and the Association of Professional Political Consultants (APPC) all revised their codes of practice. McGrath (2011) looked at how lobbying was regarded in the 19th and 20th centuries, to see how its current reputation evolved.

Garsten and Howard (2011) have also investigated how practitioners have differ-entiated the services they offer by stressing specialist and sector expertise. They list consumer, business to business, media relations, digital communications, corporate social responsibility, internal communications, investor and government relations. Indeed, this textbook follows a similar approach in splitting public relations into such specialisms in Parts III and IV. Garsten and Howard examined how these specialisms have developed over the past 25 years to try and provide insights into how they might evolve in the future.

The 2011 PR census listed sectors from where consultancies tended to get the majority of their work. Within the private sector, the sectors with the greatest demand sectors were technology; consumer services, media and marketing; general business services; financial services; and food, beverages and tobacco. On the in-house side, the majority of practitioners worked in charity/not for profit; public sector agency; and local government, the areas from which consultancies got the least work.

In his blog, PR Moment, Ben Smith (2015) spoke to several practitioners who suggested that job roles were changing and the old hierarchical lines between managers and executives were blurring. Angela Sinclair Millar, editor-in-chief at PR agency Bottle, suggested that a career is PR was 'a web of opportunity'. She added, 'Digital teams, analysis experts, trend spotters, content creators and high level strategists, have created a complex career path model.' She advised practitioners to 'throw out the rule book that tells you to race to the top. You can seek out positions that interest you, that challenge you and that allow you to build area expertise.'

Sim Mistry, development and PR director at brand and design agency the CLIP group, agreed that a career in PR was never straightforward. She said: 'I have had to learn new skills, learnt to work alongside creatives and designers and also incorporate new business development tasks along the way. It wasn't all about rising to the top, but it was more about the knowledge and experience gained, the people I have met, the clients I work with and the satisfaction of knowing that I love what I do.'

Rebecca Haynes, media and marketing specialist at agency Vantage PR started off as a PR intern: 'Clients are increasingly demanding a number of services from PR agencies that don't typically fall under the traditional PR umbrella. Everything from digital marketing to social ads can now be expected from a PR firm. What this means for a PR professional is that their career could end up going in a number of different directions that they hadn't anticipated.' She felt that this less structured approach meant 'endless learning opportunities, new skill sets, and the opportunity to become a specialist'. Do you think that a less clearly defined career path is an advantage or disadvantage? How might you find this challenging? Exciting?

END POINT

This chapter has summarised historical models of public relations and shown that there are several models for how PR might be practised. These models continue to create debate and to be compared against real-world examples. The main professional bodies have been reviewed, alongside a variety of ways that people can gain access to work in PR. Practitioner views on the skills needed show that there is no one right way to succeed. Valued qualities such as determination and creativity might be exactly the ones needed to take the industry forward so that practitioners may act in a more professional way. Some of these themes will be revisited in Chapter 4.

Professionalism and trends in PR

Alison Theaker

PR has always had an uneasy relationship with the concept of professionalism. Some practitioners have even declared that they do not see it in this way. At other times, the pursuit of professionalism seems like a way for PR people to gain respect or even just charge more for their services.

CHECK POINT

This chapter will examine:

- What makes a profession?
- What controls exist to govern public relations?
- What issues are affecting the development of the industry?

DEFINING A PROFESSION

The *Concise Oxford Dictionary* definition of profession is 'a vocation or calling, especially one that involves some branch of advanced learning or science'. Originally, the professions were law and medicine, and were practised by the sons of wealthy landowners after they had been to Oxford or Cambridge University. Later, specialised knowledge became the basis for entry (Cutlip *et al.,* 2000). Some of the characteristics of a profession are:

- an underlying cognitive base;
- practitioners;
- a disciplinary organisation;
- induction, training and licensing of members;
- rewards and sanctions for members;
- a code of ethics and accountability;
- quality assurance;
- the ability to ensure high standards of remuneration. (Elton 1993: 137)

The establishment of professional bodies worldwide has led to the introduction of codes of conduct and calls for regulation. Grunig and Hunt (1984: 4) put forward the view that 'true professionals possess a body of knowledge and have mastered communication techniques that are not known by the average citizen'. L'Etang and Pieczka (2006a) suggest that professionalisation is a simply a way to improve occupational standing, and win social approval. The Global Alliance of Public Relations Associations, founded in 2000, agreed principles which stated that a profession's characteristics included:

- mastery of a particular intellectual skill through education and training;
- acceptance of duties to a broader society than merely one's clients or employers;
- objectivity;
- high standards of conduct and performance.

The declaration also pledged the Alliance members to conduct themselves with 'integrity, truth, accuracy, fairness and responsibility to our clients, our client publics and to an informed society'.

In January 2003, the IPR was awarded DTI funding to conduct a best practice overview of the UK PR industry. The objectives of the study were both to spotlight best practice and to show how public relations contributed to the national economy and the competitiveness of British industry internationally. In early 2005, the IPR was awarded its Royal Charter and became the Chartered Institute of Public Relations.

However, Cornelissen (2008) suggests that an occupation will be seen as a profession only when it is socially valued as such. Public relations still has some way to go to achieve this. Corporate Watch (www.corporatewatch.org.uk/profiles/pr_ industry) even suggests: 'There is a considerable body of evidence ... to suggest that modern public relations practices are having a ... deleterious impact on the democratic process.' It goes on to list the achievements of the industry as putting 'a positive spin on disasters', undermining 'citizens' campaigns', gaining 'public support for conducting warfare' and changing 'public perception of repressive regimes'. The PR department is said to provide 'a line of defence ... to prevent information from slipping out'.

The Global Alliance (GA) continues to promote the debate of professional standards in PR. In 2010, the Stockholm Accords were published. These Accords put forward recommendations for the governance, management and sustainability of organisations and indicated how PR professionals contributed to the communicative organisation. Also in 2010, the 2nd Summit on Measurement set out the Barcelona Principles. They are mainly concerned with good practice in demonstrating the effectiveness of PR, but emphasise the importance of goal setting and measurement (CIPR, 2011a). Since then the Alliance has set up the Excellence in Corporate Communications microsite to encourage best practice in this area, published the Melbourne Mandate which discusses the future of organisations and communication, benchmarked Globally Accepted Practices (GAP), and begun consultation on a Global Body of Knowledge (GBOK) project (GA, 2016).

DEFINING THE PRACTICE

A Delphi survey was undertaken in 2000 to attempt to draw up a common European definition of PR but it concluded that 'it is difficult to find any pattern in the naming of the field'. It did suggest that there were four characteristics of European public relations:

- reflective – analysing standards in society to enable the organisation to adjust its own standards;
- managerial – developing plans and maintaining relationships with publics;
- operational – carrying out communication plans;
- educational – helping the members of the organisation to become effective communicators (van Ruler *et al.,* 2002).

Cornelissen (2008) suggests that 'the development of the body of knowledge is the crucial plank in the field's quest for professional status'.

CODES OF PRACTICE

The CIPR Code of Conduct was updated after a major consultation in 2000 and covers members' practice of PR; how the practitioner deals with the media, the public, employers, clients and colleagues. The Code emphasises 'honest and proper regard for the public interest, reliable and accurate information'. The member is required to 'maintain the highest standards of professional endeavour, integrity, confidentiality, financial propriety and personal conduct' and to bring neither the Institute nor the profession into disrepute. Professional activities must be conducted with 'honest and responsible regard for the public interest', and any conflicts of interest must be declared to clients as soon as they arise. Members must 'deal honestly and fairly in business' and 'never knowingly mislead clients, employers, colleagues and fellow professionals about the nature of representation'.

Members are expected to 'take all reasonable care to ensure employment best practice', which includes 'giving no cause for complaint of unfair discrimination', and safeguard confidences. Members must also be aware of legislation and regulation in all countries where they practise. Maintaining professional standards specifically encourages members to undertake the Institute's continuous professional development programme and to encourage employees and colleagues to become members also. The Code sets out a highly detailed process governing complaints relating to professional conduct.

The PRCA's Professional Charter covers similar ground. The Charter covers negotiation of terms and stresses the need for accuracy, openness about interests and regard to the public interest. The PRCA has specific codes which relate to investor relations, healthcare and parliamentary advice, which are in addition to the provisions of the Professional Charter. Those in investor relations deal with price-sensitive information and healthcare professionals have to be aware of legislation and make sure balanced and accurate information is given.

The Global Alliance's 2009 Annual Report stated that 'a majority' of members had filed the necessary certification to standardise their codes of ethics. Minimum elements that must be included are:

- an obligation to protect and enhance the profession;
- to be informed about practices which ensure ethical conduct;
- to actively pursue professional development;
- to define what public relations can and cannot accomplish;
- to counsel members on ethical decision-making;
- a requirement that members observe the recommendations of the Protocol.

Clauses on advocacy, honesty, integrity, expertise and loyalty are also required.

In 2015, the CIPR launched an interactive module on ethics as part of its CPD scheme. This consists of a 15-minute e-lesson, followed by an assessment which asks practitioners to make judgements on six scenarios, based on the requirements of the Code of Conduct (CIPR, 2016).

Despite these ideals, such bodies have no legal teeth. Codes can only affect members of these bodies, and even then are unable to force compliance – their only punishment is to expel the offender from membership. In 2015, the PRCA expelled Fuel PR International. PRCA Director General Francis Ingham (2015) felt that was important to show that 'no person or organisation is above the Code: it is the bedrock of our industry's professionalism'.

CREDIBILITY OF PRACTITIONERS

'Honesty begins at home. It is synonymous with trust and trust is the lubricant that makes our practice function.' Despite this aspiration, John Budd (1994: 5) relates the example of Hill & Knowlton chief, Robert Dilenschneider, who in 1988 warned against:

> twisting the facts 'a little'; unquestionably doing the unquestionable thing; ducking the truth, doing anything you knew 'in your bones' was wrong. Two years later [he] . . . advocates an array of highly questionable stratagems . . . publicly attack the competitor; steal his best people; insert Quislings into his ranks; and pre-empt his access to the media.

The conduct and regulation of lobbyists has been constantly debated in the media. Back in 1956, Tim Traverse Healey warned that 'the further development of public relations depends on the confidence of the community in the integrity of our prac- titioners' (quoted in Budd, 1994: 4). In 1997 a number of MPs lost their seats as a result of revelations in the media that some firms had allegedly been involved in paying them to raise questions in the House, and Ian Greer Associates, a long-standing firm of lobbyists, was forced out of business. Subsequently, Labour aide Derek Draper was accused of boasting that he could secure access to ministers for those who wanted to make their case. He was forced to resign. A media frenzy about 'spin-doctors' and lobbyists resulted in calls for more regulation and slurs cast upon public relations practitioners of all kinds, not just those engaged in public affairs.

In October 1994, the then Prime Minister, John Major, set up the Committee on Standards in Public Life under Lord Nolan. The Committee continued under the Labour government with Lord Neill as chair, and the IPR also gave evidence to the Wicks Committee on how to help clarity in political communication. Despite all this time spent in such committees, the nature of lobbying continues to be debated. Public affairs practitioners now have an extensive code which relates to their conduct towards MPs and clients. The UK Public Affairs Council (UKPAC) comprises the PRCA, CIPR and APPC.

PR possesses several of the prerequisites to be considered a profession, and the professional bodies show a clear desire to address the issues of entry, training and conduct of practitioners. They recognise that in order to achieve this, they must get the message across about ethical and professional working standards. The problem, ironically in an industry which prides itself on the ability of its practitioners to com- municate, is one of getting the message across to the relevant stakeholders in business. In February 2007, in the *PR Week* Ethics Debate, the motion 'PR has a duty to tell the truth' was defeated. The editor, Danny Rogers, paradoxically commented, 'the fact that PR people admit they need to lie occasionally is a sign of growing honesty

Kathy Fitzpatrick and Carolyn Bronstein put forward the case for responsible advocacy in *Ethics in Public Relations* (Sage, 2006). It is useful to compare their approach with Tony Harcup's examination of a related profession which is often critical of PR practitioners, in *The Ethical Journalist* (Sage, 2007).

DIVERSITY

The CIPR 2009 Benchmarking report found the majority (65 per cent) of the 1,940 respondents were female, but that 30 per cent of male respondents held boardroom positions, compared to 18 per cent of their female counterparts. The CIPR (2015) found that gender was the third most important factor in determining pay, and that this amounted to a difference of £8,348 between men and women doing the same work. Hughes (2016) concluded that the industry was in denial about embedded bias. Griggs (2016) reported that chief executives of the UK's top 50 agencies were mostly under 50, reflecting the CIPR's (2015) findings that 70 per cent of agency staff were under the age of 44. He suggested that older professionals had to move to in-house positions, and that ageism in agencies was responsible.

Edwards (2010) reported that although 12 per cent of the adult working population in the UK is from black and minority ethnic groups (BAME), only 1 per cent of public relations practitioners is from these groups.

Avril Lee, UK CEO for Ketchum Pleon, was interviewed by *PR Week* (Cartmell, 2011a) and quoted as saying: 'I don't believe the industry reflects the wider society we are in . . . It's not right and it's not good for business. If we get more diverse talent the work can only improve. If we don't have these people how can we understand these groups?'

The PR census (Gorkana, 2011) found that only 2 per cent of the industry came from BAME backgrounds. By 2015 (CIPR, 2015) this had improved to 9 per cent. However, latest figures state that the BAME population of the UK is 14 per cent, and could increase to 20–30 per cent by 2050 (Policy Exchange, 2014).

How many black PR practitioners do you know? Are there any in your company? Why is the PR industry not attractive to people from ethnic minorities? Is it a problem that the industry does not reflect the ethnic mix of the UK population?

and confidence in what they do' (Rogers, 2007). This hardly helps the case for professionalism.

FUTURE ISSUES

Several studies have examined issues which will affect the development of public relations in the future. Richard Edelman, CEO of Edelman, the world's largest privately owned PR agency, spoke at the 2011 PRSA Leadership Rally. His main theme was trust. 'We operate in a world without trust ... People see everything as spin and lies.' He believed that PR had the power to build trust. However, he felt that whilst PR was best equipped to deal with complex communications, practitioners from different disciplines, especially advertising, were competing for this position (Woodward, 2011).

Ogilvy PR Australia's CEO, Kieran Moore, declared that, 'the age of spin ... is now dead'. He was announcing agency research which suggested that PR's most significant role in 2021 would be strategic thinking and planning. The majority of respondents (76 per cent) felt that the term 'PR' would be dropped in the next decade (Ma, 2011).

A series of meetings were held with CIPR regional groups in the UK in 2011 to discuss possible future developments to 2020. The Wessex group felt that a successful future would involve a respected practice led by a strong professional body. However, the most likely scenario suggested that PR would continue to be misunderstood and that citizen control over communications would increase. Thus there remained a need for a better definition of what PR practice was meant to achieve, allied to a need to improve approaches to evaluation (White, 2011).

The 2011 Communication Director's survey (Murphy, 2011) revealed that integrating communications across the organisation was the major challenge for respondents. Because of the rise of social media, audiences are able to access information from several sources so communications must be consistent. This increased the need for new ideas, but directors felt that these most often came from advertising agencies, underlining Edelman's point above.

Dealing with new channels of communication and social media is another common topic. Zerfass *et al.* (2015) found that technology was significantly influencing the practice of PR. Whilst technology created more opportunities for communications, respondents to their survey also reported increasing pressure, feeling an obligation to be 'always online'.

The CIPR (2015) offered some positive developments, with nearly 80 per cent of practitioners stating that they contributed to their client's business strategy, and 98 per cent contributing to developing communications strategies. Half of practitioners also stated that a senior member of the communications team briefed the board on communications strategy, with a further 25 per cent saying that there was someone on the board with direct responsibility for this.

Baker *et al.* (2016) offered a 'Future PR' study by consulting with 70 members of the CIPR. Technological developments were discussed, such as: the use of messaging using WhatsApp and others; micro-payments through Blendle; the changing demographic of Facebook from teens to over 50s; live-streaming events. Another development was the use of citizen activists to spearhead campaigns, such as Kathleen Haase's petition to stop British Airways selling trips to SeaWorld whilst orcas were kept in captivity. Whale and Dolphin Conservation (WDC) launched the petition on Change.org using one of its supporters.

The PRCA (2016a) issued its recommendations for good communications, and advised practitioners to move beyond stereotypes, engaging with stakeholders based on shared interests and creating experiences. Theaker (2016) reflected that the reputation of the industry itself continued to concern practitioners, but that there did not appear to be much progress. This is especially ironic given that PR is responsible for the reputation of its clients.

ACTION POINT

Several eminent practitioners and academics were asked what they felt were the main issues that the PR industry was facing. Their replies are included below.

In the future, public relations professionals are going to have to be more aware of two major and profound changes in society which will have far-reaching implications for the profession. The first is the overall context in which their organisations operate. According to the World Economic Forum (WEF) there are five principal drivers that are making a major impact on the world and organisations. These are time compression, complexity, inter-connectivity of issues, interdependence in the global village and a shift in context – power is shifting from the west to the east and from the north to the south. Many issues facing the world today such as the continuing effects of the economic slow-down, increases in migration and instability in states and society are the result of these drivers eliding. Governments are unable to supply answers or deal with these immediate and pressing issues and in the meantime longer-term issues such as climate change and the impact on water supplies, and global health issues and inequalities are, in some cases, being put on the back burner. These complex problems in turn affect organisations and the way they need to interact with society and the demands their stakeholders are making of them to be part of the solution to these issues. The barriers between the economic, social, technological and political spheres are breaking down and organisations can no longer isolate themselves from being involved in these wider concerns. The WEF concludes that it is only by acting 'together' that there is a sustainable future. This provides a major opportunity for public relations. Contextual and commun-icative intelligence will be the new gold. Understanding, interpreting and interacting with a world of growing complexity will be a skill that will be highly prized by senior managers in the future. This has always been our role, and it will be vital for organisational survival in the future.

The second topic is the Fourth Industrial Revolution. To quote the WEF, 'We stand on the brink of a technological revolution that will fundamentally alter the way we live, work, and relate to one another. In its scale, scope, and complexity, the transformation will be unlike anything humankind has experienced before. We do not yet know just how it will unfold, but one thing is clear: the response to it must be integrated and comprehensive, involving all stakeholders of the global polity, from the public and private sectors to academia and civil society.' Already this is impacting on the way public relations is conducted because of the impacts of social media, the move to mobile, to cloud technology and to visual. But this is just the beginning. Big data is already being used to push pin-point accurate advertising to us as individuals, but it also has the potential to shape and control as well as liberate and empower lives in a way that is currently unimaginable. Those organisations who have the means to gather and interpret huge data sets such as Amazon, mobile phone companies, governments and Google will wield extraordinary power. Smaller companies will be able to do the same. The role of public relations in ensuring that their organisations are responsive and responsible to the needs to society and people will be bigger than ever. Helping them define a purpose which is contributory to society and to act to their principles (or values) always bearing in mind that people matter and have value will be one of the biggest challenges the profession faces.

Professor Anne Gregory PhD, Professor of Corporate Communications, University of Huddersfield

We have entered into different local/global/regional as well as social/economic/political spaces (environments) whose common traits appear to be economic inequality, political polarisation and social disruption. Environments (spaces) where the 'one organisation/one voice' paradigm, in tandem with the top-down as well as the bottom-up approaches to communication are progressively losing their power, perhaps and hopefully leading to a more desirable communicating-with, relationship-building, peer-to-peer process. The contradiction between these two features evokes fuzzy versus linear thinking and public relations professionals are left with the priority task of understanding and monitoring the quality of stakeholder relationships, also by evaluating the reciprocal levels of trust, commitment, satisfaction and control mutuality in every relevant relationship.

The recent concepts of diversity, sustainability, influencers, always-on, engagement, storytelling and at least as many other buzzwords have become the jargon of a profession that mirrors itself and its cultural decadence and 'political correctness'. The growing market acceptance of public relations signals the rise of power of the public discourse in the agendas of clueless and confused social, private and public organisational leaderships. The almost terminal depletion of social capital (as per Robert Putnam) induced by those three common traits, can only hopefully lead us to the concept of relationship ... resilience (another buzzword!), while we strive to improve our critical understanding of the changing environment and improve our abilities to listen, particularly by avoiding all those tools that lead to confirmation bias (listening only to what we want to hear). Specifically – as we seem to mostly confide in what we gather from our peers, and as deteriorating physical as well as digital 'spaces' lead us to depletion of our habitats – we need as professionals to focus much more on risk analysis and pre-emption than to specialise in crisis management when it 'hits the fan'.

Toni Muzi Falconi, Senior Counsel Methodos (Italy), public relations adjunct at the Vatican's LUMSA University (Rome), author and polemicist (PR conversations)

Marketing and PR: two terms that have launched a hundred thousand textbooks and several million careers. The relationship between the two has been academically scrutinised and debated in practice for decades. But are we so different? As we look to the future of our profession, the truth could be more fraternal than you might think.

I have spent almost 20 years in public relations, but more recently I have been head of content at two digital inbound marketing agencies. Inbound – or content – marketing is the latest big thing, with three-out-of-four marketers making it a priority for 2016. It seeks to engage audiences through issues, not products. Through empathy and expertise, not promotion. With content playing a central role. Sound familiar? Inbound wants to establish a dialogue, to tell a story. There is even a dedicated team that conducts media relations under the guise of 'influencer outreach'. And social media is leveraged in exactly the same way as in PR; to generate interest and facilitate dialogue.

To some in PR this probably is not news. Indeed, many in our industry have long held a broader view of PR's potential; evangelising the power of good communications in making a good business, regardless of channel. This latest convergence is fuelled by the ever greater digitisation of communi-cations. How information is being sought out, consumed and the role this all plays in influencing reputations and buying behaviour is redefining the relationship between public relations and marketing. Or not, depending on your view.

So what does this all mean for the future? For some, this blurring of traditional boundaries is heresy. But if you see the opportunities for PR presented by digital media and the power and influence of integrated, collaborative communications, I wager this won't be a surprise. Whether we call it marketing or PR can be left to the endless debates. Or perhaps the conversation should focus on if there is even a future for either as a standalone concept?

Alister Foye, visiting lecturer in PR and communications at Birmingham City University, seasoned PR practitioner, sometime journalist and current marketer

The CIPR's State of the Profession 2015 survey demonstrated alarming facts about PR – we have a problem with skills and action is needed to ensure the public relations profession is fit for the future.

The survey paints a picture of a two-tier industry in which, for the majority, PR is a technical practice. Time is largely spent on content creation or media relations. Then as practitioners progress into management, we expect people to stop being tactical and demonstrate leadership. We expect interpersonal and strategic management capabilities as well as the hard business skills of pitching, project management and financial planning. The majority of people believe they have these skills.

We need to educate and train the next generation of PR professionals to have the skills to be managers and business strategists as well as excellent communicators. The benefits could be significant in terms of the acceptance of public relations as a strategic management function.

There is evidence, perhaps for the first time, that media relations is no longer the thing we all do more of than anything else. We've talked for a long time about how media relations should not and by and large does not define our profession. Now, 'content' creation is considered more important. Content comes in all shapes and sizes, with increasingly sophisticated DIY tools and skills that capitalise on digital and social media.

The last ten years saw monumental upheaval with the advent of social media and digital communication but the next challenge is already here. The language of PR is evolving.

The consumption of video online is breathtaking. YouTube has in excess of four billion video views a day. Facebook claims more than double that. Newspapers are increasingly desperate for video content, because video drives views. The message for PR people is clear. Press releases and email remain valuable. Still images are not going away, but there is an inexorable rise in video content. It is a lexicon we must understand and adopt. It's a daunting prospect but an exciting one. With the ability to go straight to the consumer via owned media channels PR has never had a more pivotal role in communications, but we must learn and adapt.

Rob Brown, CIPR President 2016, Founder and Managing Partner, Rule 5

Public relations seems to be a profession that's always 'nearly there', but never complete. On the one hand, significant progress has been made on the way to becoming a management and leadership function; by the same token, the standards for measurement and evaluation have started to improve. On the other hand, if the public relations profession wants to gain significance in the coming decade, it still has further upgrading to do. It first needs to find its own response to the age of hyper-transparency, in which organisations are accountable more frequently than ever. Corporate governance and leadership are already being reconceptualised and PR should follow. Secondly – with PR booming in the major markets of the global East and South – a balance needs to be found between the search for joint standards and the celebration of differences between markets and cultures. This is also the goal of the Global Alliance. Thirdly, the profession – together with its educators – needs to close the quality gap that still persists between top practitioners and the bottom tier. And finally, public relations must start to better contribute to the big responses needed by humanity and society in the coming decade, including responses to global warming, ageing, automation, inequality and a slowing global trade flow.

Professor Gregor Halff, Singapore Management University and European School of Management and Technology, Chair of the Global Alliance for Public Relations and Communication Management, Chartered Institute of Public Relations

END POINT

The discussion of whether public relations can be, or desires to be, a profession, continues worldwide. In a presentation to the Public Relations Institute of Australia in 2007, I suggested that the answers to the questions, 'Can PR ever be a profession?' and 'Does it matter?' would be 'No' and 'No'. I do not feel that PR will ever have the same gravitas as law or medicine, but that as long as clients and organisations continue to see the benefits of using PR counsel to communicate their aims and value, that should not worry PR practitioners. That is not to say that I condone 'unprofessional' behaviour, nor denigrate the efforts of the global PR community to agree on good practice guidelines. It is healthy that we reflect on practice and strive to improve it. The opinions in the last section show that academics, practitioners and pro-fessional organisations are addressing these questions on an international scale.

Part II

Public relations planning

Introduction

Heather Yaxley

This Part of *The PR Strategic Toolkit* presents planning as a professional approach to strategic public relations. It reflects a need for PR objectives and activities to derive from and support the wider organisational strategy and be consistent with the mission, vision and goals set by senior management.

Being able to plan effectively and efficiently is a requirement for all public relations practitioners, regardless of where they work or how long they have been doing the job. Job descriptions and role responsibilities emphasise the wide range of competencies that are developed by being involved in planning.

Many organisations have a formal process of planning. This may follow a hierarchical process whereby a main strategic plan informs functional and operational plans. Forward planning may look ahead to guide the organisation over many years, for instance with a rolling five-year plan. Shorter-term planning is likely to involve an annual process, including establishing budgets. The PR department will be required to establish a functional plan detailing its purpose, resourcing and priorities. Operational plans need to be integrated with other functions, such as marketing and HR. Specific campaign plans are then required for projects undertaken. Consultancies may also be briefed on developing campaign plans.

The six chapters in this Part appear to support a classic linear approach to planning where a series of steps should be followed sequentially to generate a proposed plan that is then signed off and implemented. Such a process is thorough – and time-consuming. It reflects a rational approach to management whereby matters can be predicted and controlled. Yet this logical planning approach seems at odds with the spontaneous flexibility of day-to-day operations in a busy PR function. Too often plans, if prepared, are forgotten, or only reviewed and amended as part of the next cycle of planning.

In reality, planning is not something that should be reserved for annual budget rounds or major projects. It does not apply just to campaign proposals or getting sign-off to implement activities. It can be both strategic and tactical. Plans may have a single use or support ongoing operations. They may be developed as policies, standard procedures or for guidance. Or plans may emerge organically and require an ability to improvise. Planning is both proactive and reactive.

Action planning is adopted in this Part, where strategic planning is seen as a problem-solving approach. It can be used to identify new solutions and develop ways to evolve existing processes and practices. This reflects the Japanese concept of *kaizen*, which involves gradual, ongoing and continuous improvement. It is also evident in the iterative and incremental *scrum* method, which is a key component of the agile working approach that Betteke van Ruler (2016) has applied to public relations practice. Similar process improvement concepts are lean management, six sigma and total quality management (TQM).

This approach to planning supports continual professional development. It encourages practice-based learning and proactivity in improving routine operations on a regular basis. Planning is also strategically transformative when enacted as an effective process of intervention for achieving innovative and original advances throughout organisations.

The professional planning concepts considered in the next six chapters are not presented as a rigid set of procedures, or recommended best practices, to be followed without question. Plans must be contingent (dependent) on external and internal situations rather than advocating a single solution to be adopted in all circumstances. Indeed, this Part aims to equip practitioners with practical tools (from research to evaluation) to be used as necessary in planning a range of PR programmes.

Each of the individual chapters in Part II contributes in an iterative and incremental manner towards a plan-do-check-act management process. The Appendices contain supplementary materials, including checklists and pro-forma documents, which practitioners are encouraged to adapt for their own purposes.

This Part supports other chapters in *The PR Strategic Toolkit* where specialist application or engagement with particular publics is required. The framework presented reflects the two key aspects of plans identified by Mintzberg (1994):

1   Action planning (strategies and programmes) – management decisions to inform behaviour
2   Performance controls (budget and objectives) – assess results of behaviour undertaken.

PR practice has focused traditionally more on action than control, but the necessity to achieve specific objectives within agreed budgets is a fundamental aspect of professional planning and should not be ignored. It is a challenge to be both goal-directed and activity-focused, but without a clear purpose, PR actions run the risk of being superficial, disparate and undervalued. At the same time, a scientific approach that focuses primarily on the end direction and budget constraints without the ideas, inspiration and creativity required to determine effective solutions loses the art of public relations.

Integrating the two aspects of planning acknowledges that public relations is involved primarily with intangibles, such as reputation, relationships and communications. Although the processes involved can be defined and controlled to some extent, the outcomes of PR activities may be harder to pin down. This does not excuse the failure to determine objectives and undertake evaluation seen all too often in PR practice. For example, no more than a veneer of planning is evident in many published campaign case studies.

In preparing this Part, various PR planning models and emerging ideas have been reviewed. The key components within these are reflected in the following chapters:

Chapter 5 Situational analysis focuses on research skills, tools and techniques that enable PR practitioners to gain insight into organisations, issues and opportunities.

Chapter 6 Understanding public psychology brings in theories, concepts and methods that help to understand people based on undertaking quantitative and qualitative research.

Chapter 7 Setting objectives provides a detailed consideration of practical approaches, alongside a critique of common problems and errors.

Chapter 8 Strategic campaign execution tackles the implementation stage at the heart of all PR planning models. As well as creativity and tactics, a strategic approach is emphasised and what is meant by a PR strategy is explained. A framework for developing narratives (from a dialogic perspective) is presented alongside tips on pitching and gaining approval for ideas.

Chapter 9 Budgeting and resourcing offers a straightforward approach that even maths-phobic PR practitioners can adopt. It looks at identifying required resources, determining costs, presenting budgets and other skills required in performance control management.

Chapter 10 Monitoring and evaluation is presented at the end of Part II, but needs to be entwined throughout the planning process. The chapter presents an ongoing, iterative approach to guiding and adapting plans through the implementation phase. In this way it differs from planning models that imply an objective can be set, actions undertaken and success evaluated. Although it is vital to know where you are heading, planning should allow for the end goal to be reviewed and redirected if necessary.

The structure follows the simple RACE approach of Research, Action, Communication and Evaluation (Marston, 1963, cited by Smith, 2005). However, it reflects the philosophy of Baines *et al.* (2004) that planning steps are not necessarily followed in order; they may be undertaken simultaneously or revisited during the process.

Planning is ultimately about what can be done with the available time, money and resources, rather than what is ideal or desirable. Over-promising and under-delivering undermines professional PR practice and is avoided by a realistic approach that does not claim to be low cost, or free. Certainly much can be done using public relations without big budgets, but cutting corners or skimping on the time and effort required to plan is a false economy. Organisations gain real value employing public relations strategies wisely; this Part seeks to guide practitioners in achieving that aim.

Part II ends with an 'Outro' chapter. Its purpose is to present a counterpoint to managerial rationality and a scientific structured approach to planning. It considers the merits of artistic spontaneity and the dramatic freedom to act on instinct. It advocates greater use of technology as a means of freeing up resources to take advantage of opportunities where imagination and speed of response are essential. Most of all, it encourages readers to move away from the riparian edge of the certainties of the land and uncertainties of the river, to explore a multiplicity of 'intellectual tributaries' where 'there is room for emotion and absurdity' (Brown, 2015: xv).

CHAPTER 5

Situational analysis

Heather Yaxley

This chapter provides an understanding of the research skills, tools and techniques that enable PR practitioners to gain insight into organisations, issues and opportunities.

CHECK POINT

After reading this chapter, you should be able to:

- Adopt a knowledge management approach to public relations
- Apply research skills, tools and techniques to inform PR activities.

KNOWLEDGE MANAGEMENT

The action research approach applied in this chapter supports practice-based learning. It positions public relations practitioners as informed 'knowledge workers and theory generators', who apply, and develop, 'practical theories' that are 'located in and generated from everyday practices, inspired by tacit intuitive forms of knowledge' (McNiff, 2013: 4).

Practice-based learning involves an active process of professional development where people are intrinsically motivated to augment their competencies. Existing knowledge and skills are tested in real-life situations where practitioners develop personal theories of what works well and how practices can be improved. This theorising about practice can be informed by prior experience, research, scholarship and reflexivity.

Action research involves the investigation of practical situations by 'insiders' who wish to 'explore improvements in areas they think important' (Hinchey, 2008: 3). The process of action research is cyclical involving 'systematic inquiry, which includes information gathering, analysis and reflection' (Hinchey, 2008: 4). The outcome of action research should be a set of recommendations, which if implemented would result in a new cycle of action research. Stringer (2014) presents this model in three recurring steps: Look | Think | Act.

A focus on action research and practice-based learning addresses the criticism by Van Ruler *et al.* (2008: 1) that a focus on informal, *ad-hoc* research in public relations is harmful to 'its prestige and its status'. They offer a structured approach to planning, albeit one that is more flexible than traditional views of 'command and control' management.

For public relations to act as a strategic function, it needs to encourage development of capabilities in analysing issues and opportunities. The knowledge base of PR practitioners will not be respected if it is based predominantly on personal experience, intuition, common sense, methodologically weak research or habitual practice. Likewise it is not enough to know how to execute tactics without being able to provide a rationale to support a course of action.

A Public Relations Information System Management (PRISM) approach is presented in Figure 5.1. This concept incorporates objective, quantitative data (e.g. organisational performance statistics), and subjective, qualitative information (e.g. narrative analysis of social media coverage). It advocates looking beyond organisational boundaries as knowledge is increasingly co-constructed online (Phillips and Young, 2009).

Organisations increasingly recognise the value of knowledge as a strategic resource (Zack, 2002) with technology enabling information to be sourced, recorded and analysed to provide intelligence upon which decisions can be made.

Public relations practitioners could enhance their contribution towards strategic stakeholder relationships by developing organisational competence in listening. Grunig (2016) contends that: 'Perhaps, the most important aspect of public relations as a strategic management function is the research that public relations professionals do to listen to, interact with, and communicate from publics to management.' In contrast, research has been termed 'surveillance' by L'Etang (2008: 86), when organisations seek to exert power over those being monitored. Bourne (2016: 124) likewise criticises research commissioned by organisations as a means to 'manipulate stakeholders'. He observes that digital technologies have increased 'dataveillance' based on algorithms.

These arguments are supported by an international PR study by Macnamara (2015) that found listening to be a rare occurrence. When it did happen, it was used mostly to serve the interests of the organisation as functional research, complaint resolution, social media monitoring or consultation with elites or dominant parties.

Knowledge management includes consideration of the social capital inherent in the organisation's relationships. This highlights the strategic value of an intelligent stakeholder management system (compliant with data protection legislation).

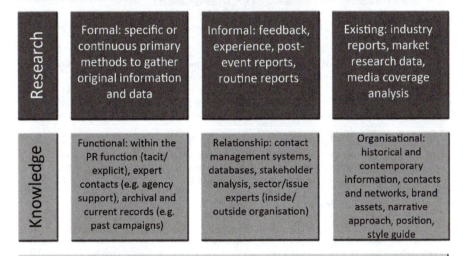

FIGURE 5.1 Public Relations Information System Management (PRISM)

Ihlen (2009) draws on Bourdieu's typology of capital in the context of public relations. This is useful for reflection on the value of the organisation's PRISM knowledge base (Figure 5.2).

Knowledge management systems should be designed around the needs of the PR function (and where relevant, the wider organisation, including senior management) for timely, relevant information to guide decision-making and address matters that arise. It should include secondary (existing) and primary (commissioned) research undertaken internally and externally, on a specific and/or continuous basis.

The starting point is existing information within the PR function, followed by information collected elsewhere in the organisation (e.g. market research). Collaboration with other functions is a cost-effective option for primary research.

Economic PR capital

- Records of resources (budget, staffing, tools, collateral materials) available to the PR function to achieve the organisation's communicative and relationship objectives

Knowledge PR capital

- Cultural/informational capital possessed by individuals within the PR function (e.g. 'professional knowledge, verbal facility, or general cultural awareness' Ihlen 2009: 72). This could be determined, monitored and managed in conjunction with the organisation's HR procedures, e.g.: appraisals, training and CPD

- Repositories of knowledge within the PR function, such as libraries, publications, reports, image and video archives, media coverage, historical records, etc.

- Procedural knowledge, for example, of financial or political processes, or how traditional and online media operate

- Human and information sources of knowledge within the organisation, such as professional standing, sector expertise, opinion leadership and competent spokespeople

- Knowledge of networks supporting co-orientation, alliance building and other PR strategies

Social PR capital

- Patterns of relationships maintained by the PR function and the wider organisation. These occur at the individual, functional and organisational levels. Capital includes the size of direct network, plus indirect relationships accessible through it

- Evaluation of exchange and communal (Grunig, 2001) relationships. Covey (1989: 55) states human assets are pivotal as 'people control physical and financial assets'. He also discusses building trust within relationships as an 'Emotional Bank Account' (p. 188) which further implies capital balances can be created and maintained

- Level of 'investment' (conscious or unconscious) put into building relationships, particularly by the PR function, plus indicators such as contact records

- Formal and informal obligations in relationships. These may only be realised in the long term and reflect a level of risk in terms of the return on investment made (Ihlen, 2009). Social capital is necessary to achieve some outcomes and in these circumstances, it has to be 'well-established' (Ihlen, 2009: 74) before any return can be realised. This can be considered in the case of CSR

- Tangible benefits, e.g. reduced costs or organisational advantage. For example, PR's role in internal communications may increase productivity by enhancing relationships between employees and management

- Knowledge capital may be accessed through the established network of relationships, and also transferred by the organisation to others in the network, thereby enhancing social capital

- Comparative information regarding similar organisations enables benchmarking

- Symbolic capital, such as reputation for being knowledgeable or well-connected is inherent in social capital and can be obtained through knowledge capital. Other elements of reputation, such as credibility or legitimacy can also be determined through analysis of relationships. Ihlen (2009) advocates qualitative analysis of symbolic capital. He argues (p. 76) that it is 'easier to secure symbolic capital through cultural capital than through economic capital'. That is, it is harder to buy a good reputation!

FIGURE 5.2 Capital value within Public Relations Information System Management (PRISM)

ACTION POINT

Commercial services are available to support construction of a PRISM structure. Freitag and Quesinberry Stokes (2009) detail the following media-related service providers:

News and information distribution networks – maintain media database information

Media monitoring companies – provide media directories, digital 'clippings' services, broadcast transcripts and statistical-analysis reports

Software providers – offer the above services and systems 'for managing public relations functions such as organizing and cataloguing collateral materials, managing contacts, monitoring legislative issues, and coordinating compliance reporting' (p. 27)

Broadcast specialists – produce and coordinate relevant materials, organise studio tours and training.

Review the services used by your employer. What knowledge is gained from using external service providers? How does this supplement information about the media gained internally within the organisation?

A PRISM set-up need not be complicated or expensive to create and maintain. Existing systems and procedures can be integrated within a more holistic knowledge management approach. What is important is that information is not left to stagnate. Phillips and Young (2009: 76) claim 'the half-life of knowledge is becoming shorter' but knowledgeable people are a valued asset. In addition to recording existing knowledge, the PR function needs to interrogate, analyse and interpret data to create new knowledge.

Stacey (2003) argues that new knowledge is often tacit and needs to be translated from its location in someone's head into an explicit form. He says knowledge is diffused between members of a team though mimicry and a process of 'discussion, dialogue and disagreement' (p. 164). Phillips and Young (2009) believe collaboration should be extended outside the organisation's boundaries, albeit whilst recognising the importance of protecting vital information. They advocate that PR should develop 'transparency policies' (p. 77), which support it as a strategic bridging function within organisations (Kim and Ni, 2010).

UNDERTAKING RESEARCH

Watson and Noble (2007) identify the first stage of PR planning as analysing the problem, which Cutlip *et al.* (2000) explain as understanding what is happening now. CIPR (2011c) suggests gaining input from analysing existing data, conducting original research, auditing the organisation's communications, as well as benchmarking and reviewing the client/management brief. A comprehensive checklist of information required in a PR brief is available in the Appendices.

In order to adopt the Public Relations Information System Management (PRISM) approach or to gain insight to inform planning, it is important to understand the basic components of research.

Formative secondary research

The purpose of initial research is to provide sufficient context to enable reflection on the nature and causes of the situation to be addressed by a PR campaign. Smith (2005) recommends formative research should analyse the:

1   Situation (problem or opportunity facing the organisation)
2   Organisation
3   Publics (Chapter 6).

Analysis starts with an orderly investigative process of fact-finding, which can also be used to monitor and adjust action plans as required. Cutlip *et al.* (2000) advise a process that involves:

*   **A searching look backward** – history of the organisation and the situation
*   **A wide look around** – publics' opinion about the organisation
*   **A deep look inside** – character, personality of the organisation
*   **A long, long look ahead** – contribution to mission, forces affecting future success.

This can be thought of as a case study inquiry. This 'reflective and very focused' research method involves investigating 'contemporary cases for purposes of illumination and understanding' (Hays, 2004: 218). The technique is used to produce 'in-depth descriptions and interpretations over a relatively short period of time' (Hays, 2004: 218). Case study research can be used to support decision-making and look for explanations in situations that may be complex or straightforward.

Parameters of the scope of the research need to be set. Case studies offer an opportunity to look at a unique or typical set of circumstances. Defining the purpose of the study and determining precise research questions ensures formative research has a clear direction. Research questions can be descriptive (what, when, where and who) or explanatory (why and how). These may generate quantitative data that can be counted or measured (e.g. opinion polls) or qualitative information (e.g. stakeholder views).

Sufficient understanding may be obtained solely via existing (secondary) sources. Alternatively original (primary) research may need to be undertaken (surveys, observation, focus groups, etc.). Primary data will be more up to date and tailored to the

ACTION POINT

Secondary sources include: archival records, meeting records, reports, books, newspapers, magazines, multimedia materials, raw data, research studies, media coverage, internet and social media search results, census studies, published reports, statistics, academic journals, historical data, media usage information, lifestyle studies (e.g. http://kantarmedia-tgigb.com/), organisational surveys (e.g. consumer or employee), online surveys (e.g. www.yougov.co.uk) and government data (www.direct.gov.uk).

Identify an issue or organisation in the news and review secondary sources to gain a deeper understanding. How did you locate these sources? What methods were used to originate the data found? How can you review the data? What insight have you gained?

specific requirements, but will be more costly, time-consuming and may require expert skills and resources to acquire.

Primary research

If existing data does not provide enough understanding, primary research may need to be undertaken. This can be done in-house, although professional research companies offer expertise in constructing objectives and questions, determining suitable methodologies, undertaking research and analysing results.

Figure 5.3 presents a three-part workflow, which allows for modification depending on the nature of the research study and how it develops.

Internet research

Online sources provide easy and often free access to an enormous volume of information. As well as secondary data, primary research can be undertaken using social media and online tools. Blythe (2006) warns that the advantages of online research are offset by concerns over its validity and credibility. PR practitioners should remember that all data (whether sourced online or by other means) need to be analysed and reviewed to provide intelligent insight.

ANALYSIS

Information obtained by research needs to be interpreted to provide meaning that can inform decision-making. Data must be prioritised, reviewed, edited and key aspects identified. This should involve an objective process, or at least, bias or subjectivity

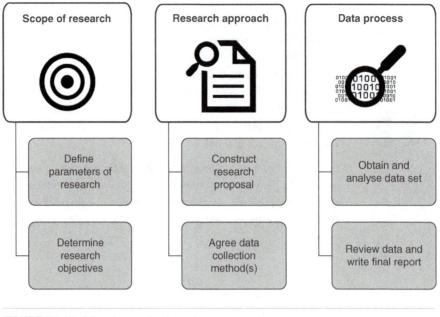

FIGURE 5.3 Workflow for conducting primary research

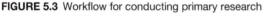

needs to be acknowledged if it cannot be avoided. Any limitations on the data, such as time dependency, need to be considered.

As part of their 'boundary-spanning' role, PR managers should provide insight into issues that could impact on the organisation to determine appropriate responses. This involves environmental scanning, scenario planning, trend forecasting and information analysis.

Scanning and forecasting

Johnson *et al.* (2005: 230) recommend that 'constant but thin' attention should be paid to changes in the organisation's environment. Scanning is inherent in PR operations (e.g. media monitoring) but should be formalised within a PR Information System Management approach to enable tracking of trends, changes and emerging issues. Regular reports can then be generated as a professional outcome from this aspect of the PR knowledge base.

- **Environmental scanning** involves gathering and processing information in order to identify and monitor issues that may affect the achievement of the organisation's aims. Sung (2007) advocates a formal environmental scanning process, which enables the PR function to provide 'an early warning system' to management (Moss and Warnaby, 1997: 61). Environmental scanning helps improve understanding of an issue and facilitates scenario planning.

TALKING POINT

FAKE FACTS

Understanding of the unreliability of online information has increased as a result of high-profile complaints about online fake news and recognition that social media and search engine algorithms influence what we see. As with any other research method, it is important to be mindful of the dangers of confirmation bias, where we look for information that supports an existing perspective.

Access may also be an issue as much online information is restricted or expensive to obtain. Search engines may favour paid-for results and everyday skills may be insufficient to undertake effective online searches.

There are ethical issues to consider when undertaking online research. The British Psychological Society (2013) publishes a helpful document (www.bps.org.uk/system/files/Public%20files/inf206-guidelines-for-internet-mediated-research.pdf).

The most important aspects, however, concern the validity and credibility of online information. It is vital to distinguish between evidence and opinion. Wherever possible statistics and other data need to be tracked to an original source. If these derive from research, then the methodology of that requires critical examination.

The calibre of the source should be checked, although this is no guarantee of accuracy. For example, many newspapers have opinion pages online that are not subject to any editing process of fact-checking. Likewise papers in many online open-source journals are paid-for or not subject to robust peer-review.

Crowd-sourced studies similarly need to be treated with caution. Participants may be chosen on the basis of convenience (often an existing relationship with the researcher) or they will have selectively decided to respond.

Even sites that purport to undertake fact-checking need to be questioned. The chief fact-checker of the *New Yorker* explained the publication's approach at the Columbia Journalism School (www.cjr.org/the_delacorte_lectures/new-yorkers-fact-checker-post-truth-facts-fake-news-trump.php).

Have a conversation with colleagues and friends about a particular topic and see where they obtain their information. Are they aware of any fake facts? How would they go about verifying that these were fake? How can PR practitioners avoid including fake or questionable data in their work?

- **Scenario planning** is a useful method of strategic thinking (Van der Heijden, 2011). It involves envisioning possible future situations that can be evaluated and compared. PR practitioners tend to take a short-term focus, so scenario planning enables them to contribute towards longer-term strategic decision-making (Sung, 2007). The process of considering possible outcomes helps address uncertainties (see Chapter 13). Scenario planning should be undertaken in partnership with other functions in the organisation, and external publics (where feasible). As a 'collective and learning process' (Sung, 2007: 191) it can be used to assist knowledge transfer between the PR function and these other parties.

- **Trend forecasting** identifies current issues and extrapolates these on the basis of previous experience or statistical predictions. It could be used to create a 'most likely' scenario or investigate how uncertainties could affect the future. One key question in trend forecasting is 'what if?' to allow creative answers to emerge. Historical data and trends may, or may not, help predict the future; disruptive thinking may be required to challenge the idea of continuity.

- **Gap analysis** involves considering variation between the existing and desired situation. Koenig (2003: 297) specifies the need to focus on what is most important rather than easiest to address. Once the nature of any disparity is identified, its significance can be determined and action taken to close the gap, if appropriate. A gap analysis can be used in conjunction with other tools such as a cultural web or stakeholder mapping which can be plotted for the current and ideal scenarios (see Appendices).

- **Force field analysis** identifies factors that support or counter proposed changes; allowing reflection on how aspects supporting change can be reinforced and those countering it can be overcome (Johnson *et al.*, 2005). The nature and magnitude of the identified forces need to be assessed and a cost–benefit analysis undertaken to determine the value of taking action.

Predicting what may happen in the future may involve human reflection or computer modelling. Gregory (2012: 67) states 'information is power' although Pieczka (2006b: 350) cautions against the belief that information creates a clearer picture; arguing any process needs 'to take account of human sense-making strategies'. This emphasises forecasting is an interpretive rather than a deductive process.

PESTEL analysis

This is a mapping tool reviewing the findings obtained by environmental scanning. It is used to evaluate the impact of Political, Economic, Socio-cultural, Technological, Environmental and Legal issues. A PESTEL analysis can be used at a big-picture (macro) level, or to examine a specific issue (micro level). As with risk analysis (Chapter 13), the likelihood of any incidents occurring and their potential consequences need to be determined. A numerical or other indicator could be used. For example, arrows could be included to identify trends, with plus/minus symbols indicating possible impact.

A checklist for undertaking a PESTEL analysis is provided in the Appendices. The first step is to determine salient issues, with additional secondary or primary research used to identify less obvious matters. Many sources of data can be used (media coverage, internal knowledge, external reports, etc.) but analysis requires answering the question 'so what?' to understand the implications for the particular situation.

Inter-relationships between various factors in the PESTEL analysis need to be considered. However, the main aim of the analysis is to consider critical issues rather than worry about the 'right' box in which to include a particular factor. It is important to use evidence in reflecting on issues and note reference sources to facilitate reporting to management and for future reference.

SWOT analysis

Insight from a PESTEL analysis can be reviewed using a SWOT analysis (see Appendices). This considers internal capabilities (Strengths and Weaknesses) as well as key issues facing the organisation (Opportunities and Threats) as a basis for developing responses. Objective data and reflection is required to avoid any over-confidence in assessing the organisation's competencies. In this way, the PR practitioner needs to enact Holtzhausen's (2002: 77) concept of the organisational activist prepared to stand up in the face of 'the normative discourse of corporate management'. When reviewing issues it is important to separate those where action is possible from those where the organisation has no control. In other cases, counsel may be that PR activities are not an appropriate response and/or the organisation needs to change its policies and practices.

Corporate communications audit

Undertaking a communications audit enables the PR function to analyse different sources of information. According to Grunig and Hunt (1984) an audit should be receiver-oriented to determine whether information has been received, understood or acted on.

A checklist for undertaking a communications audit is provided in the Appendices. An audit provides insight into the process and content of communications (distribution and feedback). It should review data relating to channels, target audiences and key messages. Communications may be categorised in terms of being direct/mediated, one-way/two-way, level of technological sophistication, ownership of

ACTION POINT

In the 1970s, the International Communications Association (ICA) undertook a longitudinal study as a model for organisational communication audits (Goldhaber and Krivonos, 1977). The model analysed communication networks and experiences. Audiences were asked to rate communication vehicles on the following scales:

Not useful	to	Very useful
Inaccurate	to	Accurate
Ineffective	to	Very effective
Untimely	to	Timely
Dishonest	to	Honest

Respondents were asked to comment on their needs and media preferences; satisfaction with amount of information received; method of communication; ability to understand that information and preferred method of communication.

All current communication vehicles were assessed for usefulness, actual use, accuracy, timeliness, comprehensiveness and perceived effectiveness. Factors relating to trust and honesty were included if required. Other factors were determined from initial exploratory interviews with select stakeholders.

How useful do you think this approach would be for understanding views towards the organisation and situations it faces? What are the problems and benefits of such research?

channel, source/control of information, involvement of the audience, reach, cost per impression, key challenges to effectiveness, etc. Research may be undertaken routinely or conducted for specific campaigns.

Content analysis

The content of communications (including media coverage) can be analysed using quantitative and qualitative methods (see Appendices). A framework should be used to categorise factual data (title, edition, date, etc. for a newspaper cutting) and methods of analysis (e.g. rating as positive/neutral/negative). An inductive counting system within predetermined categories (e.g. brand mention) could be used or a more in-depth, exploratory approach (deductive) developed to identify themes and look for meaning within the data. Coding of articles may be undertaken by humans or computerised.

Macnamara (1999) proposes a media analysis model to consider:

- **Issues** – strategic insight and intelligence into issues/trends reported in the media

- **Client** – evaluate effectiveness of media relations and PR for the particular organisation in terms of what is being reported
- **Sources** – strategic insight and intelligence into other sources in media, such as competitors
- **Public** – evaluate messages reaching target audiences – share of voice, impact on opinion.

Analysis has three steps:

1 Select the media form/genre
2 Select issues/investigation period
3 Sample content (census, random, purposive, quota, stratified composite).

It is important to consider if any sample of materials being analysed is representative and replicable, or selected for other, more purposeful reasons. For example, relating to a critical incident or issue.

Fawkes (2012b) notes discourse analysis as a supplement to media content analysis. This involves looking at the meaning of language as well as subjective experience and the context and social rules governing specific narrative use.

Other analytical tools and techniques

A list of various tools and techniques is provided in the Appendices. In determining which analytical tools and techniques to use, it is important to be clear over the purpose of the analysis. An option should not be used without careful consideration that it is appropriate for making sense of a situation and relevant data set.

It is also key to ensure that information used to populate any model can be substantiated as a credible source, and that the source is attributed to the data. A list of sources should be indicated as a valid evidence base. There are likely to be experts within any organisation who have access to more specialist information and their insight can be essential in both understanding a scenario and making sense of research data.

For instance, if looking at economic factors for a PESTEL analysis, PR practitioners should speak with their finance director, investigate the finance media, research particular topical aspects, look at economic forecasts and so on. It may not be feasible to undertake robust research on every factor. Hence, after initially scoping out the situation, more in-depth research should be undertaken for issues deemed to be priority factors. A root cause analysis can help to determine the critical incidents identified as having particular significance for the topic of inquiry (see Appendices).

Analytical models offer conceptual frameworks to guide thinking. As such they may be adapted to best fit the nature of analysis being undertaken. This is compliant with an action research approach. Brown (2015: 4) argues that 'PR is experiential and contingent', which combined with the view of McNiff (2013) that theory should not be seen as the preserve of textbooks and academics, supports a contention that practitioners should play a part in testing and updating models, theories and conceptual frameworks to best support their practical experiences.

OUTCOME OF ANALYTICAL PROCESS

Cutlip *et al.* (2000: 347) describe the situation analysis as 'the unabridged collection about everything that is known about the situation, its history, forces operating on it and those involved or affected internally and externally'. (This latter aspect is considered in Chapter 6.)

PR practitioners should summarise the findings of their research and analytical tools to produce a problem statement or insight report to be presented as intelligence to management or used to inform campaign development.

Intelligence summary

A succinct summary should include statements regarding:

- The initial problem/opportunity that research has sought to examine
- An overview of the research methodology and sources used
- Key findings and an interpretation of these
- Identification of any limitations and need for any additional research
- Insight gained into the problem/opportunity that PR activities need to address
- Appendices containing further detail, list of sources, etc.

This summary will be supplemented by the outcome of research into publics (Chapter 6). It should help inform objectives and other aspects of the PR plan. However, it should not include suggestions relating to how the issue will be addressed. Iterative research should be undertaken where feasible during the implementation phase. An update report that adds new knowledge can then be produced. In addition, research, reflection and results of any PR activities undertaken should be added to the knowledge management database.

It is particularly important when presenting the outcome of analysis that a logical and considered approach is undertaken. Whilst providing a concise overview (executive report) that clarifies the context, key findings and main issues to be addressed (problem statement), the source and detail of research undertaken should be available for reference to demonstrate a robustness of methodological approach.

END POINT

A knowledge management approach to public relations is suggested to establish a PR Information System Management structure comprising a comprehensive intelligence resource. The value of PR to the organisation is underpinned by the economic, knowledge and social capital this approach offers.

As well as providing continuous intelligence, research is the first step in PR planning. It enables information to be obtained in relation to problems or opportunities facing organisations. Analysis of the situation and the organisation needs to be undertaken (alongside analysis of publics – Chapter 6) using existing and original information (where necessary). A range of tools are available to PR practitioners to support their strategic role as 'boundary-spanners'. An organisational activist approach is recommended to ensure frank and objective reporting to management of the issues identified.

Knowledge management and situation analysis position public relations as helping organisations deal with uncertainties. That is done on the basis of competencies that are continuously developed through experience, learning and reflection.

CHAPTER 6

Understanding public psychology

Heather Yaxley

This chapter explains the importance of social sciences, particularly the field of psychology, in helping PR practitioners to understand stakeholders and publics. Methods to enable the segmentation, research and analysis of individuals and groups are outlined.

CHECK POINT

After reading this chapter, you should be able to:

- Relate social sciences, notably public psychology, to the PR strategic planning process
- Understand how to segment stakeholders and publics for research purposes
- Consider a variety of research methods to gain insight into the attitudes and behaviour of stakeholders and publics.

SOCIAL SCIENCES AND PUBLIC RELATIONS

In the 1920s, PR counsel, Edward Bernays drew on 'a hodgepodge built from various modern psychological theories' (Ewen, 1998: 169). For example, his 'Torches of Freedom' campaign challenged the taboo on women smoking by using Freud's ideas of penis envy to associate cigarettes with a challenge to male power.

White (2000: 148) suggests that PR is applied psychology because it concerns 'the way people think, feel and behave'. Indeed, Ihlen and van Ruler (2007: 243) observe that 'public relations is often studied from a managerial, instrumental perspective or a psychological, behavioral perspective'. However, they call for a broader underpinning that draws on social theorists in order to develop 'sociological oriented public relations approaches'.

A 'socio-cultural "turn"'(Edwards and Hodges, 2011: 1) developed in recent years within public relations literature has started to shift attention to the broader role of public relations in society. This reflects re-emergence of a sociological orientation evident in the US *Dictionary of Sociology* which claims, public relations' 'theories and techniques represent applications of sociology, social psychology, economics and political science' (1944: 255).

Brown (2015: 9) contends that identifying PR as a science is 'aspirational, misleading and problematic'. He favours a multidisciplinary understanding that incorporates the humanities alongside social sciences, including 'behavioural psychology, organisational theory and sociology' (p. 10).

Similarly, Ihlen and van Ruler (2009: 1) claim, 'social theory can help us to make sense of public relations at societal, organisational and individual levels'. This may be considered to offer an academic rather than a practice-based focus. However Fawkes (2015: 38) develops an understanding of PR ethics within a context that includes 'the sociology of professions'. Indeed, many themes and concepts from sociology are evident when thinking about public relations practice. For example, the basis of corporate social responsibility may be seen as the inter-relationship between organisations and society. Likewise, terms such as structure and agency, power, legitimacy, social capital, discourse, reflexivity and publics that are prevalent in the field of sociology are referenced in this Part of *The Public Relations Strategic Toolkit*.

Many other disciplines have potential for greater exploration and application in the context of public relations when seeking to understand publics. These include psychosociology, social anthropology, ethnography, biopsychosociology, neuroscience, bioethics and behavioural economics.

Further transdisciplinarity is arising from examining problems occurring at the interface of technology and society, organisations and individuals. Areas such as health technology literacy, for instance, suggest a need to examine the implications for communicating with various sectors of society, particularly those who have low levels of power or knowledge concerning health systems and technological developments.

Sociological perspectives ought to be of interest to government communicators in particular. However, the adoption of behavioural science (applied psychology) by the UK government and other public sector organisations continues to focus on influencing public behaviour through 'nudge interventions' (Oliver, 2013: 1). This raises ethical questions owing to the one-sided, covert nature of such approaches.

PSYCHOLOGY AND PUBLIC RELATIONS

Many psychological concepts have been applied to public relations in order to gain an understanding of the underlying reasons for human behaviour that can then be influenced (Fawkes, 2006). In planning, analysis of publics is included by Smith (2005) in the formative research phase. Other models, such as Gregory's 12 stages of planning (2015), place stakeholders and publics later in the process, after analysis and objective setting.

In keeping with the iterative approach advocated in this Part, understanding of publics and stakeholders is considered to be an ongoing process that has relevance at all stages of planning activities. It is also an important consideration in anticipating issues or crisis situations.

Empathetic listening

Cutlip *et al.* (2000: 344) state that 'effective public relations starts with listening' and recommend systematic research to obtain 'reliable feedback'. Similarly, Covey (1989: 237) advocates the principle 'seek first to understand, then to be understood' which is achieved by 'empathetic listening' (p. 240).

Listening and understanding relate to research and analysis of stakeholders and publics within the PR strategic planning process. Recognising the perspectives of those with whom we seek to communicate, influence, build relationships or co-orientate demonstrates a proactive, 'diagnose before you prescribe' approach, which Covey says is 'the mark of all true professionals' (1989: 243).

Learning theories

Theories looking at how behaviour is acquired or changed assume a predictable relationship between a stimulus and a response (Bettinghaus and Cody, 1994). Social learning theories suggest that people acquire mental rules relating to positive or negative outcomes which reinforce their behavioural responses. Psychologists, therefore, study the formation of attitudes (learned evaluations), beliefs (subjective expectations) and values (guiding principles) and their relationship to behaviour. These and other relevant cognitive aspects can be researched within the PR planning process.

Relationship theories

Socio-psychological theories investigate how people interact with others. They cover concepts such as credibility, social norms, social exchange, trust, loyalty, conflict, cooperation and co-orientation. Although a relational perspective of PR has been studied since the 1990s (Jahansoozi, 2006), there has been limited consideration of relational aspects within the planning process.

This omission is important given the increasingly networked nature of communications, for example, through social media. Focus has been on individuals as influencers rather than looking at gaining insight into communities that may be of interest to public relations practitioners as potential advocates or activists.

Rather than providing insight into group psychology, surveys and opinion polls tend to present aggregated opinions. Likewise, where focus groups could offer in-depth, qualitative information, this method is used in PR primarily to generate ideas or assess concepts (Edmunds, 2000). Participant selection tends to be based on demographic or other criteria rather than interpersonal relationships. The extent to which participants constitute a public is therefore questionable.

Jahansoozi (2006) notes the need to establish baseline measures of knowledge between an organisation and publics. She cites surveys of 'individual members of the public' (p. 88) used to determine variables relating to co-orientation (similar and mutual understanding of views). However, the wider complexities of organisational–public relationships, inter-public relationships and the impact of inter-organisation relationships (Chapter 20) have received relatively little attention.

Social psychologist, Donelson R. Forsyth, has studied group dynamics extensively, believing that 'to understand people, we must understand their groups' (2009: 2). He confirms that groups influence members' actions, thoughts and feelings. As well as group cohesion, Forsyth considers entitativity (perceived unity), which indicates that people may appear to be a group when they are not (or vice versa). The characteristics of a group, which can be researched, are stated as (p. 12):

Interaction: Groups create, organise and sustain relationship and task interactions among members

Goals: Groups have instrumental purposes, for they facilitate the achievement of aims or outcomes sought by the members

Interdependence: Group members depend on one another, in that each member influences and is influenced by each other member

Structure: Groups are organised, with each individual connected to others in a pattern of relationships, roles and norms

Unity: Groups are cohesive social arrangements of individuals that perceivers, in some cases, consider to be unified wholes.

The potential existence of a 'group mind' (that differs from summation of individual cognitions) suggests a need to understand psychology of the group itself. For example, individuals' own standards may vary from the group norms that they would support. Janis (1972) identifies 'groupthink' where seeking consensus overrides dissent and consideration of other options.

SEGMENTATION

Segmentation strategies are evident in interpersonal and targeted communications. There are several ways in which populations can be segmented (see checklist in the Appendices):

Demographics

Demographic segmentation is based on specific or multiple personal characteristics such as: age, gender, family size, income, occupation, education, religion, ethnicity and nationality. Although a relatively easy and popular method, categories can be broad and consequently offer limited psychological understanding. This can be seen in the use of the generational label Millennials that in the UK comprises 17 million people – a quarter of the population (ONS, 2017).

Socio-economic segmentation combines education, income and occupation characteristics (Pickton and Broderick, 2005). The traditional six-class system (based on the occupation of the head of household) is evident in ABC1 media circulation data (www.abc.org.uk), indicating advertisers' preference to reach those in the top three categories:

A   Higher managerial. administrative and professional

B   Intermediate managerial, administrative and professional

C1   Supervisory or clerical and junior managerial, administrative and professional.

The other classes (C2: skilled manual; D: semi-skilled and unskilled manual; and E: casual labourers, state pensioners, the unemployed) are traditionally less attractive to advertisers. Such segmentation can be criticised for being outdated and not taking account of other factors, for example, life stages that apply across categories.

Life stage segmentation combines marital status and family size. Segments reflect changes traditionally experienced over time (e.g. Single, Newly weds (no children), Full nest (with sub-stages depending on age of children), Empty nest (children left home), Retired, Solitary survivor). Again the usefulness of life stage segmentation can be questioned for not reflecting the diversity, complexity, dynamism and pluralism of modern society.

Geographics

Geographic segmentation is based on the area where someone lives, works, shops or other location-relevant behaviour. Various levels can be used; e.g. society, continent, country, region, town or postcode. Geographical differences have been evident in British politics, for example, in results of the EU referendum.

Another option segments by nature of the area, e.g. coastal, country, urban; whilst terms such as Third World and BRIC (Brazil, Russia, India and China) are used to describe areas similar in economic development terms. In media relations, geographic segmentation may reflect reach or distribution; e.g. BBC Local offers 60 websites covering the British Isles.

Geographic segmentation is relevant for international public relations, although increased globalisation (including travel and internet technology) affects its value.

Geodemographics

Demographic and geographic information are combined to reflect the idiom: birds of a feather flock together. ACORN (a Classification of Residential Neighbourhoods) groups UK neighbourhoods, postcodes and consumer households (www.caci.co.uk). It signifies that those living in geographic areas with similar demographic and social characteristics tend to share common lifestyles and patterns of buying behaviour. ACORN uses variables from the government population census undertaken every ten years.

ACTION POINT

REAL-TIME GEODEMOGRAPHICS

Mobile devices, wearable technologies, GPS tracking and the Internet of Things make it increasingly possible to gain real-time information about where people are (and what they are doing) at any particular time. It therefore links spatial and temporal information.

Real-time geodemographics is defined as 'the study of people according to their spatial location over time' (Aljandali, 2016: 178). The concept was first proposed by Furness (2008). He refers to 'spatially referenced data' (2008: 104) as a means of generating new classification systems. Data may be collected overtly, for example, from using mobile phone contactless payment or in-vehicle technologies. There are also reports of covert tracking of customers by stores such as Marks & Spencer (Knapton, 2016) that gather data as mobile devices search for wifi connections. This can also be used for targeted hyperlocalised communications.

Live-stream video through social networks offers further opportunities for both engaging with people and gaining information about them through real-time comments.

Review your behaviour over a 24-hour period and consider what digital trace data you may have generated. How could the data collected through real-time geodemographics be useful to public relations practitioners? What are the benefits and drawbacks of such approaches? Do you have any ethical concerns?

Stakeholders

Freeman and McVea (2005: 192) state 'a stakeholder approach to strategic management, suggests that managers must formulate and implement processes which satisfy all and only those groups who have a stake in the business'. From a corporate communications perspective, Bernstein (1984: 93) identifies nine 'separate but not discrete' groups: internal, local, influential groups, trade, government, media, financial, customer and general public.

At a broader level, stakeholders can be divided into internal or external; or more narrowly using demographic, geographic and other variables. Internal stakeholders could be segmented by occupation, department, location, grade level, union membership, length of service, for example.

Gregory (2009: 185) confirms practitioners should 'move from the general to the particular' when segmenting. She details a circular model to map stakeholders, with those with the highest stake placed nearer the centre. Prioritising may depend on the nature of the issue being addressed. For example, Johnson *et al.* (2005) identify three types of external stakeholders: economic, socio/political and technological.

A power/interest matrix (Mendelow, 1991, adapted by Johnson *et al.,* 2005: 181) creates four segments according to the extent to which stakeholders 'impress their expectations' on the organisation and 'whether they have the power to do so'.

- **High power and high interest:** key players; keep informed and satisfied
- **High power and low interest:** keep satisfied
- **Low power and high interest:** keep informed
- **Low power and low interest:** require minimal effort.

Mapping should be based on research, although some assumptions could be made. It is important to recognise variation within stakeholder groups and any interaction that could affect group behaviour or indicate a need to consider relationships within or between groups.

Stakeholder mapping can be used as a dynamic tool as part of the planning approach. This involves using gap analysis to consider action required to move from an existing to desired position for a specific issue. Models that support stakeholder mapping are included in the Appendices.

Behaviour

In marketing, behavioural segmentation generally relates to aspects of the purchasing process or consumer usage of products and services. Within public relations, Grunig and Hunt (1984: 144) suggest a 'behavioural molecule' involves publics detecting, discussing and organising to do something about issues.

Originating from socio-psychological theory (Vasquez and Taylor, 2001), the situational theory presented by Grunig and Hunt (1984) proposes four categories depending on cognitive or behavioural connection to an issue:

- **Nonpublic** – not affected by an issue
- **Latent** – affected but not aware
- **Aware** – detect an issue but not taken any action
- **Active** – discussed the issue or taken other action.

Grunig and Hunt (1984: 160) suggest using survey interviews to categorise people in relation to issues. They identify four 'patterns of publics':

- Active on all issues
- Apathetic on all issues
- Active only on issues that involve nearly everyone in the population
- Active on single issues.

Active publics can be segmented (Grunig and Hunt, 1984) into those who seek or process information once a problem has been recognised. Participation segments can be determined, e.g. whether someone comments using Twitter or joins a Facebook group. Media usage and preference is another useful way of segmenting publics for PR campaigns.

Segmentation could consider the level of engagement an individual or group has with the organisation. For example, contact and support could be plotted on an axis of friend–foe. The Fair Fuel UK campaign (Chapter 17) identified over 150 parliamentarians actively supporting its campaign, who could be further segmented by the nature of this support.

Psychographics

Psychographic segmentation groups people according to their cognitive characteristics, for example:

- Attitudes – learned evaluations (e.g. favourable or unfavourable); protect self-image
- Opinions – judgements which are narrower and less rigid than attitudes
- Beliefs – subjective expectations
- Values – guiding principles
- Interests – matters about which someone is curious or concerned
- Lifestyle – activities, interests and opinions (AIO); reflects attitudes and values
- Motivations – reasons for behaving in a particular way
- Self-esteem – evaluation of self; feelings of personal worth or confidence.

This type of segmentation is necessary for PR practitioners addressing situations where cognitive (awareness/knowledge) or affective (attitude/preference) change may be sought. For example, PR initiatives to encourage older people to use the internet could segment by attitudes towards technology, beliefs about the costs of using computers or personal interests (e.g. wish to be in contact with family members who live overseas). Patterns of characteristics can be summarised in typologies; for example, Technophobes or Silver Surfers.

A PORTRAIT OF GENERATION NEXT

Pew Research Center (2010) noted similarities in the values, attitudes, behaviour and demographic characteristics among the Millennial generation (born in the 1980s and 1990s). However, Fields and Robbins (2008: 64) state 'you have to communicate one way to one type of teenager (jock, computer geek, emo, goth, party animal, Calvinist), but then you have to communicate a completely different way to another type of teenager (surfer, headbanger, gangsta, spelling-bee freak, polka lover)'.

Millennials have grown up in a world of rapid change. They are now maturing and entering different life stages. Possibly their experience of having grown up with digital technologies will influence how they behave and communicate as they age (see www.goldmansachs.com/our-thinking/pages/millennials/). However, given the number of people who today can be classified as Millennials, the term may be increasingly irrelevant as a segment.

Attention is shifting to the younger, post-Millennial generation termed Gen-Z (born after 1993). For example, Goldman Sachs has researched this generation and other emerging themes (www.goldmansachs.com/our-thinking/pages/what-if-i-told-you-full/).

How useful do you think generational studies are for those working in public relations? What is the value in identifying subcultures within age groups? Are you familiar with the term Gen-Z? How do you feel this demographic segment could be researched in terms of psychographics for PR campaigns?

Although segmentation is important, categories must have sufficient homogeneity to be useful, recognisable and accessible. This is particularly relevant when undertaking research to inform PR activities. It should also be remembered that no group is totally homogeneous.

Individuals, groups and organisations

Groups can be segmented using demographic, geographic and other approaches discussed above. They could also be analysed by purpose (e.g. interest or pressure groups), motivation of those joining, relationship to the organisation, etc.

Segmenting organisations is useful for inter-organisational public relations (Chapter 20), where broad categories can be used, e.g.:

- Industry sector (e.g. UK Standard Industrial Classification)
- Geographic location or presence (e.g. national, multinational or international)

- Number of employees (small-medium enterprises (SMEs) defined as under 250 employees)
- Financial data (e.g. profitability, turnover, size of budget, membership of FTSE100 index).

Organisations and groups can be analysed for psychographic, behavioural and reputational characteristics. For example, employee satisfaction ratings or environmental performance may be relevant criteria.

RESEARCH METHODS

Research needs to be undertaken routinely or for specific campaigns. It is important to establish baseline data to inform PR campaigns, particularly when seeking to address cognitive (thinking) or affective (feeling) objectives. This will include factual information relating to publics, e.g. size, location, demographic composition or behaviour of relevant segments.

The most common methods (surveys and interviews) involve individual participants, although groups or organisations can be researched using the following methods (Forsyth, 2009):

- Observation (covert, overt or participation)
- Self-reporting (including sociometry, a way of measuring relationship patterns)
- Case studies (including action research, validating theory through practical application)
- Correlational studies (seek patterns of relationships between variables).

Secondary data

As part of operational management, organisations maintain records containing factual, psychographic and behavioural information regarding customers, employees and other stakeholders. Such data can be linked to the Public Relations Information Systems Management (PRISM) structure discussed in Chapter 5.

Many external sources of data on attitudes and behaviour exist. For example, the National Centre for Social Research (www.natcen.ac.uk) publishes the British Social Attitudes survey (www.britsocat.com) tracking changing attitudes to social, economic, political, moral issues.

Secondary sources may provide raw data or published summaries. Such research has been conducted for a particular purpose and could be outdated. Nevertheless, it is low cost and relatively easy to access. Raw data offer the opportunity for new analysis.

Primary research

Where existing information is inadequate or not available, original research may be undertaken. It can be used to improve understanding of publics in relation to issues or opportunities facing an organisation, or inform communications activities (e.g. communication preferences, probable responses, etc. The cost and time investment is offset by ensuring PR resources are used effectively with greater likelihood of success in achieving strategic objectives.

Saunders *et al.* (2000: 85) present a research process 'onion' enabling suitable methods of research to be considered (Figure 6.1).

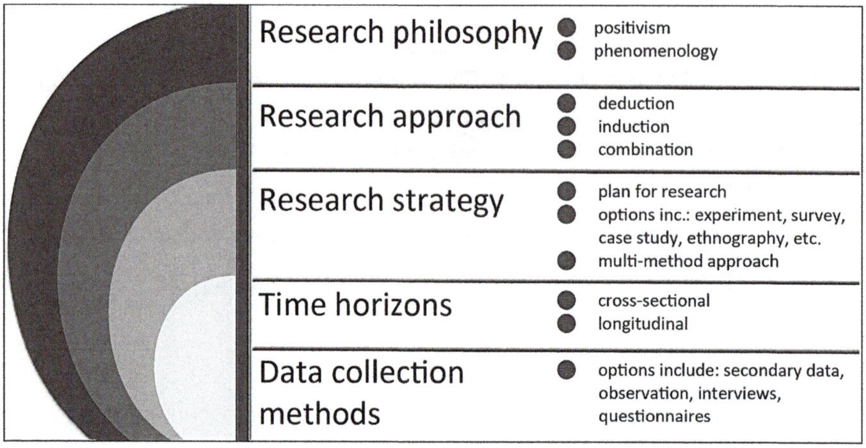

Research philosophy	positivism phenomenology
Research approach	deduction induction combination
Research strategy	plan for research options inc.: experiment, survey, case study, ethnography, etc. multi-method approach
Time horizons	cross-sectional longitudinal
Data collection methods	options include: secondary data, observation, interviews, questionnaires

FIGURE 6.1 Research process (based on Saunders *et al.*, 2000)

Research philosophy

- **Positivist:** assumes a scientific, objective perspective that seeks generalisations from research
- **Phenomenology:** assumes a social-scientific, subjective, perspective that recognises complexity and uniqueness of people and experiences being researched.

Research approach

- **Deduction:** tests hypotheses, seeks to determine causal relationships between variables
- **Induction:** builds knowledge, explores reasoning, understands context and meaning
- **Combination:** adopts deductive and inductive approaches.

Research strategy

- Plan for the research including objectives, questions, sources, constraints, rationale
- Options include: experiment; survey; case study; grounded theory; ethnography; action research; cross-sectional and longitudinal studies; exploratory, descriptive and explanatory studies
- Multi-method approach – employment of different methods to extend the value of the study, enable triangulation (increase reliability of data), reduce limitations.

Time horizons

- Cross-sectional – undertaken at a particular time
- Longitudinal – undertaken over a long period of time.

Data collection methods

- Wide range of options including secondary data, observation, interviews, questionnaires.

Key considerations include ethical aspects of designing, conducting and analysing research; credibility of findings and avoiding assumptions or errors in logic. Chapter 5 outlined the benefits of using research specialists. Such expertise is particularly useful when undertaking complex or important research; it also provides independence that can be important if findings are published. A research brief checklist can be found in the Appendices.

Sampling issues

A census researches everyone within a population (or segment). Unless this group is small and everyone within it can be accessed, a sample of participants will need to be identified. There are two main ways of sampling (Saunders *et al.*, 2000).

Probability sampling

This is used where conclusions will be drawn for the entire population from the results. A population list is required to ensure everyone has an equal chance of selection. If this is not possible, a sampling frame must be determined. For example, a full list of employees could be obtained and a probability sample taken from this. Alternatively, an email list could be used as the sampling frame, although it will omit employees without computer access.

Non-probability sampling

Various techniques rely on subjective judgement to select participants. These include:

- **Quota** – participants selected using key variables, e.g. if researching PR practitioners, the PR census (Gorkana, 2011) suggests a quota of six females to four males.
- **Purposive** – based on a specific reason, e.g. select typical or exceptional participants.
- **Snowball** –uses a network approach to identifying participants.
- **Self-selection** – voluntary participants.
- **Convenience** – anyone who is available.

Response rates

Hill and Alexander (2006) identify discrepancies between different methods of data collection and a tendency for low response rates to reflect a bias towards those with high levels of involvement (positive or negative). They cite (p. 106) 'a rule of thumb in the research industry is that a response rate above 50 per cent is sufficient to minimize the problem of non-response bias' and urge caution with rates under 20 per cent.

Surveys

PR practitioners use questionnaires to measure awareness, knowledge, beliefs, attitudes and behaviour (Szondi and Theilmann, 2009). However, surveys rely on closed questions which prevent exploration of reasons or meaning. Answers may also reflect what is salient (easily recalled) rather than most important or truthful.

Polls research individual views on issues, which are aggregated to indicate the opinion of a population. Although Brettschneider (2008) confirms the popularity of opinion polls within news reporting, surveys have greater value to PR practitioners than simply gaining media coverage.

Surveys can be self-administered or use an interviewer. Collection methods include: online, telephone, face-to-face, email, postal and delivery and collection. Research can be commissioned by the organisation or questions can be submitted to an existing omnibus survey. Surveys use standardised questions, which could seek factual, evaluative, information or self-perception responses (Grunig and Hunt, 1984). Types of questions include (Saunders *et al.*, 2000):

- **List** – choice of prompted responses. May offer a dichotomous choice (e.g. yes/no, agree/disagree) or multiple choice (list of answers). Don't know, unsure or other options can be included.
- **Category** – respondents select one response from a list of options, e.g. how often they undertake a particular behaviour.

- **Ranking** – respondents order their answers as an indication of importance.
- **Scale or rating** – evaluate attitudes or beliefs by asking respondents to indicate how strongly they agree or disagree with a statement.
- **Quantity** – requires numerical answers.
- **Grid** – lists questions in rows with responses indicated across columns.
- **Open questions** – respondents answer in their own words. These are more common in interviews, but can be included in surveys for exploratory purposes. People tend to skip questions requiring extensive reflection. Time is required to analyse and interpret narrative.

Responses can be coded to produce statistical data such as totals, averages and frequencies. Data can be investigated using cross-tabulations, factor analysis and other calculations to identify trends, correlations and so forth. Results can be presented using tables, charts, graphs and infographics.

ACTION POINT

REPUTATION ANALYSIS

Fortune magazine's list of America's most admired companies asks executives and analysts to rate companies in their industry on eight attributes: quality of products/services; innovativeness; value as a long-term investment; financial soundness; ability to attract, develop and retain talent; community responsibility; use of corporate assets; quality of management.

The Reputation Institute (www.reputationinstitute.com) examines 15 stakeholder groups in more than 25 industries covering 50 countries using a standardised measurement system to rate more than 7,000 companies. The results generate a 'RepTrak Pulse' score of 0 to 100, representing an average measure of people's feelings (reputation) for a company.

How useful do you think league tables are in understanding the reputation of organisations? What evidence do respondents use in forming their opinions? How can PR practitioners apply this information in developing plans?

Qualitative methods

Qualitative research provides a depth of understanding, particularly important when investigating complex communicative relationships and behaviour (Daymon and Holloway, 2011). This approach tends to be time-consuming and focuses on a select, small number of participants or cases where rich information can be gained. Qualitative research produces insight into individual, subjective experiences rather than statistical or representative data. The researcher is seeking meaning and plays an active role in generating, recording and interpreting results.

The interview (individual or focus group) is the most well-known qualitative research method. Themes or open questions are used as prompts to gain considered responses. Follow-up and probing questions test understanding and add further depth. Interviews can be undertaken face-to-face, by telephone or online. Video or audio recording is helpful to obtain a full record which can be transcribed to facilitate analysis.

Qualitative analysis should look for themes, similarity/differences and meaning in data. A coding structure can be prepared in advance or a more exploratory approach taken whereby a framework emerges during the analytical process.

ACTION POINT

ANALYSING CORPORATE CULTURE

Schein (1991) recommends researching corporate culture using a focus group of motivated individuals asked to identify relevant cultural artefacts. Spontaneous and prompted responses are analysed to identify shared underlying assumptions. The Cultural Web (Johnson *et al*., 2005) offers a useful framework of categories for research. Observational research and documentary analysis can be used. Diaries and other forms of reflexivity enable researchers and participants to record and analyse thoughts and experiences. See Appendices for checklist.

For example, Raz (2003) undertook observational research at Tokyo Disneyland, as well as individual interviews and focus groups. He then reflected on the findings.

Using either your own organisation or one that you can visit, use a variety of qualitative methods to gain insight into its culture. Consider issues involved in undertaking observational research and how findings can be analysed. Review your findings using the Cultural Web tool.

Motivational research

Most research involves a rational thought process, so more creative methods are required to uncover subconscious or hidden motivations that reflect emotional impulses. Psychoanalyst Ernest Dichter (1986) believed that asking direct questions produced unhelpful answers and sought to put the research problem into a larger frame of reference. Among his famous campaigns was one for Ivory soap where he interviewed 100 people regarding their bathing habits. He did not ask why they used soap but discovered a Saturday night bath ritual among women going out looking for romance. This led to the concept of freshness being used in the successful campaign. Dichter believed that a researcher's role is to interpret public behaviour as people are unaware why they do things. By talking about experiences, a proposition can be developed which is then validated by quantitative research.

Csikszentmihalyi and Rochberg-Halton (1981: x) examined 'the role of objects in people's definition of who they are, or who they have been, or who they wish to become'. They proposed that the emotion evoked by objects is symbolic of attitudes. An example is seen in an episode of *Frasier*, when the lead character replaces an old recliner chair belonging to his father who becoming upset shares memories illustrating the chair's sentimental value. By interviewing people about their homes and cherished objects, Csikszentmihalyi and Rochberg-Halton sought to infer attitudes and motivations.

END POINT

There is considerably potential to apply sociological and other theories to public relations although to date these have been under-examined. Instead, the primary theoretical base applied to understanding publics derives from psychology.

Cognitive, affective and behavioural understanding of public psychology forms part of the formative research phase of the PR strategic planning process. A range of approaches enables relevant groups of stakeholders and publics to be identified. Technological developments are offering new opportunities to gain data, particularly real-time geodemographics.

Statistical data regarding publics can be obtained using surveys. Qualitative methods provide deeper understanding although the researcher then needs to take a more interpretive role to use findings to inform PR campaigns.

The Appendices provide various helpful checklists and tools to support analysis of publics and stakeholders. Resulting insight into public psychology can be included in the concise research overview (executive report) discussed in Chapter 5.

CHAPTER 7

Setting objectives

Heather Yaxley

This chapter looks at practical approaches to setting objectives. This is a traditionally weak area for PR planning and consequently, a critique of common problems in relation to objective setting is also provided. Reference is made to the original and updated Barcelona Principles and their influence on objective setting in public relations practice.

CHECK POINT

After reading this chapter, you should be able to:

- Understand the role of objectives in PR strategic planning
- Apply practical approaches to set objectives (including reference to the Barcelona Principles)
- Avoid common problems in setting objectives.

MANAGEMENT BY OBJECTIVES (MBO)

Drucker introduced the term Management by Objectives (MBO) in 1954, with objectives conceived as 'the core of the structure of a discipline of managing' (cited by Greenwood, 1981: 161). MBO was proposed as a way of improving the effectiveness and motivation of management.

Objectives specify desired results, emphasising an important connection with monitoring and evaluation (Chapter 10). They provide direction to motivate individuals' achievements and as such, should be linked to an organisation's appraisal system.

The overview to Part II discussed a formal process of planning which involves defining the organisation's purpose and key objectives, with functional and operational objectives derived to support these. Criticisms of this hierarchical approach include:

- Limitations of a top-down, rational approach to management, e.g. impression of control that may not be possible or desirable in reality
- PR's role is presented as implementing strategy to achieve objectives (which have both been determined at the highest level), rather than contributing towards their construction as part of senior management
- Little regard paid to matters arising that necessitate a more flexible and adaptive approach
- Setting objectives in isolation of the needs/opinions of stakeholders or any relationships between them and the organisation
- Arguments that many people are action-oriented rather than goal-driven
- Resource and other constraints impacting on ability to achieve established objectives
- Objectives frequently lack any foundation in research and may not be achievable or appropriate
- Downplays the value of intuition and expertise of those undertaking specific roles within the organisation.

OBJECTIVES WITHIN STRATEGIC PR PLANS

Most planning models (including those within PR literature) place objective setting after a situational audit. This connects them to formative research (Chapters 5 and 6). However, the process of objective setting should be iterative rather than one-way, as consideration of objectives may raise a need for additional research.

Objectives answer the question: where do we need to be? At the department level, they establish the purpose and direction of PR within the organisation, with objectives set for individual employees underpinning job roles. Performance standards are required for each key objective to facilitate ongoing monitoring of achievements.

PR objectives need to align with those of other relevant functions within the organisation or with external partners as appropriate. Strategic alignment does not mean PR should be merged with other functions. Indeed, ensuring integration throughout the organisation requires PR to be more than a sub-set of marketing both strategically and in terms of its wider remit.

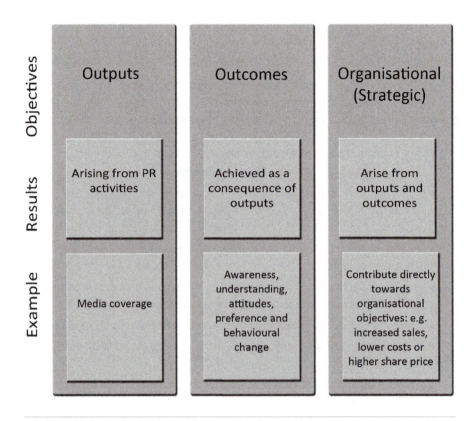

FIGURE 7.1 Illustration of objectives and results

The PR function needs to determine a set of operational and specific campaign plans, each with their own objectives. Drawing on the formative research phase, objectives can be set to address issues or opportunities relating to particular publics. Briefs for external suppliers (including PR consultancies) should detail result-oriented objectives (see Appendices). Figure 7.1 distinguishes objectives by the nature of the result achieved. It should not be presumed that output objectives would deliver outcomes or strategic results. For example, media coverage does not indicate sales have been achieved.

UNDERSTANDING OBJECTIVES

Consider the saying: 'if you don't know where you are going, any road will take you there'. Organisations, and PR practitioners, need to know where they are going, and consequently, plan how they will arrive at the destination. Objectives should specify the end point rather than describing the journey or how it will be undertaken.

Grunig and Hunt (1984) relate objectives to reasons why an organisation needs public relations: how it contributes to organisational effectiveness and the value its activities deliver. Objectives help explain the possible and actual impact of PR. Cutlip *et al.* (2000) state objectives provide:

- Focus and direction for developing strategies and tactics
- Guidance and motivation in implementing programmes
- Outcome criteria for assessing progress and impact.

Anderson *et al.* (1999: 5) specify six reasons for 'setting clear, concise and measurable objectives':

- To create a structure to prioritise, clarifying the focus and sequence of strategy and tactics
- To reduce the potential for disputes before, during and after the programme
- To focus resources to drive performance and efficiency, providing a sense of purpose that enables tactics and resources to be concentrated where they have most impact
- To identify areas for prescriptive change and continual improvement; tracking performance against properly set objectives allows for corrective action, or positive adjustments
- To support evaluation by making it easier to determine if the PR activities meet or exceed expectations
- To support the business case for PR by linking its objective to the business objective.

Setting PR objectives may involve a process that is either:

Proactive – based on the results of a situational analysis

Reactive – responding to a decision taken (inside or outside the organisation).

Consultancies, and those working in-house as PR technicians rather than managers, are commonly given objectives to achieve. This may be unproblematic if the objectives indicate an issue or opportunity to be addressed. Nevertheless, PR practitioners still need to analyse the situation and agree realistic objectives for identified publics and activities. Objectives need to be set for entire programmes and individual projects as well as at the strategic and tactical level (Gregory, 2000).

Task/process objectives

Grunig and Hunt (1984) criticise PR practitioners for focusing on processes (number of releases distributed, schedule for annual report, tactics to handle an immediate crisis) instead of effects (what the release, report or other tactics aim to achieve, such as

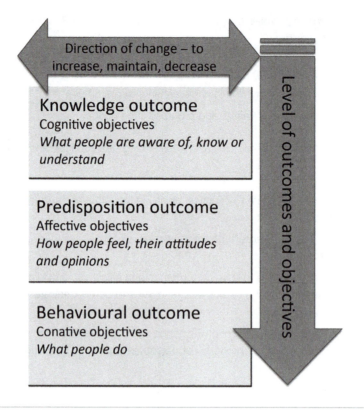

FIGURE 7.2 Matrix detailing level and direction of objectives

increased knowledge, acceptance of decisions or a behavioural change). Examples of task/process objectives are:

- to add new posts to the corporate social media accounts by 9am every weekday
- to generate six feature articles by 31 July.

Task/process objectives describe activities, but do not consider what value they deliver, such as whether social media posts are read, understood, changed opinions or stimulated action. This type of objective can help steer what needs to be done, making them useful for monitoring the implementation of its plan. However outcome objectives need to be determined, task/process objectives and relevant tactics can be considered.

Outcome objectives

To demonstrate effectiveness, objectives must be outcome orientated – i.e. specify results to be achieved. Cutlip *et al.* (2000) propose three levels of objectives and a choice of direction for the intended outcome (Figure 7.2).

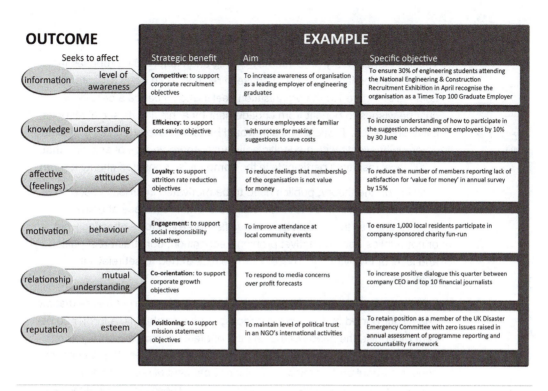

OUTCOME

Seeks to affect

		EXAMPLE	
	Strategic benefit	Aim	Specific objective
information — level of awareness	**Competitive**: to support corporate recruitment objectives	To increase awareness of organisation as a leading employer of engineering graduates	To ensure 30% of engineering students attending the National Engineering & Construction Recruitment Exhibition in April recognise the organisation as a Times Top 100 Graduate Employer
knowledge understanding	**Efficiency**: to support cost saving objective	To ensure employees are familiar with process for making suggestions to save costs	To increase understanding of how to participate in the suggestion scheme among employees by 10% by 30 June
affective (feelings) — attitudes	**Loyalty**: to support attrition rate reduction objectives	To reduce feelings that membership of the organisation is not value for money	To reduce the number of members reporting lack of satisfaction for 'value for money' in annual survey by 15%
motivation — behaviour	**Engagement**: to support social responsibility objectives	To improve attendance at local community events	To ensure 1,000 local residents participate in company-sponsored charity fun-run
relationship — mutual understanding	**Co-orientation**: to support corporate growth objectives	To respond to media concerns over profit forecasts	To increase positive dialogue this quarter between company CEO and top 10 financial journalists
reputation — esteem	**Positioning**: to support mission statement objectives	To maintain level of political trust in an NGO's international activities	To retain position as a member of the UK Disaster Emergency Committee with zero issues raised in annual assessment of programme reporting and accountability framework

FIGURE 7.3 Types of outcome objectives

This matrix suggests all PR objectives are persuasive, that is, they indicate the organisation's intention to influence what others know, feel or do. However, if organisations wish to co-orientate or build relationships with publics (e.g. adopt a two-way symmetrical communications strategy), PR objectives must reflect a less persuasive intent. Such objectives could be agreed or co-constructed using a process of discussion rather than each party seeking to achieve separate objectives. Collaborative objectives would need to reflect measures by which the relationship or outcome of the symmetrical discussion can be assessed. Figure 7.3 considers examples of outcome objectives, separating awareness from knowledge and adding relationship and reputation objectives.

Each of the cases in Figure 7.3 reflects only part of the process of achieving a strategic benefit. For example, increasing awareness of an organisation as a top employer will not automatically achieve the competitive benefit of recruiting the best engineering graduates. This highlights the importance of the situational analysis: was a lack of awareness identified as a problem in achieving recruitment objectives? If so, then the suggested objective would be an appropriate first step. At the same time, awareness lacks ambition as an objective for the exhibition, where knowledge, attitudes, behaviour, mutual understanding and esteem could also be improved.

The complex relationship between types of objectives needs careful consideration. Developing a clear rationale that explains the reasoning behind determining objectives is recommended.

SITUATIONAL THEORY IN PRACTICE

The situational theory presented by Grunig and Hunt (1984) proposes that publics may be latent, aware or active in relation to an issue (Chapter 6). Looking at Figure 7.3 the organisation seeking to influence a behaviour change wishes to benefit from engagement by achieving its social responsibility objectives. Tactically its aim would be to improve attendance at local community events with a specific activity-related objective of ensuring that 1,000 local residents participate in the company's sponsored charity fun-run.

Drawing on the theory, publics need to be motivated in order to become active as participants or advocates of the event (in the case of opinion leaders, such as the media). It also specifies three variables affecting whether or not publics become active: problem recognition, constraint recognition and level of involvement. These could be researched to set relevant objectives.

Let's say research shows 60 per cent of local residents do not realise that the charity supported by the fun-run is facing funding problems. A further 20 per cent recognise the needs of the charity, but feel constrained from getting involved. Among those unaware of the charity's challenges, 10 per cent have concerns about participating. In addition, 5 per cent of residents do not feel a personal connection to the charity or the event. These data indicate where problem recognition, constraints and personal involvement need to be addressed with specific publics. This enables sub-objectives to be set to increase awareness, change attitudes, improve knowledge or make a personal connection to the charity. These may all need to be achieved in order to deliver the overall PR campaign objective to ensure 1,000 local residents participate in the company-sponsored charity fun-run.

This example demonstrates PR plans need to be thought through carefully. It is likely that more than communication will be required to achieve objectives. For instance, ensuring that residents are able to participate in the fun-run involves considering, and where necessary removing, potential barriers relating to the nature of the event, ease of signing-up, relevance of the charity being supported and so forth.

Hierarchy of effects

The concept of levels of objectives suggests inter-related steps need to be taken in order to achieve an ultimate goal. This indicates a rational cognitive process is involved. For example, there may be a need to increase awareness before altering attitudes. Then a change in attitude is required before focusing on addressing behaviour. In the

PASSIVE SMOKING AND CHILDREN CONCERNS

ACTION POINT

A report by the Royal College of Physicians on passive smoking and children (2010) claimed that passive smoking is a major hazard to over 2 million children. Key health problems were reported to generate over 300,000 UK GP consultations, about 9,500 hospital admissions and a cost to the NHS of about £23.3 million.

Qualitative research by the University of Liverpool (Robinson and Kirkcaldy, 2004: v) used focus groups to explore parents' smoking behaviour, including 'the role of knowledge and lay beliefs about the nature and risks of passive smoking to children'. The study found:

Limited knowledge, with a belief that coughs are relatively minor and many parents unconvinced of a link to exposure to tobacco smoke.

High awareness of the association between cot death and exposing newborn babies to smoke; three-quarters of parents smoked in their homes and cited difficulties in leaving young children to go outside.

Parents relied on their existing knowledge and experiences as much as official information.

Resistance to smoking cessation indicated rejection of messages about children's health.

What type of objectives do you feel would be relevant for any PR health campaign to address this issue? Is lack of awareness or knowledge the cause of parents' smoking behaviour? Would an initial objective to increase the percentage of parents who know they should not smoke around their children by 50 per cent before the summer holidays be reasonable?

Would a hierarchical effects approach be feasible for objectives? Why might those already aware of the dangers continue to smoke? Would a behavioural objective to reduce number of parents smoking in front of their children by 10 per cent within 12 months be reasonable?

classic 'Torches of Freedom' campaign, for instance, Bernays needed to make smoking cigarettes acceptable for women before changing their behaviour.

This conceives that people progress through a linear psychological sequence that Walser (2004) dates to the 1898 St Elmo Lewis AIDA model (Awareness, Interest, Decision, Action). Parvanta et al. (2011) trace the modern usage of such thinking to Lavidge and Steiner in 1961 who outlined six steps: awareness and knowledge (cognitive), liking and preference (affective), conviction and purchase (conative). In 1969, McGuire conceived a hierarchy of effects for information processing developing from attention to comprehension, retention, and ultimately behaviour (cited by Rodgers et al., 2008).

The AMEC integrated evaluation framework draws on such models evident within PR and wider management literature (http://amecorg.com/amecframework/home/framework/introduction/). However, such logic models are simplistic, do not reflect the reality of much decision-making or recognise other psychological theories.

Figure 7.3 is intended to illustrate that PR practitioners should not presume that increasing awareness will automatically change behaviour. Knowing about the charity is no guarantee that people will sign up to participate in the fun-run. Indeed, it may be that participation in the event would raise knowledge of the charity and enhance mutual understanding and esteem. It should also be considered that, rather than a logical process of thought to inform their decisions, people may rely on an emotional reaction.

SETTING OBJECTIVES

Pickton and Broderick (2005: 420) state that 'objective setting is not an easy task', particularly for those who are unfamiliar with the exercise. They suggest referring to past experience and previous activities to determine what is achievable and realistic. However, this may compound any errors in objective setting.

SMART objectives

To return to the analogy of a journey, vague objectives would be of limited help. What is needed is, at least, a specific destination and time of arrival. Likewise, it is useful for objectives to follow the acronym SMART (Figure 7.4).

Quantitative and qualitative objectives

Figure 7.3 indicates types of quantitative measures that can be set: e.g. to decrease the number of members reporting lack of satisfaction for value for money in the annual survey by 15 per cent. In some circumstances, objectives need to be measured using qualitative methods (Chapter 6): E.g. to understand motoring journalists' experiences of international car launches.

Johnson *et al.* (2005) argue that an objective may be important but 'become absurd if it has to be expressed in measurable terms'. They use the example of achieving a reputational leadership position. However, it is possible for public relations practitioners to develop 'skill in appraising intangible factors', which Batchelor (1938: 30), likens to the analytical abilities of engineers.

Objectives and publics

In setting PR objectives, it is important to consider the publics that need to be engaged as specifically as possible. Chapter 6 discussed the importance of segmentation and research to gain an understanding of publics which can be used to set objectives. The research process can also be used to set qualitative and quantitative objectives.

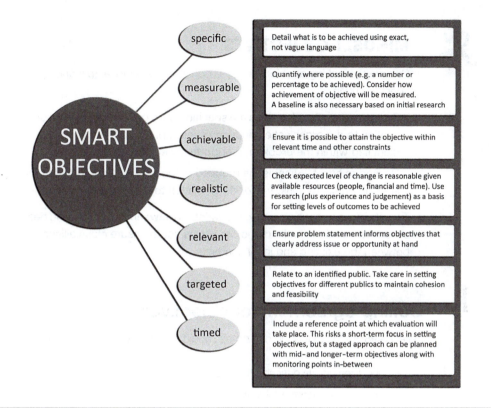

FIGURE 7.4 SMART objectives

ACTION POINT

Review the following examples of objectives to determine which can be addressed by PR activities. Which are SMART? Do they suggest quantitative or qualitative outcomes? How could they be improved?

- To increase the percentage of the electorate who know how to vote by 10 per cent, two weeks prior to the election date.
- To maintain the number of adults (aged 18–50) who feel eating five fruit or vegetables a day is good for you, over the next 12 months.
- To reduce the number of cars parked illegally in spaces reserved for disabled drivers to zero, by 31 December.
- To ensure no local residents object during the planning application process for a new factory.
- To improve recognition among politicians of the organisation as a leading employer.

MINDSET OBJECTIVES

One way of looking at objectives is to consider the mindset (psychology) of a specific public.

Current mindset – what does the specific public currently think, feel or do in relation to the organisation, industry sector, product, trends or issue identified within the problem or opportunity statement?

Desired mindset – what is the required outcome; i.e. what you want the specific public to think, feel or do in relation to the problem/opportunity?

This offers a gap analysis where the variation between the current and desired situations can be examined and objectives set to ensure close alliance between the existing and ideal mindsets.

Getting agreement for objectives

Seitel (1998) states that good objectives should stand up to the following questions:

- Do they clearly describe the end result expected?
- Are they understandable to everyone in the organisation?
- Do they list a firm completion date?
- Are they realistic, attainable and measurable?
- Are they consistent with management's objectives?

Being able to answer such questions is important in ensuring that they can be agreed with senior management or other partners in the PR programme.

PROBLEMS

Various problems with understanding and setting objectives are discussed in this chapter. Gregory (2000) lists the following barriers affecting successful achievement of objectives:

- Problems resulting from lack of capability of the PR function to carry out required activities
- Financial constraints
- Time issues – internal and external – including unforeseen matters that may arise
- Issues experienced in the decision-making process

- Difficulties arising with support mechanisms including the organisation's administrative and physical infrastructure
- Challenges relating to the specific public
- Problems caused by socio-cultural differences.

Normative objectives

The problem with normative objectives is that they suggest a common standard that should be achieved by PR activities. For example, a company may expect media releases to generate a specific response rate, reflecting a measure that is common in direct marketing. Although a calculation could be made on the basis of previous experience and set as a future target, this is pretty meaningless. Determining a PR standard result is difficult given the importance of ensuring campaigns reflect the particular needs of an organisation, the issues and opportunities it faces and the specific nature of relevant publics.

Competitive objectives

The marketing concept of share of voice may be used to set a competitive objective for PR activities (Watson and Noble, 2007). The Institute of Practitioners in Advertising (2009) identified correlation between share of voice and share of market, although it is not apparent this applies to editorial coverage. A competitive focus is evident in social media, for example, where objectives are set for number of Twitter followers or social media influence ratings (Chapter 16). A problem is in demonstrating that such competitive objectives deliver strategic benefits.

Idealistic objectives

Organisations may experience difficulties if they set idealistic objectives indicating the end result they would like to achieve. Their aspirations may be significantly different to what is realistic. Gregory (2000) criticises the PR industry for over-promising through a lack of understanding of what activities can actually achieve. This emphasises the need for accurate monitoring and evaluation of outcomes which can be referenced when setting future objectives.

Stretch objectives

Fung et al. (2008: 109) state stretch objectives seek to push people 'to do more than they think is possible'. They argue this encourages more innovative solutions. If these are viewed simply as motivational objectives, a stretch approach may be useful, but could set unrealistic expectations or prove demoralising if they prove impossible to achieve.

Inflexible objectives

It may seem strange to suggest objectives need to be flexible. However, it would be dogmatic and unrealistic to ignore any need for adaptation, particularly if the organisation is open to feedback within its PR operations.

Objective overload

Practitioners may try to do too much, with too many objectives presented for what can be achieved with the resources available. Likewise, trying to meet a long list of hierarchical objectives may prove overambitious. Another issue is trying to target every

ACTION POINT

INFLUENCE OF BARCELONA PRINCIPLES

Literature reveals many decades of academic examination of methods to evaluate public relations activities and the value of the function to organisations. However, this matter continues to be seen by many practitioners as problematic. In 2010 the AMEC Barcelona Declaration of Measurement Principles set out seven statements that encompass objective setting and measurement (http://amecorg.com/2012/06/barcelona-declaration-of-measurement-principles/).

These can seem rather obvious – for example, Principle 1 is the importance of goal setting and measurement. However, the publication of these statements received considerable attention within the industry and led to the development of additional resources intended to help PR practitioners improve their practice and secure management support for a more professional approach.

The Principles were updated in 2015 and an Integrated Evaluation Framework was published in 2016. Emphasis remains on addressing evaluation practices rather than stressing the importance of objectives. This means that, whilst more PR practitioners may use measurement methods to report on their work, without establishing objectives their plans are not being fully evaluated for effectiveness or efficiency.

In 2010 the US-based Institute for Public Relations (IPR) updated its 1999 report: Guidelines for setting measurable public relations objectives (see: www.instituteforpr.org/setting-measurable-objectives/).

Review these published materials and apply them to your own practice. Review award-winning campaigns to see the extent to which they comply with the recommendations. How do you feel that the framework of evaluation would be improved with greater focus on objective setting?

stakeholder (Chapter 6) rather than setting priorities for the primary opportunity or issue that has been identified.

Lack of benchmarks for objectives

Cutlip *et al.* (2000) confirm that, without benchmark data, judgement will dominate in setting outcome objectives. This can present problems for PR practitioners if management set unrealistic objectives. Being able to present management with reliable research data is more likely to influence them to accept more realistic, relevant and achievable objectives.

END POINT

Objectives are vital within PR strategic planning to ensure resources can be used effectively and specific outcomes achieved. They need to be focused on problems or opportunities (identified from research) that affect the organisation and specific publics. Setting objectives is not an easy process, with many possible problems that can be encountered, including a tendency to over-promise and a lack of a reflexive approach within real-world examples within published PR campaigns. Consideration of relevant quantitative and qualitative methods of evaluating objectives ensures public relations is able to offer strategic value to organisations. Recent work such as the Barcelona Principles provides a higher focus for evaluation, although it seems less attention has been directed towards objective setting.

CHAPTER 8

Strategic campaign execution

Heather Yaxley

At its simplest, planning can be considered as involving Preparation, Implementation and Evaluation (PIE). The earlier chapters in this section have considered preparation through research, analysis and reflection and objective setting. This chapter (along with Chapter 9) focuses on implementation of plans within a strategic framework, where the role of creativity and narrative development are considered alongside relevant tools and techniques.

CHECK POINT

After reading this chapter, you should be able to:

- Build a strategic framework to support the implementation of plans
- Develop campaign strategies and narrative approaches
- Consider how to identify and select relevant practical tools and techniques.

Throughout this book a comprehensive set of strategies, tools and techniques has been presented and critiqued. This chapter complements that expert focus with an overview of the components of strategic campaign execution.

This phase of the planning process considers how (strategy) the organisation should achieve its PR objectives (Chapter 7) and what it should do and say (tactics) with regard to particular publics (Chapter 6) in response to the issues and opportunities identified from a situational analysis (Chapter 5). The campaign cannot be executed without

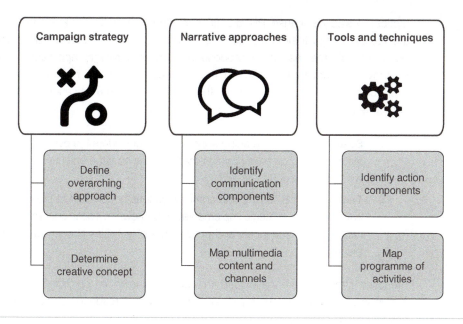

FIGURE 8.1 Public relations strategic implementation framework

considering the costs and resources necessary to implement the plan (Chapter 9) and how it will be monitored and evaluated (Chapter 10).

Cutlip *et al.* (2000) identify two aspects involved in implementing public relations strategy:

- **Action component** – what needs to be done
- **Communication component** – what needs to be said.

These are evident in the proposed strategic implementation framework (Figure 8.1) that comprises three main elements:

1 **Campaign strategy** – defining the overall approach and creative concept
2 **Narrative approaches** – methodology underpinning communication
3 **Tools and techniques** – methods by which the strategy is executed.

As already discussed, PR plans should fit within the organisation's overall strategy and the wider operation of the PR function. This ensures cohesion and consistency across all elements of the strategic implementation framework.

CAMPAIGN STRATEGIES

Within the strategic implementation framework, campaign strategies need to be considered before detailing tactical aspects. Strategy is often confused with tactics, possibly because PR practitioners find it easy to think immediately of the tactical things they could do to address a problem or achieve an objective but may lack the insight to propose an overall, strategic approach. A clear strategy is determined to achieve the required objectives. It then provides an overarching approach to support the choice of communication and action components.

- **Strategy** is the overarching approach that considers the overall game plan, main idea and creative concept that explains how the objectives as a whole will be achieved.

- **Tactics** are the actions and communications undertaken at the operational level within the strategic implementation framework. These encompass multi-media content/channels and programme of activities chosen to implement the strategy.

Proactive strategies are developed to address known or predicted issues and opportunities; reactive strategies are planned to respond to unanticipated circumstances.

ACTION POINT

STRATEGY STATEMENT

Wilcox and Cameron (2006: 162) state that 'a strategy statement describes how, in concept, an objective is to be achieved, providing guidelines and themes for the overall program'. The strategy statement provides a rationale for the tactics.

The strategic statement for the UK government's Public Health Responsibility Deal is 'to tap into the potential for businesses and other organisations to improve public health and tackle health inequalities through their influence over food, alcohol, physical activity and health in the workplace'. The government believed that a responsibility strategy requiring commercial partners to pledge action would be faster and more effective than adopting a regulatory strategy.

In terms of communications, the government has embraced the concept of a nudge strategy. John *et al.* (2011: 9) explain: 'Nudge is about giving information and social cues so as to help people do positive things for themselves and society'. Kelly (2011) says nudge reflects a libertarian paternalism philosophy and draws on behavioural economics and social psychology. It utilises the concepts of social norms, social contagion, peripheral processing (see below) and framing messages to make certain behaviours more salient. Applying the work of Collis and Rukstad

(2008) to a public relations campaign, the strategy statement for it should be concise (they recommend no more than 35 words) and comprise:

- an explanation of the main objective or goal that the strategy is designed to achieve;
- the scope or domain of the project;
- the advantage or distinctive nature of the particular project for identified publics.

Alstiel and Grow (2006) claim that a strategy statement can be simple or detailed, but needs to have a focusing element. This is what is most important and may be expressed as a positioning statement, unique selling proposition, big idea, central truth or creative concept.

Research or review a range of projects, campaigns, adverts, brands, products, organisations and so forth to determine what their single focusing element may be. How could this be developed into a strategy statement?

FIGURE 8.2 PR strategies and decision-making process

Given that many PR campaigns seek to achieve behaviour change objectives, psychological theories can be used to inform strategies. Figure 8.2 provides examples and a decision-making process.

Creative campaign concepts

Gregory (2000) explains that public relations strategy can be presented as an approach (e.g. publicity campaign), a conceptual proposition (e.g. thought leadership) or a creative idea (e.g. the Child Bereavement Charity's Mother's Day Campaign).

PR practitioners face considerable competition to be heard and so creativity concepts offer a way to stand out, as well as providing cohesion and consistency across activities and communications. A creative concept should be given an identity, which helps ensure it is memorable (easy to recall) and remarkable (worthy of discussion). Increasingly the idea may be represented by a hashtag.

A creative concept embodies the campaign strategy and is more than a list of tactical ideas. Moriarty (1997: 555) says 'the brilliant creative concept involves what some experts have called the Creative Leap' represented by a 'Big Idea', which needs to be presented in 'an exciting new way'.

The creative concept enables the strategy statement to be transformed into an engaging narrative. Ideally, it will become closely associated with the particular organisation or issue, yet remain adaptable over time.

ACTION POINT

MACMILLAN CANCER SUPPORT WORLD'S BIGGEST COFFEE MORNING

Following a successful coffee morning event by a local fundraising committee in 1990, the charity adopted the simple, yet effective idea in 1991. Since then it has raised over £60 million in total. The idea offers flexibility, enabling supporters to adapt the coffee morning concept locally. It has also accommodated record attempts (e.g. the highest and deepest coffee mornings) and attracted corporate partners and celebrity ambassadors.

The basic rules of creativity are to have an open mind, involve different perspectives, generate numerous ideas, record all suggestions, avoid early evaluation or don't be dismissive of previous solutions. Creative concepts should be:

- **Relevant** – review against research, objectives and strategy
- **Appropriate** – reflecting the organisation's culture and cognisant of its publics' sensitivities
- **Simple** – readily explained to others and easily implemented
- **Compelling** – securing buy-in from internal and external stakeholders
- **Surprising** – cutting through the clutter of other communication activities.

Smith (2005: 13) advocates 'effective creativity' and cautions that outcomes should not be forgotten in the enthusiasm of a novel idea. He argues that research and creativity are complementary, with the former supporting the creative process and validating ideas.

ACTION POINT

PUBLICITY STUNTS

Creativity is most evident at the tactical level of public relations with stunts used to attract media attention. Taylor Herring (2009) presents a Publicity Stunt Hall of Fame, with ideas including the Olympic torch relay (introduced in 1936), the Women's Institute naked calendar (1999), Tourism Queensland's Best Job in the World (2009) and Lego's model of Obama's inauguration (2008). Beyond securing media coverage, ideas need to ensure the client and its message are recalled, not just the stunt.

Social media offers the opportunity to extend the reach and longevity of an idea beyond traditional media coverage. Viral campaigns depend on word of mouth to be successful, and trying too hard to be funny or edgy can backfire. Organisations need to be prepared for the irreverent treatment of ideas online. Spoof YouTube videos, Twitter jokes and ironic Facebook groups are frequently used to poke fun at big brand initiatives, sometimes with affection, although anti-groups can be very hostile in their satire. This illustrates Moloney's point (2006: 144) that brands 'attract public attention in ways that are not always welcome to their constructors. Sometimes they are connected to popular culture in ironic, creative ways and are transformed into counter-cultural icons'.

Do some research when you spot a publicity stunt to examine who is talking about it, which channels and the tone of any comments. What elements are involved and how does the discussion around a stunt develop over time? What makes ideas spreadable?

Evaluating creativity

Creativity involves more than new ideas, which 'are only part of the equation. Execution is just as important' (Isaacson, 2011: 98). It is likely more than one idea will be generated and knowing which to adopt is a matter of judgement. This should be based on a rational decision-making process (Figure 8.3).

Issue
Opportunity
Objectives

Ideas generation process:
imagination, brainstorming,
modelling, 'What if?' question
snowball groups,word/object
prompt, scenario forecasting, etc.

Techniques to achieve a paradigm shift and
create new ideas: Instant response, reconceptualise the
issue/opportunity, big picture and detail perspectives, change the
operational parameters, co-create with others, apply thinking models
(intuition, logic, etc.)

ideas - ideas - ideas - ideas - ideas - ideas - ideas

Ideas review process: gradual process to nurture, select
and test using instinct, research, costings analysis,
originality test, etc.

Techniques to develop ideas, ensure
core concept is protected, gain
agreement, identify implementation
and risk factors, etc.

Implement
preferred
idea

FIGURE 8.3 Creativity decision-making process

NARRATIVE APPROACHES

Alongside the campaign strategy, a strong narrative approach is required. This provides a framework for determining what needs to be communicated within a campaign. Narrative mediates human experience enabling thoughts, attitudes, values

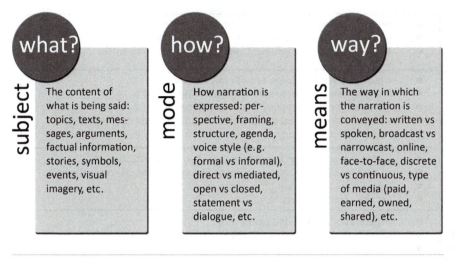

FIGURE 8.4 Core aspects of a narrative approach to public relations

and meaning to be expressed through communications. It is a broader concept than key messages, which tend to reflect slogans, headlines and other statements. Key messages are part of the communication component, rather than its entirety, as is implied by many PR planning models.

Figure 8.4 illustrates the three core aspects to consider in developing a narrative approach. These aspects need to be researched and considered as part of the communicative element of strategic plans. They also need to be connected to the campaign objectives (Chapter 7) and resources available (Chapter 9).

The narrative approach for any campaign needs to be derived from the narrative position of the organisation. This should include how communications are managed and organised, authority levels, procedures and so forth. The narrative position will draw on the organisation's brand profile and corporate principles (Figure 8.5). The organisation's style guide should inform the narrative position or be informed by it if one doesn't exist. The narrative approach, position and style guide should be part of the Public Relations Information System Management discussed in Chapter 5.

Shaping narrative

The narrative approach needs to be distilled into concise, clear and engaging communications. It needs to be shaped into a framework for production of written and multimedia materials, and participation in dialogue or conversations.

Construction should reflect natural, human language rather than the corporate speak of key messages. The purpose is to guide thinking and understanding, not rigid use of slick slogans or defensive position statements.

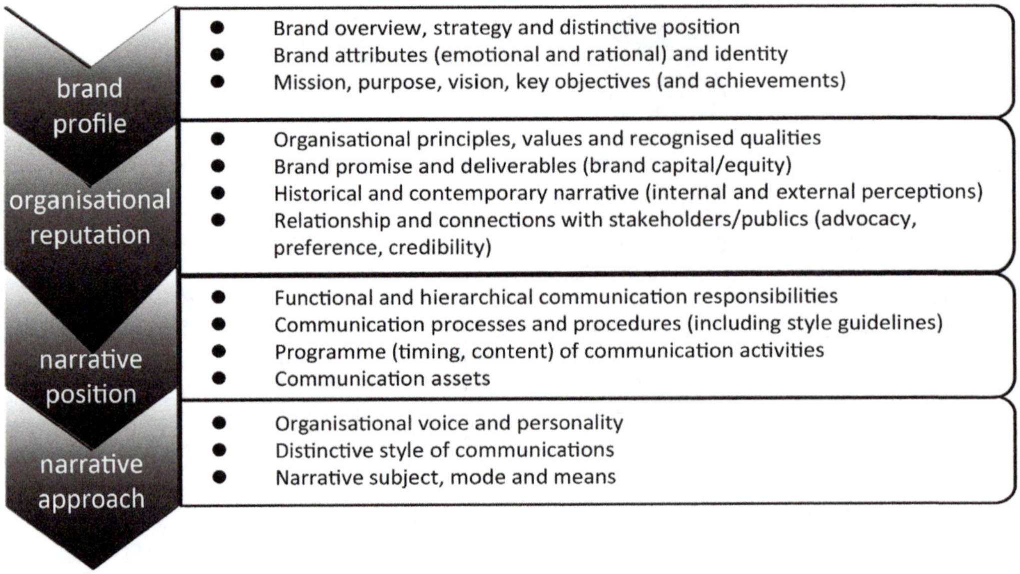

brand profile
- Brand overview, strategy and distinctive position
- Brand attributes (emotional and rational) and identity
- Mission, purpose, vision, key objectives (and achievements)

organisational reputation
- Organisational principles, values and recognised qualities
- Brand promise and deliverables (brand capital/equity)
- Historical and contemporary narrative (internal and external perceptions)
- Relationship and connections with stakeholders/publics (advocacy, preference, credibility)

narrative position
- Functional and hierarchical communication responsibilities
- Communication processes and procedures (including style guidelines)
- Programme (timing, content) of communication activities
- Communication assets

narrative approach
- Organisational voice and personality
- Distinctive style of communications
- Narrative subject, mode and means

FIGURE 8.5 Narrative process

Indeed, the corporate narrative should allow for polyphony, where many voices are heard and different conversations are taking place. Christensen *et al.* (2008: 196) call for organisations to challenge the established principles of corporate communications that seek to 'orchestrate their symbols and messages consistently across different situations and different audiences'. This approach can be extended outside an organisation where stakeholders and publics may be involved in the content creation, curation and co-construction of communications.

Traditionally, a key message approach (also reflected in message grids or a message house) involves creating consistent statements comprised of predetermined words, phrases and/or sentences, which can be monitored as outputs to be deemed as a measure of successful communication. This reflects a transmission approach to communications. That is, the focus is on what the organisation wants to say, rather ensuring others understand, gain a positive impression or empathise with the communications.

It is helpful to determine the priority point(s) that need to be understood, and identify examples, imagery, facts and other ways in which a story can be illustrated, remembered and accepted. PR practitioners need to be the architect of the design and construction of this narrative framework. Their role is to plan communications that are shaped by purpose and context; whilst allowing flexibility in application within the framework. This is indicated in Figure 8.6 with a template for shaping narrative in the appendices.

Rather than looking to control the shaping of narrative, PR practitioners need to allow scope for other functions and people inside and outside the organisation to be involved in the process. Guidelines can be produced to help illustrate the organisation's narrative and allow for wider input and development.

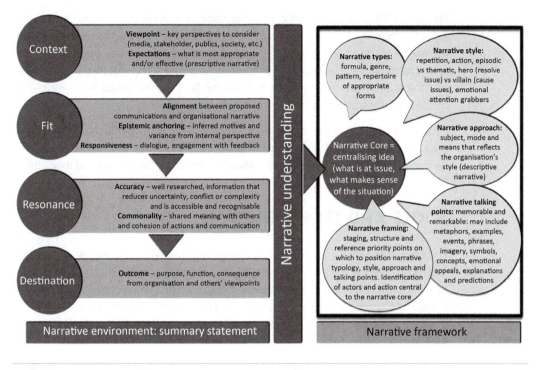

FIGURE 8.6 Shaping narrative

Memes

The narrative approach can accommodate the concept of a meme, proposed by biologist Professor Richard Dawkins (Green, 2010). A meme is a cognitive concept involving transmission of cultural information between humans. It is 'an idea that behaves like a virus – that moves through a population, taking hold in each person it infects' (Gladwell, 2000). It is applied to information that possesses the dynamic potential to be spread between individuals.

From a PR perspective, this means that narrative elements need to be memorable and replicable, i.e. easily passed on by word of mouth or through social media. The concept emphasises that organisations need to avoid jargon and language that is difficult to recall or repeat. Memes may incorporate multimedia as well as written elements.

Green (2010) highlights three aspects of a meme proposed by Dawkins:

- **Longevity** – the meme must survive; to be remembered, recalled and transmitted
- **Coherence** – memes have the strength to replicate themselves; sticking in someone's head even against their will
- **Copyability** – others must be able to make a cognitive copy of the meme (although it may not be identical to the original).

He argues PR practitioners need to make communications coherent, copyable and robust to benefit from the features of a meme. Stories, slogans, images and brand identities can be strong forms of cultural information. To enable these and other elements of the narrative approach to harness the power of memes, they need to hook into the public's existing psychology (Chapter 6). It is also useful to consider the diffusion process by which ideas spread throughout society.

PR practitioners can produce meme-friendly communications, in formats that facilitate easy distribution (Figure 8.7), but cannot guarantee they will become viral. It should also be remembered that, once communications spread, they take on a life of their own.

TOOLS AND TECHNIQUES

The campaign strategy and narrative approach provide guidance regarding the tools and techniques involved in what needs to be said and done. Implementation needs to occur in a responsive and responsible manner to ensure that campaign objectives and measurable outcomes are achieved. Tools, techniques and tactics are considered throughout *The PR Strategic Toolkit,* providing expert insight into the effectiveness of various options.

Figure 8.1 details that communication and action components need to be identified before a process of mapping occurs. This includes mapping of multimedia content and channels as well as a programme of activities. A checklist covering relevant tools and techniques to implement these tactical elements is included in the appendices.

Gregory (2000) suggests two tests for tactics:

- **Appropriateness** – Will they reach the target publics? Will they have the right impact? Are they credible and influential? Do they suit the message? Are they compatible with other communication devices the organisation is using?
- **Deliverability** – Can they be implemented successfully, within the budget and required timescale? Are the right people available to implement them?

Chapter 9 details methods for determining a timeframe, costs and resources to execute a planned programme of tactics.

Health and safety

Campaign plans need to consider legislation constraints including health and safety issues. This may involve compliance with existing policies or contractual arrangements, ensuring adequate public liability insurance is in place, training and documenting procedures. Risk management needs to be part of this stage of the process. At times, constraints may need to be overcome for the successful implementation of tactics. This requires professional negotiation and possibly revision or adaptation of plans.

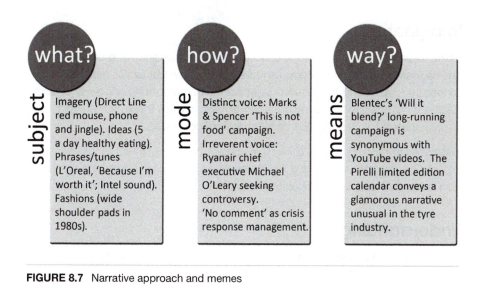

FIGURE 8.7 Narrative approach and memes

SECURING APPROVAL

All the work involved in research, setting objectives, developing a strategy, building a narrative framework and preparing a programme of tactics will be wasted without securing approval to implement the plan.

In addition to understanding the validity of recommendations, decision-makers need to understand how proposals relate to organisational objectives, integrate with other functions and seek to have an operational impact. For example, plans may involve action outside the PR function's remit to address problems or maximise opportunities. They may also require the support of external partners, suppliers, stakeholders or publics, which needs to be detailed within the report.

Discussion with managers while developing the plan can be a useful way of engaging them and understanding what they are looking for. In general, senior managers are persuaded by arguments that draw on evidence (logic), imagination (creative) and understanding (theory).

Evidence

The use of evidence – research, statistics and other analysis – shows a logical and intelligent basis for your campaign. Ensure evidence is credible and presented in a coherent and considered way. Creative elements need to be supported by proof of viability and likely success rather than just being clever. Feedback from a focus group, for example, would be helpful insight into public reception of ideas and narrative elements.

Imagination

As discussed above, a campaign concept provides cohesion for proposed ideas. An imaginative campaign strategy, narrative and/or individual tactics must be clearly connected to achieving the required objectives. When proposing original or unusual ideas, it is important to acknowledge potential risks and how these can be minimised. A risk management checklist can be found in the Appendices.

Ideas need to be presented in a way that enables the management to visualise their impact. Ensure mock-ups of any visuals are executed professionally and feedback from research is also clearly understandable.

Understanding

Use of theoretical concepts and models demonstrates that a body of evidence supports suggestions, although care needs to be taken to avoid unfamiliar academic terms. Showing appropriate use of tools and studies in developing recommendations demonstrates intelligence and builds the credibility of plans.

Proposals

Plans may be produced as a written report or a presentation. Organisations may have specific requirements for the style and content of proposals, such as a one-page summary, a detailed report (including supporting evidence), credentials and details of previous experience (in the case of a consultancy pitch document) or samples of specific tasks or tactics to be undertaken within the campaign.

The proposal needs to detail next steps or dates by which a decision should be made. Murray and White (2004) note concern among senior executives that PR practitioners do not demonstrate 'a good enough "radar" for emerging issues'. These authors urge practitioners to articulate more clearly to CEOs their strategic role. This underlines the importance of using research and analysis to provide intelligent insight into issues and opportunities affecting the organisation.

A report or presentation should demonstrate recommendations are both goal-directed and activity-focused. It is normally a good idea to structure a plan chronologically reflecting inductive reasoning. This is a process whereby a rationale argument is built leading to recommendations and conclusions. Research and analysis would start the report to highlight understanding and insight into the situation. That would lead onto specific objectives, strategy and tactics before detailing required resources, method of evaluation and a summary of the recommendations at the end of the report.

Given the pressures on management time, it is likely that such a structured report will be preceded by an executive summary that presents a standalone overview of the entire campaign, which could be referenced in isolation of the more detailed report.

The key to a successful report is to ensure that essential information can be easily found, with appendices, references and sources noted for further information if it is required. If presenting an action plan (rather than a campaign proposal), it should include details of tasks to be executed alongside responsibilities and deadlines by which they should be completed. Contingency plans may also be included to anticipate events that may occur and enable a 'plan B' to be followed.

Presentation needs to be professional, with high-quality materials reflecting the standard of work involved. The proposal may be an initial recommendation subject to change on the basis of management feedback or additional research. The impact of any changes needs to be understood, particularly on budget and required outcomes. Consultancies need to be clear over issues of intellectual property and confidentiality.

Approval is likely to involve a process of discussion, and additional information or responses to questions may be required. This may require adaption of initial recommendations; although the implications of such accommodation need to be understood. There are also times where proposals may challenge existing practices or management's expectations. Presenting a situation using informed, rather than emotional arguments is more likely to be successful.

To gain support from members of senior management, knowledge of their challenges, requirements, psychology and interests can be used to ensure the proposal is an effective form of communication. This is an important opportunity to build strong professional relationships and identify ways to engage key influencers in the work of public relations.

END POINT

A strategic implementation framework is proposed to inform PR strategies, narrative approaches and selection of the actions that need to be executed to achieve strategic objectives. A rational decision-making approach is recommended, alongside recognition of the need for creative approaches. This combination of evidence, imagination and understanding underpins campaign proposals to ensure executive approval of recommendations.

Budgeting and resourcing

Heather Yaxley

This chapter provides a straightforward approach to budgeting and resourcing. This includes consideration of planning requirements, costs, financial reporting and other skills involved in performance control management.

CHECK POINT

After reading this chapter, you should be able to:

- Take a practical management approach to planning budgets and resource requirements
- Understand the process of performance control reporting.

HUMAN RESOURCE PLANNING AND MANAGEMENT

Public relations generally requires human resources to implement a strategic plan of action. Activities may be undertaken by internal personnel or an external resource (freelance or consultancy) may be employed to provide operational support. To determine the nature of the required human resources, the nature of work involved in executing activities must be considered. The capability of any internal PR function to plan, manage and execute the project should be assessed alongside requirements to manage routine operations. If the campaign cannot be handled internally, consultancy resource needs to be sought. Roles and responsibilities need to be determined and built into the detailed planning process (see below).

Consultancy resource

External PR support offers expertise and additional human resources. A consultancy may be contracted to provide:

- Strategic advice
- Execution of programmes (independently or alongside in-house teams)
- Retained PR services (with a monthly fee) at an agreed level
- *Ad-hoc* or routine project work.

Organisations may appoint consultancies for one-off projects or to deliver activities over a longer contract term. Rather than one dedicated consultancy, organisations may draw on a roster of firms for specific purposes or used on rota.

A detailed PR brief (see Appendices) specifies the requirements for any campaign (including specific objectives) prior to agreement of a proposal/quote and an official contract. Details of the agreed programme of work, budget, resources and so forth should be set out in a contract, alongside financial paperwork (such as purchase orders enabling prompt invoicing). Even when long-standing relationships exist, this professional approach helps to avoid misunderstanding and minimise risk (Chapter 13).

When responding to a client brief, a PR consultancy will put together a team to undertake the contracted work. Its members will require relevant levels of knowledge, experience and skills. The team may comprise an account director or manager (primary client contact), a number of executives and support personnel (full- or part-time), plus specialists and experts for specific elements of any project. The consultancy accepts responsibility for managing the assignment work, and needs to update the client regularly on progress. Status reports (see Appendices) detail work undertaken and budget allocation. Consultancies may outsource key functions (e.g. media planning, multimedia production, event management, etc.) or utilise their internal resources as appropriate.

The cost of employing a consultancy is based on the time dedicated to the account or project. Personnel are charged at an hourly or daily rate, with the team completing time sheets to monitor how long is spent on individual tasks. This is not simply to ensure that clients are charged accurately, but it enables performance to be monitored. Budgets are calculated on the basis of forecasting time required (which is likely to be based on previous records). Clients may quote a fixed cost, based on an estimated or specific time involvement. Should the nature of the project change, consultancies should review the plan or budget (or both) with the client.

The client–consultancy relationship can be a fractious one. This is most notable in respect of consultancy claims of over-servicing accounts and client counter-claims of exaggerating billable time or under-delivering on promised results. Pieczka (2006a) highlights a third perspective, that of the consultancy's personnel, who experience a long-hours culture without paid overtime. This is evident in the results of the PR census (Gorkana, 2011), and debate in the industry regarding paid internships (Cartmell, 2011b).

Consultancies need to account for incidental services including costs of materials, phone calls, travel costs and other expenses. A mark-up may be charged on bought-in costs, subject to agreement with the client. This normally reflects the accounting consequence (and possible risk) of the consultancy making payments on behalf of clients.

In-house resources

Even if public relations projects are executed in-house, human resource requirements need to be determined. Appropriate staff and skill sets need to be identified, with work on the project scheduled alongside other responsibilities.

External consultancy staff are normally charged on an hourly basis or a per day rate. It can be useful to consider the cost of internal staff in order to make comparisons against the costs of external resources. The full cost of maintaining an internal resource includes salaries, fixed costs involved in providing a professional working environment, plus costs of training, holiday entitlement and other employee benefits. Charges for equipment (computers, telephones and so on) as well as postage, photocopying, travel and other ongoing costs may be hidden within the accountancy process, but still need to be covered by the organisation. Where organisations view their PR function as an internal consultancy, they will cross-charge PR support to other departments. The PR function may also be charged if it utilises other personnel or internal services.

Time management

Working in PR requires multitasking – which means having good time management, administrative and prioritising skills. In some organisations, even when working at a senior level, the PR practitioner may not have additional staff and be required to implement rather than just plan activities. Research by Moss et al. (2004) reveals that most senior managers retain personal responsibility for important elements of technical craft work, such as writing speeches for senior executives or handling highly critical/sensitive tasks such as releasing financial information.

Covey (1989) provides a useful matrix plotting tasks in relation to urgency and importance, which is helpful in looking at time management and workload in PR (Figure 9.1).

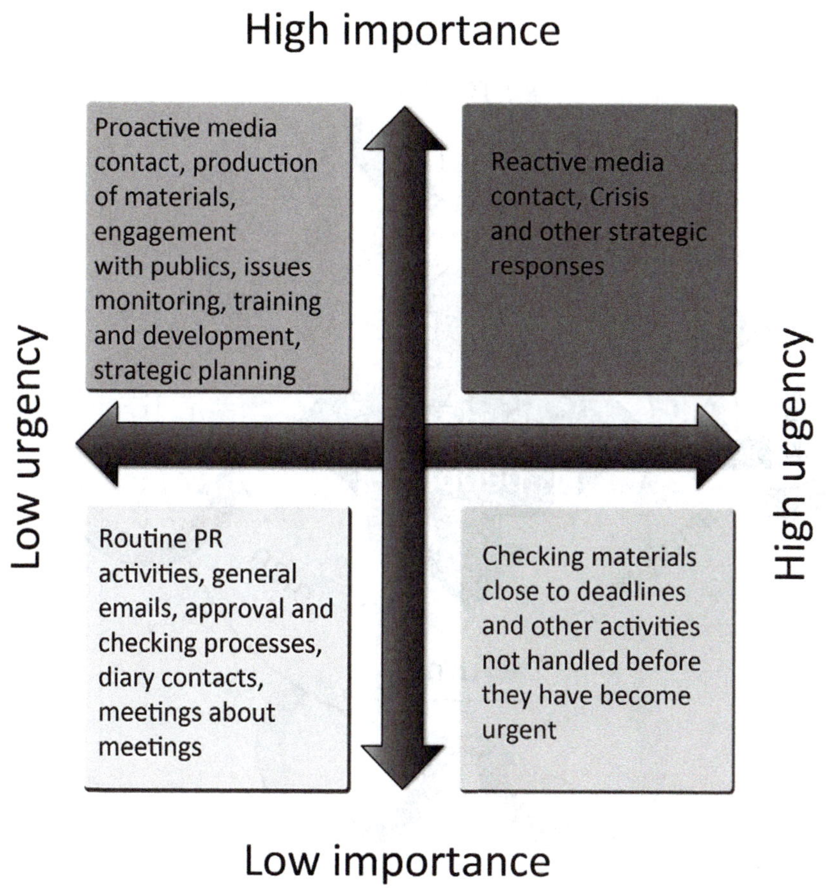

High importance

Proactive media contact, production of materials, engagement with publics, issues monitoring, training and development, strategic planning

Reactive media contact, Crisis and other strategic responses

Low urgency

High urgency

Routine PR activities, general emails, approval and checking processes, diary contacts, meetings about meetings

Checking materials close to deadlines and other activities not handled before they have become urgent

Low importance

FIGURE 9.1 Time management matrix (based on Covey, 1989)

Time planning

Any campaign will comprise a series of activities that need to be scheduled. This requires assessment of how long such tasks will take to be planned and implemented, as well as the required skills to undertake the allocated activities.

The timescale within which the PR campaign is to be executed can affect resource requirements. For example, if a situation is urgent, additional human and financial resources may be necessary. If there is sufficient time to plan ahead, it may be possible to deliver a campaign with fewer people or more efficient use of resources. Figure 9.2 details considerations involved in developing a timeframe for a campaign.

Mapping the tasks to be undertaken enables consideration of human resource requirements, the deadlines of external suppliers and internal approval processes.

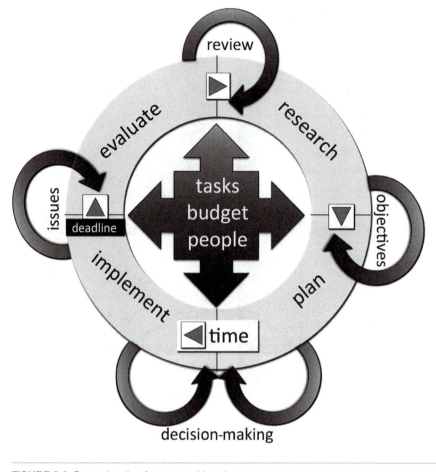

FIGURE 9.2 Campaign timeframe considerations

It also provides a sanity check on the detailed programme of activities in terms of its feasibility. If too many tasks have been proposed within a short period of time, additional resources may be required or the campaign may need to be revised. A flexible approach is necessary as it is likely circumstances will arise and affect the planned schedule, even if it has been accurately mapped.

Roles and responsibilities need to be allocated for individual tasks, with deadlines that are monitored during the planning and implementation stages (see Appendices).

In determining a suitable campaign or programme of work, the manager needs to have a clear understanding of time availability and what is achievable before any fixed deadlines. Any campaign will comprise a series of activities that need to be scheduled and this requires reflection on how long such tasks need to be planned and implemented. It is necessary also to consider the skills and experience of the people undertaking the allocated activities.

The timescale within which the campaign or programme of tasks has to be realised can affect resource requirements. For example, if the situation is urgent, additional human and financial resources may be required. If there is sufficient time to plan ahead, then it is feasible that the same campaign can be delivered by fewer people or with more efficient use of resources.

It is important to establish priorities and ensure that time is managed in relation to achieving specific targets. Recognition of key outcomes and how a task will be evaluated is also important in determining how best to allocate time. Where other people or organisations are involved in a campaign, their time management also needs to be considered. Where aspects of the campaign are outsourced or approval is required from management, a reasonable allowance of time, including contingency, needs to be determined.

In order to understand the amount of time required for a task to be undertaken, previous experience can be used as an indicator. Detailed time-diaries, such as those used in consultancies, can be very useful for planning purposes. It is important also to maintain accurate files for previous projects as these can provide a helpful guide to future activities. Other people who have undertaken similar activities or published examples of case studies may also be consulted. Aspects such as meetings, travel, status reports, administration and routine communications on any activity need to be built into plans. Time also needs to be allowed for research, analysis, planning, securing agreement from management, evaluation and a final review of outcomes.

Critical path analysis

This process considers which elements of a campaign take the longest time and so affect when the project can be completed. It also enables reflection on which tasks are dependent on the completion of others and which can be undertaken simultaneously. It will be necessary to factor in constraints of external resources (e.g. suppliers' deadlines) and available internal resources (who is able to undertake various tasks). Decisions about use of resources and what can be achieved in a particular timeframe or to meet a deadline can then be made. Computer systems such as Microsoft Project enable tasks to be planned, resources considered and progress monitored. Tools such as a GANTT chart or PERT can be helpful in planning complex tasks (see Appendices).

Project calendars

Another option is to map out tasks and key deadlines on a project calendar (see Appendices). This can be particularly helpful for larger campaigns or those with a longer timeframe (e.g. annual plans). A timetable of activities by date enables a clear visual picture of the scope of the project to be understood and any conflicts or potential resource constraints identified at an early stage. Peaks in activity may highlight the need to plan for additional resources. Holidays and other personal and ongoing departmental commitments can be factored into the plan.

BUDGETING

Resources and time are two key elements in effective campaign management, alongside cost control. These three elements need to be considered alongside the scope and quality requirements (Wysocki, 2011) for the campaign. Figure 9.3 illustrates the relationships between these five aspects. Requirements in one or more of these will impact on other aspects, indicating a need to determine the ideal balance, as well as the consequences of issues that are likely to arise.

A financial budget may be presented as a fixed element of a campaign. This is particularly the case when budget cuts may have been made year-on-year with expectations of delivering the same results for lower investment.

The budget needs to include the cost of people resources as discussed above. Some organisations have a formal procurement process whereby consultancies (and other suppliers) need to be approved prior to work being undertaken. Quotes for services are used in building a budget.

The cost of PR consultancies varies significantly, depending on factors including size, expertise and location, as well as the level and competency of personnel undertaking the campaign. Bought-in goods and services may include print and design costs for

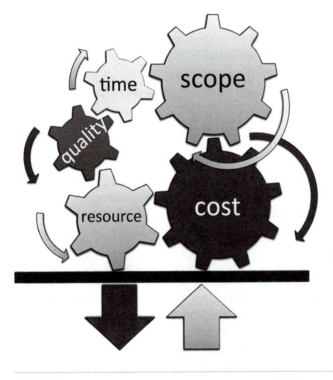

FIGURE 9.3 Balancing resource, time, cost, scope and quality

materials, audio-visual services, external suppliers (on retainer or project basis), event organisation, photography, staging, hospitality, travel, etc.

Budgeting to the penny is not advisable since it is unlikely that cost predictions will be 100 per cent accurate at the outset, although reasonable estimates are possible. Rather than adding a certain percentage figure to a budget to allow for contingencies (unexpected or unforeseen costs), clients/managers expect to be consulted on any additional costs as they arise. If these can be anticipated, the proposal should set out the options, enabling clients to plan accordingly.

The budget may be affected by the time available to plan and execute the campaign. If time is short, premium prices may be charged. This can be built into the critical path analysis and clients/managers informed in status reports of the implications of any slippage.

Some budget areas may be covered by overall or departmental costs depending on how the financial resources are determined by the individual organisation. Costs such as postage, stationery, etc., may be covered on a corporate basis, an 'overhead' charge may be placed on the department or coding used to recharge exact costs. The cost of expenses incurred by internal personnel also needs to be calculated.

Control processes

When planning a budget, it is important to consider control processes, which are likely to also be a budget item (e.g. evaluation). Cole (2004) outlines the key steps in establishing a budget control system:

- **Forecast** – statements that determine probable costs and other relevant data
- **Budgets** – based on the analysis of previous experiences that include any income generation and variable, fixed or capital costs
- **Departmental and corporate budgets** – managers are required to produce overall departmental budgets, beyond those for specific campaigns or purposes. These are fed into overall corporate budgets that take account of the organisation's total income and expenditure, profit objectives and so on
- **Period budget statements** – these inform management about performance against targets in relation to relevant periods of time; and specify costs incurred and accruals (costs for which invoices have not been received)
- **Action required** – if any issues are identified in relation to budgets, action will be required to resolve such problems.

Cutlip *et al.* (2000) suggest three useful guidelines:

- Knowing the exact cost of what is required in undertaking the activities
- Communicating the budget in terms of what it costs to achieve specific results
- Using computer programmes (spreadsheets) to track costs of individual projects matching actual against projected.

BPM (BUSINESS PROCESS MANAGEMENT), WORKFLOWS AND PLAYBOOKS

BPM focuses on the governance and improvement of 'essential business processes' (Jeston and Nelis, 2014: 4), which may be facilitated by the use of technology. The development of automation technologies in the mid-to-late 1990s was evident in public relations primarily through media databases that could be managed in-house or accessed through various service providers.

These improved the work management – or workflow – of the operations and tasks involved in contacting journalists/titles and keeping up to date with changes in the media landscape.

Today the use of technology has the potential to simplify and streamline many aspects of the PR workflows. This includes the management of people, services and financial resources.

Technology can be particularly useful for managing repetitive and routing activities. Plotting the components of tasks within any process of work helps to identify the activities that it may be possible to improve using technology. This may be best undertaken in respect of a live project, but if this is not possible, then getting a team together to document the process will suffice.

A step-by-step guide can be produced. This can be developed into a playbook to inform sustainable professional development (Yaxley, 2015). A playbook may involve flowcharts detailing the process to be followed (e.g. in responding to media inquiries). The extent to which the process is prescribed depends on the nature of the situation. The more predictable the process is, the more likely it can be automated.

Where processes require 'ad-hoc functionality to solve unpredictable events' (Jeston and Nelis, 2014: 60) dynamic capabilities will be required. This is a challenge for automated technologies currently. Hence, these aspects of a plan are where human resources should be devoted.

Where technologies (including software) can help to improve the efficiency and effectiveness of processes and procedures, these need to be researched. This is an ongoing process as technologies are developing continuously. Over time the functionality of technologies tends to increase and their costs decrease. This may mean that further processes can be automated.

Check out the following useful guides to improve a workflow that you have responsibility for executing:

PR workflow modernisation – the essential guide (2016): www.frederikvincx.com/how-to-modernize-your-pr-team-workflow-the-essential-guide/

PR Stack #1 and #2: https://prstack.co/#/

PR software: the complete guide: www.prezly.com/pr-software

Unfortunately, such resources soon become dated owing to the speed of development of online technologies. Research companies can be a more useful way of keeping up to date, for example:

Gartner: www.gartner.com/technology/home.jsp

Forrester Research: https://go.forrester.com/

Methods of setting budgets

Budget planning involves securing agreement on costs required to execute proposed action to achieve specific objectives. Different organisations have different approaches to setting budgets:

- **Arbitrarily** – a budget figure is allocated without any analysis
- **All you can afford** – the organisation decides what it can afford to spend on PR. This may be arbitrary or related to surplus over expenses
- **Historical basis** – a figure is allocated relating to what has previously been spent
- **Competitive necessity** – the PR budget is set in relation to the standard in the industry or to address a competitive weakness/opportunity
- **Percentage of income** – PR budgets may be agreed as a certain percentage of sales income (or fundraising income in the case of charities) or in relation to the marketing budget
- **Experiment and testing** – the budget may be allocated dependent on proving its effectiveness
- **Modelling and simulation** – there may be a formula used to predict the required budget
- **Situation driven** – budget may be allocated according to a particular situation, such as to support launch of a new product

- **Objective and task** – this is the best approach in terms of determining what needs to be done to achieve the objective. There will obviously be constraints according to what the organisation can afford and the strategic relevance of the activities.

Setting a budget may seem complex but it is a simple matter of determining what needs to be done and researching what it will cost. This is an iterative process as the costs calculated may raise questions about the planned activities and either the plan or the budget needs to be amended.

Presenting budgets

Organisations may have budget forms and systems that need to be followed. In general, easy to understand tables are used (normally spreadsheets) where costs are specified for individual tasks and an overall cost is calculated (see Appendices). Within a campaign proposal, the key elements of the budget would be detailed and managers could expect to be questioned on both the overall figure and specific items. Sufficient detail is necessary to ensure managers understand the financial and resource implications of recommendations. Additional detail would be included in campaign plans, with an operational budget used to track ongoing and final expenditure.

Proposals need to include budgets that reflect the level of expenditure advised by the client, or if no budget was set, it needs to be reasonable for the anticipated results. Detailed explanation can be included to clarify specific aspects or outline options that can be determined before proceeding.

As well as ensuring that any budget takes account of all the tasks included within the plan (including research and evaluation costs), it needs to be sanity checked in relation to the objectives that are to be achieved. Simple calculations such as a cost per head to attend an event can be made. In addition, brand standards of the organisation need to be factored to ensure that budgets are commensurate. For example, the Royal Bank of Scotland reduced its corporate hospitality budget by 90 per cent in 2011, reflecting expectations of a state-owned rather than public sector organisation.

Any project needs to be reviewed to consider whether the objectives could have been achieved at a lower cost, to ensure that ideas proposed are not disproportionate in terms of return on investment.

PERFORMANCE CONTROL REPORTING

The management of campaigns and programmes of work involves an understanding of time planning and allocation of budgets and human resources. This requires organisational skills and an ability to produce effective plans to enable others to work efficiently and effectively on tasks. In addition, PR planning and management involves control and reporting of standards of performance and the achievement of desired outcomes.

Management information systems enable reports to be produced, utilising quantitative and qualitative data from a variety of sources. As discussed in Chapter 5, the PR Information Management System (PRISM) can be used to inform management decision-making. The strategic campaign planning and execution process outlined in Part II includes documents and information which can be included in the PRISM approach and support ongoing management.

The five elements of effective campaign management (Figure 9.3) need to be monitored and reported, with consideration made of the impact of any variation from plans.

Human resources

The performance of individuals (whether in-house, consultants or other suppliers) needs to be monitored, controlled and reported. Meetings and status reports are used to monitor progress within the campaign. If a project management system is being used, the consequences of any variance in human resource performance can be considered in respect of impact on finances, time management, etc. In addition, regular team reviews, including official appraisal systems, enable individual performance to be assessed and corrective action implemented. Acknowledgement of achievements is a key component of personnel performance management.

Individuals should also be encouraged to monitor their own performance as part of a proactive career management strategy. As discussed in Chapter 16, some organisations are using gamification systems to motivate personnel through suggestion schemes and appraisal programmes.

Time

Time management has been discussed earlier in this chapter. Monitoring progress on a timely basis, using critical path analysis and project calendars, is recommended. In addition, updating daily task plans and monitoring any slippage is a useful monitoring approach. Close management of suppliers, particularly those with whom there is no existing relationship, is important. Printers, for example, are notorious for missing deadlines. Contracts can include penalty clauses to help minimise the risk of slippage, or at least help manage the financial consequences.

Cost

Performance control reporting includes review of monthly (or more frequent) financial statements of proposed and actual expenditure. Controls on finances also need to indicate where action is required and determine return on investment made.

Scope

Monitoring and managing the scope of the planned campaign involves determining progress towards achieving the specified objectives. Reports should be produced to determine the attainment of specific deliverables or milestones in a campaign. Remedial action can be identified to accommodate any problems incurred. Adjustment where necessary of the objectives can be made or other elements of the plan altered as appropriate.

Quality

Standards of performance can also evaluate the quality of work undertaken. Any issues or problems arising need to be addressed (Chapter 13).

Reporting

As well as producing reports to monitor progress of a campaign, regular reporting to management is recommended to demonstrate a professional approach to PR management. Simple one-page documents conveying key indicators could be produced (see Appendices). It is important to be open and honest regarding any problems or issues that have been experienced, with implications and solutions outlined.

PRACTICAL MANAGEMENT CONSIDERATIONS

Although there are many valid reasons to take a planned approach to public relations, it may not be feasible or possible to adhere to such processes in all circumstances. Practical limitations and considerations include:

- **Real-world complexity:** The process of planning may create an illusion of control by focusing on a set of steps to be undertaken. The complexity of actually executing plans is a reminder of the importance of an adaptive approach where flexibility needs to be built into plans to accommodate changes in the internal or external environment.

- **Partnership effects:** The planning approach largely focuses on actions for a particular organisation, but the actions and objectives of stakeholders and publics need to be considered. This is to be considered particularly when undertaking campaigns in partnership with others, seeking to build relationships or engage in two-way communications. Involving others in the planning process and considering the impact of their actions is advised.

- **Unforeseen circumstances:** Some circumstances cannot be anticipated when decisions are made, or things may not go to plan. Risk, issues and crisis management (Chapter 13) should be undertaken, especially for any campaigns that are of significant strategic importance.

- **Intended vs realised strategy:** Mintzberg and Waters (1985, cited by Henry 2008) distinguish between the intended strategy (the one chosen for the campaign) and the realised strategy (the one actually carried out). This reflects an adaptive approach, where managers use experience and learning to develop and implement an emergent strategy (which becomes the realised strategy). It is important to recognise such developments and identify factors that affected execution of the intended strategy. There may have been inherent problems with the original proposed strategy or other reasons offering lessons to be learned for future planning.

- **Limitations:** Planning is ultimately about what can be done with the available time, money and resources, rather than what is ideal or desirable. If the problems discussed in Chapter 7 regarding objective setting have not been avoided, PR activities would not have been able to achieve the unrealistic aims set for them. The plan may also have been compromised by cuts or issues emerging that affected the time, money and resources that were foreseen during the initial planning stage.

- **Lack of planning:** In the case of routine or *ad-hoc* opportunities, PR activities may not warrant a full plan as discussed in this section. The principles of thinking before acting remain important and the consequences of failing to plan can be surprisingly impactful, even resulting in crisis situations.

- **Irrationality:** Practitioners may prefer to rely on experience and knowledge, to act intuitively without a rigorous process of research or planning. Instincts can be useful, but could reflect irrationality and be a faulty guide to future behaviour. Feelings and gut instinct are not always the most reliable or professional approach to good management.

- **Zeitgeist** – Changes in society, cultural considerations (especially for international or localised campaigns) and timing issues can have an impact on the implementation of campaigns. It is possible that plans can be hugely successful sometimes and an absolute failure another time owing to factors that may seem to be entirely outside our control, and simply reflect a changing zeitgeist.

END POINT

An organised approach enables management of five key elements of campaign plans: human resources, budgets, time, scope and quality. Information management systems and processes help to predict, monitor and report on each element. The successful implementation of plans to achieve the required objectives can still be affected by a number of practical considerations, emphasising the importance of an adaptive approach. Technology is increasingly enabling processes to be automated and made more efficient and effective. Workflow mapping is suggested as a means of investigating where technology may be deployed.

CHAPTER 10

Monitoring and evaluation

Heather Yaxley

This chapter presents an ongoing, holistic approach to monitoring and evaluation that is directly connected to objective setting. Assessment of contemporary public relations practice is examined alongside thoughts on future challenges and opportunities.

CHECK POINT

After reading this chapter, you should be able to:

- Examine historical, contemporary and future developments in PR evaluation
- Understand the value of pre-emptive, formative and summative evaluation in strategic PR management
- Adopt a practical approach to monitor and evaluate PR campaigns.

DEVELOPMENT OF PR EVALUATION

Watson (2011) demonstrates that evaluation has a long history, with social science methods evident in the 1920s and 1930s. Indeed, he notes a full circle (with 'new' techniques echoing those in use almost a century ago) following decades of resistance by practitioners. Despite this heritage, the prevailing attitude within public relations has been that evaluation is difficult and the real measure of success is a happy client.

Batchelor (1938) notes the Roosevelt Administration monitored changes in political attitudes to assess the reception of its publicity activities. He observes that the Works Progress Administration achieved 'great local publicity' (p. 212) but little coverage of its real objective to put unemployed men back to work; this misunderstanding became a 'political liability'. A revision of the communications policy altered the emphasis of media materials, increasing favourable editorial coverage from 10 to over 40 per cent. The in-house PR operation of the Bell Telephone System was cited as typical of large-scale business in monitoring and responding to critical letters published in local newspapers to correct inaccurate allegations. These simple examples illustrate early practical use of monitoring and adaptation to achieve specific outcomes.

Gregory and White (2008) note progress in evaluation within PR has been slow despite attention paid to the matter in the 1990s. Momentum was gained by the *PR Week* Proof Campaign in 1998 (which urged 10 per cent of budgets be allocated to research and evaluation). Likewise a joint industry PRE-fix initiative published a Research and Evaluation Toolkit that clearly set out a planning and evaluation framework. However, Pieczka (2006a) notes such enthusiasm for evaluation didn't last owing to economic constraints.

What impact does historic and ongoing resistance to evaluation have on the industry's reputation? How would you suggest this can be addressed?

PR practitioners need to stop hiding behind excuses or poor practices and accept evaluation as normal operating practice. Relevant concepts and methods concerning measurement and evaluation have been developed and promoted in recent years. Nevertheless, some practitioners still call for a single, simple method of evaluation as the Holy Grail of public relations. Others claim that a substantial budget is required for effective research and evaluation. Another argument is that management only require a simplistic number (see below) to evaluate the PR function.

Opposition to robust measurement misses its real purpose, which is to help improve performance and make best use of available resources. From an organisational perspective, the intention of evaluation is to be able to assess the contribution made by public relations towards achieving organisational goals. Given the extensive scope of public relations as evidenced throughout this book, developing a range of key performance indicators is more useful than presenting a single measure of communications activities or their output.

The publication of the AMEC Barcelona Declaration of Research Principles in June 2010 emphasised the importance of evaluation and sought to guide practice in

AVE, SOCIAL MEDIA METRICS AND ROI

The notion of Advertising Value Equivalents (AVEs) involves calculating a financial figure for media coverage on the basis of what this would have cost if bought as advertising. Published advertising rates are used to produce a financial measure for the number of column centimetres achieved by media relations activities. McKeone (1995: 149) states that AVEs 'represent an early effort to assign spurious monetary values to media relations activities'.

Research by AMEC (2011) found the majority of PR practitioners (55 per cent) use AVE measures. More positively, a survey undertaken by *PR Week* and PRCA in the UK in 2017 revealed that the metric continues to be used by 35 per cent of PR agencies and 23 per cent of in-house teams.

Whilst slow, the decline in use may reflect developments such as the Barcelona Principles (see above) and banning AVE measurement in the award programmes of both CIPR and PRCA. This suggests some realisation among practitioners that the AVE approach is inappropriate. Reasons why AVEs are not a good measurement include:

- Advertisers do not evaluate the success of their work by what it costs; they use recall, attitude and behavioural change measures.
- Multipliers of three to seven times (McKeone, 1995) applied on the basis that positive media endorsement or even general editorial coverage is more 'valuable' than advertising are not justified or proven by research.
- AVE values public relations on the basis of fluctuating advertising rates.
- AVE does not accommodate brief mentions or neutral/negative coverage, let alone where PR practitioners have acted to ensure negative coverage is not published.
- AVE does not allow for publications without advertising.
- AVE does not apply to broadcast or online media.
- AVE may be counterproductive, as some short pieces of coverage can be very influential, whereas a large article may not be read.

Media coverage can be evaluated in ways other than AVE. Simple checks include the relevance of media in which coverage is obtained. Content analysis can be used to check whether aspects of the campaign's narrative have been used, and identify any negative aspects (which can be addressed going forwards). Media evaluation companies offer a range of measurement services, the cost of which should be built into PR budgets.

It may be the case that greater use of online communications has shifted focus away from AVE. However, similar simplistic measures are evident here.

This suggests that greater education of public relations practitioners is required concerning more robust measurement methods. The notion of measuring the influence of social media users has gained significant attention. However, this hasn't been related to academic models concerning influence. Rather measurement of influence tends to be reduced to numeric scoring, ranking or simplistic metrics such as number of followers, reach, etc. Considerable data can be generated from digital communications. Such information should not be confused with intelligent insight into the impact and value of online communications.

Watson and Zerfass (2011: 11) observe that the term ROI (Return on Investment) is commonly used in PR practice and literature, although it reflects a 'fuzzy concept'. They argue that 'the complexity of communication processes and their role in business interactions means it is not possible to calculate Return on Investment in financial terms. Consequently. public relations practitioners should refrain from using the term in order to keep their vocabulary compatible with the overall management world.'

Which of the above arguments do you find most influential in arguing against the continued use of AVE? Why do you think AVE and similar simplistic metrics have proven to be popular in PR? What are the benefits and drawbacks of using the term ROI when discussing PR practice?

the industry. These were revised in 2015 to respond to feedback and developments (see: http://amecorg.com/how-the-barcelona-principles-have-been-updated/).

In particular, the revised principles emphasised the contribution (impact) of PR/communications to the wider organisation, the role of qualitative as well as quantitative methods of research and the scope for evaluation across channels of communication. Reference is also made to transparency, consistency and validity of research methods.

An integrated evaluation framework has also been proposed by AMEC (see: http://amecorg.com/amecframework/) that encompasses core elements discussed in its objectives. Similarly, the Institute of Public Relations has developed the Public Relations Research Standards Center (www.instituteforpr.org/public-relations-research-standards/), with a vision that 'Excellence in public relations is enabled by excellence in research, measurement and evaluation'.

Looking forwards, monitoring and evaluation will be even more complex owing to multimedia developments and technological developments such as the Internet of Things (see Chapter 16). At the same time, technologies will emerge that facilitate tracking and measurement of communications and relationships. Inevitably budgets will be required to take advantage of such options, with do-it-yourself becoming more difficult.

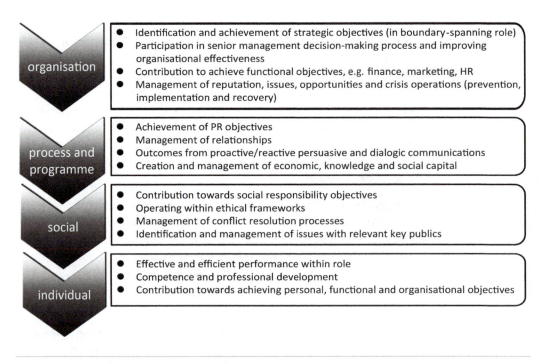

organisation
- Identification and achievement of strategic objectives (in boundary-spanning role)
- Participation in senior management decision-making process and improving organisational effectiveness
- Contribution to achieve functional objectives, e.g. finance, marketing, HR
- Management of reputation, issues, opportunities and crisis operations (prevention, implementation and recovery)

process and programme
- Achievement of PR objectives
- Management of relationships
- Outcomes from proactive/reactive persuasive and dialogic communications
- Creation and management of economic, knowledge and social capital

social
- Contribution towards social responsibility objectives
- Operating within ethical frameworks
- Management of conflict resolution processes
- Identification and management of issues with relevant key publics

individual
- Effective and efficient performance within role
- Competence and professional development
- Contribution towards achieving personal, functional and organisational objectives

FIGURE 10.1 Pre-emptive, formative and summative evaluation at organisation, process and programme, social and individual levels

PRE-EMPTIVE, FORMATIVE AND SUMMATIVE EVALUATION

Pre-emptive evaluation involves assessment of campaign plans prior to implementation. This is an important stage to check feasibility and assess risks. As a reflective process, pre-emptive evaluation helps anticipate problems or issues. Chapter 13 considers risk assessment in detail, with useful checklists in the Appendices.

Formative evaluation is undertaken during implementation of a campaign. It encourages reflexivity and adjustment of the plan. Specific stages or milestones may be set as points when formative evaluation takes place. Alternatively, feedback loops may offer continuous evaluation. Care needs to be taken in interpreting the significance of information at this point in the plan.

Summative evaluation takes place at the end of a campaign or when a major component has been completed. It involves robust consideration of all aspects undertaken to date.

Pre-emptive, formative and summative evaluation can be applied to task and outcome objectives. The contribution of PR programmes can be determined at organisation, process and programme, social and individual levels. These approaches are illustrated in Figure 10.1.

Pre-emptive evaluation

Pre-emptive evaluation involves the assessment of plans prior to their implementation. This should check for validity and risk within the planning process as well as reviewing the viability of proposed communications and activities. If insurance is required to minimise the impact of any risk, this needs to be included in the campaign budget. A brief risk assessment should be included in campaign proposals and ongoing management reports.

The research stage of planning (Chapter 6) should provide foresight as well as insight. This suggests an iterative approach with research undertaken into plans prior to their implementation. Such information is useful in supporting recommendations and enabling adjustments. Different options can be proposed, tested and reviewed.

Task/process evaluation

Chapter 7 distinguished task/process and outcome objectives. This same approach is required for evaluation. Measures assessing, for example, whether or not a Twitter account was set up, press releases distributed or an annual report delivered to schedule, do not reflect the impact of the action taken.

Pickton and Broderick (2005: 357) state that evaluation of tasks should consider:

- Efficiency – doing things right
- Effectiveness – doing the right things
- Economy – doing things within a specified budget.

These present operational performance indicators that can be useful when assessing processes, suppliers, the PR function or individual team members. Similarly, Eiró-Gomes and Duarte (2008) focus primarily on functional aspects of evaluating PR activities:

- Conceptualisation and design
- Implementation
- Impact and efficiency.

A comprehensive post-campaign review offers a summative assessment opportunity. Findings may suggest action that needs to be taken, for example, to inform future plans or suggest development needs for team members. Reviews provide useful research within the Public Relations Information System Management (PRISM) approach (Chapter 5).

Performance also needs to be monitored during the execution of activities. This formative review is important to identify any problems or issues where remedial action can avoid incidents or crisis situations (Chapter 13). Pre-emptive evaluation pulls this assessment forward prior to implementation.

Outcome evaluation

To demonstrate the effectiveness of a campaign, the results specified in outcome objectives must be achieved. Figures 7.2 and 7.3 outline levels of objectives and relevant measures. Relevant outcomes are:

- Knowledge: evaluating awareness, knowledge and understanding
- Predisposition: evaluating attitudes and opinions
- Behavioural: evaluating what people do
- Relationship: evaluating mutual understanding and co-orientation
- Reputation: evaluating trust and other relevant dimensions.

Methods of research to set benchmark objectives before a campaign is undertaken are considered in Chapters 5, 6 and 7. The same approaches should be used for formative and summative assessment.

REVIEW AGAINST MANAGEMENT OBJECTIVES

Management by Objectives (MBO) is proposed as a way of improving the effectiveness of management (Chapter 7). Achievement of campaign outcomes can be linked to objectives for the PR function and individual team members enabling review within the organisation's appraisal system. Similarly, management of external suppliers, including PR consultancies, includes assessment of results, alongside evaluation of processes and the relationship with the organisation. Evaluation can also consider the value of resources invested in the campaign.

Any evaluation provides a snapshot in time and may need to be followed up to consider any long-term impact. It is essential for a campaign to demonstrate internal integrity, which requires recognition that the sum of the individual parts add up to a compelling solution to the issue the organisation faces. This means a Gestalt approach to evaluation, assessing campaigns holistically as well as reviewing individual aspects.

If the PR campaign is integrated with activities of other disciplines such as marketing or human resources, it may be difficult to isolate the impact of particular activities. Likewise separating the impact of various communication channels can be problematic. Nevertheless, suitable research and evaluation must be undertaken so the overall programme of activities can be assessed and any change in knowledge, attitude and behaviour of the target publics identified. Agreement on evaluation and reporting measures with other functions and for all channels of communication is important.

At the organisational level, evaluation needs to demonstrate how PR activities represent a strategically valuable use of resources by contributing towards the wider objectives of the organisation. Evaluation can also indicate compliance with the organisational culture, Mission/Vision and overall aims. Other management in the organisation should understand the value of public relations and, where feasible, integrate PR activities and outcomes into their operations. For example, quotes generated from media coverage can be used within marketing campaigns (with permission).

Indeed, in many cases, to achieve a strategic difference, the PR campaign must involve early discussion with other functions and be prepared to tackle any operational or other aspects of management that either caused the issue to occur or are acting as barriers to achieving change. Reporting on such processes can be included within evaluation reports.

EVALUATION METHODS

The first step in evaluation is to determine the methods that need to be used for formative and summative assessment of progress against the stated campaign objectives (Chapters 5, 6 and 7). In addition, a variety of technologies and specialist agencies offer means of adding a scientific perspective to the challenge of evaluation.

The evaluation methodology used should be included in a campaign proposal, with details of ongoing and key stage assessment as well as final evaluation of results at the natural end of the campaign. If a programme of activity is ongoing, recommendations should be made for regular points at which measurement can be undertaken as part of the continuous PR management and planning cycle.

The methodology needs to identify how key lessons from the campaign will be learned and how remedial action can be undertaken should plans not proceed as predicted or other factors and issues arise.

Setting clear, SMART, objectives, makes it much easier to evaluate PR campaigns (Chapter 7). The value of the initial research (Chapters 5 and 6) is underpinned by an ability to revisit it to identify significant change as a result of the programme undertaken.

Evaluation may be undertaken within the PR function or by employing external experts who will assess campaigns using measures that may reflect industry standards, competitive perspectives or tailored for the client's specific purposes. Evaluation should focus on the effect on the receiver:

- Output – what messages went out and who did they reach?
- Outtake – to what extent is the audience aware of the information sent out, what do they understand/recall and what do they feel about it?
- Outcome – to what degree did the PR activities change the opinion, behaviour and attitudes of audiences?

This approach highlights the importance of what was achieved by the campaign rather than what was done in implementing it. Figure 10.2 provides information on

GCS EVALUATION FRAMEWORK (https://gcs.civilservice.gov.uk/ guidance/evaluation/ tools-and-resources/)

The UK Government Communication Service has adopted an approach that seeks to help standardise a set of evaluation measures to be used by communications throughout government departments. This framework offers a range of useful guides that are publicly available.

This model draws on approaches evident in literature and the AMEC integrated evaluation framework discussed above (see: http://amecorg.com/ amecframework/). The focus is on objective setting and a series of staged measures encompassing:

- Inputs (what is done before and during an activity)
- Outputs (what is delivered/target audience reached)
- Outtakes (what the target audience think, feel or do to make a decision)
- Outcomes (the result of activities on the target audience)
- Organisational impact (the quantifiable impact on the organisation goals/KPIs).

It is notable that the term 'audience' is used. This can be seen as a passive descriptor rather than recognising those with whom PR practitioners wish to communicate as participants, legitimate stakeholders or aware/active publics.

The framework defines an audience/target audience as a specified group within a defined public targeted for influence. This is clearly a persuasive perspective of communications. Indeed, its definition of audience engagement simply states this as: 'The extent to which the target audience interacts with the content. Typically takes the form of enquiries, calls, clicks, shares, downloads, etc.' Again this implies a narrow range of behavioural responses that would be exclusively directed towards the organisation.

Review the GCS and AMEC frameworks to identify their strengths and weaknesses. What opportunities do you feel these present to address limitations in current objective setting, measurement and evaluation practices? How do you feel the frameworks could address criticisms evident of existing planning approaches in this section? How could the approaches be adapted to take account of these and your own observation of their limitations?

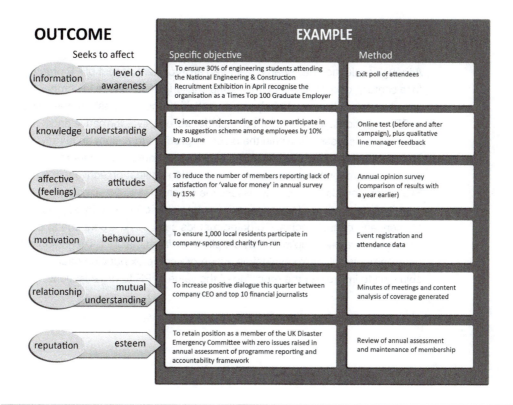

FIGURE 10.2 Evaluation methods and objectives

several possible evaluation methods linking them to various objectives considered in Chapter 7.

The cost of all evaluation needs to be included in the budget for the campaign, with human resources also considered (Chapter 9).

One final word on evaluation is to remember the Pareto Principle. In 1906, Italian economist Vilfredo Pareto created a mathematical formula which purports 20 per cent of something is always responsible for 80 per cent of the results. Gronstedt and Caywood (2011: 19) claim this can be applied to public relations activities stating:

> 20 percent of all journalists account for 80 percent of the media coverage of the company, and 20 percent of all shareholders own 80 percent of the company. The critical few are, in most cases, the most cost-effective group to target with communications.

Whether or not this is true, it indicates the importance of prioritising efforts throughout the planning process and suggests evaluation should identify the key elements that have contributed most to the end results.

END POINT

Although evaluation has been considered an important aspect of PR practice for a century, debate about methods and challenges continues to hamper the use of methods that would help inform activities and demonstrate the value of PR operations. It is important to include pre-emptive, formative and summative assessment within the planning process to ensure an iterative approach helps to review and refine practices. An outcome-oriented approach is recommended based on evaluation against objectives. Evaluation can also be used to assess the planning process itself and contribute towards performance reviews of in-house PR functions, practitioners and consultancies. Outdated metrics such as AVE continue to be used and have been replicated by simplistic online measures. Technological developments will make evaluation ever more complex but also offer solutions to improving the reporting of the value of PR to organisations.

Outro

Heather Yaxley

The considered approach to public relations strategic planning underlying the preceding chapters in Part II reflects a pragmatic perspective, encouraging flexibility, a proactive stance and adaptation to particular circumstances.

Where reference is made to managerial rationality and a more scientific structured approach to planning, the intention is not to advocate a rigid linear model whereby plans are developed in isolation from practice or practical considerations.

Some PR practitioners may welcome this stance as supporting their rejection of the concept of planning in favour of intuition, instinct and imagination. Like Apple's Steve Jobs (Isaacson, 2011), they may believe in their own insight to guide decision-making. On the other hand, other practitioners may reflect another of Jobs' characteristics, a stubborn, perfectionist nature, displaying a tendency to micro-manage rather than benefit from the expert deployment of resources that a dynamic planning process offers.

This short chapter presents a counterpoint to both perspectives. It considers the merits of artistic spontaneity and the dramatic freedom to act on instinct. Yet it champions greater use of technology in the planning process. This is viewed as a means of freeing up resources to take advantage of opportunities where imagination and speed of response are essential.

It may seem heinous or professional heresy to be challenging the evangelistic movement that is propagating a robust planning approach in public relations predicated on a measurement gospel. Indeed, in 2013, Norwegian academic Øyvind Ihlen did just this at a PR and Disruptive Society conference in London as he recollected that he had 'particularly enjoyed throwing a bomb into the audience by declaring that I don't care for measurement. The shock! The horror! Tweets were flying: #prdisrupt'.

Similarly, Robert E. Brown (2015: xv) argues against the search for a 'universal theory of PR' that he contends positions public relations as 'a container for managerial abstractions – objectives, strategies, tactics'. His contrary perspective is that PR is 'the lived, dramatic experience of human beings in the social world'. Therefore, he proposes understanding PR 'more deeply than what happens in and of and for organisations' (p. xvii).

Interestingly both Ihlen and Brown are among authors who draw on the arts in the language they use to examine contemporary public relations. Christensen *et al.* (2008) join Ihlen in using the musical term polyphony (to indicate organisations as comprising multiple voices). Polyphony creates texture through different ways of expressing a melody (arrangement of notes) which Alves (2013: 27) notes are able to 'weave around one another'. Brown (2015) prefers a dramatic metaphor for public relations prac- titioners as actors, whilst noting that PR can be made 'audible as a series of voices' (p. 91): prophetic, academic, humanistic and artistic.

Turning to the arts offers an alternative conceptualisation of planning to the mechanical, systems approach derived from management thinking about organising and evaluating public relations work. An artistic process involves practice, rehearsal and performance. Whilst some artistic endeavours are individualistic, others involve an ensemble cast which emphasises a plurality of roles and competencies.

This thinking has been applied to professions such as surgery (Kneebone, 2009), and similarities can be noted with responsive occupations such as emergency services where expert training develops an ability to deploy appropriate activities according to particular circumstances. A learning culture is evident in arts and emergency services, alongside emphasis on reflective practice, which Holmström (2004: 122) notes as reflecting a 'poly-contextual perspective' and 'sensitivity and respect for the socio-diversity'. Such ideas are under-examined within public relations scholarship and practice but seem worthy of further consideration. As such, new insight may be gained into problem areas noted within traditional models supporting public relations as organisational planners (Gregory and Willis, 2013).

Rigid planning approaches may be viewed as unethical, particularly when used to achieve persuasive objectives or where there is an imbalance in the financial or political power between the organisation and publics. However, a considered approach enables PR practitioners to adopt an ethical decision-making framework within plan- ning processes. In relation to strategic public relations, planning offers a set of essential tools that can be used wisely.

Likewise planning needs to be sufficiently flexible to help address situations within PR practice where research and analysis will not be helpful or possible, particularly when timeframes are short. Decision-making may require an immediate response.

Indeed, Gladwell (2005) argues snap judgements can be more effective than caution and deliberation. This instinctive capability may be underpinned by experience, expertise, knowledge or the reverse – an ability to avoid existing preconceptions and previous practices. It would be useful to examine this phenomenon within the context of public relations. The skill of informed improvisation within the arts and emergency services may offer an interesting model for instance.

Ultimately, decision-making is subjective, particularly in public relations, where recommendations are frequently a matter of opinion. Sometimes, practitioners feel they know what is the right thing to do to achieve the best outcome without engaging with a formal planning process. This may reflect expertise, although reliance on habitus, instinct and commonsense rationality can be the wrong approach.

Planning is not an exact science, no matter how carefully it is undertaken. Making a decision involves taking a risk (Chapter 13); and many people, and their employers, are risk-averse or reluctant to expose themselves to unchartered waters. A professional approach to planning is believed to reduce the risk of errors of judgement and reflects responsibility, particularly when it involves documented evidence as required by quality management systems. This may not actually result in better performance, but is likely to be useful in demonstrating responsibility and protecting an organisation's reputation in crisis response situations.

Being a maverick may seem appealing, but PR practitioners need to ensure their counsel is understood, valued and accepted. This means management has to trust and agree to what is being recommended. Planning accommodates those who require evidence as well as those who are looking for creative solutions. When it is necessary to challenge prevailing views or present counterintuitive ideas, planning helps justify any argument being made.

Ultimately, we need to remember, as Sutherland (1992: 3) contends, 'people are very much less rational than is commonly thought'. This applies as much to PR practitioners and those involved in the planning process as the publics they seek to engage. Planning foregrounds rational thinking. It is predicated on a positivist view of the world as behaving in predictable ways. In reality, we live in a messy, fuzzy, ever-changing world. Chance, human nature and capriciousness can scupper the best laid plans.

The fallibility of human involvement in planning supports an argument for greater use of technology in the planning process. As discussed elsewhere in this section, artificial intelligence, automation and developments such as the Internet of Things are offering new ways to practise public relations. Where appropriate, technology should be viewed as a means of freeing up resources to enable practitioners to take advantage of opportunities where imagination and speed of response are essential. There are many ways in which people add value and rather than viewing technology as eliminating public relations work, it should be viewed as playing to the strengths of strategic practice.

Part III

Corporate communications

Introduction

Heather Yaxley

This Part includes chapters looking at various specialist areas of communications undertaken by organisations. It offers thought-provoking insight both for those without expert knowledge or experience as well as for practitioners who are familiar with the individual areas. Whilst it is termed 'corporate communications', the Part does not exclusively focus on corporations – that is, the contents are relevant for those working in the public and not-for-profit sectors as well as a wide variety of private sector organisations. Likewise, it is not exclusively concerned with communications as it includes a wider remit for public relations in terms of building relationships and planning activities.

The six chapters within this section focus on areas that reach across a number of stakeholder groups (see Part IV). They also draw on considerations of public relations (Part I) and a planned approach (Part II). Chapter 11, 'Brand management' examines the complex matter of brand identity and image, including how brands can be damaged and rescued. Chapter 12, 'Effective media relations', covers the value of the media and media relations, including writing releases, targeting and the impact of developing technology. Chapter 13, 'Risk, incidents, issues and crisis management', provides insight into short- and long-term approaches to respond to negative influences on organisations. Chapter 14, 'Corporate social responsibility', considers issues relating to this important aspect of reputation management including the practitioner's role, Martin's Virtue Matrix model, cause-related marketing and integrating CSR into the organisation's operational management. Chapter 15, 'International considerations', looks at a number of aspects of the global practice of public relations. This includes views on cultural differences and questions to address when operating across international boundaries. Chapter 16, 'Digital public relations', offers a technological perspective on public relations and how practitioenrs can keep ahead of digital developments from a personal and organisational perspective.

Together these chapters provide many of the most important tools required by PR practitioners working in a contemporary, changing corporate communications environment.

CHAPTER 11

Brand management

Alison Theaker

There has been much discussion about what constitutes corporate identity and corporate image and the difference between these two concepts.

CHECK POINT

This chapter starts with suggested definitions for these two terms, and then:

- Defines branding
- Examines the concept of the corporate brand
- Explores Balmer's concept of corporate marketing
- Questions the various elements of good corporate branding practice
- Looks at two examples of corporate branding
- Discusses how an organisation can rescue a tarnished brand.

There is no established definition of corporate identity, although Balmer (2001) suggests: 'The mix of elements which gives organisations their distinctiveness: the foundation of business identities'. He goes on to define these elements as 'culture ... strategy, structure, history, business activities and market scope'. Image on the other hand is more difficult. Balmer (2001) feels that the creation of a positive image is an objective of effectively managing a business identity and that the term 'corporate reputation' is more useful. The latter he defines as 'the enduring perception held of an organisation held by an individual, group or network'. Bernstein (1984) went further when he said that image 'cannot be manufactured ... (it) can only be perceived'. It would seem that identity is to do with the things that can be controlled within an organisation, whereas image is the 'net result of the interaction of all the experiences, beliefs, feeling, knowledge and impressions that people have about a company' (Worcester, 1980, in Bernstein, 1984: 40). Wood and Somerville (2012: 128) sum this up: 'corporate identity is what the organisation communicates (either intentionally or unintentionally) via various cues, whereas its image is how its publics actually view it. An image is a perception and exists only in the mind of the receiver.' We will see that consistency is held to be vitally important for a successful identity, but that a company may have many different images amongst its stakeholders.

BRANDING

A brand is the value of a name of a product or company and affects people's buying behaviour. It is often called an intangible asset, although strong brands enable corporations to add price premiums, such as Heinz baked beans, which can retail for 68p against a supermarket's own label at 24p. In some cases, the company name is the brand, such as Virgin, Sony or Kodak. Association with a corporate brand like this may affect consumer decisions. In others, the brand names are well known, such as Fairy Liquid, but the parent company less so, such as Unilever or Procter & Gamble. Companies may produce different brands which may compete in the marketplace which can be thought of as a cluster of values that promise a particular experience. Morgan (1999, cited in Willis, 2014) suggested that brands have four attributes: they have a buyer and a seller; they have a differentiating name, symbol or trademark; they have association for consumers apart from their product characteristics; and they are created rather than naturally occurring.

'Nobody in the world ever bought anything on price alone', states L. D. Young (2006). Young quotes a blind test of Heinz ketchup against an own-label brand, where 71 per cent of consumers preferred the own label. However, when they saw the label, 68 per cent preferred the Heinz ketchup.

Naomi Klein feels that 'the role of branding has been changing, particularly in the last 15 years ... the brand itself has increasingly become the product'. Thus 'Nike was about "sport" not shoes; Microsoft about "communications", not software' (Klein, 2000). Companies are now projecting their brand onto many different products. Klein links this increase in branding activity to the tendency of multinationals to shift actual production away from where the goods are bought. She quotes the protests in Paris and Seattle, where rioters attacked McDonald's and Starbucks, as evidence of a backlash against global brands, where brands were seen as the embodiment of exploitation.

Branding means everything that surrounds a company's offerings, and both rational and emotional elements underpin the most enduring brands. Frohlich (2016) defines it thus: 'A Brand is the promise a business makes to its customers and its reputation reflects the delivery of that promise – be it positive or negative.'

Al and Laura Ries, having published *The 22 Immutable Laws of Branding*, turned their attention to public relations in 2002 with the controversially titled *The Fall of Advertising and the Rise of PR*. They state: 'You can't launch a new brand with advertising because [it] has no credibility ... You can launch new brands only with ... public relations.' They also redefine advertising's role as brand maintenance, and public relations' as brand building (Ries and Ries 2002: xi, 266). Schneider & Associates (2001) found that product launches were more likely to be successful if they included PR in the launch strategy.

Using an existing brand name to promote a new product is referred to as a brand extension, transferring brand values onto new products. Thus Richard Branson has diversified into air travel, insurance, train travel, weddings and skin care using the same Virgin name and brand as his original record stores. Keller and Aaker (2003) indicated that using an existing brand in this way directly benefited the acceptance of new products by consumers.

Corporate Branding (2011) put forward the brand triangle as a way of defining the characteristics of a brand. Functional values – they suggest that this might be responsibility for the Co-op Bank; belief in respecting children's rights for UNICEF; innovation for Tesco's – are combined with emotional values – concern, integrity, concern for employees – to produce a corporate promised experience. They also warn that stakeholders select between brands based on a small number of characteristics, so that it is best to form the brand promise from only two or three values.

Corporate branding

Palotta (2011) says: 'Brand is your strategy ... calls to action ... customer service ... the way you speak ... the whole array of your communication tools ... your user interface ... your people ... your facilities ... your logo and visuals too ... every interaction anyone is ever going to have with you, no matter how small.'

Hunt (2011) quotes Bhargava who says, 'We all want to do business with people we like.' Core attributes of likeability are honesty, simplicity and being human.

A corporate brand encompasses a name and the perceived qualities or personality that are attached to it. Knox and Bickerton (2003) define it as: 'A corporate brand is the visual, verbal and behavioural expression of an organisation's unique busines model.' Balmer (2001) suggests that the corporate brand is a mix of 'cultural, intrictate, tangible and ethereal elements'.

Davis (2004) refers to three kinds of corporate brand. An attribute brand refers to beliefs about functional attributes associated with the name – is it reliable? Marks & Spencer relies on perceptions of quality, whatever product they are selling. An aspirational brand might recall the enviable lifestyles of buyers. A Rolex watch or Lexus car suggests that the owner is successful. An experiential brand plays on emotions and other associations. Virgin encompasses innovation and value for money. The corporate brand should be portrayed as a unified image by both the marketing and PR functions.

Moloney (2006) suggests public relations is the distribution system for the corporate brand, presenting the ideal of the organisation for its own advantage. Keller and Aaker (2003) noted that corporate marketing activity can provide a direct marketing benefit by building on a strong corporate brand, rather than using a new brand name.

Moloney (2006) warns that brands attract public attention which may not always be welcome. Brands such as McDonald's have non-intended meanings, connected to popular culture. He also questions whether the paradigm of two-way symmetrical communication applies to corporate brandings, stating that the construction of the brand is asymmetrical and assumes acceptance by others. Thus brands can have both positive and negative connotations.

BRAND MANAGEMENT

Knox and Bickerton (2003) add 'competitive landscape' to the normal trilogy of vision, culture and image to set the context of corporate brand management. They also stress the need to look at the current image of the organisation and compare it with the future competition, and do the same with current culture and future vision. They build on Van Riel's concept of common starting points (CSPs) as the central values which form the underpinning of corporate communication and Knox and Maklan's 1998 framework for brand positioning. This sets out four elements:

- Organisation attributes – purpose, commitments and values, or what it exists to do, what's important and what guides its actions;
- Performance benefits – products and services, what it does and what it delivers;
- Portfolio benefits – product brands and customer, the outward faces of an organisation and who it serves;
- Network benefits – contacts and mechanisms, networks and how they are used.

This brand position then needs to be consolidated and communicated to both internal and external audiences in a consistent way. At this point, the business processes can

CORPORATE MARKETING

John Balmer (Balmer and Greyser, 2006) distilled his own corporate marketing structure into six elements. These 6 Cs are:

CHARACTER encompasses the organisation's philosophy and ethics, what it stands for and how it undertakes its activities, as well as its product, price, place, performance and positioning. Thus most of the general marketing elements are clumped together to make one entity which distinguishes it from another.

CULTURE is Balmer's take on personality, and how employees feel about the company they work for. This provides the context for staff to engage with each other and customers.

COMMUNICATION includes promotion, advertising, PR, all the communication channels used by an organisation to all its stakeholders. He also adds in word-of-mouth and media commentary. This could also be related to corporate identity.

CONSTITUENCIES recognises that customers may belong to many stakeholder groups, and that organisational success and 'license to operate' depends on meeting groups' expectations.

CONCEPTUALISATIONS includes the perception of the organisation by its stakeholders. This could include the concept of corporate image.

COVENANT embodies the promise underpinning the corporate brand and the experience its stakeholders have.

Balmer's co-author, Stephen Greyser, suggested three types of relationship in the market. His original three models were:

MANIPULATIVE – where marketers would force consumer's choices, persuading them to buy their products and may even have acted as the consumer's adversary.

TRANSACTIONAL – these relationships started to see more balance between marketers and consumers, with the goal of true consumer choice, marketers working in partnership with their customers.

SERVICE – these model relationships tended to give more power to the consumer, marketers became their servant and aimed to cater for their needs.

Greyser (Balmer and Greyser, 2006) then added on a fourth model:

CORPORATE – this gives sovereignty to consumers and other stakeholders, broadening the emphasis from simply customers.

The organisation has to balance a range of needs and profits are not the only focus. This links with the idea of corporate social responsibility discussed later in Chapter 14.

Balmer and Greyser (2006) then put forward the idea that corporate identity, branding, communication and reputation should all be integrated under the umbrella of corporate marketing.

Burghausen (2013) added two more elements to the mix:

CONTEXT: corporate environment, what we are dependent on, influenced by and part of.

CUSTODIANSHIP: Corporate marketing management, how we lead and challenge.

Balmer (2013) suggested that corporate brand orientation occurred in an organisation when they 'orient (ed) themselves around their brand', and that 'the focus is on employee/organisational member identification'. The corporate brand should underpin all communications, and be 'an explicit covenant between an organisation and its key stakeholder groups', and that marketing should have a 'stakeholder and societal CSR orientation'.

How useful are these ideas in the real world? They try to simplify the elements of branding, and also suggest that attention be paid to more stakeholders than simply customers. However, they appear to have a narrow focus on public relations as simply one element of communication.

then be reviewed to check that they are aligned with the brand position. They also recommend brand conditioning, or the need to 'review (the) corporate brand on a continuous basis'. This ensures that the brand benefits continue to be linked to customer needs.

Van Riel (1995) offered one of the most useful models of managing corporate identity. He suggested that examining current image and comparing it to desired image should be the first step. If there was a gap between the two, then he put forward eight steps to address it. Starting with analysing the problem and ending with evaluation, the model includes researching current positioning, external image and competitive marketing analysis and feeding the answers back into the corporate identity mix. This mix is made up of personality, behaviour, communication and symbolism.

There are several suggestions for lists of ingredients that create good corporate branding practice. Goodman (2010) gives five:

1 **Use the same images, logos and writing style across all communication channels for strong brand recognition**

2 **Actively manage the people who represent your brand**

3 **Separate the personal from the professional on social media**

4 **Combine different communication channels to tell the brand story**

5 **Monitor social media and customer review websites.**

She suggests that a brand differentiates a business from its competition and thus good communication is vital.

MacLeod (2011) suggests that core elements of a good reputation are like ABC:

- Advocacy – endorsements from employees and customers create trust.

- Behaviour – communications is about stimulating a desired response and behaviour from stakeholders.

- Coherence – there must be a match between values, communications and action.

Wood (2016) stresses that research is key to managing corporate identity. Senior management and stakeholders' views should be sought, and an audit of whether the corporate identity matches the communication of the desired image.

Hutcheon (2016) reviewed 'challenger brands' which shook up accepted views of particular products, such as easyJet and Virgin Atlantic making air travel accessible to more people by their different pricing structures. He suggested that there are five attributes needed to be a challenger:

1 Own a new truth and a new language – focus on an unnoticed consumer need and use new words to describe what your brand is;

2 Be a thought leader – share opinions and personality;

3 Have a superstar product – make it less hassle for the consumer and more fun;

4 Take on the villain – stand up against existing brands in the market;

5 Go long – take risks to be noticed.

He added that super-fans should be used to promote the brand and campaign on issues.

Are there any others that you might add? Examine the case studies in this chapter to see what elements of these checklists were met.

ACTION POINT

A BRANDING JOURNEY ... WITH PLYMOUTH UNIVERSITY

FIGURE 11.1 University of Plymouth old logo

INNOVATE WITH PLYMOUTH UNIVERSITY

FIGURE 11.2 Plymouth University new logo

The new 'with Plymouth University' brand captures the institution's pioneering spirit, its collaborative approach to working and its forward-thinking community. Instead of a static logo, the new identity can be tailored and used to communicate directly with different audiences. By putting the message in the hands of the communicator, it opens up new possibilities.

The finished article tells only a fraction of the story, however, as to how and why the University embarked upon this journey to rebrand after 19 years. The process of rebranding after 19 years with its old logo took 18 months, and drew upon the talents and energy of students, staff and stakeholders to define the values at the heart of the University's identity.

The branding project team, which comprised both academic staff with industry experience and professional services members, established a set of guiding principles. These included a commitment to make evidence-based decisions; to harness internal resources and expertise wherever possible; to create a holistic brand that would encompass tone of voice, HR processes, induction events, etc.; and that there would be minimal expenditure during the roll out – the project had to be cost neutral.

The first action was to gather evidence to establish whether the University's corporate identity was still fit for purpose. Using the market research skills of undergraduate and postgraduate business studies students, they established that there was a discrepancy between the way the University was perceived and the message it conveyed through its logo. They also learned:

- 54.8 per cent of students did not like the logo, and 70.6 per cent said the brand needed to be modernised.
- Among teachers, there was a 100 per cent rejection of the current logo, with 87.5 per cent agreeing to modernisation of the brand.
- In the business population, 60 per cent did not like it, and 80 per cent wanted a change.

Concurrently the project team was also conducting research into what people did like about the University itself. They approached 30,000 people and asked them to provide five words that summed up the institution. 5,000 people responded, and from this pool of 25,000 words, certain themes and consistencies were immediately apparent. Through a series of workshops and focus groups involving people from both inside and outside the University, these ideas and words were refined and distilled down to a set of values. They were:

- Expert
- Connected
- Creative
- Spirited
- Empowering.

The project team specified that any design agency that was to work with the University had to be connected with it in some way, two agencies emerged as frontrunners. Between them, they had four Plymouth graduates working as directors, ensuring that their connection to the University was evident at the very top.

The University asked the two if they would collaborate in an enterprising partnership. They were engaged to create a compelling, effective and inclusive brand identity, one which reflected the

University's 'real-world' approach. The litmus test applied at every milestone was:

- Are we creating something ground-breaking?
- Does it reflect our collective power?
- Does it communicate with our stakeholders?

The agencies pitched two approaches. The first was an evolutionary approach which took the most memorable elements of the existing brand and created a refreshed identity. The other took to its heart the aim of the University for people to say they were proud to be associated with the institution. From that, the importance of the word **with** was evident. This would change the sentence 'I am studying mathematics at the University of Plymouth' to 'I am studying mathematics with Plymouth University'!

It was suggested that 'with Plymouth University' became not only the brand, but also the basis of a new identity that could communicate different messages.

- *Pioneer* with Plymouth University
- *Endless possibilities* with Plymouth University
- *Succeed* with Plymouth University.

The two versions were taken to key stakeholders for testing, all of whom backed the radical approach, and plans for the roll out commenced. Staff engagement sessions were held. For reasons of cost and sustainability, it was agreed that existing marketing collateral would continue in use until existing stocks were used up. In addition, by drawing upon internal expertise for the formulation of the strategy, and student resources for market research and testing, rather than engaging external agencies, the University had calculated it had made significant savings.

Finally, after an 18-month journey which had examined the values of the institution, the new Plymouth University brand was unveiled at the Vice-Chancellor's Public Address in 2011.

Andrew Merrington, Senior Media and Communications Officer, Plymouth University. Andrew Merrington was a journalist at a Midlands-based press agency. He then moved into internal communications with Capital One and Experian, and now works in media relations in the higher education sector. With around 30,000 students, including those studying at its partner FE colleges throughout the South West, Plymouth is one of the largest universities in the UK.

DEVON AIR AMBULANCE TRUST: BRANDING THE SKY

Devon Air Ambulance Trust (DAAT) is the charity which raises the funds to keep Devon's two air ambulances airborne. Costing in the region of £5.5 million annually, and proud to be independent of Government and National Lottery funding, this means that every penny comes from the community, businesses and friends of Devon.

This is the DAAT-agreed form of words to be used in response to any request from a publication or media source for information about the charity. From October 2016 DAAT operates one of its aircraft (based in Exeter) from daylight right up to midnight and the other North Devon-based aircraft for up to ten hours a day. Devon is the only county to have two air ambulances, a response to the characteristics of Devon and the distance which needs to be travelled to get casualties to the nearest hospital on winding and narrow roads, but also a testament to the support from the people of Devon. The charity not only owns both of its EC135 aircrafts but it also holds its own Air Operating Certificate, giving it total independence and putting it in control of its future plans and developments.

Initially the charity adopted a red livery because that was the colour of its leased craft, but by adding its own blue and white branding elements, the brand has developed into a distinctive marque. DAAT sees its brand as a tree, developing from its roots – its vision to be an outstanding and efficient service relieving sickness and injury – to its fruit – what is achieved, lives saved. In between are the trunk – the core values of community, professionalism and independence; the branches – personality, reliable, friendly and reassuring; foliage – corporate identity, signage and livery; and blossom – how the DAAT is experienced, acknowledging volunteers, donors and suppliers.

The DAAT has resisted branding its aircraft with a sponsor's name, The only organisation name DAAT carries on its aircraft is that of the BBC Radio Devon Air Ambulance Appeal, a joint fund and awareness-raising campaign between DAAT and BBC Radio Devon on its GDAAN aircraft, in recognition for the BBC Radio Devon Air Ambulance Appeal which raised the final £800,000 needed to complete the purchase of the aircraft, and the South Western Ambulance Service Foundation NHS Trust crest who employ the paramedics who form the aircrew. This mention is smaller than DAAT's own branding, which declares 'Founded by the Ceri Thomas Appeal' and 'Funded by the People of Devon'. Thus DAAT benefits from its links to BBC Radio Devon and keeps its own brand intact.

A comprehensive document listing the Brand Guidelines has been produced, comprising a guide to producing consistent and creative marketing

Devon Air Ambulance Trust

www.daat.org
Registered Charity No: 1077998
Company No: 3855746

FIGURE 11.3 Devon Air Ambulance Trust logo

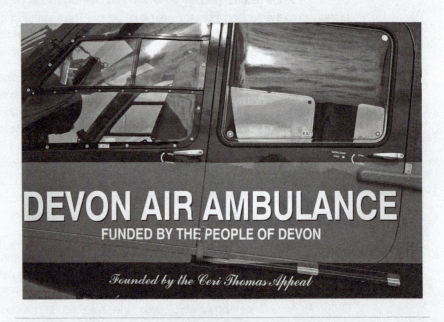

DEVON AIR AMBULANCE
FUNDED BY THE PEOPLE OF DEVON

Founded by the Ceri Thomas Appeal

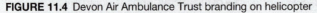

FIGURE 11.4 Devon Air Ambulance Trust branding on helicopter

communications for the DAAT. 'Our marketing communications are a visual expression of our organisation and all it stands for,' says Chief Executive Helena Holt. 'They set the standard for how we communicate our values and messages to the broad range of people we work with. We have a fantastic brand. Clear, consistent, high quality communications reinforce our reputation.'

FIGURE 11.5 DAAT Helipad newsletter

The Brand Guidelines contain sections on why the brand is so important, and what words should be used to reflect the DAAT's qualities. Key words include: open; transparent; professional; honest; friendly; accountable; integrity; truth. Key phrases are: by and for the people of Devon;

independent of Government and National lottery funding; funded totally by the community, businesses and friends of Devon; real people, saving real lives. The Guidelines also include information on the DAAT badge and how it may be used, with examples of full colour and single colour usage, minimum size, the DAAT Helicopter Strip which must be used at the bottom of all corporate documents, pantone references and fonts. Examples are also included of newsletter covers, fundraising posters and images which can be used from the photo gallery.

RESCUING A DAMAGED BRAND

O'Rourke (2011) uses the example of Tiger Woods, who lost lucrative sponsorship deals after his extramarital affairs became public knowledge in 2009, as an illustration of how important reputation is to the bottom line. He states that reputation is worth £460 billion of shareholder value to UK FTSE350 firms. Other corporations who have found this out to their cost are BP, whose share price crashed by 50 per cent after the Gulf disaster and News Corporation, whose shares have lost more than 20 per cent of value due to the UK phone hacking scandal. He quotes Echo research which shows that a 5 per cent increase in reputation will lead to a 1.8 per cent increase in the market cap of a public company.

Discussing which brands had suffered most in the wake of the riots in the UK in 2011, Jo Slatem, MHP Communications deputy head of brands, said that brands could be victims of their own success. 'The more mainstream a brand, the more likely it is to get dragged into these things' (Magee, 2011c). Top five tips for dealing with negative associations outside the organisation's control included:

- Assess the brand damage – is it really eroding sales?
- Proceed with caution – don't tell people not to use your brand. This can cause unwanted attention.
- Be prepared – what does your brand enable? Do a people-based risk assessment. What could people do to your brand if they wanted to cause damage?
- Do not overreact – don't accept the blame for what people are doing.
- Be consistent – brands don't change overnight, so stick with your brand messages.

Nick Hindle (2011) was McDonald's UK vice-president for communications and was tasked with dealing with the company's reputational problems after *Fast Food Nation* in 2001 and *Supersize Me* in 2004. Jamie Oliver was also crusading for higher quality food, and McDonald's became associated with obesity. Hindle advocates taking the long view, striking a balance between sales and investing in how the company communicates what it does. Honesty is vital. McDonald's commissioned research to see exactly how much the negative connotations were costing it. Finally, he stresses that advertising is not the answer and that fundamental problems must be fixed to rebuild trust. To do this, McDonald's started by changing their menus to reduce fat, salt and sugar. Journalists and stakeholders were taken to see where core ingredients were sourced, and the company started to communicate that it only used British and Irish beef from 16,000 farms and that all eggs were free range. Restaurants were remodelled with softer lighting and natural materials. Communications had to change and be less defensive.

The company also paid attention to its internal communications and policies. *Fast Food Nation* had introduced the term 'McJob' to mean a dead-end job with no prospects. McDonald's challenged this and made it possible for employees to take basic qualifications through the company and became an accredited examination body. They became the biggest provider of apprenticeships in the UK and trained 70,000 volunteers for the London Olympics in 2012.

A website was launched called, 'Make up your own mind', where the public were invited to ask questions of the company. CEO Steve Easterbrook took part in a debate with the author of *Fast Food Nation*, Eric Schlosser, live on BBC *Newsnight*. This was followed with discussions on 5Live, Sky, the *Today* programme and *Tonight with Trevor McDonald*. Journalists from the *Sun* were invited to work shifts in restaurants. Local franchisees were recruited as brand ambassadors, and over 100 were trained to be advocates in the regions.

The company experienced 19 quarters of growth up to April 2011, as well as a 20-point improvement on trust scores since 2006. Customers rose by 80 million in 2009–10. Even Jamie Oliver said, 'I can't believe I'm telling you that McDonald's UK has come a long way.' All these are 'important milestone(s) on the road back to brand health'.

McDonald's built on this strategy in the US by setting up the McDonald's Nutrition Network, using a dietician at regional Meetups for parents, linking with community organisations and encouraging them to apply for grants, and engaging with bloggers. This initiative won the *PR Daily* 2012 Best Use of Social Media Award (*PR Daily,* 2012). And even through Thring (2013) declared that he was 'no convert', he admitted that 'it's now possible to eat a relatively healthy meal in McDonald's'.

END POINT

Brands are made up of a combination of physical attributes and emotional connotations and brand management is a complex business. Having a good corporate brand is not just about having a great logo. So, changing brand perception is not simply a matter of communication but also of examining what the organisation is doing. This makes a compelling argument for the need for public relations practitioners to be involved in corporate strategy, not just in communicating corporate decisions.

CHAPTER 12

Effective media relations

Alison Theaker

As discussed in Chapter 3, public relations has its origins in the field of media relations. In fact, media relations and public relations are repeatedly used as interchangeable terms, especially by journalists. The latter often express a knee-jerk antagonistic reaction to public relations – one journalist has even been heard to remark, 'Without PR people, journalists would be the lowest organism in the food chain.' Early practitioners were press agents whose main aim was to gain 'free' press coverage at any cost, and the truth was not allowed to get in the way of a good story. With the development of the internet, practitioners have had to take on board the need for openness and accessibility to companies' affairs.

CHECK POINT

This chapter will cover:

- Why use the media to get your message across?
- Basic media relations principles
- How to write good media releases
- The importance of targeting
- The impact of developing technology

WHY USE THE MEDIA?

One of the reasons why public relations practitioners use media relations to get their message across is the media's role in forming public opinion. The agenda-setting theory of Lazarfeld and Katz (quoted in Wilcox *et al.*, 2003: 213) puts forward the idea that the media determine what people think about by selecting the stories which go on the front page or are included in nightly television news programmes. For the public relations practitioner, getting something onto the media agenda is the first step. In some situations, the media can also tell people what to think. If people cannot get access to other points of view, they can become dependent on the media's slant on a story. This often happens in a war situation, where limited news is available and often heavily censored by the military. While it is now easier to gain access to different points of view via the internet, most people's information will come from the mass media, leading to a tabloidisation of the issues. On the other hand, if the public relations practitioner for an organisation is the main source of information on a subject, say a new drug or scientific development, it is possible for them to shape the tone of the debate. Framing can also magnify the effect of media dependency. Wilcox *et al.* (2003) cite Tankard and Israel's work analysing the news coverage of the Bosnian war, when 'Ruder-Finn framed the issue as Serb genocide against Bosnian muslims'. The media picked up on this and started to use emotive phrases such as 'ethnic cleansing'. Lastly, cultivation theory suggests that events in the news are packaged into highlights. Repeated often enough, and given the media's tendency to concentrate on conflict and crisis situations, people get a false view of what is actually happening. Whenever a child abduction hits the news headlines, the media tend to emphasise the number of child molesters who have been released from prison and warn parents about 'stranger danger', rather than concentrate on the facts that most children are harmed by someone they know.

THE BASICS OF MEDIA RELATIONS

One of the earliest users of this method was Ivy Ledbetter Lee (see also Chapter 3), who in the early 1900s worked for coal operators in Philadelphia threatened with strike action by the United Mine Workers Union. He issued a Declaration of Principles, which stated, 'We aim to supply news ... Our matter is accurate.' The Declaration went on,

> Our plan is, frankly and openly, on behalf of the business concerns and public institutions, to supply to the press and public of the United States prompt and accurate information concerning subjects which it is of value and interest to the public to know about.
>
> (Quoted in Grunig and Hunt, 1984: 33)

Wragg argues (in Bland *et al.,* 1996: 66–7) that

> The purpose of press relations is not to issue press releases, or handle enquiries from journalists, or even to generate a massive pile of press cuttings. The true purpose of press relations is to enhance the reputation of an organisation and its products, and to influence and inform the target audience.

While it is largely of a tactical nature in practice, good media relations can contribute to longer-term strategic objectives, such as:

- improving company or brand image
- higher and better media profile
- changing the attitudes of target audiences (such as customers)
- improving relationships with the community
- increasing market share
- influencing government policy at local, national or international level
- improving communications with investors and their advisers
- improving industrial relations.

As such, media relations forms part of most strategies in the following chapters in Part III. It is still the activity on which the majority of PR practitioners spend most of their time. In the PR census, general media relations was found to feature in 85 per cent of PR roles, with 21 per cent of practitioners considering it their main task. Nearly half of respondents stated that media relations strategy planning had increased in importance over the previous two years (Gorkana, 2011).

What exactly does media relations consist of? There are a multitude of books and blog posts which deal with the mechanics of contacting the media, how to write press releases in a specific format that conforms to the needs of journalists, and the best ways to target and distribute this information. Most stress the five Ws (who, what, where, when and why), and the need to make the release appropriate to the style and content of the targeted publication or broadcast. Media releases can be supplemented by press conferences, media briefings, exclusive interviews, feature articles and photo opportunities. Advice is also offered on targeting, which is covered later in this chapter. Bailey (2014) suggests that a press release has to pass the 'so what?' test, to check whether the story is of interest to those outside an organisation.

Hitchins (2003) makes a distinction between 'techniques' used to create media interest and 'tools' which help the process once interest has been created. He includes the following list of tools: news release, press conference, informal media briefing, exclusive interview, media tour, facility visit, as well as online press office, virtual press conference and photo call. These could now be supplemented by streaming video, blog posts, podcasts and the use of social media forums.

Techniques are used by the practitioner to create news, 'turning routine and long-running development into new acts or news pegs'. *News vehicles* are events created to gain media coverage, planned not spontaneous, and their success is measured solely by how much coverage they obtain. Examples include 'surveys, research reports, media launches, announcements, anniversaries, awareness days, celebrities, awards and publicity stunts'. *Linking statements to the current media agenda* can also aid coverage. Thus pharmaceutical companies could link news of developments of their products to combat flu or hay fever to the relevant season. This method must be used with care, however, so that organisations are not thought to be capitalising on tragedy. Anecdotally, a media relations practitioner for Kelloggs' Hot Pockets in the USA was thought to have had the bright idea of publicising them immediately after the 11 September 2001 disaster in New York, with the emphasis on the fact that Americans would want to stay at home and eat comfort food that had not been tampered with. *Campaigns and special pleading* are the third way to frame a message. By appealing to the media's appetite for conflict and confrontation, organisations can emphasise their work to change legislation or fight to preserve the environment. Demonstrations and other stunts provide the media with a visual event to cover. *Headlines, slogans and stereotypes* can be used to convey the essence of the message quickly and simply. Hitchins quotes a study by the Royal College of Psychiatrists into depression in men across Europe which was called Men Behaving Sadly. Finally, *selective targeting* and tailoring news to specific media interests ensure that priorities are set regarding which media to approach and that their needs dictate public relations activities.

READING POINT

Lecturer and blogger Philip Young's chapter in the latest edition of the *Public Relations Handbook* (Routledge, 2016) discusses 'Media relations in the social media age'. He looks at the PR practitioner as a creator of news and how practice has changed with recent developments. He also raises the question of the ethics of media relations.

More information about how to use social media in public relations is also given in Chapter 16.

WRITING THE NEWS RELEASE

A news release is a simple document which sets out, as clearly and straightforwardly as possible, information which a journalist could use to write or broadcast a story. Traditional layout rules were drawn from the era of hot metal presses, when releases would be marked up by a sub-editor and sent to a compositor for setting. Originally practitioners were advised to use one side of the paper, double spaced type, clearly marking the date of issue, the source of the material and further contact details.

Releases are now normally inserted directly into the body of an email. The subject line is used for the headline and provision of contact information should be considered in the same way as in conventional releases. Double spaced text is no longer used as this increases the need to scroll down to find out the news story.

The cardinal rule of content – always get all the important facts in the first paragraph – was born from the practice of cutting the release from the bottom if space was limited. However, in a world where journalists suffer from information overload, it still serves as a useful way to get their attention when a release may be just one of multiple sources of news. Keeping clichés and 'puff' to a minimum ensures that the story is not buried in irrelevant information that reads like an advert rather than news.

PR practitioners have to learn to spot the story in the release and make sure this is the first thing covered. The subject of a release is almost never the organisation that is sending it out. Countless releases start with the date, which again is rarely the news. It is more likely to be the 'what' of the 5 Ws, such as a new bank account designed for students for example. And even then it might be that the account would lead to better degree results because it would enable students to spend less time worrying about their money. The benefits rather than the features of a new product should be emphasised.

Survey results make good news stories, and releases should start with the results, making sure that human interest is to the fore. 'Over 500 jobs have been created in the South East over the last six months, according to a report published today.' Local media need a local slant to a national news story, such as: 'South West businesses are already recovering from the recession, local HR consultancy BestPeople has found.' These stories could be illustrated by the experiences of local job seekers and employers.

To get media coverage the PR practitioner has to supply information which fits the journalist's needs. It may require the practitioner to tell the client that giving an oversized cheque to a local pre-school is not likely to make national news pages, or maybe even the regional TV news programme. The story must be interesting and specific to the readers, viewers or listeners that the journalist is aiming to capture. Often supplying an interesting picture can garner coverage. Early in my teaching career *PR Week* covered my own use of a local consultancy to update my skills because it was accompanied by a picture of myself surrounded by people wearing oversized alligator suits – one of the consultancy's clients was Alcan whose mascot was AliCan. All ten of the mascot suits had happened to be in the office at the time for cleaning. The caption mentioned my employer, Leeds Metropolitan University, the consultancy, BRAHM PR, and the client.

Quotes are often used in a release, but have been derided by journalists as often sounding stilted and too much like an advert. Good quotes further the story and are an opportunity to express an opinion. They can also make it look as though the journalist has interviewed someone, even if they did not have time to.

Using press releases alongside other activities can help to promote a new organisation. This case study shows how media relations and social media can be integrated.

HELPING A NEW ORGANISATION GET THE MESSAGE OUT

Beach Schools South West (BSSW) was a start-up Community Interest Company (CIC) with a budget of almost nothing, a big heart, an enormous message, coming from a standing start. They needed to reach the widest possible community and market swiftly to rocket fuel not only bookings but awareness too. No one before had done this kind of outdoor learning in any kind of formal, organisational way so it was important to get reams of information into the public domain for schools and parents and to establish credibility very swiftly.

The aim was to reach the widest possible audience in the shortest period of time and so articles in established newspapers and magazines needed to be combined with information through social media channels and educational magazines. Focusing on the key messages was imperative not only to help people understand what the company was all about but to give it credibility too. BSSW also needed to establish that they were an organisation that could stand up to scrutiny and that its core values and commitment to outdoor learning were shared by others. They needed their concept simplified – Beach Schools South West was chosen as a descriptor title for the CIC and the tagline 'we teach on the beach' was another snappy headline designed to help audiences understand easily what they did. They aimed to reach local audiences and national audiences, but particularly those in their region as that was where their market lay.

The first thing that BSSW did was identify their key messages and work out what the benefits of outdoor and curriculum-linked learning on the beach were and how to best describe their company to people who had never heard of it before. In advance of any media campaign, the whole team were clear on what they were doing, why they were doing it and who they were doing it for. Strategic communications on all levels need this kind of clarity backed up by evidence-based arguments. In this case academic studies provided BSSW with the statistical evidence they needed to add weight to their key messages. Pre-launch planning also involved taking high-quality, high-res pictures and preparing a video to give their online presence depth. They established Twitter, Facebook and Instagram presences, and a website as their central internet platform. PR strategies covered newspapers, magazines, TV, radio, social media and public speaking that had at their core the same message but could easily be adapted to the specific audience each platform served. Very quickly articles appeared in regional newspapers and magazines. The *Western Morning News* covered the launch day twice, then *Devon Life* and ITV Westcountry. BSSW was featured in *Primary Times*, and made themselves available as spokespeople if someone needed an opinion on outdoor learning and its benefits.

Social media platforms were repeating and complementing more traditional media, giving the company a far greater reach. Having pictures and video in-house proved invaluable. Above and beyond this BSSW submitted their work to, and were nominated for, a number of independently judged awards to open themselves up to public and objective scrutiny. So far, BSSW has won the Venus Award Devon for Green Business; Venus Award National for Green Business; Western Morning News Business Award 2015 for Community Contribution; Green Apple Award for Environmental Education. They were finalists for the Devon Environmental Business Awards 2014.

Having their key messages, content, photos, videos and spokespeople consistently primed and ready made BSSW quite quickly a 'go to' for journalists. The organisation was reliable, media-friendly, accurate and provided excellent facts and interviews plus outstanding images. Bookings were being made without any spending on advertising. Articles appeared in the regional press and on regional television, which was reaching the exact audience needed for the potential market. The awards nominations and applications gave the company positive coverage, as even from a very early stage they were being judged as outstanding and either becoming finalists or winners in prestigious regional, national and international awards. Savvy PR strategy and sensible communications legwork set the foundations for an extremely successful awareness-raising campaign.

BSSW is now an award-winning, well-established CIC which is growing year-on-year. Having a well-thought-through, multi-level, cross-output, media campaign strategy which was put in place before the launch day helped to create this. Pre-planning of communications, key messages and media relations meant they were always ready to respond to journalist requests, always had a photo to share, a video to send, an article almost written at the tips of their fingers – and someone available to be interviewed. This pre-planning galvanised staff members who had asked themselves all the pertinent questions before entering the public domain. The strategic communications success for Beach Schools South West could be summed up in 3 Ps: preparation, people, pictures.

FIGURE 12.1 Beach Schools South West teach on the beach

THE IMPORTANCE OF TARGETING

The important thing to remember in media relations is that blitzing hundreds of journalists on a press list (however up to date the contact names might be) may hit a few right targets but is likely to miss more, and antagonise many. This is probably one of the practices which has fuelled anti-PR feeling amongst journalists. Journalists are still individuals and have their own singular preferences. One may prefer to have a pitch made by telephone, another may find it irritating.

Journalists have perennially complained about media releases being addressed to the wrong people and poorly targeted. In my 1997 survey, the majority of journalists felt that too many releases were being sent to them which were not relevant to their publication or programme. The most common complaints were that the information was irrelevant (66 per cent) or not newsworthy (65 per cent). The use of mass email lists has not improved this problem. It is all too tempting to add names to an email media list, especially as it costs nothing to send out. Press offices can now subscribe to services such as Vocus which enable them to search worldwide media lists and classify contacts according to location or subject. Monaghan (2011) suggests that 'blast emails … don't work'.

Instead of sending formal media releases by email, journalists are now used to receiving more personalised pitches from PR practitioners. This approach can often result in more in-depth, quality coverage in a few more influential titles. Stateman (2003) quotes Fox 4 News reporter Jeff Crilley, who says, 'Don't pitch 300 people. Pitch three of the most important journalists you need.'

Levco (2011) advises that each pitch should be tailored to the recipient. Print media should receive a first paragraph which could appear in the publication, showing that you have researched the kinds of stories that are covered and the editorial style. The next paragraph should put the story in context and demonstrate why it's newsworthy, and the pitch can finish with a quote.

PR Week asked several journalists how many pitches they received and how many were used. Most received 100–50 pitch emails a month and used one or two, although the consumer writer used up to six or seven. Pet hates were faux personalisation (Good morning, hope you're enjoying the sunshine), referring back to the previous week's column (already covered, now looking for the next thing), gimmicks, waffle and irrelevant information. Most wanted timely, concise comment; statistics; exclusive research; case studies that brought the national news agenda to life; and the opportunity for great interviews. Tips included: reading the publication and tailoring the pitch appropriately; being concise and focused; eliminating basic grammar and spelling errors; making sure the PR practitioner knew the pitch inside out and having an interviewee available for comment (Blyth, 2011).

Be careful about attempting to control the content of the coverage, though. The *Guardian* updated its editorial code and included a new clause which stated that journalists should not agree to promote products in order to secure interviews. This has often been the case in the area of celebrity PR, where access to actors and writers is restricted and depends on them being able to plug their latest book or film. The *Guardian* explained that the clause had been introduced after complaints from readers (Wicks, 2011).

Despite these problems a 2011 survey of 500 journalists across 15 countries found that PR agencies (62 per cent) and corporate spokespeople (59 per cent) are still the top source for news content. In an environment of staff cuts, almost half were having to produce more content and a third were working longer hours, so there was still a need for relevant, targeted information from PR practitioners (Oriella, 2011).

The views of Paul Douglas, then editor of internet title, *.net*, are still relevant:

> Journalists source newsworthy stories in a number of ways, but the role of the PR agency in setting up interviews, supplying photography and clarifying background information makes an important contribution. Tactics such as the sending of tacky gifts and glossy press packs are no substitution for a clearly written press release that has been tailored to the readers of the publication to which the material is being submitted. Wrongly targeted press releases tend to annoy and reflect badly on a PR agency, as does calling a publication with a possible news story when one hasn't read the publication being approached.

Using meaningless phrases in press releases, such as 'the complete internet solution for the cost-conscious SME' in an attempt to sound au fait with the market, is unlikely to get a press release noticed. Getting to the point and saying 'a low-cost piece of kit that can benefit many small businesses' is likely to receive a more favourable response.

(Chipchase, 2001)

Attention must be paid to the specific needs of the media outlet. Johns (2016), the producer on the BBC Radio 2 *Jeremy Vine Show*, states that knowing the content of the show is vital. He also makes a plea to keep the story pitch to four sentences maximum.

ACTION POINT

This case study shows the importance of cultural awareness and targeting.

QUR'AN MANUSCRIPT DISCOVERED IN BIRMINGHAM

In July 2015 the University of Birmingham announced to the world's media that one of the earliest known manuscripts of the Qur'an had been discovered incorrectly bound within a later manuscript in its Cadbury Research Library (Figure 12.2). The Qur'an had been radio carbon dated to the period 568–645, within the lifetime of the Prophet Muhammad. According to Muslim tradition, the Prophet Muhammad received the revelations of the Qur'an between the years 610 and 632. This discovery had significant potential to provoke debate in scholarship of Islam and religion, and also within the Muslim community.

FIGURE 12.2 Qur'an manuscript

The press team were tasked with managing the media relations around the announcement and also of helping to organise the exhibition of the manuscripts at the University in October. The team had to react to incoming media requests and also maintain the momentum between July and October when the manuscript went on display. The key objectives were:

- Manage the media relations on 22 July when the story was issued to the press, ensuring widespread coverage for the University.
- Maintain momentum after the initial announcement ahead of the exhibition in October.
- Ensure that the public were given all the necessary facts about the manuscript.
- Publicise the exhibition in a culturally sensitive way.

A detailed communications strategy was developed ahead of the announcement. This included a number of streams, internal, external and social. Internally the nearly 3,000 University staff were sent an email on the morning of 22 July giving detailed information about the story and informing them of the upcoming exhibition with details of tickets and opportunities to view the manuscripts. Staff were asked not to visit the manuscript on that date to allow for the large number of filming and interview requests.

The external communications strategy included the social media campaign which was to supplement the main channels of communication. It was decided not to have a hashtag in the social media campaign as it could be deemed culturally insensitive to use, for example, '#quran'. In the end '#birminghamquran' was generated on Twitter through other users commenting on and sharing the story. This was then taken up by the digital team and used for later communications of the story.

The initial announcement was a short-term campaign with short-term goals, namely to gain press coverage for the University. This was achieved by securing an exclusive with the BBC for a piece on *BBC Breakfast*, and BBC News Online. The press release was embargoed for after the broadcast on *BBC Breakfast* and no media outlet received the story other than BBC radio stations. This was an effective strategy as it meant that all major BBC programmes and channels had been covered and interviews prerecorded before the press release was issued, allowing the spokespeople to be interviewed by other media targets over the course of the day.

The nature of the story meant that there would be a lot of interest from people with a religious interest in the Qur'an. Due to the incredibly sensitive nature of the story attempts were made to include the local Muslim community. The Imam, chair and manager of Birmingham Central Mosque were invited to see the manuscripts before the announcement was made public. The information regarding the history of Islam was checked by experts in the field. Fact sheets were produced on how ancient inks were made and how to test their age; how parchment was created in the 7th century; and radio carbon dating and its accuracy. These were not circulated externally, but were used by members of the team to ensure all information given was correct.

Local Muslim and political stakeholders were invited to a pre-launch viewing of the exhibition (Figure 12.3). Early ticket orders had highlighted the large number of Muslim people coming from all over the world to visit the manuscript. As a result, prayer rooms were set up near to the exhibition and halal food was sourced by the University caterers. A souvenir brochure was produced so that visitors were able to take home a memory of their experience, fact checked by a panel of experts and providing as much information about the manuscript as possible, without taking away the religious context and importance. Articles about the physical history of the manuscript and how it came to be in Birmingham were included, information about preservation of ancient texts, plus a double-page pull-out version of the manuscript. A board was positioned at the exit so that visitors could reflect on their experience.

FIGURE 12.3 Community leaders viewing the manuscript

The fragments of the manuscript were incredibly sensitive therefore the press team were unable to facilitate more than one day of filming. This meant that the vast majority of foreign press were unable to attend the press day. A video was produced so that raw footage could be given to outlets unable to come. The video included the Imam of Birmingham Central Mosque reading the manuscript and discussing the history of Islam, presenting the manuscripts as a treasure of Birmingham, not just of the University. The video footage allowed the University to include foreign journalists and to communicate the story around the globe. Spokespeople for the University, who were made available to the media for interview were: a Professor of Islamic and Christian History; the Head of the Cadbury Research Library; and the PhD student who was working on the manuscripts when their age was discovered. They were chosen to cover the academic background, institutional information, how the manuscript came to Birmingham, what will happen to it, and academic authority on ancient manuscripts.

A second press day, predominantly for foreign press, was arranged for October, before the exhibition opened to the public. This included crews from all over the world, including Egypt, Brazil and the Middle East. The British press were more interested in the history of the manuscript and future plans for it. The international press, particularly those from predominantly Muslim countries were much more interested in the religious aspect of the story. Spokespeople were targeted to different journalists so that each outlet was able to tell the story they wanted to tell. Every journalist was given a press pack which included detailed information on all key aspects of the story, including fact sheets about the production of the manuscript, its individual history as a document and its significance in the history of Islam.

During the initial story, in July, the press team were inundated with calls from both the media and the public. Many of the public callers wanted further information on the Qur'an manuscript and were keen to come to see it. A list of non-media callers was created and dealt with after the media frenzy died down.

The exhibition was free, with tickets allocated on a 30-minute timed basis to control the crowd. It also meant that those who were at the event for a religious experience could view the manuscript without overcrowding.

The video footage enabled a far larger group of media outlets to run the story than just those crews who were able to come to the University campus. The story had 2.5 million unique views on the BBC website in its first 24 hours, and made the front page of the *New York Times*. Tickets for the exhibition in October were taken up within minutes for an internal preview and the University had to provide 800 extra tickets over the closing weekend due to demand. The video uploaded to YouTube by the University was viewed over 90,000 times.

The exhibition allowed the University to welcome people from all over the world to campus to share in the experience of seeing the manuscript. All feedback from both press and public was very positive, complementing the University on how it had produced the exhibition. International museums and galleries requested to display the Qur'an manuscript.

The campaign was evaluated in two ways. Using media monitoring services to track coverage, sentiment was analysed alongside value and reach. Social media mentions were also analysed and used to keep track of the conversation online regarding the University and the Qur'an, alerting the team to any potential negative comments. The exhibition was analysed by ticket take-up, and the benefit to the institution in terms of visitor numbers. The comments board in the exhibition, while providing a forum for people to comment on their experience, also offered the University an opportunity to understand and reflect on the individual impact of each visit.

With thanks to Faye Jackson. Faye works at Imperial War Museums as a Corporate Press Officer. Prior to this she worked as Media Relations Assistant at the University of Birmingham with responsibility for regional media and digital research communications.

KEEPING UP WITH CHANGE

When I started out in PR in 1980, press releases were typed up, photocopied and sent out in the mail. Little change was noted in a survey I carried out in March 1999. Three hundred questionnaires were sent out to journalists working in the UK national and regional press. At that time, only 21 per cent received over 100 releases. Nearly half (48 per cent) preferred to receive information by mail, as opposed to 15 per cent who preferred email.

The world has certainly changed now. The use of the internet has affected media relations as journalists are able to obtain information straight from a website rather than waiting for press releases. The internet streamlines every stage of the process – from making proactive contact by email to providing timely material for download. Social media enables PR practitioners to form and build relationships with individual journalists and to share useful information. The Edelman Media cloverleaf model (2011, cited in Willis, 2014: 335) distinguishes between four elements:

Traditional – radio, TV and print.

Hybrid – media companies which focus on niche audiences and issues, such as the Huffington Post.

Owned media – media channels controlled by an organisation such as website, blogs, podcasts and apps.

Social media – platforms that allow information about an organisation to be distributed by the organisation but also by employees, consumers, partners, suppliers and competitors.

Momorella and Woodall (2003) listed several elements which could be included in an online newsroom. They suggested a library of archived press releases, background documents, downloadable graphics, a calendar of events, contact information, audio and video and current news to make the journalist's job easier. Seiple (2016) adds the following requirements for a social media press room: links to pages which expand on information raised over social media; links to all the organisation's social media channels; podcasts; feeds to the company blog.

Blogging is another channel that organisations can use to humanise what they are doing. All too often, though, corporate blogs are written by the PR practitioner, whilst being credited to the CEO. These fake blogs do nothing to enhance the reputation of the organisation or suggest that it is willing to engage in real conversations with its audiences. Seiple (2016) advises that news release content needs to be rewritten so that it is less formal and more conversational in tone for inclusion in a blog. Whilst company news and updates can be included, she advises that it is best to 'be humble when talking about yourself'.

Shaw (2016) reports the results of an SNCR survey which found that 57 per cent of journalists find Twitter credible and 47 per cent use it to assist with reporting. However, whether information is shared by posting material on an organisation's blog, sending direct messages through Twitter and Facebook, emailing or phoning will all depend on the personal preferences of the journalist you are trying to reach. Knowing these preferences is part of your task as a media relations professional.

Some publications have used social media to determine content. *More* magazine produced an issue in June 2011 that had been written and edited by its Facebook fans. The magazine had higher numbers of followers on Facebook than Twitter, so celebrated its 100,000th fan on the site by offering them the chance to influence magazine content. At the same time, PR practitioners were involved by offering competition prizes and discounts on client products.

END POINT

This chapter has covered the main elements in contacting the media. It has reviewed how the ways in which PR practitioners contact journalists have changed, but several of the elements of media relations have remained the same since the early days. Researching the target news outlet, approaching them with stories relevant to their audience, sending journalists information in their preferred format, sending information in a timely fashion, all these elements remain the same whether using hard copy, telephone, email or social media. Media relations will reappear in subsequent case studies as it continues to be a major element of the PR practitioner's role. *With thanks to Alexis Bowater, Bowater Communications*

CHAPTER 13

Risk, incidents, issues and crisis management

Heather Yaxley

This chapter provides insight into short and long-term approaches to respond to negative influences on organisations.

CHECK POINT

After reading this chapter, you should be able to:

- Assess risk factors and trends affecting organisations facing various scenarios
- Review how competencies, plans, processes and procedures help public relations practitioners anticipate and react to incidents, issues and crisis situations
- Examine the impact of the changing communicative environment on managing risk, incidents, issues and crisis situations.

RISK MANAGEMENT

In public relations, risk management is important at an operational level (e.g. in campaign planning and event management). Moreover, the strategic ability to evaluate potential risk and develop effective responses is vital across an organisation's operations. It contributes towards ensuring an organisation's licence to operate in wider society.

In the modern risk society (Beck, 1992), there are many uncertainties that have potential to impact on organisations as well as the publics, communities and wider society affected by their operations. Being able to identify and mitigate such influences is a key aspect of public relations. Additionally, PR plays a key communications role in circumstances where risk cannot be avoided or is necessary to achieve beneficial outcomes.

The Institute of Risk Management (IRM) specifies that risk may feature positive and negative aspects, consideration of which should be central to an organisation's strategic management to ensure its activities provide sustainable value. IRM recommends formal reporting of risk management to stakeholders, which should detail control methods as well as processes used to identify, monitor, manage and review significant risks. The benefits of formal risk management are advocated as:

- protecting the interest of stakeholders
- discharging the duties of senior management to direct strategy, build value and monitor organisational performance
- ensuring management controls are in place and performing adequately.

Hopkin (2017: 4) further argues that risk management provides 'structured information to assist with business decision making'. It contributes towards effectiveness and efficiency of an organisation's strategies, processes, and both routine and exceptional operations.

An integrated approach to risk management adopted across the organisation enables policies to be created that detail processes and procedures, specific responsibilities and compliance within other policy areas (e.g. Health & Safety).

Public relations contributes to such an approach by considering the position of stakeholders and the potential impact on the organisation's reputation. An understanding of the risk tolerance of stakeholders and their potential responses to specific policies and practices is valuable input into decision-making. Further, public relations can develop communications and relationship strategies and actions that address particular risk situations.

Methodical approach

Understanding the risks facing an organisation requires a methodical, continuous approach, starting with asking three questions (Garrick and Christie, 2008):

1   What can go wrong?
2   How likely is that to happen?
3   What are the consequences if it does happen?

Risk analysis enables organisations to identify possible problems affecting the implementation of policies and procedures and increase the likelihood of success without significant legal, financial or reputational consequences. Such a proactive approach demonstrates responsibility rather than simply hoping that an incident will not occur and being forced to respond after damage has been done.

Responding proactively to potential dangers can be costly and it may not be responsible to allocate resources to address risks that have a low probability of occurring. However, assessing the potential consequences of such risks may increase recognition of their importance and justify investment in time and cost to address these.

Risks may occur in the external environment and/or as a result of strategies the organisation adopts to achieve its aims. It may also be inherent in the nature of the organisation's operations. Potential risks need to be identified and, if they cannot reasonably be avoided, contingency plans should be devised.

In some cases, risk may be part of the organisation's strategy. This is the case where the organisation builds a reputation for being innovative, outspoken or appealing to a non-mainstream public. Organisational values can also be a source of risk if aligned to issues that are viewed as contentious by some sectors of society. In such circumstances, a plan of action is required that includes monitoring reactions and addressing problems that may arise before they threaten the organisation's operations. This may include defending a position or adopting changes, for example, in the face of a boycott or online campaign.

Where risk relates to the organisation's operations, compliance to regulatory and governance frameworks normally would be expected. However, looking at the ten trends identified by Deloitte (2016) as affecting risk management (Table 13.1), it is clear that the pace of change, particularly concerning technological developments, is challenging existing frameworks. Nevertheless, strategic and operational management would need to have a system of appropriate policies and procedures in place in order to demonstrate accountability for any issues that may arise. The common thread concerning digital technologies that is evident in these trends is discussed further in Chapter 16.

In addition to accommodating such changes, public relations offers a wide perspective of risk management. The function is well positioned to consider the organisation's values, as well as ethical expectations of, and moral responsibilities towards, key stakeholders. Being responsive helps to enhance the organisation's reputation by engaging stakeholders and influencers, understanding their particular concerns and ensuring these are considered within risk analysis.

As with issues and crisis management, risk management requires the commitment of senior executives who are responsible for the strategic direction of the organisation. They should ensure that proactive risk awareness and management is part of the culture with responsibilities and accountability allocated to individual functions. This underlines the importance of public relations being accepted as part of the strategic management team.

TABLE 13.1 Trends affecting risk management (based on Deloitte 2016)

Trend	Benefits	Concerns
Artificial intelligence, cognitive technologies and behavioural data analytics	Help to detect, predict and prevent risks	Reliance on unproven methods and ethical concerns
Sensor-enabled smart devices (The Internet of Things)	Enhance detection, control and insight into risk	New risks, data overload and cyber-security concerns
Inter-disciplinary research including neuropsychology	Greater understanding of behaviour and avoidance of cognitive bias	Complexity and ethical concerns
Focus on vigilance and resilience	Detect patterns that indicate or predict risk and improve ability to contain and reduce impact	Reduced agility and increased time, cost and other resources
Investment in risk-transfer mechanisms (such as contracts and/or insurance)	Share or transfer risk to other organisations (for example, suppliers)	Potential for increased cost and supply chain issues
Pace of innovation outpacing political and regulatory controls	Reliance on self-regulatory frameworks	Increased risk of problems and need to educate regulators
Risk viewed as an enabling performance and value rather than something to be avoided or driven by compliance	Create risk-intelligent culture where risk is associated with opportunities	Increased risk of problems and processes/procedures being ignored
Connected and collective risk management occurring across existing networks and/or using crowd-sourcing initiatives	Reduce costs and gain wider perspective on acceptable risk and possible solutions	Security concerns, need to evaluate suggestions and manage expectations
Recognition of the value of disruption to encourage risk to be taken	Potential for breakthrough and new opportunities	Challenge to existing culture, increased risk and costs
Greater convergence and mobility of technologies	Improve monitoring and proactive, targeted crisis management	Accelerate and amplify risks

Hopkin (2017: 22) advocates creating a standard matrix to encompass 'compliance, hazard, control and opportunity' risks. A template gap analysis matrix, enabling risk likelihood and consequences to be examined, and control mechanisms to be indicated, is included in the Appendices.

Risk communications

McComas (2010: 462) states that 'effective risk management includes risk communication with affected publics'; which she defines as 'a purposeful, iterative exchange of information among individuals, groups and institutions related to the assessment, characterization, and management of risk' (McComas, 2010: 462). Contemporary best practice approaches emphasise building trust, transparency and respect for others, with ongoing communications acknowledging the uncertainty of risk situations (Palenchar, 2010).

A need for proactive dialogue is encouraged within 'the modern dynamic, complex, 24:7 global communications environment' (Yaxley, 2012b: 154) where 'the immediacy and interconnectedness of mobile, online and social media are able to amplify what might otherwise be matters of low or no significance'. The flexibility this necessitates needs to be factored into risk management procedures.

ACTION POINT

The UK Health and Safety Executive (www.hse.gov.uk) has developed a five-step approach to risk assessment. It advises adoption of precautions and control measures that are easy to implement. Although specifically considering risks relating to hazards in the workplace, the HSE's advice can be adapted for a public relations risk assessment.

The Institute of Risk Management (www.theirm.org) has developed a risk management standard setting out a best practice approach against which organisations can assess their own activities.

Action templates based on these recommendations are included in the Appendices to facilitate undertaking risk management for an organisation, PR function and specific activities.

Operational PR risks

A planned approach (see Part II) enables PR activities to be assessed for potential negative outcomes. Contingency plans can be developed to minimise or address areas of risk if they cannot be eliminated.

In some cases, such as organising events, risk may be managed by appointing an external supplier with experience and expertise. A written contract, setting out key responsibilities for risk management, provides legal protection when appointing suppliers, including PR consultancies. It is important to check that suppliers have professional indemnity and public liability insurance. Specific insurance is advisable for events and campaigns to cover the risk of unexpected, often costly, occurrences.

Senior management may decide that the 'opportunity cost' of accepting a risk is worthwhile. This means that the benefits of taking action outweigh possible consequences, or that the cost (in time and resources) involved in managing a risk is considered to be better spent undertaking the campaign. In such circumstances, a contingency plan needs to be in place, particularly to manage any possible crisis that could arise.

In 2003, confectionary company, Cadbury, launched its 'Get Active' initiative in partnership with the charity Youth Support Trust. The campaign was endorsed by the government sports minister and included funding to support teacher training and increase activity resources within schools. It featured six stages:

- Training for 5,000 teachers as sports specialists with resource cards and curriculum aids.
- Free unbranded sports kit up to £9 million in value available through a promotional voucher collection scheme.
- A free public activity day at the NEC in Birmingham involving 14 sports and activities, including the opportunity to run with Olympic champion, Paula Radcliffe.
- Commissioning Paula Radcliffe, Darren Gough and Audley Harrison to be sports ambassadors and highlight the positive aspects of sport and its impact on their lives.
- Employee involvement including community 'adopt a school' fundraising 'token match' and volunteering 'count yourself in'.
- Research in conjunction with Loughborough University studying children's activity levels, interest and response in schools.

Cadbury claimed that 40 per cent of UK schools registered for the programme (with 18 withdrawing as a result of subsequent media criticism). Over 40,000 hours of activity was recorded by 13,500 children and adults at the Get Active Day. Schools were adopted by 264 employees, 160 employees fundraised through sponsorship and 170 volunteered for the Get Active Day.

However, the scheme was criticised by media, politicians and the Food Commission for encouraging children to eat large amounts of chocolate in exchange for sports gear. Calculations were made regarding the total fat and calories of all the promotional chocolates and amounts of bars required to obtain sports equipment. For example, acquiring a cricket set would require vouchers from 2,730 bars.

Use this example to walk through the risk management process to determine whether the negative outcome could have been anticipated and avoided. What was the operational risk of this campaign? Consider the consequence of removing the promotional product element of the campaign and whether a different approach could have been taken to provide positive financial and marketing benefits.

INCIDENTS, ISSUES AND CRISIS SITUATIONS

Incident management

Incidents are generally small matters that occur within everyday activities without affecting the strategic operation of the organisation. For example, travel delays, technical issues, special requests or unexpected changes may threaten the success of a planned event. Risk assessment may anticipate such incidents within plans and allow for back-up options, although the range of eventualities could make this unfeasible.

Routine incident management involves preparedness for changes in circumstances and demonstrates how working in PR requires an adaptive nature where practitioners are able to consider and accommodate emerging situations.

PR practitioners need the knowledge and experience to handle problems. Remaining calm and being able to work out solutions whilst acting promptly and efficiently are important skills to develop. Building strong relationships with those who can affect the successful delivery of PR programmes will enable situations to be resolved promptly.

The risk of minor incidents emphasises the importance of ensuring plans and requirements are detailed in writing. Key documentation includes briefing reports, action plans, timetables, movement schedules, detailed roles and responsibilities, event programmes, records of meetings, media lists, budgets and contracts. These demonstrate a responsible, professional approach and provide a means of ensuring prompt action if a problem occurs. For example, if a venue fails to equip a room as specified, reference to a contract can ensure responsibility for remedying the situation is recognised and resolved immediately. It is also important to document matters arising and solutions implemented in campaign and other reports for future reference.

Although most PR practitioners are unlikely to experience a major crisis situation, they will face routine incidents throughout their career. This highlights the need to develop the competency to prepare for, handle, reflect and learn from minor incidents in a professional manner.

A formal system of recording and analysing incidents that have occurred, and documenting response processes (and where/when these require updating) helps to create a shared incident management culture within a PR function. Learning can also be developed across the team and reports created to inform management on actions taken to avoid more serious issues developing.

Issues management

Where an incident is a routine problem to be resolved, an issue involves a matter that may present a significant risk or opportunity for the organisation where there is a difference of opinion over the most appropriate action to be taken.

ACTION POINT

The Health & Safety Executive (HSE) report into a high-speed crash involving former BBC *Top Gear* presenter, Richard Hammond in 2006 investigated the planning, preparation and training undertaken by the BBC and PTLE (owner of the jet-powered modified drag racer being driven by Hammond), as well as examining the vehicle and its tyres. Whilst acknowledging precautions that were in place, the report 'identified failings in the BBC's safety management systems relating to risk assessment and the procurement of services from others, and by PTLE in their risk assessment for the services they provided'.

The investigation noted issues that are relevant for PR practitioners involved in organising activities that contain an element of risk. A detailed summary of the investigation is available at www.hse.gov.uk/foi/releases/richardham-mond.pdf.

Issues monitoring needs to involve more than a 'surveillance' approach (L'Etang, 2008: 86) and should take account of different stakeholder perspectives. Yaxley (2012b: 163–4) advises that recognising specific concerns 'enables responses to be developed to meet particular needs or to engage with the most frequently raised aspects of the issue'.

Undertaking a situational analysis (Chapter 5) enables existing or emerging issues to be identified and addressed. This may mean working with other functions on operational responses or implementing appropriate communication strategies (Chapter 8). Trend analysis and scenario forecasting are useful techniques for identifying possible issues although, as with risk management, the likelihood and consequences of such eventualities need to be assessed.

Issues that affect an organisation's licence to operate are likely to require public affairs or lobbying strategies. Similarly, issues where organisations have expertise may offer an opportunity for thought leadership that contributes towards informing public opinion or policy decisions.

Issues management can be considered as 'opportunity management' (Jaques, 2002: 142) or a defensive precursor to crisis management. PR practitioners require a range of competencies in identifying and managing such issues. Research and analysis is the most obvious skill set alongside the ability to develop flexible and adaptive strategies (with identification of risk/opportunity factors and resource requirements) that can be agreed by senior management.

Traditional communication competencies of PR practitioners are relevant in issues management with regard to determining approaches to inform, persuade or engage stakeholders and publics.

Charities, NGOs and groups of active publics, as well as commercial and public sector organisations, use agenda-setting campaigns to raise the profile of issues or

UNDERSTANDING SOCIETY
(www.understandingsociety.ac.uk)

Understanding Society is a longitudinal study of how life in the UK is changing. It researches individuals' social and economic circumstances, attitudes, behaviours and health. The 2016 Insights report (www.understandingsociety.ac.uk/2016/11/10/new-insights) highlights public debate around identity, social divisions, income inequality, barriers to opportunities and 'resentment by those who feel left behind, geographically and economically' (p. 4). These issues are noted to relate to 'the nature and conditions of employment and the fairness of employment contracts'.

Education and health issues are also discussed in light of the EU referendum result and other developments, such as faster home broadband. It notes an ageing population and long-term health conditions, including disabilities, for those of working age. In particular, mental health problems are discussed. The study argues that there is a 'complex relationship between work and health' (p. 19).

Such reports provide a useful context to identify issues affecting organisations – consider the viewpoints expressed in this and similar publications and how they suggest matters that could affect your own organisation or one in the news.

stimulate crisis situations to get their voice heard and change public opinion (Bourland-Davis et al., 2010).

Whilst activist groups may use confrontation and civil disobedience as an issues management strategy, most organisations would face reputational risks from being seen to act outside the law. Their issues management strategies, both reactive and proactive, tend to be more restrained.

Heath (2002: 210) presents issues management as 'stewardship for building, maintaining and repairing relationships with stakeholders and stakeseekers'. It encompasses strategic planning and corporate responsibility in order to develop multidisciplinary processes and procedures that 'make the organisation smarter, more nimble and visionary' (p. 211).

According to Kelly (2001: 283) stewardship is a continuous process of public relations (in contrast to time-limited campaigns and programmes) which 'promotes ethical behaviour by practitioners and their organisations'.

Issues management is, therefore, considered as an integral aspect of public relations that recognises and addresses situations (opportunities and threats) on a proactive and

ISSUES MANAGEMENT USING A COALITION STRATEGY

Forming coalitions enables organisations to co-orientate with others on issues of common concern. One example is the Motor Ombudsman (formerly known as Motor Codes) that was set up by the motor industry in 2008 to act as the self-regulatory body for the automotive sector.

The strategy was adopted in response to a National Consumer Council (NCC) paper claiming that shoddy vehicle repair work cost consumers £4 billion a year and called for the automotive industry to obtain full Office of Fair Trading (OFT) approval or be subjected to legislation. The poor image of the service and repair sector was an issue of concern to a wide range of organisations.

The establishment of Motor Codes (rebranded as The Motor Ombudsman in November 2016) reflects a coalition strategy aiming to alter public opinion and improve the industry's reputation (see www.themotorombudsman.org).

In November 2011, Motor Codes received full OFT approval for its Service and Repair Code following recognition that it had been effective in reducing consumer complaints.

What are the benefits and drawbacks of co-orienting with other organisations to address issues of mutual concern? What role does public relations play in ensuring that such initiatives are a success?

reactive basis. It is concerned with relationships and accountability. This means the focus extends beyond addressing a particular issue using communications.

Crisis management

In May 2014, the British government and the British Standards Institute (BSI) launched BS 11200, a new British Standard of Crisis Management – Guidance and Good Practice. It replaced the Publicly Accredited Specification (PAS) 200 introduced in September 2011 to help organisations implement systems to detect, prepare for and respond to crisis situations.

BS 11200 defines a crisis as an 'abnormal and unstable situation that threatens the organisation's strategic objectives, reputation or viability'. BS 11200 provides guidance to ensure competence in dealing with crises. It details practical steps that organisations can take within an operational framework. The principles of BS 11200 reinforce the importance of effective communications with internal and external stakeholders on an ongoing basis.

Rather than presenting a prescriptive solution to every eventuality, crisis management is acknowledged as occurring in complex and challenging environments. As Edward P. Borodzicz, professor of risk and crisis management at the University of Portsmouth, confirms (Bovingdon, 2011), there is a 'need to empower the right individuals to break rules to deal with a crisis effectively'.

The recognition of a need for flexibility echoes the argument of Gilpin and Murphy (2008: 5) against 'overly rigid crisis planning procedures'. Yaxley (2012b: 170) supports 'consideration of the actual situation being faced by the particular organisation at a specific time', with public relations 'capable of working as proficiently as possible' rather than being presented as 'controlling the crisis'.

This is evident in Jaques' issues and crisis management relationship model (2010: 442), which presents four inter-related components of effective crisis management:

1   **Crisis preparedness**

    - planning processes
    - systems, manuals
    - training, simulations.

2   **Crisis prevention**

    - early warning, scanning
    - issues and risk management
    - emergency responses.

3   **Crisis event management**

    - crisis recognition
    - system activation/response
    - crisis management.

4   **Post-crisis management**

    - recovery, business resumption
    - post-crisis issue impacts
    - evaluation, modification.

This model presents a proactive, dynamic approach to crisis management. Further it illustrates the wide-ranging capabilities required by PR practitioners. Coombs (2015: 1) notes in particular a requirement for 'small-group decision making, media relations, environmental scanning, risk assessment, crisis communications, crisis plan development, evaluation methods, disaster sociology, and reputation management'. He further highlights the importance of writing as a crisis management competence, and the use of social media (where appropriate).

Crisis management capabilities within an organisation may be categorised as follows:

Intellectual: including ability to analyse situations, set strategy, determine options, make decisions and evaluate their impact

Organisational: including structures and processes needed to translate decisions into action and review their impact

Cultural: reflecting willingness of staff to share and support the intentions and policies of senior management

Logistical: ability to support solutions by applying the right resources in the right place at the right time.

Public relations practitioners need to be competent in offering counsel in relation to each category. Indeed, Yaxley (2012b: 171) calls for a 'new approach involving continuous learning', citing Robert and Lajtha (2002: 181), 'to equip key managers with the capabilities, flexibility and confidence to deal with sudden and unexpected problems/ events – or shifts in public perception of any such problems/events'.

Learning and adaptation are important in building organisational resilience. Kayes (2015) suggests a process of questioning concerning what can be learned from previous situations. This echoes the concept of reflective practice introduced in Part II, which can be deployed by those who have been identified and trained prior to involvement in crisis management.

When the future of the organisation is at risk, senior personnel will drive crisis management. It is vital that they recognise the strategic role of public relations at the earliest stage. As well as offering informed strategic advice, PR practitioners should ensure executives are prepared as credible spokespeople capable of taking a high profile in the case of serious crisis situations. However, ensuring that senior personnel recognise and reflect professional public relations expertise in their communications can be a challenge. This was seen in the case of BP where its CEO and chairman made ill-considered statements during the 2010 Gulf oil spill crisis.

The focus of crisis management training within public relations is primarily on communications. Traditionally this has concerned preparation for media interviews. More recently, the use of social media is emphasised, not least for their ability to 'amplify what might otherwise be issues of low or no significance' (Yaxley 2012b: 154).

It is vital to ensure an organisation-wide capability to recognise potential trigger points through monitoring of all sources of intelligence relating to a crisis situation. This builds understanding of where and how situations are likely to escalate. This highlights the importance of effective internal relationships and mechanisms for public relations. Further the function should take a broad stewardship perspective in a crisis scenario encompassing policy formation, relationship building, reputation management and stakeholder communications inside and outside the organisation.

Stakeholders and publics form a complex web of interconnection, meaning that messages and organisational narratives need to be coherent, consistent and credible. In determining credibility, organisations are increasingly expected to live up to any stated values. Similarly, senior executives are judged not simply on their position or expertise, but on their personality and communicative competence.

Broadcast media offer particular challenges, being less easy to be 'crafted' by public relations experts than written communications. Live and informal situations may generate video or audio recordings of prepared spokespeople or others, including general employees. Additionally such materials may be created and uploaded online by members of the public rather than professional media. Professional training is helpful but needs to engender the ability to respond in a human not a mechanistic manner.

Additionally, it should be recognised that there is increasing media and public knowledge of crisis management. This includes scepticism of the 'apology phenomenon' (Lazare, 2005: 7) where a lack of sincerity is detected. Indeed, the public and media may view apologies as important primarily as a form of 'power-rebalance' or entertainment.

In a contemporary crisis situation, many narratives and points of view may be heard. In addition to monitoring these, PR practitioners need to decide which are worthy of response. Given the multi-layered, interconnected nature of communications during contemporary crisis situations a polyphonic approach is recommended. This allows for different voices, meanings and representations of reality and experience to be understood and addressed.

Crisis communications

The planning approach detailed in Part II offers a framework for developing a crisis communications strategy and action plan based on situational analysis, clear objectives and a monitoring and evaluation process.

Effective crisis communication approaches include stakeholder engagement, although Freeman and McVea (2005) go a step further in arguing for stakeholder partnerships. This has the advantage of developing a strong relationship whereby partners not only give an organisation the benefit of doubt (at least initially) in a crisis situation, but also act as advocates in extending the reach and credibility of crisis communications.

Five levels of stakeholder engagement should be considered:

1   Inform all key stakeholders, including staff, to help dispel myths and rumours and present a positive message about the organisation's ability to deal with a crisis.

2   Monitor constantly for new stakeholders and reactions from known stakeholders to adapt communications strategy as needed.

3   Consult with staff and key stakeholders to disseminate key messages and gain feedback on analysis, alternatives and/or decisions.

4   Involve staff and key stakeholders, where possible, to ensure concerns and aspirations are considered in the decision-making process.

5   Collaborate with key stakeholders to aid decision-making and develop alternative solutions.

Online technologies also need to be incorporated in any crisis strategy. In particular, information needs to be available via relevant channels of communications, including the organisation's owned or created media.

The immediacy of online, social and mobile technology requires that consideration of an appropriate response needs to be rapid. This does not necessarily involve an instant response to anyone communicating about an incident. It is important for the organisation to be prepared and able to deploy a strategic approach rather than tactical reactions.

A series of tools to support crisis communications can be found in the Appendices, including development of a triage system and a crisis playbook.

CASE STUDIES

It is easy to find opinions online and in printed publications concerning how public relations practitioners have managed crisis situations. Largely these are critical and written in a manner that positions the writer as having greater expertise than those involved in a crisis.

Speakers and presenters at conferences on crisis management are similarly those who have experienced a high-profile situation who are willing to share their experiences. The same is true for biographies where authors recollect their involvement.

In such cases the critics are writing as outsiders of a situation, whereas those who speak from an insider perspective arguably share 'best practice' advice only as a result of ineffective crisis planning.

Although crisis cases are often included in textbooks, there is a lack of published examples using a robust case study methodology. Neither are there ethnographic studies of developing crisis situations to offer insight into lived experiences. Likewise, it is rare to see research of where crisis situations were averted or ameliorated through effective planning.

Instead, case studies are presented as dramatic narratives that may be:

• Critical of public relations practitioners on the basis of failings to demonstrate perceived 'best practice'

- First-person recollections constructed to illustrate particular 'survive and thrive' stories
- Selective examples intended to contrast mythologies of heroes and villains.

It is also difficult to investigate a crisis situation on the basis of publicly available materials. Media reports may be sensationalised, whereas materials produced by organisations as a crisis unfolds are framed according to legal and other organisational constraints and objectives (such as minimising media coverage).

In a large organisation, experiences of crisis management by public relations practitioners within an organisation may vary. For example, those operating at a national or local level will be implementing a strategy developed by a global or central head office function. Likewise materials published on websites or to inform media coverage may be centrally controlled or tailored specifically for a local context.

The majority of case studies concerning crisis situations tend to focus on large organisations and atypical situations. These generally affect private sector organisations, although public sector bodies and charities may be the focus of critical attention. There are fewer examples of small-medium enterprises or situations that typify common rather than exceptional crisis experiences.

Moreover, awards that recognise effective communication in an issues or crisis management context select high-profile situations that may not reflect the experiences of the majority of PR practitioners. They will also be examined and communicated only in relation to entry criteria. This means they are presented as examples of achieving successful outcomes where lessons learned in respect of where things went wrong are omitted.

Any case study narratives should be subject to critical examination. It should be remembered that these are constructed realities developed to convey particular messages or lessons about crisis management. Certain examples are used to illustrate a particular 'wrong way'; others are presented as exemplars of the 'right way'. This tends to reflect a simplistic approach that ignores the complexity of managing a crisis situation.

The difference between reactive and proactive issues management may not be recognised. It is also likely that the difficulties of assessing risk and determining possible or actual causes are not appreciated. Moreover, it is unlikely that any crisis situation will exactly replicate any other.

Further, the limited involvement of communication practitioners should be considered, as PR is not the only function involved in addressing risk, issues or crisis situations. Ultimate responsibility lies with senior management who may constrain the ability of the PR team to respond.

From an educational, life-long learning and professional development viewpoint, it would be helpful to have a wider range of insightful case studies using a variety of research methodologies. Without these, examples should be viewed as anecdotal evidence that relies on personal interpretations reflecting varying degrees of expertise and potentially be of limited value.

END POINT

Risk management involves identifying and mitigating uncertainties that impact on an organisation's effective operation. The PR function needs to be part of the formal analysis of risk and examine the relevance of trends affecting organisations. Risk communications should build trust and acknowledge uncertainty with a dialogic approach.

Incidents, issues and crisis offer different levels of situations faced by PR practitioners, which may represent an opportunity or a threat. When managing incidents, planning and an adaptive approach are important. Issues management addresses more significant risks, predicated on competencies to undertake ongoing situational analysis and develop particular solutions with the agreement of senior management. These should reflect stewardship in building stakeholder relationships through strategic planning and corporate responsibility.

Crisis management likewise requires competency in handling complex situations and providing strategic counsel. It is recommended that more robust studies of crisis scenarios are developed with acknowledgement of where things go wrong as well as when the ability of public relations practitioners to advise senior management is constrained.

CHAPTER 14

Corporate social responsibility

Alison Theaker

As consumers become more demanding, organisations have sought to differentiate themselves. With the use of new technology increasing transparency, one of the elements of differentiation has been to adopt socially responsible methods. How much of this is doing good to be good, or doing good to look good?

CHECK POINT

In this chapter we will:

- Define corporate social responsibility (CSR)
- Examine the Virtue Matrix
- Consider the practitioner's role in advising management on CSR
- Look at cause-related marketing and how that is different from CSR
- Examine two case studies where CSR is integral to the business.

DEFINING CSR

First, here is a definition of corporate social responsibility (CSR): 'Corporate social responsibility describes the role a company has in society' (www.ipr.org.uk/member/ PRguides/CSR). This does not really tell us much about what CSR should look like. In the 1990s, Jerry Wright, Lever Brothers' marketing director, called Persil's support of

High	Self-interest	Low
Philanthropy	Social responsibility	Pure philanthropy
Low	Cause-related marketing	Enlightened self-interest

FIGURE 14.1 Enlightenment matrix

Source: Cannon (1992)

the Funfit scheme for 3 to 11 year olds 'enlightened self-interest – a combination of a worthy cause and an opportunity to target heavy detergent users such as the parents of young children' (C. Murphy, 1999: 20).

'A corporation can gain competitive advantage by having the goodwill of local communities', suggest Werbel and Wortman (2000: 124). These arguments were a reaction to the economist Milton Friedman, who declared that business could not have responsibilities, that only people could have responsibilities (1993). He declared that CSR was a 'fundamentally subversive doctrine', and that 'there is one and only one social responsibilty of business – to ... increase its profits'.

However, Tench (2014: 49) states that CSR is 'an organisational's defined responsibility to its society(ies) and stakeholders'. He adds that, 'organisations ... are part of the infrastructure of society and as such they must consider their impact on it'.

Dauncey (1994) devised a scale of 'Shades of Green' to assess how committed an organisation was to being more environmentally friendly. Green Trimmings were just a symbolic nod, a few green products which were marketed more than the unenvironmentally friendly ones. The scale rose through Green Cuffs (basic recycling, turning off lights), Green Clothes (conducting an environmental audit) and Green Body (redesigning the product line to eliminate non-recyclable materials) to Green Brains (having a long-term business plan to achieve sustainability), Green Heart (encouraging social ownership for local offices) and finally Green Soul (overall goals of the organisation consider how they will benefit the planet and pursue higher goals).

Moloney (2006) draws a distinction between CSR and philanthropy. While public relations draws attention to CSR activities to enhance an organisation's reputation, this goes against the private altruism of philanthropy. Cannon (1992) set this out in the Enlightenment Matrix (Figure 14.1).

This puts social responsibility at the confluence of both philanthropy and self-interest. Where self-interest is low and the main aim is to do good, that would be considered pure philanthropy. So most writers see social responsibility as having benefits for the organisation as well as for the recipients.

Worcester (2007) stated: 'No modern corporation can exist for long, much less thrive, without taking responsibility for its actions.' Bowd (2005) suggests that a healthy business requires a healthy community and that CSR is generally held to increase profit or improve reputation. The benefits of operating in an ethical manner can include goodwill, customer and staff loyalty and strong stakeholder relationships which can result in a competitive edge. Thus the motivation for being seen as socially responsible is to attract sales, reputation, donors and supporters. Moloney (2006) queried whether such statements of social reponsibility are genuine or 'window dressing'. He quoted research by Christian Aid in 2004 which concluded that companies frequently use such initiatives to defend operations which come in for public criticism.

The UK Labour government's vision, published in 2004, encouraged businesses to take account of their economic, social and environmental impacts. The Companies Act (2006) obliged listed companies to include a business review in their annual reports. Key performance indicators had to demonstrate the effectiveness of environmental, social and community policies (Gray, 2007). The EU carried out consultation on CSR in 2014, and the Directive on non-financial reporting is set to come into effect in 2017, requiring companies to report on their sustainabilty performance (see Talking Point, below).

Research by Price Waterhouse Coopers (www.csreurope.org, 2002) found that 79 per cent of CEOs thought that CSR was vital to their companies, and 71 per cent said they would sacrifice profits in the short term in favour of long-term shareholder value. However, the London Business School reviewed 80 studies on CSR. Of these, 42 made a positive impact, 19 found no link with reputation, 15 gave mixed results and four were negative.

Yaxley (2009) divides an organisation's stakeholders into different groups. She suggested that focusing on employees, customers and suppliers is simply about survival, whilst thinking about shareholders and government as well means that profitability was important. If a company engages in philanthropy for good causes, this showed that it is considering its community. Social responsibility suggested an agenda which took wider society into account. She listed the expectations of different stakeholder groups (see Table 14.1).

The line between CSR and business success is not always clear. Jones *et al.* (2009) describe how Primark was voted the most unethical retailer in 2005 and the subject of a *Panorama* programme in 2008 highlighting the wages received by employees of its suppliers. Instead of responding to the BBC, Primark built a microsite to answer consumers directly. At the time over 42,000 members were registered on its Facebook fan page and many customers responded to activist sites criticising the store defending its low prices. Stern (2009) points out that Primark sales rose by 18 per cent in the last quarter of 2008. He also defends Sir Terry Leahy's announcement to Tesco's suppliers

TABLE 14.1 Expectations of different stakeholder groups

Customers	Want to buy from companies who share their views
Employees	Want to share their values with their organisation
Communities	Want jobs and revenue to be created locally as well as environments in which they want to work and live
Suppliers	Want to partner with companies with sound business practices and reputations
Government	Want business to support its aims for society
Media	Want organisations to deliver public expectations
Investors	Want to see added value and avoid damaging crises

that they needed to cut prices by saying: 'The truly responsible thing to do is to run a good business competently.'

Maybe the problem is trying to justify CSR by using a business rationale. Rangan *et al.* (2015) state that the main goal of CSR must be 'to align a company's social and environmental activities with its business purpose and values' rather than demand that CSR programmes deliver business results. They suggest three 'theatres'. The first focuses on philanthropy whereas the second aims to improve operational effectiveness. Thus donations and volunteering fit into the first arena, whilst sustainability initiatives would fit the second. Lastly, the third theatre creates a new business model, where a business is formed specifically to address social or environmental challenges. Project Shakti, developed by Unilever in Hindustan, recruits village women to sell soaps and detergents door-to-door. More than 65,000 women now participate, receiving access to micro-loans and training whilst doubling their household income and by increasing rural access to hygiene products contributing to public health. Miccio (2015) suggested that as some entrepreneurs develop products for 'the sole purpose of societal benefit', the lines between for-profit and non-profit companies will become blurred.

READING POINT

Martin (2002: 69–75) suggests referring to his Virtue Matrix to assess whether it is worthwhile engaging in a particular activity. He found that consumers, investors and business leaders were all urging corporations to 'remember their obligations to their employees, their communities and the environment, even as they pursue profits for shareholders'. He put forward the view of corporate responsibility as a product, subject to market pressures. By examing the drivers of corporate virtue, he found there were two main elements, compliance and choice. Furthermore, CSR activties could either be instrumental – explicitly enhancing shareholder value – or intrinisic – simply because it was the right thing to do.

Martin then devised his matrix, with four quadrants, The bottom two he called the civil foundation. This is made up of norms, customs and laws and companies may either choose to observe them or may have to legally comply with. Companies operating here do no more than meet society's basic expectations of how they should act. When they move beyond this, this is what Martin calls the frontier. This is above and beyond the call of duty, so to speak. Practices that benefit both society and shareholders are termed strategic and those that benefit society but not shareholders are called structural, because there is thus a structural barrier to corporate action here. Some actions which start by being in the frontier, such as Prudential Insurance's introduction in 1990 of viatical settlements to allow people with AIDS to tap into death benefits in their life insurance to pay medical expenses, create so much goodwill for the companies concerned that others
follow suit and this kind of behaviour can migrate to the civil foundation. In the US, only a handful of companies once offered healthcare benefits to employees' dependants, but because this created so much goodwill, others soon followed and eventually this became included in government regulations.

The upper limit of the civil foundation is therefore not fixed. In strong economies it may move upwards as more social benefits become the norm, but it can shrink if times get hard. Martin also raises the question of international companies who comply with the civil foundation in their area of operation, but not in their home country. Thus Nike complied with local customs in its pay and practices in south-west Asia, but was criticised in the US and Europe because this did not agree with expected standards there.

How does this help an organisation considering its own CSR and what policies to introduce? There will be certain good practices that it will have to comply with, and some that have become accepted as normal in the society in which it is operating. So complying with environmental laws or providing an on-site nursery win no brownie points. To earn 'public credit' a company has to be in the frontier. Most policies would tend to be strategic, giving some benefit to shareholders as well as society, but Martin makes a compelling case that companies should consider moving into the structural frontier to satisfy their publics.

> No consortium of energy producers has come together to formulate and execute a strategy to reduce greenhouse-gas emissions. Pharmaceutical companies have not yet crafted a plan to halt the worldwide spread of HIV infection. Media companies have failed to take concerted action to stem the tide of vulgar trash that too often passes for children's entertainment. ... the inability or unwillingness to deliver these obvious benefits create a powerful sense that corporations are not doing enough.
>
> (Martin, 2002: 72)

CSR EUROPE: THE EUROPEAN BUSINESS NETWORK FOR CORPORATE SOCIAL RESPONSIBILITY

CSR Europe is a European business network for corporate social responsibility (CSR), with 50 multinational corporations and 45 national partner organisations as members. The organisation was founded in 1995 by senior European business leaders in response to an appeal by the European Commission President Jacques Delors. It has since grown to become a network of business people working at the very forefront of CSR across Europe and globally. CSR Europe's network of national partner organisations brings together 45 membership-based, business-led CSR organisations from 30 European countries. In total, the network reaches out to more than 10,000 companies throughout Europe.

Enterprise 2020

In October 2010, CSR Europe launched a joint Enterprise 2020 initiative to address societal challenges through collaborative action and shape the business contribution to the European Union's Europe 2020 strategy for smart, sustainable and inclusive growth. Since its launch, Enterprise 2020 forms the umbrella for all CSR Europe activities.

Two major campaigns

In order to help companies to progress towards Enterprise 2020, CSR Europe has implemented two major campaigns:

1   **Sustainable Living in Cities** aims to create local and regional alliances and encourage collaborations between public and private, city and business. Presently 75 per cent of Europe's populations live in urban areas. CSR Europe's vision is 'By 2030, the European urban population will be living in sustainable cities that can provide economic opportunities, reliable infrastructure and a high standard of living.'
2   **Skills for Jobs** has a goal of engaging with 5 million people to equip them with skills to compete in the job market. To date, 3 million people have been equipped with STEM skills and 1.5 million with entrepreneurial skills.

CSR Europe also aims to help companies engage with the EU Directive on non-financial information disclosure. The first reports will be published in 2018, referring to activities in 2017 (www.csreurope.org/participate-eu-platform-diversity-charters-high-level-event-23-october).

CSR Europe's model sets out several elements to sustainable business growth, dealing with climate change, changing demographics, resource scarcity, population growth, global trade, environmental degradation, urbanisation and poverty, education and equality. Should businesses be involved in these areas, or is this the job of governments? What happens if only some organisations get involved, at cost to themselves, and their competitors do not?

What is the role of the PR practitioner in advising management whether to engage in CSR or not? James and Larissa Grunig gave a lecture at the 2010 PRSA international conference where they put forward the view that public relations was about communal relationships between organisations and their stakeholders and that 'we do what we do in the interest of the relationship more than the self-interest of the organisation that employs us'. They felt that the developments in social media meant that stakeholders could initiate a conversation with an organisation, and that 'better ways to listen' needed to be put in place.

CAUSE-RELATED MARKETING: A MORE HONEST APPROACH?

In the Enlightenment Matrix above, cause-related marketing (CRM) is high in self-interest and low on philanthropy. Sue Adkins (2006), of Business in the Community, states that research shows that '67% of the general public and 42% of business journalists agree that industry and commerce do not pay enough attention to their social responsibilities'. She adds, '83% of the general public feel that it is very or fairly important' that organisations should demonstrate that they are taking their social responsibilities seriously. Consumers are more inclined to purchase a product which is donating a proportion of its price to charity. BITC's latest CR Index (2016) includes examples of 'responsible companies' and benefits of participation in its initiatives. Fritz (2017) suggests that CRM had grown into a $2 billion industry in 2016.

CRM is different from CSR in that it is obvious that both parties have a commercial interest in the partnership. Whilst Marks & Spencer's partnership with Breakthrough Breast Cancer raised £1.45 million for the charity, it also raised the company's profile and led to the development of a new product range for those living with or having survived breast cancer. Adkins (2006) says: 'core components of today's effective cause-related marketing programmes, . . . (are) a win for business, a win for the cause or charity and a win for the consumer'. She added,

Cause-related marketing is a marketing-driven activity. Parties, be they businesses, charities or good causes, enter a cause-related marketing relationship in order to meet their objectives and in order to receive a return on their investment, where that investment may be in cash, time or other resources, or a combination of all.

Adkins warns that CRM, whilst having clear business benefits in raising consumers' sense of trust in an organisation and its products, must not be undertaken lightly. If it seems like a bolt-on rather than related to business values, such schemes can backfire. Cadburys received much criticism for its Get Active scheme where children could save wrappers to exchange for sports equipment for their schools. This caused a backlash when the media highlighted how much chocolate a child would have to eat to claim a football. Whilst Cadburys denied that it was designed to boost sales and that the people collecting vouchers were families and the wider community, it phased out the wrapper collection part of the initiative (Williamson, 2004).

There are only a few charities that could afford to work without corporate support. Fritz (2017) warns that non-profits lending their name to for-profit activities carries a risk and might weaken the charity's trustworthiness: product strategies could outweigh humanitarian ones, and larger non-profit organisations who are more marketing savvy could eclipse smaller, just as worthy ones. See also the discussion in Chapter 21.

The two case studies chosen illustrate organisations where it would be hard to separate the social responsibility element from the business itself. Both have taken social responsibility to heart as part of their mission and business values.

ACTION POINT

LOVING THE BEACH – VENUS CAFÉS

Founded in 1995 by Michael and Louisa Smith and Lee Porter, The Venus Company is one of the UK's leading beach-based cafés and takeaways. They began life at Blackpool Sands and have kept beachgoers fed and watered for 21 years. They serve locally sourced, tasty food with minimum impact on the environment and an emphasis on sustainability. They have six sites across the West Country including Blackpool Sands, East Portlemouth, Bigbury on Sea, Tolcarne, Watergate Bay and their only inland café at The Shops at Dartington.

Previous initiatives include raising over £30,000 from 2001–6 in support of local green lanes heritage conservation, from 500,000 customers opting to pay 5p on a cup of tea or chocolate flake. In 2011, they also collected 5p from every filter coffee to send to the Children of Sumatra Aceh (where the coffee comes from) to pay for six to eight cleft palate and harelip operations. The company was a corporate member of Devon Wildlife Trust in 2003 and in 2006, setting up the Venus Beach Wildlife Fund with the Trusts in Devon and Cornwall. The VBWF enabled over 250 primary school pupils from local schools to visit a Venus beach and learn about marine wildlife and conservation. From 2006 to 2011, customers' donations of 5p from each cup of tea and chocolate flake raised another £30,000. Other activities included litter picks by Venus staff and rockpool rambles with DWT staff.

Michael, Louisa and Lee wanted to create a business to encompass their interest in environmental issues, but also bring the professionalism of high street catering to a beach setting. They were enthusiastic about creating a brand known for both quality and corporate responsibility. At the same time they had clear business objectives to establish market leadership in the UK as the greenest beach café and shop operator. Michael says: 'As a company situated in some of the South West's most beautiful locations we strive to minimise the harmful effects our business and its operations has on the environment.'

The Venus Company's philosophy is best summed up by the phrase 'Loving the Beach', they even use it in their web address. They have twice won the Queen's Award for Sustainable Development (in 2005 and 2010). They are one of only ten companies throughout the UK to have been awarded a sustainability honour in 2010 and one of only eight companies to have achieved the award in 2005. Over the years they have increased their sourcing of local food and drink products to over 40, with over 90 per cent of food and drink products sourced from the South West, predominately Devon and Cornwall. Suppliers are chosen for their environmental and ethical values. Michael, Louisa and Lee endeavour to work with producers who have a similar ethos to them.

'There are so many fantastic benefits associated with sourcing produce locally', Michael says. 'As a family run business we are keen to support our surrounding economy, its farmers, producers and other related businesses too, this is one of the main factors which drives us to source our products from the region. That and its outstanding taste and freshness, of course.'

Wall-mounted maps (Figure 14.2) promote the local provenance of food and drink at each café. 'Both locals and visitors want to eat local food', Michael adds. The Venus Company is also very keen to collaborate and work with local producers who share a similar ethos to them. A recent collaboration is with Totnes-based brewery, New Lion Brewery, which has seen them create a Venus Ale.

The Venus Café

FOUNDED 1995

At Venus, we are really passionate about quality local food and, where available, organic. We believe tasty nutritious food is the right of all. Although we serve over 600,000 customers a year, we strive to maintain that very high quality, and taste, each and every time.

We make nearly everything on the menu. From humous to burgers, chicken tikka to brownie, pâté to bruschetta, gluten free drizzle cake to carrot cake, veggie burger to crab bisque – we make it all from scratch. This way we know exactly what ingredients are being used and that they are nutritious, healthy and tasty. We NEVER compromise the quality or nutrition for cost savings. Despite all business challenges we have stuck to our guns through thick and thin.

Our meat is all sourced from Devon and from farms we know and trust. We only use organic and free range animals knowing well developed muscle is the key to taste and flavour. The Devon beef for our burgers comes from Chorolais Cross (South Devon & Angus) single farm cattle which are grass fed. This provides higher nutrition to the animal and well formed muscle and marbling. Our organic steaks from grass fed Devon Aberdeen Angus are hung for 28 days.

We take equal care with all other products. We use grass fed dairy product – milk, cheese, cream – again this ensures higher nutrition and a natural taste which does away with the need to add ingredients and flavourings. You can taste the difference.

We do not rest on our laurels. We know we can still improve and that it doesn't go right all the time. If we have done a great job let us know. More importantly, if we mess up let us fix it here and now – we want you to leave happy and satisfied. If we don't know, we can't put it right.

We hope you enjoy your meal with us today and look forward to seeing you again in the near future.

If you have any questions please do email at Michael@venuscompany.co.uk. We would be delighted to hear from you.

Michael & Louise Smith, Lee Porter

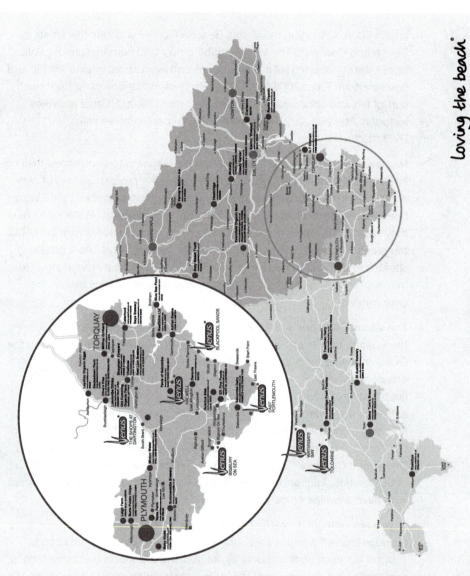

loving the beach

FIGURE 14.2 Suppliers map 2016

In 2008, Michael took over as chair of the board of directors for Food & Drink Devon, an organisation founded with the aim of representing like-minded businesses dedicated to producing food and drink of the very highest quality. Michael served as chair until 2016, The Venus Company remains a proud member of the organisation and sponsor of the Food & Drink Devon Awards.

Michael, Louisa and Lee are passionate about working closely with other local businesses, developing strong relationships with local tourist information centres and accommodation providers. Once a year they hold an evening for South Hams-based tourist information centres and accommodation providers to showcase Venus' food and drink. During the evening West Country producers are invited to speak and share their passion and enthusiasm for their products. As well as working closely with local producers and accomodation providers The Venus Company recruits and trains local management and seasonal staff wherever possible as well as employing the expertise of Devon-based agencies such as RAW PR and Marketing and specialist food photographer Guy Harrop.

The Venus Company is regularly featured along with their beaches in both the local and national press (Figure 14.3). A recent example has been the launch of their free children's activity bag which is supplied to children with every children's meal. The activity bags not only keep children entertained but increases their awareness of the sea and shoreline and communicates key environmental messages.

FIGURE 14.3 The Venus Café at Blackpool Sands

In 2011 Venus launched a fully compostable hot drink cup and lid (Figure 14.4). The lids, which had previously accounted for almost 9 per cent of Venus' non-recyclable waste, are now made from a biopolymer made of natural plant sugars which compost in 60 to 90 days. The sugar is taken from cane grown for industrial use and the production of the biopolymer uses 60 per cent less greenhouse gases and 50 per cent less non-renewable energy than traditional polymers. 'We used media relations to tell the story of the cup,' says Michael Smith. 'It does cost more than traditional polymer lined disposable cups. We wanted to demonstrate to customers that by looking after the beach, we were looking after their enjoyment of our café locations, and felt that this was the best way to get the message across.'

FIGURE 14.4 The Venus biodegradable cup

The launch of the new cup helped to reinforce to customers and the media that Venus are continuously improving their commitment to sustainability. Being one of the first users of these cups in the UK, it shows that Venus are at the cutting edge of sustainable innovations. Not only will it allow Venus customers to help look after the environment, it will also educate the wider population on what alternatives are available and will hopefully encourage them to seek the same environmental awareness and commitment from other café and restaurant chains.

With thanks to The Venus Company and RAW PR.

PENNYWELL FARM – DEVON'S FRIENDLIEST DAY OUT

Pennywell has been a farm attraction for 26 years and started as a bare field site. Visitors can have a go at activities like goat milking, bottle feeding lambs and cuddling pygmy pigs. Pennywell has grown from a staff of two with a few thousand visitors a year to a team of over 100 in the main tourist season and now attracts nearly 90,000 visitors each year.

The target market has traditionally been families with children under 11 but in recent years more adults are choosing to visit without children and there are guided visits for schools with a choice of different themed days to tie in with the National Curriculum. The focus is still animals and the hands-on experience. There are more than 200 animals as well as four farm rides and a different activity, show or display every half hour.

Pennywell endeavours to be completely sustainable and has won many awards for Green Tourism over the years, recently being awarded 'Best Sustainable Business' in the South Devon Tourism Awards and has held the Gold Award in the Green Tourism Business Scheme since the scheme was introduced to Devon over 20 years ago.

Sustainable features of the buildings include low-energy lighting in the Main Barn and hand washing by press taps, cutting down on the amount of water used. The lavatory system can be switched to use grey water. The Coffee Cabin is a recycled building, formerly a TA hut in Paignton. It uses Fair Trade products. Initiatives are in place to recycle as much of the café waste as possible. Noah's Barn was designed and built by a local company and utilises natural light, almost eliminating the need to use the installed low-energy lighting. The foundations for the building were slate from the woods across the road and the pathways are made from recycled, crushed concrete from local brown field sites. The Pennywell Tower is made from local wood, designed and built by a local craftsman. The solar panel and wind turbine on top of the tower are used to power the voice box which gives information about this green initiative and also explains the local history and wildlife that can be viewed from the top. The Toddlers Play Farm is home to a wind charger which plays nursery rhymes for the younger visitors. It drives a battery which in turn runs a voice box playing recordings of nursery rhymes for children.

Three years ago Pennywell invested £200k in 210 ground and roof mounted solar photovoltaic panels, ensuring maximum energy production. Mastervolt is used for daily PV monitoring and monthly readings are taken for electric. A 17ft high solar tracker shows visitors and schoolchildren how it tracks the sun and is compared to a real sunflower.

Around the site, the Run Rabbit Go Carts produce no noise, burn no carbon fuels and cause no pollution. The three ponds are filled with run-off water from the car parks filtered through a reed bed system (Figure 14.5). The Willow Maze is grown on site. The Pennywell animals are all used to demonstrate ways of sustainable living, whether it is learning about fibre, such as with the Angorra goats and Alpacas, dairy products from cows, goats and sheep or ferrets used for hunting. Goldfish in the water tanks keep them clean and the land is farmed organically with chemical fertilisers or pesticides. Dung from the Pennywell animals is collected by a neighbouring farmer for use on his organic farm.

FIGURE 14.5 Wildlife ponds at Pennywell

A lack of formal qualifications is no barrier to employment at Pennywell and all the current management team have worked up to their positions from elsewhere in the business, giving every employee the chance to reach their maximum potential. Staff come from the local area and many car share to work or make use of on-site mobile homes. Pennywell provides funding for a youth worker in the local town of Buckfastleigh and supports many local schools and charities by providing prizes for fundraising raffles (Figure 14.6).

FIGURE 14.6 Presenting a cheque to THHN

Each Thursday morning Pennywell hosts a free breakfast and interdenominational prayer meeting which is open to anyone and has up to 80 local people attending.

Pennywell owner Chris Murray was awarded an Honorary Doctorate in Business for his work in sustainable tourism in 2012 and has recently been made a Fellow of the Royal Agricultural Societies in recognition of his distinguished achievement in the agricultural industry. Chris regularly gives talks and tours to tourism students from both Exeter and Plymouth Universities about sustainable tourism and is a Director of Visit South Devon. He is also on the marketing committee of the Devon Association of Tourist Attractions. His Christian beliefs underpin his commitment to social responsibility. 'We consider we have a duty of care towards the environment and our fellow man. This is the only truly win–win strategy for the business and for the planet. A day at Pennywell lasts a lifetime.'

END POINT

Corporate social resposibilty is often quoted as one of the major issues that PR will have to deal with in the future. This is not just about communicating what an organisation does to be sustainable, but advising organisations on how to improve their credentials and earn their 'licence to operate'. This chapter has reviewed attitudes to CSR policies and presented two case studies where CSR cannot be separated from the mission and values of the business. Public relations is the function which is most involved with communicating with key stakeholders and is therefore in the best position to find out their views and expectations of how an organisation should interact with its environment.

CHAPTER 15

International considerations

Alison Theaker

Globalisation and the challenges of operating in a diverse world have been on the agenda for the practice of public relations for some time. Here we have a look at some useful writing on cultural differences and some case studies to illustrate how practitioners tailor their communications when dealing with different global groups.

CHECK POINT

This chapter covers:

- How several writers have attempted to map cultures
- Thoughts about how organisations operate globally
- Does PR follow development or lead it?
- Case studies where communications had to be changed in different environments.

THE GLOBAL PR COMMUNITY

Public relations is growing across the world. Wilcox (2006) stated, 'Reed's Worldwide Directory of Public Relations now lists 200 public relations professional societies in 70 nations with an aggregate membership of 150,000 members'. He went on to describe China as the 'new frontier', with 20,000 practitioners, and 2,000 public relations firms. Falconi (2006, cited in Molleda, 2009) estimated that there were any-where from 2.3 to 4.5 million public relations professionals globally.

Heath (2001b) stated that practitioners would need to examine behavioural and communication theories, the mass media, interpersonal communications, research methods, markets and public policy arenas as cultural differences could make or break successful campaigns.

Wakefield (2001) felt that international PR (IPR) is similar to domestic work in that it is strategic, dealing with media relations and promotions. PR practitioners will still communicate with targeted publics, deal with issues and crises, and develop com-munity relations.

By 2005, the Ford Vice President of Communications declared at the ICCO summit: 'There is no such thing as local, globalisation is a reality.' However, the CEO of Weber Shandwick was equally forthright when he said that: 'All PR is local' (Crush, 2005).

DEFINING INTERNATIONAL AND GLOBAL PR

Szondi (2006) makes the distinction between global PR, which he defines as the internationalisation of the profession, and IPR, which is the 'planning and implemen-tation of programmes involving two or more countries'. He also suggests that IPR can be preparative (cultivating the environment), situational (dealing with a single issue or situation) or promotional (supporting global marketing). Verčič (2014) reminds us that 'both management and public relations are concepts of Western origin', and that 'it is impossible to translate the term "public relations" in many languages'.

Only 5 per cent of countries have homogeneous cultures (Jandt, 2004). Post-communist Russia contains 148 million people from 100 nationalities, living across 11 time zones. In countries with high levels of immigration such as Australia and the US, it was assumed that children of immigrants would simply assimilate. But learning the language of the host country can take three generations. Moreover, whilst people learn the dominant culture and language they do not lose their original one. Teaching in the US, I found that of the 30 students in my Masters class on Global PR who were American, all had another culture they related to and often spoke another language at home.

The cultural background of targeted publics can change which media channels practitioners should use. In the US, gaps have narrowed between ethnic groups in how they use the internet. Whilst 78 per cent of blacks and 81 per cent of Hispanics use the internet, 85 per cent of whites and 97 per cent of English-speaking Asian Americans are familiar with the Web (Perrin and Duggan, 2015).

Asian cultures are also different. Clarke (2000) outlined the differences between the religious, royalist culture of the Thais; the assertive, workaholic culture of Hong Kong; the international sophistication of Singapore; and the heavily restricted media in Japan.

MAPPING CULTURES

Several writers have tried to list characteristics of different cultures and put them into groups and themes. Sebenius (2002: 80–1) offers 11 things which people need to find out when dealing with a different culture:

- Greetings – how do people greet and address each other? What role do business cards play?
- Formality – will I be expected to dress and interact formally or informally?
- Gifts – are gifts exchanged? What is appropriate?
- Touching – what are the attitudes towards contact?
- Eye contact – should this be direct?
- Deportment – how should I carry myself?
- Emotions – is it rude, embarrassing or usual to display emotions?
- Silence – awkward or expected? Insulting or respectful?
- Eating – what are proper manners? Are certain foods not allowed?
- Body language – are certain gestures expected or offensive?
- Punctuality – should I be on time or are schedules fluid?

Anthropologist Edward Hall's *Silent Language* from 1960 suggested variables that may drive behaviour:

- Relationships – if the focus is on relationships, deals arise from already developed relationships. If it is on the deal, relationships develop after it has been agreed.
- Communication – whether indirect, high context with non-verbal cues or direct and low context. In the US, communication should be to the point, whereas in China people like very detailed data.
- Time – monochronic or polychronic? Anglo-Saxon schedules are fixed, people do one thing at a time. Latin schedules are fluid, interruptions are common, interpersonal relationships take precedence.
- Space – moving too close in some cultures produces discomfort, and in others, backing away may convey disdain. (Sebenius, 2002)

Hofstede (Schneider and Barsoux, 2003: 87–91) built on Hall's *Silent Language*. Based on an employee opinion survey of 116,000 IBM employees in the 1960s, across 40 different countries, he identified four value dimensions. Power distance is the extent to which unequal distribution of power is accepted. Uncertainty avoidance refers to society's discomfort with uncertainty and preference for stability. Individualism/collectivism looks at the individual or group focus and masculine/feminine reveals the bias towards masculine assertiveness and competitiveness as against feminine nurturing, quality of life and relationships. On studying Asian cultures, a fifth dimension appeared, referred to as long-term orientation, reverence for persistence, thrift and patience. A table of rankings was produced for each country, showing that the US ranked most highly in individualism and Japan was the most masculine culture. Arab countries were less masculine orientated than both of them. Greece was ranked highest in uncertainty avoidance and Malaysia in power distance. High power distance is reflected in more levels of hierarchy and centralised decision-making. High uncertainty avoidance results in more rules and procedures and risk avoidance. High collectivist organisations prefer group decision-making. High masculinity rates task accomplishment higher than social relationships. The rankings were then translated into country clusters: Anglo, Nordic, Latin and Asian.

While actions can be copied, understanding is more difficult. In Britain and the US, a contract is a document that should be adhered to once signed. In Japan, it is a starting document that can be modified as needed. In South America, it is regarded as an ideal which is unlikely to be achieved but which is signed to avoid argument.

Marx (2001: 47–57) suggests that there is no right or wrong, but that in order to be effective, people must adapt their methods of doing business according to the cultural context.

Stevens suggested the following cultural profiles:

- Anglo/Nordic: Village market. Decentralised, entrepreneurial, flexible, delegation, informal personal communication. Output control.
- Asian: Tribe or family. Centralised, paternalistic, strong social roles, personal relationships. Social control.
- Germanic: Well-oiled machine. Decentralised decision-making. Narrow span of control, compartmentalised, throughput control. Efficiency.
- Latin: Traditional bureaucracy. Centralised decision-making, less delegation, pyramid of people, elitist, input control.

Selmer, in 1998, added a Viking form of management, with decentralised decision-making, emphasis on consensus and avoiding conflict, informal channels of communication and long-range objectives. These cultural preferences affect how information circulates and is shared. In French companies, the flow of information between groups is limited, as information is a source of power and not easily given away. In Sweden, communication patterns are much more open and informal, whereas information sharing is not widely practised in Russia, especially with outsiders, in case of misinterpretation. In Japanese companies, intensive and extensive discussion is encouraged at all levels (Schneider and Barsoux, 2003: 92–3).

Ransom (2011) shared her own views of what makes a successful multicultural campaign, but this related mainly to an exhortation to research attitudes to products and services and avoid stereotypes. Payne (2011) started by warning about differences in language and steering clear of brand names which could be misinterpreted. He quoted the Ford Pinto's launch in Brazil, where the name means 'small male genitals'.

So we can see that there is no universal 'best practice', and no shortcuts to simply doing thorough research into the different cultures of targeted publics.

ACTION POINT

INTERNATIONAL CONSIDERATIONS IN VIETNAM

Public relations practitioners have to be able to interact with diverse target groups and handle different types of relationships. Certain strategies may work in one culture but not in others. It depends on our ability to understand the culture of the target group and on our capacity to observe the norms guiding their interactions. To be successful in Vietnam's cultural environment, it is essential for PR practitioners to learn to act by the social rules, which are not always explicit or spoken.

International partners have different expectations about formality, gifts and punctuality when they come to Vietnam.

Formality

Formality in Vietnam depends on the context of the interaction, the nature of the work and the degree of relationship. One is expected to act formally for the first meeting and gradually become less so as one gets to know more about the Vietnamese partners. Sometimes guests feel awkward or uncomfortable in such settings and expect something less formal. Vietnamese tend to act more informally after they have shared food and drink. Rules will be broken when they accept you more as a 'friend' than a partner.

Generally, Asian partners expect a higher level of formality than Europeans. Korean partners feel comfortable in formal settings as they consider this an indication of their importance. Likewise, they appear happier when they are invited to luxury restaurants with a group of staff at their service. On the contrary, European partners, especially English and German, may feel awkward in this context. Long-term partners would request a street restaurant or traditional one, where they can feel real life and touch the culture rather than an expensive one in Western style.

As the relationship grows, you are expected to act informally or try to act as if you are friends. The secret to success in international cooperation and public relations is to learn the expectations of the partners and live up to them without compromising one's own.

Gifts

Exchanging gifts is part of Vietnamese culture. A Vietnamese saying goes, how you give is more important than what you give. The value of the gift is not only in the gift itself but also in the attitude of the giver. Neutral gifts are often given for first-time contacts and personalised ones will be given to known contacts. Corporate gifts have now become more common in Vietnam because it creates the sense of standardisation and equality.

At AJC, the practice of gift giving follows certain rules. The gift must be Vietnamese-made, representing the country's culture. Silk, porcelain or wooden products are popular choices. International guests sometimes receive a present that they can use rather than keep. Vietnamese coffee and tea are given because they are world famous. There will also be an explanation of the meaning of the gift, which adds spiritual values to it.

Vietnamese people show their appreciation when they receive a gift in return. Again, it need not be a big thing but something of spiritual meaning or practical use. Decorations, a notebook, book, pen or plaque are good to give. If you want to convey that the Vietnamese partner is special to you, personalised gifts are needed. I was once given a number plate by my American 'buddy' and a PhD bear by my English 'older sister' upon the completion of my dissertation.

We offer gifts to all the partners who are at meetings as a sign of hospitality. Gifts are given equally to each guest. However, it is acceptable if partners only have one gift for our side. Often the partner's only gift is presented to the most important person in the team. Long-term partners gradually recognise our patterns and prepare small gifts for everybody. The staff in my office are happy when they receive the small presents as a token of appreciation.

A German professor comes every year to teach students. Every time he comes, he brings plenty of gifts such as pens and nail clippers. However, he does not know that nail clippers are considered inappropriate gifts in Vietnamese culture. It is a traditional belief that sharp things are bad for the relationships because people are linked with one another with invisible strings. Next time, I will explain this to him as we are close enough to let the other know the little things in our culture. Handkerchiefs, mirrors and combs are bad to give because they are associated with separation. During the wars in Vietnam, these things were prepared for soldiers going to the front and many of them never returned.

Punctuality

Vietnamese people are quite flexible with time and may be 'in time' more than 'on time'. Punctuality applies more to business meetings and important events than social gatherings. In Vietnam when you receive a message, 'I am coming', to a party from a friend, he may just be leaving his own house. The safe rule is to be on time.

Some international partners are late for the meeting because of traffic. Traffic jams in big cities, especially Hanoi, happen not just at rush hours. It is good to get advice from your partner on how to get to the venue. People understand if you apologise for being late because of the traffic. Some of my Austrian partners could not understand at first why they were asked to leave their hotel at 8am for the meeting at 9am. The distance of 10 kilometres may only take 20 minutes in their countries, but can take at least an hour when they cross the city in the morning.

Japanese and German partners are trusted for their punctuality. German partners often make a plan one year ahead of time and I have never seen anything out of the blue. If they say they will come for the lecture in September next year, they will do it. They are upset when agreed arrangements are broken. Vietnamese people tend to regard time like air, which is flexible, while Germans consider it a limited resource.

The PR industry in Vietnam is going through rapid development with the debut of many domestic companies and the appearance of more international ones. While Vietnamese companies need to update international professional standards, foreign ones need to understand local traditions and customs. The practice of PR should be localised to meet the expectations and requirements of the local market. A lot of opportunities for cross-culture cooperation are emerging, which not only enhance mutual understanding but also foster business growth.

Dr Van Vu is Director of the International Office at the Academy of Journalism and Communication, Hanoi.

Key principles

Verčič (2014) advocates that certain key principles should be borne in mind when trying to deal with the 'rainbow' of cultures and worldviews. First, in a complex environment, practitioners should concentrate on bringing simplicity by focusing on common values. He suggests that whilst public relations needs to be represented at the top level of the organisation, 'communication ... can only work at the bottom' by using local teams to provide a local context. He underpins the general belief that good external communications needs to be based on good internal relationships. Lastly, he asserts that, whilst the channels for global communications have been changed by technological developments, true communication is always cultural.

Moss *et al.* (2010) suggest that techniques that practitioners use may not vary that much in different countries. What can vary, though, is the purpose of PR. They also observed that social responsibility has become increasingly important, with the rise of pressure groups calling for more accountability by governments and corporations. This can be linked to the spread of the internet and use of social media which has affected how people get information and form attitudes. People can now generate news and post opinions on goods and services, and this is a global phenomenon.

TALKING POINT

DOES PR FOLLOW OR LEAD DEVELOPMENT?

Sriramesh and Verčič (2009) relate the development of public relations to three elements in the infrastructure of a particular country. They feel that public relations thrives on public opinion, and so is most developed in democratic systems. It is most common in developed countries, where suppliers have to compete for public attention, approval and support. Activism, which provides opportunities for public relations in putting both sides of the case, is unlikely to be high if the bulk of the populace are more concerned about where their next meal is coming from. In addition, in developing countries, the media may reach only a small, homogeneous group because of illiteracy and poverty. Thus practitioners may have to adapt to using traditional and indigenous media.

In addition, Africa is a vast and untapped market of 800 million people across 53 states. These countries vary enormously in wealth, although the average share of GDP is US$684, compared to US$780 in China and US$440 in India. Gyroscope developed an Africa Communications Index (ACI), examining range and reach of media, the existence of a professional PR body and the ease of access to trained staff. Countries most developed according to the ACI are South Africa and Egypt, with the lowest scores earned by Mozambique and Ethiopia. Wells (2006) suggested that countries could not develop without an effective communications industry.

The events of the 'Arab Spring' in 2011 changed the political map in the Middle East and Northern Africa. Many of these political movements were sparked by single incidents, communicated by individuals via social media. Public relations cannot be said to have had a hand in these changes, and indeed PR consultancies have more often come under fire for representing the previous regimes to the West. Whilst Lerbinger (2001) stated that 'The essence of PR is cultural context', it seems that most public relations practice in developing countries is geared towards preserving the status quo. This raises the question of whether PR really is intrinsically in the public interest or is irretrievably wedded to corporate and governmental reputation.

Taking account of different cultures is integral to the success of global projects. This can be a lengthy process.

ACTION POINT

NATIONAL GEOGRAPHIC'S GENOGRAPHIC PROJECT

In 2005, I joined *National Geographic* along with a newly created team of international scientists and IBM researchers to develop and launch a flagship scientific effort to trace the history of humankind using DNA as a study tool, over 60,000 years.

It was a huge undertaking; the scientific consortium were asking big questions through their research 'where do you **really** come from? And how did you get to where you live today?' using cutting-edge genetic and computational technologies to analyse historical patterns found in DNA from participants around the world to better understand our human genetic roots. *National Geographic* would aim to tell the broader story; we are all related.

The three main components of the five-year project were to invite indigenous and traditional peoples to learn about the project and provide their genetic information to our researchers; to invite the general public to join in by purchasing a Genographic Project Public Participation Kit; and to use proceeds from kit sales to fund the Genographic Legacy Fund which supports indigenous educational and revitalisation projects. Genographic is anonymous, non-medical, non-profit and all results are placed in the public domain following scientific peer publication.

It was and is a huge project with a mass of multiple-layered internal and public communicating for many audiences across the world – and most particularly in explaining the project and its regionally approved ethical frameworks with locally accountable review boards to interested indigenous and traditional peoples, people who historically have not been well-respected by some scientists. Much of what we did differently was in how we thought about how we wanted to work; collaboration is the touchstone of every major phase of the outreach. Much of what we changed was in how we learned from the communities about how to talk with them.

Before any trip is planned, researchers at each of the regional centres around the world reach out first with local collaborators and leaders in individual communities not just to explain the Genographic Project, but also to better understand how and if those communities are interested in learning about their migratory history, before any other planning takes place. This work is relationship building. It is structured and transparent and it takes the time that it takes. At the same time it is truly iterative, in that we will follow and adapt to feedback and better practice as advised – all communities are unique.

Actual contribution of DNA takes place only when consultation – which may take weeks and months – is complete, and there is both collective and individual interest in participating. All consent is based on the principle of free, prior and informed consent (both written and oral). Individuals own the rights to their own samples and can withdraw from the study at any time and ask for their data to be removed from the database. This right extends to communities where the consent has been communal in character. The generic, non-individualised research generated by the project is meant to be shared; the Genographic Project research centres release the resulting genetic data (on an anonymous and aggregate basis) into the public domain to promote further research. The genetic data is not patented.

The collaborative relationship continues into the results phase of the analysis. The researchers work with the communities to determine if, when and how they are interested in sharing the collective information from the analysis of the group's genetic data. Researchers will then go back to the communities to talk through the results and the stories around them and hear more from the communities. We are very clear in presentation from the beginning that we are offering an additional understanding around peoples' and communities' origin stories, not seeking to replace them.

Most of what we knew back in 2005 about anthropological genetics was based on DNA samples donated by approximately 10,000 indigenous and traditional people from around the world. While this information gave us a broad view of the patterns of human migration, it represented just a small sample of humanity's genetic diversity. The project is still under way and new data have already helped support mapping of world migratory patterns dating back some 150,000 years and fill in the huge gaps in our knowledge of humankind's migratory history.

Today the language of DNA and genetic anthropology is more familiar to many of us than a decade ago, and many of the ethical and privacy issues are more clearly understood by the global community.

For more information about the Genographic Project: https://genographic.nationalgeographic.com/genographic/index.html.

Impact

- Published 25 papers in leading scientific journals with more manuscripts in development.
- Approximately 500,000 indigenous and public participants from over 130 countries – around 420,000 kits have been sold so far.
- To date, granted over $1.5 million from kit sales to revitalisation and educational Legacy Fund projects around the world.
- Educational programme integrated via online lesson plans and swabbing events in universities and schools.
- E-newsletter subscriber base of 60,000+, annual global exhibits and speaking events.
- User-generated content – migration stories from the public make up part of *National Geographic*'s award-winning website.
- Widely seen as a genuinely successful, informative and 'real-time' scientific engagement initiative. Genographic continues into the next phase …

Lucie McNeil is a Vice President in National Geographic's Explorer Programs and Strategic Initiatives, based in Washington, DC. She began her career in communications as a student in the first year of Leeds Metropolitan University's four-year public relations degree, graduating to work in the British government as a media advisor for various departments including the Prime Minister's, and later as Director of News and Public Affairs at Harvard University.

READING POINT

For those working internationally, management literature provides some good overviews of different cultural considerations. Jandt's 6th edition of *An Introduction to Intercultural Communication* (SAGE, 2009) is a good place to start. *Management across Cultures: Challenges and Strategies* by Steers, Sánchez-Runde and Nardon (Cambridge University Press, 2010) sets out some general themes which global organisations need to deal with and suggests some strategies for cross-cultural communication. Moss, Powell and DeSanto (Routledge, 2010) offer descriptions of a variety of PR campaigns in *Public Relations Cases*.

In their 2010 lecture to the PRSA International Conference, James and Larissa Grunig put forward a suggestion that there should be generic principles of public relations which would apply internationally, and specific applications which would then be carried out by people familiar with the local culture. They felt that the financial problems of the West had pushed sustainability up the agenda, and that this had increased the need for PR to be a strategic management functions in organisations (PRSA, 2010). Read more about corporate social responsibility in Chapter 14 of this Toolkit.

ACTION POINT

CHINA: THE 'NEW FRONTIER' OF PR?

Wilcox (2006) called China the 'new frontier' of PR due to the fact that the industry is growing rapidly there. Other writers have also looked at the Chinese cultural context for the practice of PR. Chen (2013) looked at the concept of *guanxi* and the importance that the Chinese place on a network of relationships. The 'human touch' is very important in Chinese society. However, she found that the purpose of PR here is often likened to high level receptionists entertaining guests, or using young women to sell products. There is some awareness of how PR is related to advertising and marketing, but generally the emphasis is on persuasion.

Wilson (2016) suggests that the Communist Party of China (CPC) still operates from the belief that 'the best way to control people is to maintain an iron grip on the flow of communication'. This is not that far from Bernays' belief that the elite manufacture consent.

One of the main issues is the state control of the media. There is no tradition of investigative journalism and official newspapers present news from the CPC point of view. Dantz (2015) notes that there are independent papers which are more consumer driven. She adds that many journalists are inexperienced and so appreciate traditional press conferences to gather information. On the other hand, because of the growth of digital media, they struggle to keep up with the pace of content delivery. This can result in press releases being published verbatim if they are from respected sources. PR practitioners are unlikely to have a background in journalism, as 80 per cent have not worked in the media.

Waddington (2015) counters that social media platforms in China are more advanced than those in Europe and the US, with new entrant Weixin combining elements of Instagram and Snapchat to attract over 600 million active users. In addition, QQ is the largest network, the third largest in the world, and Weibo, a mix of Facebook and Twitter, also with 600 million users. Whilst some sites are censored, such as Facebook, Google, Instagram and Twitter, others like LinkedIn, Amazon, WhatsApp and Wikipedia are not.

Mellalieu agrees. He says: 'One of the reasons why the digital scene in China is so vibrant is exactly because people know that print/broadcast is controlled. There are much higher levels of participation in social media in China than in virtually any other country in the world. China is changing – fast' (personal email communication, 2016).

As the largest media landscape in the world, with 2,200 newspapers, 9,000 magazines, 2,000 radio stations and 3,000 TV stations (Dantz, 2015), along with the online platforms mentioned above, China offers plenty of opportunities for PR practitioners.

The following campaign shows how taking account of cultural considerations in China and skilful use of social media can produce great results.

ACTION POINT

HAPPISTACHIO NEW YEAR

China is crazy about nuts. Chinese eat more nuts than anyone else on earth, thanks to a fast-growing middle class with a healthy appetite for nutritious foods. So, in a nation of nut lovers, how difficult could it be to raise brand awareness of the California pistachio brand, Wonderful? The brand had an appealing name, but it was up against two better-known nuts on the snack menu of Chinese New Year – walnuts and chestnuts, cheaper must-haves that comprised 93 per cent of all nuts consumed in China. Ketchum set out to drive sales by breaking Wonderful pistachios from the pack. The Chinese name for the pistachio, *kaixinguo*, literally means 'happy nut', because its split shell resembles a smile. A nut named 'happy' would be a winning proposition.

For clients Cal Pure Produce Inc, Ketchum sought to position California as the source of the best tasting pistachios and Wonderful pistachios as the must-have healthy snack to increase sales over the critical Chinese New Year festive season. This is one of the major holidays of the year and a time for tradition and family togetherness. Mums over the age of 30 manage the family's groceries and are willing to enlarge the menu of must-have holiday snacks. Eating better is a major goal of the country's growing middle class. The benefits of tree nuts to the heart, brain and kidneys are well-promoted, but mums are more easily convinced by recommendations from friends than nutritionists.

Taking advantage of the name 'happy nut', Ketchum aimed to give Wonderful pistachios a happy place in the cultural life of China by associating the brand with traditional Chinese New Year rituals. There was an opportunity to zero in on tension-filled moments at festive family gatherings when young adults are badgered by their well-meaning older relatives with questions about their love life and when they are going to get married. So-called 'push for marriage' (*cui hun* or 催婚) questions at family gatherings are a well-recognised slice of family life that horrify young men and women across China. To break through the promotional holiday clutter, however, the idea had to be powerful, bold, fun and targeted.

Family gatherings, sending festive greetings, and having your fortune told for the year ahead all feature traditionally at Chinese New Year. An integrated two-month campaign was created, geared for maximum visibility and impact. The video 'Happy Nuts and the Single Girls' (http://v.qq.com/boke/page/n/0/b/n0182mlfwfb.html) presented California pistachios as the secret weapon of two bachelorettes who are being tortured by 'push for marriage' questions from relatives. The flavour and the fun of cracking open shells of the happy nut are the perfect distraction that transports them to the Californian sunshine and puts a smile back on their faces. Partnerships with four social media Key Opinion Leaders (KOLs) were formed to share tailored posts and the video was posted on WeChat and Weibo to drive clicks.

A dozen seasonal California pistachio emoji social media stickers were created featuring popular Chinese New Year phrases for consumers to save and share over the festive season. They were published on the brand's official Weibo account and leveraged KOLs' platforms to spread the word. A pistachio-themed HTML 5 fortune-telling game was launched on the Weibo platform of Uncle Tongdao, an astrologer with 4 million followers. Content integrated California pistachios and astrological signs, and encouraged gamers to play. Gamers were then guided to the Wonderful brand on the WeChat platform of Yihaodian, a popular online grocer.

To push sales on e-commerce platforms Yihaodian and also Tmall, 17 KOLs popular with young mums were engaged to spread the word about Wonderful products on social media feeds. Teaser posts in different formats included creative long stories, comics, entertainment gossip and other hot social topics with links to the e-commerce sites. A healthy New Year grocery shopping storyline was used in a paid placement on *36.7 °C*, one of the most popular TV programmes on healthcare among middle-aged women in China. The Director of the Department of Clinical Nutrition was invited to explain the health benefits of California pistachios alongside other nut categories to help position California pistachios as a must-have snack during Chinese New Year. Earned media coverage was secured using two light-hearted and humorous feature article pitches and supporting creative images targeting mainstream media.

Results

In just 14 days (16–31 January 2016), the campaign drove nearly a half-billion impressions, 25 million page views – and a 300 per cent increase in sales over the previous year. In addition: the video went viral, reaching 11.8 million viewers, receiving 2.8 million clicks and leading to 8,374 interactions in just five days. The emoji series garnered 10 million in social media reach and over 4.5 million views. Through the support of only one social media star, the HTML 5 game was played over 23,000 times and drove nearly 18,000 consumers to the online shopping link, a 75 per cent conversion rate.

The e-commerce push led to over 25 million page views and nearly 170,000 engagements. One of the posts ranked among both the list of 'hot search content' and 'recommended content' – ahead of Chinese celebrity posts – within one hour on the Sina Weibo platform. Over 30 earned feature placements were generated from influential portals such as Sohu and Sina to lifestyle guides including iWeekly and iLady. Audience reach was 424 million. With the correct choice of programme and strong preparation of the programme script the segment on *36.7 °C* reached 885,100 households, 75 per cent higher than the programme's average viewership.

With thanks to Stephen Waddington, Chief Engagement Officer, Ketchum.

END POINT

Again we have seen that there is no one size fits all to working in international public relations. The various models of cultural awareness can help to understand why messages may be misconstrued when operating in different cultures. As more research into different ways of doing public relations in different countries is carried out and published, a fuller picture will be revealed. Organisations will need to deal with the emerging international markets to stay competitive in the global economy.

CHAPTER 16

Digital public relations

Heather Yaxley

This chapter offers a technological perspective of public relations and how practitioners can keep ahead of digital developments from a personal and organisational perspective.

CHECK POINT

At the end of this chapter, you will be able to:

- Engage with digital technological developments as an individual PR practitioner and on behalf of organisations
- Understand the implications of emerging technological developments for public relations as an occupation.

There are several ways of examining digital public relations and many of these are threaded throughout this book. Here we consider how PR practitioners learn about the latest developments and how digital technology affects PR practice, the organisations they work for and wider society.

DIGITAL PUBLIC RELATIONS IS NOT NEW

The technologies, practices and concepts underpinning this aspect of public relations have developed over several decades. However, Watson (2015: 1) argues that the majority of practitioners have failed 'to appreciate the benefits of technical advances in communication and held doggedly to print-based models of mediated communication'.

Developments are absorbed into practice over time by 'cautious sense-makers' being influenced by early adopters who advocate for change and create niche specialisms within the field (Yaxley, 2016: 455). Ease of adoption is important, with Eyrich *et al.* (2008: 413) observing that PR practitioners have been 'slower to integrate more technologically complicated tools' into their work.

Familiarity with technologies, particularly through use of mobile devices, has normalised use of certain tools and social media channels in public relations practice. Grunig (2009: 1) warns that:

> many practitioners are using the new media in the same ways they used the old – as a means of dumping messages on the general population rather than as a strategic means of interacting with publics and bringing information from the environment into organisational decision-making.

This suggests that digital PR is focused on everyday delivery of multimedia information within a 24/7 global online communications environment rather than realising its broader potential.

One perceived barrier in engaging with technology is age (Prensky, 2001). Kitchen and Panopoulos (2010: 226) suggest that organisations may fail to develop the skills of more experienced PR practitioners in favour of employing 'young well-informed, technologically sophisticated professionals'. The distinction proposed by Prensky (2001) between digital natives and digital immigrants (the former having grown up in a digital age) is arguably no longer helpful. Whilst those starting their careers today are competent in using social media and other technologies, they need to learn how to apply their skills and knowledge within a professional public relations context. In contrast, older practitioners have developed competencies through training and assimilating technologies into their work.

A more useful concept is that of the 'digital natural' conceived by Åkerström and Young (2013) to indicate 'individuals who are comfortable in an online environment, equipped through experience and exposure to both its cultural norms and the technological competencies required to operate effectively'. This concept avoids Prensky's binary division and acknowledges how 'nearly everyone has some digital competence' as we are able to use 'an array of online tools in our daily lives, even if few of us are completely comfortable in this new environment' (ibid.).

Likewise, most organisations have adopted digital technologies and established an online and social media presence to some extent. This is not to say that they have all done so enthusiastically or with a commitment to integrating existing and emerging technologies as part of normal organisational practice. Those who equate management with control are likely to perceive technological developments as a threat rather than as an opportunity for enhancing organisational communications and relationship building. They may view the immediacy and interconnectedness of mobile, online and social media as problematic, particularly as mistakes and misunderstandings can be exposed in the glass box of online communications where everything can potentially be accessed, and shared, by anyone.

The open, multifaceted system of online communications challenges a simple linear model of transmitting messages from sender to receiver. Instead, information is exchanged, and even jointly constructed in real time within networks of participants. Duhé (2007: 57) envisages this online environment as a 'conduit for transparency and complexity' that necessitates a flexibility of response that she believes resonates with PR practitioners.

DIGITAL PR STRATEGIES

The continuing evolution of new technologies affects PR practitioners as much as organisations. Theaker (2007) viewed competency with new technology as a requirement for everyone working in PR and today we expect anyone to be able to easily 'add, change and share content with others' (Phillips and Young, 2009: 103). The question is how individuals and organisations should best identify, assess and assimilate emerging technologies into their digital PR strategies.

Personal adoption strategies

Rogers' diffusion process provides a useful framework for considering adoption of emerging online technologies by PR practitioners. Diffusion is 'the process by which an innovation is communicated through certain channels over time among the members of a social system' (Rogers, 2003: 11).

Five types of adopter (innovators, early adopters, early majority, late majority, laggards) can be considered in relation to PR practitioners' engagement with emerging digital technologies. Innovators welcome change and engage with others at the leading edge of technological developments. Monitoring innovators is useful in keeping up to date with the latest technologies and their relevance for organisations and PR practice.

Early adopters tend to be more influential than innovators. They adopt technologies once they have been tested and proven of value. Early adopters promote technologies by writing articles in trade media, advocating through PR networks (professional bodies and so forth), running training courses and demonstrating the value and ease of adoption. This opinion leader strategy has benefits of credibility, influence and the potential rewards of enhanced reputation and business opportunities.

The early majority of users recognise advantages of specific developments but need them to have been widely reported and made simple to use. As discussed above, this category seems to apply to assimilation of technologies within public relations. Once adoption becomes normal practice, the late majority follows, either voluntarily or by force of expectation. Those who do not adopt common technologies (laggards) may be in denial over the benefits of such developments, or they may lack the knowledge, skills or resources to use them.

TALKING POINT

There are two key aspects of technological developments: underlying principles and emerging tools and techniques.

UNDERLYING PRINCIPLES

In 1999, publication of the Cluetrain Manifesto (www.cluetrain.com/book/) offered a series of theses setting out how the internet challenged traditional mass communications. The essential argument is summarised in the statement that:

> A powerful global conversation has begun. Through the Internet, people are discovering and inventing new ways to share relevant knowledge with blinding speed. As a direct result, markets are getting smarter – and getting smarter faster than most companies.
>
> (Levine *et al*., 2009: xiii)

Searles and Weinberger revisited the seminal text in 2015 with the addition of New Clues (http://newclues.cluetrain.com). They warn that many organisations have failed to understand the potential of the internet, whilst others see it as 'theirs to plunder, extracting our data and money from it'. They argue that people have been apathetic to how institutions are transforming the internet and call for greater recognition of its power for 'connection without permission' where people 'can make of it whatever we want'.

Initially innovators saw the internet as a place for 'fostering conversation and connection between people' (Levine *et al*., 2009: 25). Those who followed tended to seek the 'commercialization of cyberspace' (Curran and Seaton, 2003: 235) and reflected the 'aggressive, competitive, hyperbolic, selling mind-set' of marketing (Hutton, 2010: 510).

Discuss with others the principles on which online communications were founded and consider how these have been affected by greater commercialisation, attempts to control conversations, development of apps, growth of major social networks and concerns about privacy and security.

DEVELOPMENT OF TOOLS AND TECHNIQUES

There are many useful sites that have tracked technological changes over time and provide insight into trends. For example, Fred Cavazza (https:// fredcavazza.net) has considered developments and offered predictions for over a decade. (Note this site is written in French – you can translate it using the Google Chrome browser.)

Specifically looking at how developments affect public relations are the PR Stack crowd-sourcing initiative (https://prstack.co/) and the Prezly guide into PR Software (www.prezly.com/pr-software). Whilst aiming to help PR practitioners improve their workflow practices, unless these sites are updated, their value soon diminishes.

Review your own approach to keeping up to date with latest developments. What online resources do you use and find most helpful? How does your approach compare with that employed by friends and colleagues?

Emerging technologies may require adaption or disruption of traditional PR practice, necessitating a continuous, long-term process of adoption (Kitchen and Panopoulos, 2010). Practices that start as innovative eventually become the norm. This means that, whilst organisations may initially offer training in new technologies, it is not long before competency is an expectation of all practitioners.

This highlights two key areas where practitioners need to develop personal digital PR strategies in relation to technological developments:

1   Willingness to identify and adopt emerging technologies for professional digital PR purposes as innovators, early adopters or early majority practitioners.

2   Develop learning strategies to enhance technological competencies within a framework of professional development and career planning.

Learning strategies

Regardless of their knowledge and experience of existing and new technologies, PR practitioners face a continuous need to learn about the latest developments and their impact on practice. Heads of PR teams also need to create a proactive learning culture that helps to attract and retain talented PR practitioners who are capable of adapting to the changing communications environment. This 'middleness' position underlines the importance of investing in sustainable professional development that connects existing digital PR competencies to new skills and abilities through effective ways of learning.

Developing self-efficacy ('the conviction that one can successfully execute the behavior required to produce the outcome', Bandura, 1977: 79) is particularly relevant for anyone who may lack confidence in understanding, utilising or managing emerging digital technologies.

Gangadharbatla (2008) identifies internet self-efficacy as a key factor in influencing the adoption of social networking, alongside a need to belong and collective self-esteem. Communities of practice (Wenger and Snyder, 2000) within offline and social networks enable practitioners to share experiences and engage in debate about technologies. However, without the initial confidence or skill to join such communities, practitioners may not be in a position to benefit from this peer-group learning.

ACTION POINT

PR-PRAXIS PROFESSIONAL DEVELOPMENT FRAMEWORK (YAXLEY, 2015)

Proactive management of professional development helps to ensure effective and sustainable performance in digital public relations. Yaxley (2015) proposes a *PR-Praxis Professional Development Framework* (PDF) comprising six elements (that form the acronym PRAISE):

- Professional development needs (of individuals and teams)
- Review processes that monitor continuous and incremental learning
- A proactive learning culture and community of practice
- Identification of available and suitable developmental strategies
- Specific learning objectives, responsibilities and expectations
- Evidence of performance improvements to support career progression.

This framework offers a cyclical approach that helps PR managers to develop a learning culture and supports individuals' continuous learning. It encourages personal and organisational adoption of a practical *Professional Development Programme* (PDP). This involves establishing an evidence-base for professional development that helps to justify investment in learning about new areas of digital public relations practice and improving competencies.

The PDP's starting point is a one-page professional development résumé as a useful statement of learning intent for any individual, team or project (see Appendix). This acts as a snapshot of the current position, intended outcome(s), learning methods to be adopted, and milestones for determining progress.

SMART objectives and learning outcomes (LOs) set in relation to key performance indicators (KPIs) or competencies support assessment of learning. The Global Alliance is developing a Global Capabilities Framework for public relations that includes a detailed list of knowledge, skills, abilities and behaviours (KSABs) that practitioners may find helpful in identifying potential areas of improvement (see www.globalalliancepr.org/ capabilitiesframeworks/).

Five levels of evaluation of the effectiveness of learning are proposed from the work of Kirkpatrick (2007) and Phillips (2011):

Level 1: Reaction – engagement, relevance and satisfaction with learning experiences, perceived achievement of LOs, anticipated change

Level 2: Learning – change in knowledge, skills, attitude, confidence and commitment resulting from the learning experience (immediately and through later reflection)

Level 3: Behaviour – application of learning in practice (on-the-job) that can be monitored, reinforced, rewarded, and encouraged

Level 4: Results – tangible and intangible benefits resulting from change including leading KPIs and desired LOs

Level 5: Return on Investment – calculation of the efficiency and effectiveness of devoting resources to the particular learning activities.

A template learning evaluation sheet and cost–benefit analysis is provided in the Appendix.

The PDF provides a robust planning approach. As well as supporting long-term, strategic and sustainable learning, it is able to integrate participative, iterative, agile and reflective learning using the Dynamic Planning Model discussed in Part II of this book.

Learning should not be considered solely for its immediate work-related benefits. Indeed, Jarvis (2007: 100) observes an 'overlap' between vocational and non-vocational life-long learning whereby 'non-vocational learning may have beneficial results in the work situation and learning in the work-place may also serve a non-vocational learning function'.

Using the set of professional learning and development documents included in the Appendix undertake the following tasks:

- Set LOs and KPIs to improve your digital public relations competence
- Identify suitable learning activities and resources
- Map your personal professional development programme.

Professional development of digital public relations competencies is an immersive process. For example, Noor Al-Deen and Hendricks (2011: 133) clarify that 'social media provides the opportunity to interact with and contribute to the knowledge being created and disseminated'. This offers the advantage of learning within the environment being studied, which could be beneficial to those practitioners familiar with technologies, but not necessarily how they can be used within a professional PR context. However, when such participation takes place in a live situation any errors would be public and could potentially be open to criticism of the organisation as well as the individual practitioner.

Nevertheless, it is useful to develop technological skills by gaining hands-on experience. This could, for example, be through personal use, although Bridgen (2011) warns of the potential dangers of blurring professional and personal identities online. Another option could be to undertake volunteer work with a local not-for-profit organisation to gain experience and hone skills.

As well as self-efficacy and peer-group support, practitioners can draw on a range of texts and courses or work with experts to adopt technological advances. These learning strategies tend to be more appropriate for those who are early-to-late majority adopters of new technology, with innovators preferring to experiment and learn by doing.

A number of professional development approaches, activities and resources are indicated in the Appendix. Regardless of which learning methods are adopted, practitioners are advised to plan their learning within the PR-Praxis Professional Development Framework discussed above (Yaxley, 2015).

Professional development should be documented within a paper-based or digital learning diary to encourage reflection on experiences as well as recording skills and knowledge development. Many employers and professional bodies (such as CIPR) offer an opportunity to record learning progress through appraisals or professional development schemes. A checklist to help find or set up such an initiative is included in the Appendix.

Organisational strategies

According to the Office of National Statistics, home access to the internet has increased from 9 per cent of households in 1998 to 89 per cent in 2016. Over 40 million adults (82 per cent of the population) use the internet every day, with mobile/smart phones being the most popular device. In 2016 one in five adults used smart televisions and other devices (such as games players, e-book readers or smartwatches) to connect to the internet.

Understanding how and why publics and stakeholders access online data is a key consideration for effective digital public relations. Objectives and strategies should be developed in conjunction with other functions in an organisation. Individual functions will have their own requirements for using digital technologies but it is important to ensure that an integrated approach is taken to consider impact on internal and external stakeholders and publics.

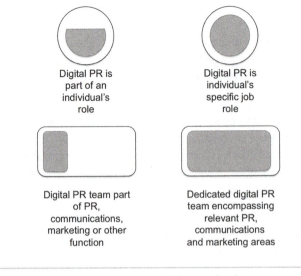

FIGURE 16.1 Model of options for digital PR within organisations

Public relations practitioners also need to be involved in an organisation's crisis management plans to anticipate and react in the event of issues that are caused by, or affect, technological operations (see Chapter 13).

In respect of how digital and technological competencies are deployed within the organisation and specifically the PR function, there are many possible options. The choice of which to adopt depends on factors such as the size and nature of the organisation, the role and size of the PR function and the competencies of team members. Possible options are indicated in Figure 16.1. In addition, digital PR may be outsourced to agencies or independent practitioners.

Looking specifically at social media teams, a survey by Altimeter (2011) of 144 global US corporations with over 1,000 employees revealed that they employed an average of 11 people within their primarily cross-functional, social media team. In contrast, Go-Gulf (2012) indicated that in 42 per cent of organisations a single person works on social media whilst just 9 per cent had teams comprising six or more staff.

Further Go-Gulf (2012) noted that only 27 per cent of organisations have a dedicated social media team, with 3 per cent outsourcing social media activities and 5 per cent using both internal and external teams. The majority (65 per cent) assigned social media tasks to individuals on top of their current job responsibilities. Grunig and Grunig (2010) argued against creating a specialist function, while Altimeter (2011) believed a core team is required for coordination purposes, although its form will change going forwards.

Three-quarters of organisations are reported by Go-Gulf (2012) as preferring to employ those with communication or public relations degrees to work on social media. It should be noted, however, that these data derived from a Ragan.com survey and may therefore bias these disciplines in the research population. Given the speed and nature of digital technology development in recent years, the validity today of such statistics is questionable. Indeed, finding accurate information is difficult and often seems to reflect the focus of those undertaking the research.

Despite considerable discussion of the need for organisations to develop a social media – or digital PR – strategy, there is a lack of clarity over what this may involve. One complication is the cross-functional nature of the online environment and determining the optimum approach for individual organisations. Yaxley (2012a: 417) argues that 'a holistic organisational approach enables a wide range of perspectives and skills to be involved in the process and ensures greater support for the resulting strategy'.

As with any other strategy (see Part II), the starting point needs to be the overall purpose and aims of the organisation, and in turn, how its communications and PR strategies contribute towards achieving those objectives. Organisations should also consider their adoption strategy (as above), with use of technologies diffusing at different rates within individual countries and sectors.

Given the dynamic nature of digital PR and the technological environment, this chapter does not detail how to set up and use specific existing and emerging technologies. Instead, it is recommended to monitor websites such as MIT Technology Review (www.technologyreview.com/) and identify innovators in social media channels for particular areas of interest. Additionally, guidance is offered in the online help centres for individual technologies concerning any updates. Some organisations also offer online training such as Facebook with its Blueprint e-learning courses: www.facebook.com/blueprint.

Likewise, any attempt to present 'best practice' would be fraught with dangers as accepted behaviour online is subject to change and interpretation. For example, the mantra of openness and engagement can be countered by examples of when keeping silent and allowing an issue to quietly dispel is a better approach.

IMPLICATIONS OF EMERGING TECHNOLOGICAL DEVELOPMENTS

Although it is difficult to predict the future, the implications for public relations have been considered in respect of the following aspects of technological development.

Multimedia and specialist competencies

Creativity and collaboration are important competencies 'developed by tech-savvy learners in the Digital Age' (Sanabria and Arámburo-Lizárraga, 2017: 487). This can be seen in public relations where there is an ongoing need for practitioners to be competent in technologies that support engaging multimedia communications. However, their involvement extends beyond the skills involved in creating copy, graphics, images, augmented-reality experiences, live-stream and recorded video and audio communications. Essential knowledge encompasses regulatory frameworks, ethical behaviours, cultural impacts as well as the privacy and security matters that are involved in creating and curating technological content.

Such implications for public relations need to be examined as a result of technologies that are increasing media and channel convergence in addition to enabling greater interactivity with and between publics. This includes the co-creation of multimedia, multi-channel materials and the concept of transmedia storytelling.

Transmedia storytelling crosses over multiple channels of communication and types of media. It has a rhizomatic nature, being multidirectional, fragmented, interconnected and incomplete. Thanks to search engines, algorithms and shared content we are most likely to encounter a story in its middleness rather than where it began. Whether or not it has an ending may currently be unknown. The vast archive of information readily accessible online offers knots of past/present/futuredness where dimensions of time, place and human agency are intertwined and offer numerous entry points and future directions to explore a story.

Drawing on the language of music, transmedia storytelling is polyphonic. Simultaneous variation in voices, narrative, tone, interpretation, content and technique have the potential to create layers of complexity within the story being told. Those who are fully engaged will follow the story and the texture that develops in understanding through their personal exploration and possible participation. Others will rely on the partial impression gained from their exposure to part of the story.

Consequently public relations practitioners need to understand how to craft, monitor and support these varying forms of storytelling and ways of accessing them. There will be multiple opportunities to contribute and participate (rather than simply to construct, disseminate and control) the story and how it is encountered.

Aspects of the story may be told in the form of news, feature articles, editorial opinion or thought leadership. It may be shared as information, education, marketing, gamification or entertainment. It may combine elements of paid (bought and sold), owned, shared, earned and hijacked media. It may spread through forum debate, social media sharing or automation through algorithms. It may also extend offline including through word of mouth communications. Some aspects may need intervention to correct misinformation, stimulate additional interest or slow down momentum. Individuals and groups (both publics and stakeholders) may act as advocates and support the organisation's perspective through positive contributions. Or they may provide input that could be perceived as criticism or activism. Positions may change through engagement with others (including media and influencers) or direct with the organisation.

Transmedia storytelling offers an opportunity to extend the reach of public relations narratives using multimedia content, knowledge of multiple channels of communication and the networked behaviour of online individuals and communities.

The intention is to craft a coherent story that uses multiple media types and channels, but allowance should be made for multiple access points and how that story can be retold and reinterpreted by others.

Specialist competencies are required to execute multimedia communications and transmedia storytelling. Expertise may be found within the organisation or externally. Moreover, PR practitioners are required to act as the orchestral conductor or film producer and bring together all the required specialisms. They need to be multimedia literate in order to produce briefs and manage holistic, integrated communications and relationship building programmes.

Automated, embedded and intelligent communication technologies

Yaxley (2016) discusses a range of technological developments that are enhancing access to, and participation in, digital communications. In particular, assistive technology (Wendt and Lloyd, 2011) is supporting people with disabilities with low-cost and accessible devices and appliances. These feature integral technologies as well as applications and software.

Additionally, the concept of the Internet of Things (IoT) indicates how a wide array of objects utilise embedded technologies. Beyond the estimated 25 billion objects already connected online worldwide (anticipated to rise to 50 billion by 2020; CISCO, 2011), and developments in wearable devices and interconnected vehicles, the Internet of Things – also known as the Internet of Everything – is being applied to wider societal infrastructure, for example, in health, transport and energy.

Looking forwards blockchain technologies will be connected to IoT. The concept of blockchain relates to secure and trusted database technology. The blockchain is defined as a distributed ledger (Government Office for Science, 2016) or record of data that can be 'shared across a network of multiple sites, geographies or institutions' (p. 5). Whilst each network participant has their own identical copy of the ledger, if any changes are made in one record, all other copies are updated almost immediately (subject to the agreement established between all participants). The content is encrypted and so its accuracy and security can be ensured.

The blockchain is best known through the peer-to-peer virtual currency Bitcoin, but its use has been extended to other forms of assets including communications that can be secured with smart contracts, digital signatures and other emerging tools.

Blockchains are underpinned by algorithmic technologies that help ledgers accommodate a wide range of transactions. The technology is being adopted within public services such as taxation and healthcare. They are also used in the commercial sector to verify the identity of goods and intellectual property. This is a new area of development and its potential for public relations and the organisations that practitioners work with it is underexplored. For more information see: http://blockchain.open.ac.uk.

The Internet of Things, blockchains and algorithmic technologies are increasing automating processes and services. Their impact on communications and wider society is a matter that needs greater investigation by PR practitioners and academics. Increasingly technology itself is communicating with publics.

We can see this with interactive voice response technologies (IVR) that use speech recognition to enable people to interact with computers verbally. Auditory interfaces are found in a range of devices (such as smart cities, homes, cars and communications devices). As well as responding to human voice instructions, the devices verbalise feedback on human behaviour and their surroundings. For example, car companies are developing technologies that can automatically gather information and advise car drivers of road hazards such as potholes. It is not a great leap to consider the wider PR implications of such technologies for hyperlocalised communications. Conceivably such information could be conveyed autonomously or as news reports or briefings to politicians as part of a campaign to call for greater investment in road repairs.

Similarly, a human–computer interface is evident in facial and image recognition software. This is already relevant for public relations communications in respect of images that can be interpreted through content recognition software. For example, technology can already describe images to the millions of people with visual impairments. Likewise, machine-learning algorithms can also be used to scan video footage and blur out faces to protect individuals' identities where their permission for inclusion has not been possible to obtain.

A wider issue concerning technology is the potential for unforeseen consequences that affect public debate and may cause issues or crisis situations. For example, Koerber (2000: 68) notes how visualisation technologies have altered debates around abortion and consumption of alcohol during pregnancy by enabling clearer foetal scans. Similarly, issues around pornography, stalking and cyber-bullying raise questions around anticipated equality within the online public sphere created by social media and other technologies.

This discussion illustrates the need for much greater understanding of how emerging technologies affect PR practice and particularly the implications for communications, relationship building and issues concerning societal responsibilities. See David Phillips' blogsite (http://leverwealth.blogspot.co.uk) where he is exploring such issues and developments.

Technology and contemporary careers

The PR census (Gorkana, 2011) emphasised the long-hours working culture of public relations. Social media use has further blurred personal and professional boundaries (Bridgen, 2011), meaning that practitioners could be viewed as working 24/7. Mobile phone technology increases the expectations and pressures to respond to email, phone calls and social media updates round the clock. At present, engagement 'out of hours' seems to be mainly voluntary, but this will need to be addressed by policies that either formally recognise a need for a 24/7 PR function or establish regulations regarding expectations on engagement.

The ability to work at any time and place illustrates the flexibility inherent in recent career concepts that emphasise boundaryless, protean and multidirectional patterns. These view the individual as a 'free agent' (Baruch, 2004: 70) rather than an employee who is tied to any one particular organisation or career path. A boundaryless career is one that offers 'mobility across physical and psychological boundaries' (Sullivan and Arthur, 2006: 20). This is evident in public relations work where there are few barriers to making career moves. Career independence is evident in the protean concept first used by Hall (2004: 1) in 1976 to reflect self-determined 'career orientation'. Baruch (2004: 58) argues that these trends encourage a multidirectional pattern of careers, whereby people may take 'a sideway move, change of direction, of organization or inspiration'.

Technology supports such flexibility within employment in public relations. The use of mobile phones and personal computers make it easy for practitioners to manage a 'work portfolio' (Handy, 1989: 146) comprising salaried or independent assignments alongside non-paid work (including leisure, family commitments, education, business development or volunteerism). This 'fragmented' (Inkson, 2007: 142) perspective of careers is under-examined in relation to public relations.

Likewise, Mainiero and Sullivan (2005: 108) suggest a kaleidoscopic model for women who face 'career interruptions, employment gaps, top-outs, opt-outs' and have long reflected a boundaryless approach to careers 'out of necessity'. Again technology supports the need for women to purposefully 'blend their work and nonwork lives' (Mainiero and Sullivan, 2005: 111). This may facilitate independence but could also be seen as encroachment of working time into personal lives.

More specifically, disruptive technological developments open up new career opportunities for entrepreneurial PR practitioners as specialisms can be created within the occupation. At the same time, some aspects of existing PR practice will disappear. This is already happening in professions such as law and accountancy where automation can manage routine processes more efficiently and effectively than people.

Further, digital technology enhances geographic mobility and is evident in the concept originated by Makimoto and Manners (1997) of a digital nomad. This can be seen in Bridgen's (2011) observation that social media enable remote working by public relations practitioners. Likewise technology has driven the growing trend for public or other co-working spaces (Hickey, 2015) that support the nomadic PR practitioner. Here the focus primarily relates to working practices, rather than how digital technologies open up new career paths and opportunities.

The use of technology enables individual PR practitioners to develop career paths working within virtual teams. They may be employed or contracted by organisations or agencies or work more independently. One potential issue of this position is that the

PR practitioner becomes invisible within a 'gig economy', employed only when working on specific projects.

One further consideration is how adoption of technology means that PR practitioners may find themselves undertaking an increasing amount of shadow work (Lambert, 2015) that involves unpaid tasks that may previously have been the responsibility of support personnel or offer potential for career development purposes (such as blogging or participating in crowd-sourced initiatives).

There are a lot of issues created by increased technology concerning the nature of work in public relations, how it is executed and the implications for careers in the field. These are largely unexplored but are likely to present increasing and new challenges or opportunities as technological developments continue to affect public relations practice.

END POINT

PR practitioners need to consider whether they, and the organisations they work with, require strategies to engage with digital technologies as innovators, early adopters or early majority users. There are risks and benefits associated with early involvement. Self-efficacy and communities of practice are recommended as ways for individuals to improve their knowledge and skills in social media.

The PR-Praxis Professional Development Framework is proposed as a model for developing sustainable learning cultures within organisations and supporting individuals in enhancing their digital PR skills.

The wider implications of technological developments suggest the need for PR practitioners to gain multimedia and specialist competencies and be capable of managing increasingly complex projects and transmedia storytelling.

Additionally, automated, embedded and intelligent communication technologies will undoubtedly affect PR practice, organisational communications, relationship building and wider society. Further, technology has a notable impact on the way that PR practitioners work and build their careers.

These areas are under-researched currently and it is important that public relations practice and academia addresses the tendency for the occupation to be slow in recognising the benefits and addressing the implications of technological advances.

Part IV

Stakeholder engagement

Introduction

Alison Theaker

This final Part looks at different sectors of public relations. The chapters look at different stakeholder groups and show the different ways of engaging with an organisation's stakeholders, with insights from a variety of practitioners working in the field.

A 'stakeholder' is a more specific term than a 'public', but both are hard to define. Publics tend to relate to issues. They grow up around issues of concern, such as wanting to be more 'green' in how they choose products, parents' groups and consumer activists. The same person may be a member of several publics. Grunig and Hunt (1984: 160) define four kinds of publics:

- publics active on all issues;
- publics apathetic on all issues;
- publics active only on an issue or small number of issues that involve nearly everyone in the population;
- publics active only on a single issue.

Stakeholders are essentially anyone who can affect or be affected by an organisation. Burkitt and Ashton (in Wood, 2012: 113) explain that 'many interest groups may be said to have a "stake" in certain activities … these stakes should be recognised by those whose actions impinge upon them'. The concept of stakeholders was taken to heart by the New Labour government in the UK. Rather than simply focusing on shareholders, businesses were encouraged and in some ways forced to have concern for other groups in society, such as their community, employees, competitors, the media, customers and suppliers.

Sometimes, the two terms are used interchangeably, so how do we tell the difference? Grunig and Repper (1992: 124) suggest that 'Publics form when stakeholders recognise ... consequences (of the actions of an organisation) and organise to do something about it.' A 'public' seems to be distinguished by the recognition of a problem, although we can see from Grunig's own model above that some publics are deemed to be passive.

How are these concepts helpful to the practitioner? Rather than waiting for publics to form around issues, PR practitioners could be investigating and identifying stakeholders, and thinking ahead to how they may be affected by the organisation. Cornelissen (2008: 51–7) sets out ways of mapping different stakeholder groups, helping practitioners prioritise which groups should be communicated with. He goes on to distinguish whether awareness and understanding is the objective of these communications, or involvement and commitment. Awareness could be achieved by sending out newsletters, whereas involvement and commitment require consultation and collective problem-solving. This shows the development from stakeholder management to stakeholder collaboration, where it is more important to build long-term relationships.

Political relations provides an understanding of public affairs and government relations, for both those seeking to engage in the process and those working in it. Links between public affairs, the media and lobbying organisations are examined. Public opinion and the role of political bloggers are considered. Restrictions on those working in government and those targeting it are discussed alongside a debate on codes and regulation.

Financial and investor relations provides an overview of the role that financial PR plays in society and the nature of communications with key stakeholders and influencers. Some of the basic tools such as annual reports and shareholder meetings are set out. Finally how recent developments in this area to improve corporate governance have impacted on PR's role is considered.

Internal communications studies one of the most important groups of stakeholders. As well as examples of good practice in the field, this chapter covers the importance of good internal communications and the goals of employee communications. The qualities needed to be a good practitioner in this field are set out. Business to business provides an understanding of working with, and for, organisations where there is a focus on engaging other organisations as the primary public. Community relations sets out the activities which could be included in a good programme to engage with an organisation's neighbours and distinguishes it from cause-related marketing. Consumer PR gives an insight into working in one of the biggest sectors in PR, looking at working with the marketing function and the role of creativity in the face of ever-changing channels of communication.

CHAPTER 17

Political relations

Heather Yaxley

This chapter provides an understanding of political communications, public affairs and lobbying. It includes a particular focus on issues-related campaigns, monitoring public opinion and engaging with the political process. The implications of the cultural context of 'post-truth politics' are examined in relation to populist movements and professionalisation of political relations.

CHECK POINT

At the end of this chapter, you should be able to:

- Outline the purpose of political communications, public affairs and lobbying
- Understand approaches to initiate issues-related campaigns, monitor public opinion and engage with the political process
- Recognise implications of 'post-truth politics' on populist movements and the professionalisation of political relations.

POLITICAL COMMUNICATIONS AND PUBLIC AFFAIRS

Politics and governance in society

Getting to grips with the practice of political relations is complicated by the myriad of terms used and a lack of clarity in how these may be defined. Table 17.1 presents an

TABLE 17.1 Overview of politics within a society

Politics	
Activities undertaken by citizens, interest groups and organisations concerning disputed matters of public, private, altruistic and partisan interest in a society.	Activities undertaken by entities involved in making decisions concerning the governance of a society by use of policies, laws, norms, communication and behaviour.

Means of resolving disputes arising from interactions between citizens, interest groups, organisations and government institutions within a society.

Exercise and effect of **power**	Promotion and preservation of **values**

overview of politics in relation to governance in a society as a basis for understanding relevant concepts and the relationships between these.

Political relations can be understood as the interface between various citizens, interest groups and organisations in a society and entities that are established to manage the governance structure of that society.

Public involvement is essential, as explained by Dalton (2014) who writes that:

> Democracy should be a celebration by an involved public. People should be politically active because it's through public discussion, deliberation, and involvement that societal goals should be defined and carried out. Without public involvement in the process, democracy loses both its legitimacy and its guiding force.
> (Dalton, 2014: 37)

In most societies a range of goals, opinions, ideas, interests and issues are discussed and contested. Where disputes arise these might need to be resolved by referral to the society's governance framework that comprises an established set of norms, regulations and laws.

However, this framework may favour the political power base of certain sections of society whilst adversely affecting others. For example, historical and cultural restrictions on the right to vote signify who has political power. Since the late 19th century, political campaigns have been undertaken to seek electoral reform and extend voting rights on the basis of gender, race, class and age. As well as communicative activities, at times such power struggles have involved violence on the part of organisations, individuals, activist groups and the state.

The ability to use power to influence political decision-making privileges the interests of particular individuals, groups and organisations in a society. An alternative perspective on how political disputes are resolved can be seen as value-driven. From this position, pressure to change how society is governed indicates the importance of political ideology. For example, social justice campaigns that argue for equal rights in society reflect the idea that all individuals and groups within society should be treated with respect and fairness. In contrast, the ideology of neoliberalism favours concepts such as individualism, freedom and choice, with enlightened self-interest seen as driving social responsibility.

TALKING POINT

It is common for government bodies to work with non-governmental organisations (NGOs), charities and commercial concerns. For example, the UK government body the Food Standards Agency engages with a wide range of industry organisations, charities and other NGOs as part of its campaign to reduce salt consumption. This practice highlights how political access is more readily available to some organisations.

Similarly, the ability to employ specialist PR/public affairs advisers and deploy other means of direct political influence enables certain individuals and organisations to progress their particular interests. This means that less powerful members of society may struggle to get their voice heard, particularly if they lack resources or are not articulate, media savvy or conversant in political processes and procedures.

There are also concerns about ideological links in politics. For example, in the UK there are traditionally close ties between businesses and the Conservative party and unions and the Labour party. As well as sharing values, such relationships commonly involve financial support and privileged access that may present opportunities to influence policy decisions.

Are you aware of any examples of political discussion where power and values are evident in the positions taken by different participants? How is any conflict resolved in terms of influence on legislation and/or societal norms?

Political communications

In a democratic society, a *trias politica* model of government is common. This comprises three separate areas of governance: legislative, executive and judiciary. A wider perspective of government in the context of the UK would include entities such as devolved parliaments, central government departments, local authorities, directly elected officials (e.g. mayors and police and crime commissioners), public sector organisations (e.g. NHS, education establishments and emergency services), executive agencies and non-departmental government bodies.

These institutions have a legal and moral duty to 'inform the population and the media about policy decisions and issues affecting everyone in society' (Yeomans, 2009: 578). Lees-Marshment (2014: 2) observes that politicians and other political actors use 'marketing tools and concepts to understand, respond to, involve and communicate with their political market in order to achieve their goals'.

However, Lilleker and Jackson (2011: 167) contend that a political marketing approach concentrates primarily on 'gaining visibility through public relations activities' with a focus 'on media management and gaining hype by being "loud"' (p. 171). They favour a broader strategy for political PR that is based on building relationships (rather than attracting attention). This approach encompasses reputation management activities including: 'corporate image, community relations, issues management, crisis management, corporate social responsibility, investor relations, and lobbying' (Lilleker and Jackson 2011: 171). A similar multi-dimensional perspective is evident in McNair's (2011: 4) use of the term 'political communications'. His definition of 'purposeful communication about politics' (p. 4) includes:

- All forms of communication undertaken *by* politicians and other political actors for the purpose of achieving specific objectives.
- Communication addressed *to* these actors by non-politicians such as voters and newspaper columnists.
- Communication *about* these actors and their activities, as contained in news reports, editorials and other forms of media discussion of politics.

McNair (2011: 4) acknowledges that his focus omits 'interpersonal political communications' that occur in private. Such activities are an integral aspect of how organisations, individuals and interest groups seek to influence policies and engage in the political process. His concentration on 'political discourse' (p. 4) also ignores direct action movements and challenges to traditional forms of communications from networked and largely unregulated social media environments.

Public affairs

Moloney (2009) explains public affairs as an approach that enables organisations and groups to talk with each other and government, both publicly and privately, about public policy. From an organisational perspective (inside or outside of government), public affairs may be seen as a strategic function operating at 'the nexus of politics, management and communication whereby an organisation seeks to deal with external public policy challenges' (McGrath *et al.,* 2010: 336). Consequently, organisations need to appreciate the strategic relevance of relations with their political stakeholders, as well as the wider public context within which their policies are developed and implemented.

Attempts to shape politics date back centuries, with Ancient Greece acknowledged as pioneering the Western political tradition (Cartledge, 2009). Britain has a long history of successful political campaigning. For example, social reformists in the 18th century included the anti-slavery movement and Quakers such as Elizabeth Fry who campaigned to improve prison conditions. Organisations that are involved in influencing political decisions today include political parties, think tanks/advocacy organisations, trade unions and professional bodies, consumer and grassroots groups, interest groups (who lobby on particular topics or causes), religious bodies, charities, non-governmental organisations (NGOs), universities/academics and activist/pressure groups.

Within government, political decisions are influenced by other parts of government. This may involve communications where common goals and joint initiatives are involved (see Chapter 20). However, there has been some concern regarding public sector bodies seeking to lobby central government. Similarly, criticism has led to legislative restrictions on the ability of charities and trade unions to engage in political activity. Nevertheless a dialogic process remains legitimate within civil society and may be a more effective practice than top-down communications throughout government and the wider public sector.

Moreover, government and public sector communicators increasingly work in partnership with each other and counterparts in the commercial and not-for-profit sectors. Such activities range from publicity and public information campaigns, to crisis preparedness and issues management. In addition, internal communications frequently require engaging employees of private and charitable organisations that are contracted to deliver public services. In addition, commercial organisations, either independently or through trade bodies, engage in the political process. Alliances may be formed with a range of other organisations and groups to help build a strong case for a cause and increase pressure on policy-makers through collective and collaborative action (see Fair Fuel UK Action Point below).

Lobbying

The term lobbying indicates 'direct attempts to influence legislative and regulatory decisions in government' (Cutlip et al., 2000). Organisations, groups and individuals have a legitimate right, within certain parameters, to attempt to influence the actions of governments that have a direct or indirect impact on them and the environment in which they operate. Building relationships with political influencers may be undertaken by an organisation's public affairs function or an appointed consultancy (or independent consultant).

Somerville and Ramsey (2012: 47) cite Milbrath's 50-year-old definition that highlights how lobbying is undertaken by 'someone other than a citizen acting on his own behalf'. They recommend a wider perspective on lobbying than direct advocacy, including 'monitoring and intelligence gathering' using media relations, as well as 'building relationships and coordinating activities with other actors engaged in pursuing the same interest or promoting the same cause' (p. 48).

Lobbying is directed at decision-makers – such as portfolio holders (e.g. ministers), elected members, executive staff or their representatives – or those who are directly able to influence them. This applies across all levels of government from local to international. Lobbying can be defensive (to avoid legislation) or offensive (to press for action). It is used to shape opinions (political and/or public) before government policy or regulation is agreed or to secure amendments to existing legislation.

A pejorative view portrays individual lobbyists and lobbying consultancies as working for any cause if paid enough. Likewise, critics reflect a belief that lobbying unduly favours private interests. It is accused of doing so through secret or underhand approaches (such as providing gifts or favours) in order to directly influence political decision-making. Legislation governing lobbying consultants was introduced in 2014 (see Case Point below). However, there is no requirement in the UK to declare the amount spent on lobbying activities. Parvin (2007: 10) stated that the 'public affairs industry' in the UK was worth £1.9 billion based on a calculation that around 30 per cent of wider PR activity can be defined as public affairs. Applying the same logic today would indicate a figure of £3.9 billion with 24,900 people involved in public affairs work (using data from the PR census: PRCA, 2016b). The validity of this estimate cannot be substantiated, however.

TALKING POINT

OFFICE OF THE REGISTER OF CONSULTANT LOBBYISTS

Statutory lobbying legislation was introduced for the first time in the UK as part of the Transparency of Lobbying, Non-Party Campaigning and Trade Union Administration Act 2014. This involves a register of consultant lobbyists (first published in March 2015) that as of September 2016 comprised 129 organisations (95 of which undertake consultant lobbying). Each is required to pay an annual registration fee of £1,000 and submit Quarterly Information Returns (QIRs) to the Office of the Register of Consultant Lobbyists. In November 2015 the first Civil Penalty Notice amounting to £2,000 was issued to an organisation for non-compliance.

The intention of the Register is to ensure transparency regarding the work of consultant lobbyists when engaging with government ministers and permanent secretaries on behalf of their clients. Whilst names of clients are required in the Register, there is no requirement to detail the nature or frequency of any communications. Details of the registration/QIR process – and circumstances affecting exception from the Register – are complex and can be found at: http://registrarofconsultantlobbyists.org.uk.

The Register has been criticised for various reasons including:

- Its narrow definition of those involved in lobbying meaning that corporate in-house lobbyists, individual firms and small consultancies, SMEs (small–medium-sized enterprises), trade associations, charities, NGOs, legal firms, auditors, management consultants and think tanks are not required to participate.

- Issues in determining what activities need to be disclosed – the Registrar has issued further guidance on such matters.

- Necessity to disclose clients only when direct contact has occurred with a minister or permanent secretary, meaning that other lobbying activities are exempt.

- Shift in the nature of lobbying consultancy to supporting clients to make their own representations (that are exempt from the QIR) rather than meeting directly with government contacts.

- Cost of compliance and operation of the Office of the Registrar, which is expected to cover its costs (although as at the end of 2016 it has not done so).

- Distinguishing contact made with individuals in their personal rather than professional context.

- Issues involved in verifying accuracy of reported information.

Such issues suggest that it is unlikely that the UK Register will be able to achieve its original purpose and address concerns about a lack of public trust in access and influence on politicians. Indeed, registers in other countries, including the US, Canada and Australia, are claimed to be more useful and informative.

Legislative process

Political structures and processes vary from country to country and within different levels of government. Knowledge of how relevant decisions are made is essential. Specialists in public affairs and lobbying are expected to be informed about relevant political stakeholders, have previous experience of engaging politicians and other contacts, and ensure they have up-to-date understanding of developments in the political arena.

The legislative process generally develops from initiation (deciding to act on some matter) to consultation (seeking views) and, where relevant, formulation (shaping laws). A law may then be enacted. In the UK parliament (Westminster) this involves passing through various stages in the House of Commons and House of Lords and concluding with Royal Assent. Passed laws are enforced through the judiciary system to ensure compliance.

Individuals and organisations can influence law making at a number of points. The UK government regularly launches public consultations that follow the Cabinet Office's code of practice (see: http://consultations.direct.gov.uk/). In terms of UK legislation enacted at Westminster, influence may be sought through participation in think tanks, green papers, white papers, party manifestos, the Queen's speech, Acts and Bills. Other opportunities to present a position include: online petitions, Private Member's bills (proposed/championed by an individual Member of Parliament), reaction to events (e.g. calling publicly for legislation), issues emerging with existing laws, rulings by the Supreme Court and other legal precedents (case law).

ENGAGING IN THE POLITICAL PROCESS

Issues-related campaigns

Where lobbying can be seen as a behind the scenes approach to influencing political decision-making, issues-related campaigns raise matters of interest (opportunities or threats) through public debate. Such debate takes place in the public sphere, which is a concept originated in the 1960s by Habermas. Burkart (2009: 142) notes that the public sphere 'comes into existence when citizens communicate, either face to face or through letters, journals, and newspapers and other mass media in order to express their opinions about matters of general interest, and to subject these opinions to rational discussion'. Social media may be thought of as providing an additional public sphere for debate.

The direct lobbying approach favours 'insiders' who are viewed by politicians as having a legitimate right to participate in the political process (Grant, 2004: 408). They can be thought of as possessing a high level of 'political capital', which is an asset that develops as a result of 'political expertise within an individual's network of relations' (La Due Lake and Huckfeldt, 1998: 567). Indeed, Lochbihler (2009) argues that personal networks are more valuable for public affairs practitioners than the reputation of the organisation that they represent. This is evident in the 'revolving doors syndrome' (L'Etang, 2008: 111) discussed later in this chapter.

In contrast, campaigning involves an indirect approach that can be undertaken by 'outsiders groups' (Grant, 2004: 408). These individuals or organisations may be unfamiliar with 'the language of government and civil servants' (ibid.) and lack the experience or networks that help to develop political capital. Consequently they may struggle to attain recognition as a legitimate participant in the political process and fail to secure a place in either formal or informal consultations.

However, outsiders are able to undertake issues-related campaigns where they can utilise an agenda-setting strategy. Baumgartner (2001: 288) defines the political agenda as 'the set of issues that are the subject of decision making and debate within a given political system at any one time'.

The profile of an issue can be raised through activities that make use of what Szondi (2009: 123) proposed as a tripolar model of agendas: media, public and policy agendas. He also cites Watson's (2003) addition of the corporate agenda and proposition of a 'dynamic, and often imbalanced, relationship between the public, policy, corporate and media agenda' (Szondi, 2009: 123). This tension within communicative interactions between citizens, interest groups, organisations and institutions within a society may call for a political response.

Yaxley (2012c) argues that the development of social media challenges and extends the agenda-setting model as detailed in Figure 17.1. The idea is that social media channels serve to increase debate and consequently pressure on politicians to act as they

- offer a public arena in which debate is able to take place;
- act as an influencer on the public, media, policy and corporate agendas;
- provide a global, 24/7 dynamic environment in which legacy, current and emerging issues are discussed.

In addition to providing a place where anyone can engage in an online public sphere (provided they have access and ability to do so), digital developments have created new influencers and opinion leaders. One example is the political blogger Paul Staines (who describes himself as 'a campaigning journalist who publishes via a website'). As well as developing his Guido Fawkes concept as a leading political blogsite (http://order-order.com/) and wider media platform, Staines is involved in digital businesses that offer consultancy advice to a range of clients.

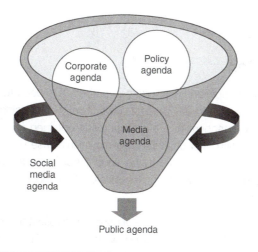

FIGURE 17.1 Dynamic agenda-setting model incorporating social media

2016 US ELECTION AND BREXIT REFERENDUM

TALKING POINT

D.G. Lilleker and colleagues (2016) published an analysis of the November 2016 US election within 10 days. In itself, the speed of publication, comprising contributions from 83 authors, confirms the role of online communications in this ground-breaking election.

As with the Brexit referendum concerning the UK's membership of the EU in June 2016, polarised positions were established among the electorate largely around a narrative of insiders and outsiders within the political system. The use of social media was important in both cases with Donald Trump's use of Twitter routinely setting the public, media and political agendas, and frequently forcing a response from corporate organisations. For example, Trump used Twitter to attack companies such as Ford for their plans to move jobs to Mexico and then to claim credit for corporate responses after his victory.

Review the US election analysis publication to identify political strategies used by Trump and Clinton and how these affected the media, public, policy and corporate agendas.

How do you think that the Brexit result challenges the ability of 'insiders' and 'outsiders' to influence policy-making as the UK negotiates its position on leaving the EU?

Public opinion

The concept of public opinion is important in politics. It is used to reflect an overall consensus or an aggregation of individual views. It may be considered the outcome of debate in the public sphere or a statistical result obtained from opinion surveys. The opinion of individuals or vox pop interviews may also be used to illustrate or support a particular perspective. Opinions may be sought from a wide number of people, a representative sample, or using a purposeful sample of those with personal experience or expertise on an issue.

Individuals' opinions may be the outcome of considered reflection or expressed as an immediate reaction to a topic. Social media have been argued to create a 'filter bubble' (Pariser, 2015) affecting the development of opinions. The likelihood of someone being exposed to a range of perspectives is adversely affected by:

- algorithms – the rules governing what content appears to users of social media;
- influence of networked contacts – who are predominantly reflecting homophily (the tendency of individuals to be connected with others similar to themselves);
- confirmation bias – paying attention to information that supports existing viewpoints.

Where opinion polls have been thought of as able to predict public behaviour, they have been judged to be failures in relation to the 2016 US election, the Brexit referendum result and both the 2015 UK election and Scottish Independence Referendum. Such criticism may indicate problems relating to the methodologies employed by polling companies. Alternatively, it may signify phenomena such as 'shy voters' who are unwilling to reveal publicly their actual voting intentions, and the 'filter bubble' of many commentators in predicting voting results from selective data.

It is not yet clear whether such concerns will change the way that public opinion is used to inform political decision-making. Social science research is used typically as evidence in influencing, developing, implementing and evaluating political policies. For example, politicians and other decision-makers may use public opinion to justify taking action on the basis of anticipated acceptance by a majority of people.

Young *et al.* (2002: 218) argue that 'in the traditional or ideal type of policy process, policy research is used as an instrument of the problem-solving process, to aid the making of choices'. Public opinion data may be included as objective evidence, although it is important to acknowledge that it can be 'dynamic, fluid and a *shapeshifter*' (L'Etang, 2008: 100).

Public opinion is researched primarily through commercial surveys commissioned by various organisations. Although Price (1992) identifies that such research plays a role in public debate, Young *et al.* (2002: 218) caution that 'it is infused with values'. Understanding the research brief, methodology employed and process of analysing and interpreting results is important in determining the validity of any survey. However, these matters are sometimes ignored in favour of selecting evidence to fit with political goals or for agenda-setting purposes.

In-depth analysis of detailed responses within opinion research may be more useful than focusing on averages or totals. Likewise other methods, such as content analysis, ethnography or depth interviews, may be more appropriate for understanding an issue and public opinion (see Part II).

Public affairs techniques

Details on getting involved in the Westminster political process can be found at the website: www.parliament.uk. This site also provides information on parliamentary business, arranging visits and free training for organisations wishing to know more about the work of Parliament and politicians.

Online information can also be referenced for local authorities and other public sector bodies, including the devolved regional administrations:

- Scotland: http://home.scotland.gov.uk/home;
- Wales: www.assemblywales.org/;
- Northern Ireland: www.niassembly.gov.uk/.

In addition, social media enable monitoring and engagement with politicians and political entities. Keeping up to date on developments in the political landscape can be achieved by monitoring online and offline media for:

- speeches, leaks and 'flyers' to test public opinion;
- reports of think tanks and other influential groups;
- political discussion at a local, regional, national and international level;
- opinion poll results (see above);
- statements and draft documents issued by government, politicians (especially those who have special interests), select committees and so forth.

Research should form part of a formal situational analysis (see Chapter 5) to inform public affairs plans and selection from a range of tactics (see Figure 17.2).

FIGURE 17.2 Public affairs techniques

Many of these techniques can be carried out using digital means of communication (see Chapter 16) that enable wider discussion of issues of public concern. Such debate may support consensus building or result in entrenchment of views among groups of online publics, as discussed later in this chapter.

ACTION POINT

FAIR FUEL UK (www.fairfueluk.com/)

The Fair Fuel UK campaign was established in March 2011 to lobby for a reduction in vehicle fuel taxation by Peter Carroll, whose company, Why not Campaign Ltd, previously ran the Ghurkha Justice Campaign resulting in a change in the law. Developments in technology, alongside moves to open up government since the late 1990s, offered new methods to raise issues with MPs who were keen to show they were listening and responding to the public following the 2010 expenses scandal.

An integrated, planned approach was used in the Fair Fuel UK campaign. In particular, opportunities to raise the issue with MPs enabled those interested in the topic to be identified. Fair Fuel UK claims over 150 parliamentarians supported its initial campaign that involved a range of insider and outsider tactics including:

A recognisable spokesperson: motoring journalist, Quentin Wilson;

Traditional and social media activities to communicate and engage with supporters;

Stunts such as unveiling a banner outside the Houses of Parliament depicting a graphic of a fuel tanker showing the proportion of fuel cost accounted for by tax;

A website and other use of technology to facilitate and monitor participation by individuals and organisations;

Tailored emails sent to individual MPs by grassroots supporters of the campaign;

Inter-organisational support from the motoring organisation, RAC, and two trade bodies, the Road Haulage Association and Freight Transport Association;

Radio, television and print media interviews;

A Westminster Hall debate with MPs;

An e-petition calling for planned fuel duty increases to be scrapped and for a mechanism to stabilise prices at the pumps, attracted 135,000 supporters. This enabled a debate to be scheduled in the House of Commons, leading to a successful motion asking the Government to 'consider the feasibility' of price stabilisation.

In his Autumn Statement to Parliament on 29 November 2011, the Chancellor of the Exchequer cancelled a planned fuel duty rise in January 2012 and reduced a promised rise for August 2012.

Fair Fuel UK welcomed the successful outcome of its initial campaign and has continued to use a range of techniques to ensure that the issue of lower fuel duty remains high on the political agenda. The organisation claims to have saved road users £57 billion in tax between 2011 and 2016.

IMPLICATIONS OF POST-TRUTH POLITICS

In 2016, the Oxford Dictionaries' word of the year was 'post-truth'. This is defined as 'relating to or denoting circumstances in which objective facts are less influential in shaping public opinion than appeals to emotion and personal belief'.

Six years earlier, David Roberts (2010) coined the term 'post-truth politics' in an online article where he argued that members of the public 'don't generally know much about politics or policy' and hence use 'crude heuristics to assess legislative proposals'. The heuristic-systematic model originated by Chaiken (1980) is a dual-process theory that distinguishes between conscious and unconscious methods of thinking. Heuristics processing requires little cognitive effort and relies on the 'availability, accessibility and applicability' (Chen and Chaiken, 1999: 74) of persuasive cues.

This intuitive response echoes the notion of 'peripheral' processing of information in the Elaboration Likelihood Model (ELM) developed by Petty and Cacioppo (1986). ELM proposes that when faced with complex situations people may be expected to engage in central cognitive processing, involving critical or systematic thinking. Reflection enables people to evaluate messages or arguments and use evidence to establish their position. Alternatively someone may simply react without much thought (peripheral cognitive processing) to superficial aspects such as the attractiveness of the source of a message, how ideas match existing views (with rejection of contradictory aspects) and reliance on immediate emotional reactions.

When people do not examine information and use heuristics (mental shortcuts) to either accept or reject messages, it can be difficult to change their opinions. If confronted with facts that conflict with what people already know or believe, they may experience cognitive dissonance. This means that new information would be rejected unless someone is prepared to consider alternative views further and be open to revising a current viewpoint. Indeed, people may accept information as factual even when it has little or no basis in truth because it feels right to them.

This situation can be found when examining the rise of populist movements. In addition, superficial thinking may be encouraged by the use of political marketing techniques to influence the public and media agenda. This has been driven by, and further stimulates, a rise in the power of social media. For example, search engine algorithms, social network endorsements and confirmation bias (paying attention to information that supports existing viewpoints) create a 'filter bubble' (Pariser, 2015) that offers a limited ideological frame and inhibits 'unbiased self-reflection' (Magala, 2017: 2).

At the same time, decline in the power and influence of traditional broadcast and print media has affected the role of journalists in society. They are no longer accepted by many people as critical gatekeepers who are trusted to check on the veracity and validity of political information, policies and politicians' decision-making behaviours.

The implications of the cultural context of this post-truth era of politics are examined in the conclusion of this chapter in relation to populist movements and professionalisation of political relations.

Populist movements

Populist movements are concerned with 'public participation in collective decision-making in a democratic society' (Smith, 2014: xi). As such, this is not a new concept and can be seen in activism and what Moloney (2012: 2) terms 'dissent and protest public relations'. He defines dissent PR as 'the dissemination of ideas, comment-aries, and policies through PR techniques in order to change current, dominant thinking and behaviour in discrete economic, political and cultural areas of public life' (Moloney, 2012: 2). The goal is to promote change 'in the political economy and civil society' and is not restricted to any particular philosophical or organisational per-spective. Protest PR goes further in seeking to ensure that change is enacted within the political process.

Smith (2014) identifies a number of factors influencing populist movements. These include existing grievances, opportunities for collective action and emotional responses to how issues are framed in communications. She observes that the internet supports 'an entirely new form of social movement politics' (p. xxvii). Clearly publics may form movements as a result of different kinds of pressures, uncertainties, pro-blems and opportunities or combinations of these.

The notion of populist politics is conceptualised in different ways. The above discussion concerns the phenomenon whereby people come together as a grassroots or social movement. Additionally, the concept encompasses attempts by politicians to mobilise those who are disgruntled with the current situation. Adopting a polarised position and using populist rhetoric or elements of propaganda may stimulate the formation of a populist movement among those who feel excluded in society.

Public relations techniques may be employed by participants in populist political movements and by politicians seeking to stimulate a populist reaction. Edwards and Hodges (2011: 2) reflect this view of public relations as 'a social and cultural practice', encompassing the practice within types of organisations or movements that are more commonly presented as activist opponents to government or corporations (Coombs and Holladay, 2012).

Rather than seeing populist movements in a negative way, Brunner (2016: 237) calls for public relations practitioners to adopt 'civic professionalism' as a means of community engagement. This indicates a 'socio-cultural "turn"' (Edwards and Hodges, 2011: 1) that seeks to shift attention to the broader role of public relations in society.

Nevertheless, the context of post-truth politics presents a challenge to arguments that practitioners have 'a higher duty and responsibility to the community' (Brunner, 2016: 238). Indeed, public affairs practitioners, and especially lobbyists, are seen as predominantly serving the interests of, as being part of, political and business elites in society (Miller and Dinan, 2008). This positions them as partisan and unable to act in the public interest.

Professionalisation of political relations

There is little demographic or career-related information regarding those who work in public affairs or as professional lobbyists. The occupation has a tripartite structure with practitioners working as independent practitioners or employed in-house or for a specialist consultancy.

Those working in the lobbying field tend to have gained experience within politics and have a relevant University degree. This is likely to have contributed towards the establishment of a fairly homogeneous occupational population over time. Indeed L'Etang (2008: 111) observes a 'revolving doors syndrome' that involves purposeful career movement between 'prestigious jobs' (Pieczka, 2006a: 325) in journalism, politics and public relations. This suggests inequity of career opportunity.

Anecdotally, public affairs practitioners who are studying the specialist Public Affairs Diploma awarded by the CIPR reflect a wide range of backgrounds and experiences. Not all have a first degree and most of those have not studied politics or a related subject. Women and ethnic minorities are well represented among cohorts. Their age range is slightly older than for the equivalent public relations qualification, which is likely to reflect their prior experience before attaining roles in public affairs.

Indeed, Parvin (2007: 10) reports there is an 'enormous number of other consultants, advisers, and experts in other professions and sectors who provide public affairs support in one way or another'. Moreover, non-professionals may develop skills and knowledge to undertake lobbying activities. For example, celebrity chef Jamie Oliver has championed improved funding for school dinners over recent years.

Whilst anyone can potentially work in public affairs, and certainly develop relevant competencies in order to influence political decision-making, it is useful to consider the implications of professionalisation of political relations, particularly in the context of post-truth politics.

The point is not to determine whether or not the occupation of public affairs (or lobbying) constitutes a profession. Rather professionalisation relates to formalising practices and approaches to political communications. Moreover, it enables critical examination of political processes and systems as well as consideration of the activities and strategies of political actors. This is the context in which the CIPR Public Affairs Diploma qualification has been developed.

Papathanassopoulos *et al.* (2007: 10) present 'the idea of the professionalisation of political communication' as encompassing:

- Rational organisation of political communications with focus on improved skills, effectiveness of operations and efficient structures.
- A process of ongoing modernisation viewed as supporting – and being supported by – pluralism, 'differentiation and secularisation taking place within contemporary societies' (p. 11).
- Deployment of a range of skills and techniques as required to achieve 'objectives of gaining and sustaining power' (p. 11).
- The 'mediatisation of politics' whereby, rather than acting solely as 'channels of communication between the worlds of politics and the public' (p. 11), the media are part of the political process.
- Specialisation of skills and activities 'that are used in the context of the persuasion and mobilisation of individuals as citizens, voters and consumers' (p. 11).

In summary, Papathanassopoulos *et al.* (2007: 12) highlight 'the convergences as well as interdependencies between the political and communication systems'. It is apparent that these ideas concerning the professionalisation of political communications position those working in public affairs and lobbying as expert insiders in respect of *both* politics and communications.

Within the cultural context of post-truth politics the implications of professionalisation may be seen as enabling adaptation of political communications practices, approaches, processes, systems, activities and strategies to fit (or indeed drive) the new environment. However, when post-truth is recognised as a euphemism for lying, this highlights the importance of ethical practice and the dangers of accommodating rather than challenging deliberate deception.

Further, if professionalisation enhances the involvement of experts in managing public affairs and political communications, it raises a number of concerns. These include space for public involvement in politics as discussed above. Importantly, professionalism needs to be seen as involving more than a process of best practice with ethical considerations providing guiding principles for political relations practice.

Fawkes (2007) emphasises the importance of examining ethical and power dimensions of communications. This encompasses:

- The ethical values of communicators, including senders, media and receivers as individuals, groups or organisations
- The ethical culture in which communicators operate

- Professional codes and practices
- Ethical expectations and values of publics and wider society.

Clearly the current political environment presents new challenges for those engaged professionally in political relations. Indeed, it underlines the vital importance of political communications, public affairs and lobbying for organisations and civil society.

END POINT

Public affairs and lobbying are undertaken by various organisations, groups and individuals either directly or by employing specialist consultancy services. The aim is to influence public opinion and policy decisions using public or private communications. This raises concerns about privileged access for those with money and/or influence in society.

Public relations practitioners working for government and public sector organisations seek to inform, persuade and engage the population and the media in policy decisions and issues affecting everyone in society.

Issues-related campaigns may use social marketing or agenda-setting strategies. The development of a social media agenda extends and challenges debate beyond existing media, policy, corporate and public agendas.

The emergence of 'post-truth' politics underlines the importance and challenges of contemporary professional, ethical practice.

CHAPTER 18

Financial and investor relations

Heather Yaxley

This chapter provides an overview of the role that financial PR plays in society and the nature of communications with key stakeholders and influencers. It considers technical developments alongside the impact of global economic and political issues on financial PR.

CHECK POINT

At the end of this chapter, you should be able to:

- Understand the role of financial PR and the nature of communications with key stakeholders and influencers
- Identify the key components of financial communications, including annual reports and shareholder meetings
- Consider technical developments and the impact of global economic and political issues on financial PR.

ROLE OF FINANCIAL PR

Financial public relations is 'one of the most profitable and highly paid sectors of the PR industry' (Phillimore, 2012: 311). The problem with this perspective is that it reinforces an image of financial matters as complex, mysterious and beyond the mathematical abilities of many PR practitioners (Fleet, 2006). Further, if viewed as a specialist function playing 'a fundamentally important role in any modern listed business' (Bowd, 2009: 465), financial matters are separated from other areas of corporate public relations, and presented as the preserve of those with expertise in the stock market and its operations.

There are three reasons why this approach is inappropriate:

1   For public relations to be recognised as playing a strategic role within the dominant coalition (whether or not that means having a seat on the board), senior practitioners must understand the financial operations of organisations.

2   An ability to discuss key financial metrics is essential for PR practitioners to be able to engage equally with other senior managers, particularly the financial director.

3   Financial public relations should be applied to all organisations rather than the narrow perspective of publicly listed firms, where the focus is on communications, relationship building and reputation management with stock market investors and those who influence their opinions.

Financial performance is of relevance to a wide range of stakeholders, including internal and political ones, and concentrating on investor relations ignores the importance of these other interested and influential parties. Indeed, there is a complex web of influence on the financial performance of any organisation that increasingly crosses international boundaries and reacts to the opinions of those with little direct contact with the financial markets. Likewise, the financial performance of an organisation impacts on its ability to achieve its strategic goals and contribute positively to wider society.

Financial PR is traditionally viewed as supporting public listed companies, although these represent a small fraction of the 5.5 million private sector businesses operating in the UK (Business Population Estimates, 2016).

A total of 2,267 companies had shares listed on the London Stock Exchange (LSE) in December 2016, with a combined market value of more than £4.5 trillion. This includes the Main Market comprising the largest firms and the Alternative Investment Market (AIM) that lists smaller expanding companies seeking access to growth capital. LSE is one of 60 major stock exchanges in the world. Sixteen of these (including the LSE) have a market capitalisation of more than US $1 trillion and account for 87 per cent of global market capitalisation (Desjardins, 2016). Some companies are listed on several exchanges around the world, whilst others may be subsidiaries of multinational or international companies whose shares are listed in countries where the organisation has its global headquarters.

There are two main types of individuals or other entities participating in financial stock markets, both of which are required to ensure their effective functioning:

Traders – The focus of traders is on the performance of the overall market. They seek to profit from short-term price movement in shares, specifically those of commodities that are responsive to supply and demand.

Investors – The focus of investors is on particular companies. Through the purchase of shares of companies listed on the stock market investors become part-owners, known as shareholders (or stockholders). They take a longer-term view than traders and are interested in the value of shares in relation to a firm's growth potential.

In addition to the importance of existing shareholders, Phillimore (2012: 315) identifies potential and past shareholders as investors and notes that institutional shareholders include 'pension funds, insurance companies and investment banks'. He also details new capital sources (hedge funds, private equity and venture capital) as innovations over the last few decades.

This is Money has published a lexicon of terms providing a useful reference point. See www.thisismoney.co.uk/money/article-2004837/Financial-glossary.html.

Spangler (2016) observes the risks, potential rewards, criticisms and political scrutiny of such developments that are now an established part of the financial landscape. He reports the lack of transparency of the private equity and hedge fund industries, noting the preponderance of partisan 'rumors and accusations and public relations banter'.

In contrast, the Investor Relations Society (2016) argues for the importance for public listed companies to build relations with those who invest in their shares. Likewise, organisations operating in the private sector that are not publicly listed (as well as those within the not-for-profit and public sectors) need to communicate with relevant stakeholders regarding financial performance.

Bowd (2009: 466) identifies three categories of stakeholder for publicly listed companies:

1 National and international regulators of the exchange of money

2 Those who exchange money (institutional and private shareholders, private client brokers, and investment and merchant banks)

3 Those who influence or communicate about the exchange of money (analysts, financial and business media, regional media in major cities, broadcast and online media, wire services and trade media).

In the case of a public sector body, the government provides financial budgets using income generated from taxpayers. For a charity, grants and donations from the public may be the main source of income.

Financial reporting is undertaken in one form or another by most organisations. For example, details of financial operations will be required by a small business requesting a bank loan. Charities are required to present an annual report to relevant stakeholders including the Charities Commission, which publishes these online (www.gov.uk/government/organisations/charity-commission).

Public relations may be involved in ensuring that organisations establish and maintain a reputation for financial probity. This could include producing an informed narrative in financial reports or communicating financial results with key publics.

ACTION POINT

The Open University offers a free course: called Organisations and Management Accounting (www.open.edu/openlearn/money-management/organisations-and-management-accounting/content-section-0). This short online course considers different types of organisations and their financial goals. Research the following examples to find out their purpose, how they obtain their funds and the financial relationships they have with various stakeholders.

- Firms listed on the London Stock Exchange (www.lse.co.uk/companyLookup.asp), e.g. Walkers Crisps plc (www.wcgplc.co.uk/).

- Public utilities providing essential services such as water, electricity or telephone: some are publicly owned, e.g. Scottish Water (www.scottishwater.co.uk/); others are privately owned, e.g. Thames Water (www.thameswater.co.uk/).

- Government agencies (www.gov.uk/government/organisations), e.g. the Environment Agency (www.gov.uk/government/organisations/environment-agency).

- Public sector bodies such as hospital trusts, police authorities and universities.

- Franchise networks (www.thebfa.org/), e.g. Molly Maid (www.mollymaid.co.uk).

- Centrally owned chains of medium-sized companies, e.g. John Lewis Partnership (www.johnlewispartnership.co.uk/).

- Private providers of health, education or environmental services, e.g. Nuffield Health (www.nuffieldhealth.com/), Eton College (www.nuffieldhealth.com/), Ecover (www.ecover.com).

- Not-for-profit organisations including charities, e.g. Scope (www.scope.org.uk/).

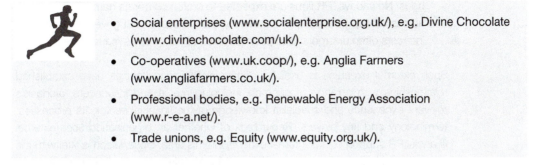

- Social enterprises (www.socialenterprise.org.uk/), e.g. Divine Chocolate (www.divinechocolate.com/uk/).
- Co-operatives (www.uk.coop/), e.g. Anglia Farmers (www.angliafarmers.co.uk/).
- Professional bodies, e.g. Renewable Energy Association (www.r-e-a.net/).
- Trade unions, e.g. Equity (www.equity.org.uk/).

Financial PR practice

The starting point for understanding the role of financial PR in respect of an individual organisation is its relevant regulatory framework. This will cover its establishment, operation, reporting requirements and controls on matters such as mergers and acquisitions.

Regulations vary across countries. In the UK, Companies House registers limited companies. The Financial Conduct Authority (FCA) is the regulator for financial services firms and financial markets. The independent regulator, the Financial Reporting Council is responsible for promoting high standards of governance and reporting through the UK Corporate Governance Code. Its website (www.frc.org.uk/) contains a range of reference publications.

Financial PR involves working with specialist financial broadcast, print and online journalists. Chapters 12 and 16 provide guidance on media relations and online PR respectively. Journalists and other communicators who specialise in financial reporting will be cognisant with the language and operations of the sector in detail. However, pressures on the media and ease of publishing online mean that non-specialists are increasingly covering financial matters (particularly around major announcements). Access to online information has expanded the reach of such communications to non-specialist audiences. Consequently, PR practitioners require an understanding of relevant financial terminology, alongside an ability to communicate financial matters in everyday language.

Financial public relations for publicly listed companies is primarily undertaken in the UK by specialist consultancies, often working with internal corporate or financial affairs functions. Additionally, high-wealth individuals employ such firms. Phillimore (2012: 312) reports that the major financial PR consultancies also 'provide government relations and regulatory support'.

The *Financial Times* (2016) states that:

> Leading financial communications companies from New York to Hong Kong are responding to growing demand for 'whisperers' with global, political and digital

nous. Nowadays, PR firms are expected to craft a corporate narrative that works across different markets, to handle complex relations with governments whose interests often diverge and to provide rapid-response crisis management.

Such external expertise is useful as financial PR consultancies have established relationships with a range of contacts including media and influencers, alongside relevant experience and specialist knowledge of the financial sector, its processes, terminology and key players. Regardless of whether an organisation uses external financial PR support or has internal expertise in this area, close liaison is vital with the dominant coalition (particularly the CEO and finance director) and other relevant board members.

Shareholder activism

Issues and crisis management is important in relation to financial affairs. Knowledge of shareholders and their interests is an important aspect of a strategic situational analysis (Chapter 5). This was apparent when, in 2006, British Airways faced a crisis after banning a check-in employee from displaying a cross over her uniform. The *Daily Mail* reported 'condemnation from an overwhelming alliance of Cabinet ministers, 100 MPs, 20 Church of England bishops and, finally, the Archbishop of Canterbury' who 'threatened to sell the Church of England's £6.6million holding of BA shares', forcing the company to back down on its policy.

Companies may also face challenges from activist shareholders. Individuals or pressure and interest groups may purchase shares in order to protest about behaviour of companies they find socially unacceptable. Alternatively, existing shareholders may become active publics in response to strategic changes about which they feel strongly.

Activist shareholders may develop high-profile public relations campaigns; including disrupting AGMs with stunts or raising motions against the incumbent directors. However, Gong (2014: 2) argues that 'the full potential for shareholder activism has not been realized', going on to criticise the 'passivity of some institutional shareholders' who prefer to sell shares rather than hold a firm's board to account over poor decisions.

TALKING POINT

OUTSIDER AND INSIDER ACTIVISM

In April 2010, 30 Greenpeace activists dressed as 'orangutans' appeared outside Nestlé's AGM, campaigning for the company to address concerns regarding the Indonesian rainforest. Inside the meeting other activists abseiled from the ceiling before unfurling two large banners stating 'Nestlé – give orangutans a break', a play on the slogan of the company's Kit-Kat chocolate bar. Greenpeace wanted 'shareholders to use their influence to change Nestlé's policies and stop using palm oil and pulp and paper products from destroyed rainforests and carbon-rich peatlands'.

This action was part of an integrated campaign which included 200,000 emails, hundreds of phone calls and Facebook messages sent to Nestlé. A website (www.greenpeace.org/kitkat) featured a video that was watched 1.5 million times. Two months after the start of the campaign, Nestlé announced a new policy committing to identify and exclude companies from its supply chain which own or manage 'high risk plantations or farms linked to deforestation'.

Greenpeace adopted an outsider strategy that targeted Nestlé and its shareholders using a public campaign. In contrast, PETA (www.peta.org) offers an example of an insider activist strategy in purchasing shares to effect change from within a company. The organisation encourages 'cruelty-free investment' among its supporters and has also undertaken shareholder activism campaigns since 1987.

PETA has owned stock in over 80 companies. By becoming a shareholder, the organisation is able to present proposals or resolutions at an company's annual meeting. It claims that such actions 'can open the door to discussions with companies' upper management and top scientists' and as such 'represent a powerful tactic for educating company management, boards, and investors about important animal-related issues, which can lead to long-term change'.

This approach has been used recently in targeting the fashion industry's use of exotic animal skins. In 2015, PETA stepped up its campaign against the sale of alligator and crocodile products by Hermès by purchasing a single share in the company. In 2016, PETA protested the use of ostrich leather by Prada by again following public campaigning (including a video exposing treatment of the animals circulated through social media as well as a 'whose head is really in the sand?' stunt at the opening of the firm's flagship Vancouver store) with purchase of a single share. When Prada refused to allow a representative from PETA into its annual general meeting in Milan, this provided further opportunities for protest and publicity outside the venue.

The same outsider–insider approach was launched against LVMH in January 2017 to campaign against the use of crocodile skin from Vietnam by the firm's Louis Vuitton brand.

What are the benefits and drawbacks of an activist campaign targeting shareholders? How does mobilising the public online contribute to persuading an organisation to alter an existing strategy? What benefit is gained from an insider shareholder strategy? How might an organisation prepare for such activist targeting?

PR FOR FINANCIAL BODIES

In addition to considering financial communications with an organisation's stake-holders, it is worth reflecting on the role of PR within financial bodies. Customers of banks and other financial institutions may be thought of in relation to consumer PR (Chapter 22) although the importance of financial decision-making is different from low-value products that are the primary focus of most consumer PR campaigns.

The financial sector has been high-profile since the global economic collapse in 2008. This has required ongoing issues and crisis management as well as a strategic need to rebuild trust and reputation in the financial sector and specific institutions with a wide range of stakeholders.

Post-2008, the financial sector has been subject to regulatory reforms on a global basis. Tafara (2012: xi) notes that reforms were necessary to address 'an evolution in markets and financial services' that included:

- Mobility of capital on a global basis
- Intense competition within the sector
- Removal of barriers that traditionally separated 'financial products, sectors and actors'
- The effect of complexity in the sector on the ability of 'investors, financial entitles and regulators' to monitor behaviour and risk
- Emergence of 'large and relatively liquid unregulated institutional financial markets'.

Johnson *et al.* (2016: 1867) further argue that the financial crisis can be traced in part to the nature of the sector that reflects 'a culturally homogenous elite prone to herd behavior, group-think, and affinity bias'.

Whilst it is debatable whether the culture of the financial sector has altered significantly in recent years, a range of voluntary and regulatory changes has been implemented. Stringfellow (2016: 19) discusses a 'social dialogue approach' to diversity manage-ment where organisational transformation is argued to result from enabling 'margin-alised groups to play an active role in defining, developing and sustaining equality initiatives' (p. 20). This suggests that participative internal communication is an important element in driving such change in the sector.

However, recent political developments (as discussed below) are set to reduce regu-lation in the financial sector. It may be a challenge for those operating in financial PR to address any resulting public concerns. Indeed, whilst the 2016 Edelman Trust Barometer indicates that trust in the financial services industry in the UK continues to improve, it remains the least trusted industry in the survey.

Notably those who have a higher level of education, disposable income and engage-ment with the media (informed public) report a much higher level of trust than the general population. The extent of this gap is increasing, which indicates the importance of reaching a wider audience with financial communications.

FINANCIAL COMMUNICATIONS

Bowd (2009) cites Grummer's observation that most aspects of financial communication which are legally required to be produced are issued according to a calendar:

- **Interim results** (half-year results in the UK) – providing a financial account of performance over the previous six months and expectations for the second half of the year in a Chairman's report.
- **Preliminary results** – the first opportunity for financial audiences to gauge whether performance matches expectations.
- **A profits warning statement** – may be issued prior to releasing either of the above results if performance is notably below expectations. This can be framed to reduce the impact of the published figures with the aim of preventing a lowering of share price, reduced confidence and negative impact on reputation of the organisation's performance.
- **Annual report and accounts** – provides an in-depth account of the reporting year's financial results with further information felt to be of relevance and interest to financial stakeholders. There has been a move towards Triple Bottom Line reporting covering social responsibility and environmental performance alongside the financials. This is being superseded by Integrated Reporting (see below).
- **Annual general meeting (AGM)** – offers an opportunity for shareholders (individual or institutional) to ask questions of the company's management; although few investors tend to attend such meetings having voted in advance by postal ballot.

Annual reports

The preliminary report provides a shortened version of the full annual report that must reach stakeholders no later than four months after the company's financial year end (Phillimore, 2012). Financial results are issued via one of the approved regulatory wire services to ensure that the release of such sensitive information is coordinated to be available to all investors simultaneously.

Although the numeric data included in financial reports is audited for accuracy, companies will frame the accompanying narrative to highlight key aspects and influence media reporting and public opinion regarding performance.

Surma (2006: 58) analysed narratives in corporate social responsibility reports written to inform stakeholders of performance in this area. She identified that PR practitioners tend to create narratives that serve only the interests of the organisation and do not provide 'a voice' for less powerful stakeholders. Fekrat *et al.* (1996: 178) cite a *Financial Times* (15 April 1992) article stating a similar view: '[environmental reporting] exhibits the glossy hand of the public relations experts'. This approach to generating a one-sided, persuasive narrative can be found also in the text accompanying financial reports.

The counter side of this perspective is that annual reports present an opportunity to present a favourable image of the organisation. This is useful as the annual report will be published on the company's website where it acts as 'a marketing tool and can be used to introduce the business not only to potential investors, but also to potential customers' (Phillimore, 2012: 321).

ACTION POINT

The International Integrated Reporting Council (IIRC) aims to develop global reporting standards for a range of challenges facing capital markets, including sustainability and climate change. This involves considering organisational strategies and decision-making processes.

The International [Integrated Reporting] Framework, published in 2013, offers a broad perspective on value created by human, social, natural, intellectual, manufactured and financial resources. As such, it encourages a long-term perspective that evaluates organisational performance beyond economic and financial data.

IIRC has been criticised, however, for failing to incorporate sustainability sufficiently in the framework. There have also been calls for better communications by organisations regarding their sustainability priorities and how these are being addressed. Further the extent to which investors draw on information concerning multiple capitals in assessing current and future corporate performance is under-researched.

Nevertheless, over 1,000 companies worldwide have adopted this multiple capitals system of reporting. The intention is that the model will see principles of corporate governance and stewardship accepted as best practice across global capital markets.

The multiple capitals concept proposes the measurement and reporting on social, economic and environmental performance – also known as Triple Bottom Line reporting (Elkington, 1997). Thomas and McElroy (2016) present a Multicapital Scorecard (www.multicapitalscorecard.com/) comprising six elements:

Environmental bottom line: [1] Natural capital (natural resources and ecosystem services).

Social bottom line: [2] Human capital, [3] social and relationship capital and [4] constructed capital (including intellectual).

Economic bottom line: [5] Internal economic capital (financial and non-financial) and [6] external economic capital (financial and non-financial).

What role could public relations play in communicating organisational performance in these areas? What are the challenges of a formal reporting system in reporting multi-capitals performance? Which stakeholders would be interested in such measures? How do you think that non-expert audiences could be engaged in understanding triple bottom line reporting? How may this help address their reported lack of trust in organisations?

Shareholder meetings

The primary formal shareholder meeting is the annual general meeting (AGM) held each year. It is a legal requirement for public limited companies (PLCs) to hold an AGM within six months of their financial year end. The meeting may be held either at the company's head office or another suitable venue. The AGM offers an opportunity for shareholders to ask direct questions of the company's senior management. At the AGM, the annual report needs to be formally accepted, directors re-elected and auditors appointed. The company may use the opportunity to make a presentation on the results and plans for the year ahead.

Private companies legally do not need to hold an AGM (unless their Articles of Association specify otherwise). Guidance on AGMs and other meetings for charities can be found at: www.charitycommission.gov.uk.

In relation to an AGM:

- Written notice must be sent to directors and shareholders 21 days in advance for public companies with traded shares (14 days' notice for private companies, unless the Articles state otherwise). Shorter notice can be given provided 95 per cent of shareholders agree (90 per cent for private companies)
- Copies of the company's accounts do not need to be sent to shareholders prior to the AGM, but must be sent before filing with the registrar of companies
- Ordinary resolutions can be passed by a simple majority with special resolutions (which must be filed at Companies House: www.companies-house.gov.uk) requiring at least three-quarters of those eligible to vote in favour.

Other financial issues

Specialist advice or expertise is involved in managing PR around several other types of activities:

- **Flotations:** This is when an organisation decides to have its shares listed on the stock exchange. Formally known as an Initial Public Offering (IPO), a broker and corporate financier will be appointed to manage the technicalities and marketing of the offering to institutional investors (Phillimore, 2012). PR support helps handle media relations and reputation management during the process.

- **Mergers and acquisitions/divestments:** Companies may consider merging or acquiring/divesting another company as part of a growth/consolidation strategy. Johnson *et al.* (2005) state the number of acquisitions tripled during the 1990s, with many involving cross-border deals. Johnson *et al.* (2005: 351) note that 'in the majority of cases' flotation 'leads to poor performance or even serious financial difficulties'. They suggest as an alternative organisations may form strategic alliances where resources and activities are shared as a joint venture – although around half of these are said to fail.

- **Hostile takeovers:** May be launched when the directors of one company resist the advances of another. These can be complicated and very bad-tempered, with PR representatives of both sides engaging in a war of words through the media, analysts or direct with stakeholders.

These strategic moves require corporate PR expertise alongside financial PR in order to engage all stakeholders, particularly employees. They are also subject to supervision and regulation by the independent Panel on Takeovers and Mergers (www.thetakeoverpanel.org.uk/). An in-depth enquiry could also be undertaken into a merger by the Competition Commission (www.competition-commission.org.uk/), another independent public body.

Governments may decide to float or deregulate public sector organisations to become public listed companies. In the 1980s, the Conservative government privatised British Telecom and British Gas (a record £5.6bn flotation), with more than 40 UK state-owned

READING POINT

Annual reports, company press releases, corporate videos and other communications can be located for hundreds of companies at the Financial Times Company Content Hub (http://markets.ft.com/research/Markets/Company-Content).

Company websites should also contain information relevant to shareholders, which Phillimore (2012) advises may include webcasts and presentations as well as feeds to enable updates to be received by interested parties.

businesses employing 600,000 workers switching to private ownership whilst Margaret Thatcher was Prime Minister (Groom and Pfeifer, 2011). The UK coalition government introduced the Postal Services Act 2011, leading to privatisation of the Royal Mail between 2013 and 2015.

GLOBAL ECONOMIC IMPACTS

The Investor Relations Society (2016) notes how 'increasing harmonisation of international regulation and global markets is resulting in permeable borders; a company listed in one country will often find its share price influenced by events in another'.

Similarly, traders and investors increasingly operate on a global basis. Madura (2016) indicates three factors that have facilitated international trading and investment:

1   Reduction in transaction costs as a result of electronic communications and stock exchange alliances cross-listings that enable easy purchase of shares across different stock exchanges.

2   Reduction in information costs due to easy access via online channels of communication. This facilitates decision-making without requiring purchase of information about foreign stocks.

3   Exchange rate risk can be ameliorated by hedging (such as selling future contracts).

The second factor relates to the role of financial PR using digital and social media communications. In particular, the continuous news cycle supports immediate communications, but also challenges the controlled release of information. Leaks and rumours through online channels present a further difficulty in managing financial PR.

Automated technology affects both financial services operations and communications about financial matters. It enables easier access to affordable advice for stakeholders (as customers or investors). It also ensures consistency of information, which is important for financial organisations to avoid allegations of mis-selling, which cost UK banks £880 million between 2003 and 2015.

Financial reporting increasingly uses automated technologies to improve accuracy and transparency. This helps in production of financial accounts and release of statements to regulatory authorities and other stakeholders.

Going further, since 2015, the Associated Press (AP) agency has published financial earnings updates using automated technology. Data from corporate financial result statements, stock market estimates and additional AP sources feed algorithms that generate stories (written in AP style) using its Wordsmith software. Journalists and editors may add human insight to supplement the raw data-generated story. Going forwards, it is likely that natural language technologies (similar to Alexa, the Amazon Echo cloud-based voice service) will improve the user interface by humanising financial reporting and conversations for non-expert publics.

Automation also highlights the importance of crisis management for financial PR. Markets are responding to both small and major news items, including information on social media. For example, automation of foreign exchange markets has increased the speed, and extent, of reactions to unexpected and expected events. Market volatility as a consequence of the largely unpredicted EU referendum result saw London traders relying on human expertise rather than algorithms that may create an immediate over-reaction.

Social media monitoring by public relations practitioners is increasingly important in protecting organisations from stock market reactions to breaking news or commentary. Sentiment analysis algorithms tracking social media channels have been noted to affect investor trading behaviour. For example, when the newly elected President Donald Trump criticised firms such as Boeing, their shares initially fell in value.

This trend underlines how global markets have reacted since the economic crisis began in the final quarter of 2008. Share prices have risen and fallen rapidly and frequently on numerous occasions, indicating a crisis of confidence among investors. Indeed, established, long-term reputations may be no guarantee of a stable share price for any organisation.

Financial insecurity looks certain to continue as a result of the US election and preparation of the UK to exit the European Union, among other political developments. As organisations seek to plan their activities in response to such events, they require strategic public relations management to avoid negative reputational impacts. This is not reserved for companies listed on stock markets, as the not-for-profit and public sectors, alongside small–medium enterprises (SMEs) are also affected by global economic and political issues.

END POINT

Financial public relations should be considered from a wider perspective than a specialist focus on investor and shareholder relations. This recommendation emphasises the need for all PR practitioners to engage with the financial operation of organisations in order to work at a strategic level.

Stakeholder activism and PR for financial organisations also need to be included within the scope of financial public relations. Traditional financial relations activities operate to a calendar of activities including annual general meetings and publication of financial results, which are also relevant for non-listed companies.

Attempts to extend financial reporting to cover multi-capitals have the potential to enhance PR's strategic role in organisations. Additionally, the impact of technological developments as well as global economic and political issues, enhance the need for financial PR, including issues and crisis management.

CHAPTER 19

Internal communications

Alison Theaker

One of the most important groups of stakeholders is a company's employees. Organisational rhetoric may declare 'our people are our most important resource', but companies can survive without taking the needs of their workforce into account. However, it is generally agreed that an informed workforce is more likely to be productive.

CHECK POINT

This chapter will examine:

- The importance of good internal communications
- Goals of employee communications
- Using the cultural web
- The qualities needed to be a good practitioner in this field
- Suggestions for best practice.

WHY ARE INTERNAL COMMUNICATIONS IMPORTANT?

Crystal Interactive (2006) suggested that 67 per cent of employees were unhappy with communication within their company. This led to increased staff churn at a cost of

£943 per employee per year. Jack Morton Worldwide's (2006) survey across the US, UK, Australia and China found that only 33 per cent of employees were happy with the quality of internal communications. Workers wanted more frequent and engaging communications and better information on how to do their jobs. The most popular forms of communication were contact with their immediate supervisors and meetings.

Watson Wyatt (2006) found that companies with effective communication were more likely to have higher market share and the best organisations had shareholder returns more than 50 per cent higher than the worst. They concluded: 'Effective communication is the lifeblood of successful organisations.' *Harvard Business Review* (2013) found that 71 per cent of organisations rank employee engagement as very important to achieving overall organisational success, but just 24 per cent of respondents said that they considered most of their employees to be highly engaged.

Communication can flow downwards from senior directors and management to workers, upwards from the shop floor, and between groups and individuals. Some routes may work well, others may be blocked. When communication does not work, the grapevine steps in to fill the gap. Problems can arise if the grapevine is seen as more reliable than information sent by management.

THE GOALS OF EMPLOYEE COMMUNICATION

Most literature in this area stresses that good communication leads to bettter staff performance, emphasising the needs of the organisation. As we saw in the chapter on CSR, doing good is again a way of serving the company's self-interest. Cutlip *et al.* (1985: 315) says 'the goals of employee communication are to identify, establish and maintain mutually beneficial relationships between the organisation and the employees on whom its success or failure depends'.

Hendrix (1995) set out a variety of impact objectives, such as:

- to increase employee knowledge of organisational activities and policies;
- to enhance favourable employee attitudes towards the organisation;
- to receive more employee feedback.

Output objectives could be:

- to recognise employee accomplishments in employee communications;
- to distribute communications on a weekly basis;
- to schedule interpersonal communication between management and a specific employee group each month.

Once objectives have been set, appropriate techniques can be selected. Evaluating the success of different methods will help lessons to be learnt for the future.

Management often try to show an interest in employees' concerns by organising attitude surveys and suggestion schemes. But if there is no response to this information, employees may be more dissatisfied than before, as their expectations will have been raised. *Harvard Business Review* (2013) states that 'Leading companies devote significant resources to carefully crafting employee engagement surveys so they ask pointed, clear questions that go beyond measuring "satisfaction." They use this information to inform strategy and policies going forward.'

INTERNAL COMMUNICATION METHODS

It is important that techniques match the needs of employees. It is no longer good enough to rely on a few dated techniques, such as noticeboards, memos and company newsletters. Employees expect more interactive media, such as meetings, forums, video conferences, email, intranets and social media. McNamara (2011) gives a detailed list of downward and upward communication methods, from giving all employees a handbook, job description and organisation chart to holding regular staff and team meetings and making sure that management acts on feedback.

Different methods will be used depending on the company's objectives for its internal communication programme. If the goal is simply awareness, noticeboards, memos, annual reports for employees and email may be sufficient. If understanding is needed, more feedback and information tailored to a specific group must be added. Roadshows, video conferencing and presentations to groups will start to allow interaction and participation. If employees' support is sought, their acceptance of company objectives is necessary and business forums and training events can be added.

Involvement needs dialogue rather than one-way communication. Team meetings and feedback forums encourage employees to share their opinions. If commitment to a new strategy is needed, employees must feel a sense of ownership and involvement in developing that strategy. Interaction, team problem-solving sessions, forums, intranets and social media could work here. Management must demonstrate willingness to listen and accept feedback.

Quirke (2001) suggested that the way to demonstrate the value of internal communications was to make the link between business problems already on the agenda. Problems such as: low retention of customers; high cost of customer acquisition; high cost base; need for greater internal collaboration; need to stimulate greater cross-selling and customer service; falling market share; increased cost of administration; high employee turnover could all be 'points of pain' for a business. He also advised that the problem had to concern the internal client. 'If (they) do not feel something is a problem, nothing that is done … will feel like a solution.' He points out that internal communication can only increase staff retention if that is a problem. Whilst IT organisations may need to keep their staff because of shortage of skills, a retailer may accept the seasonal migration of young shop assistants.

Watson Wyatt (2006) set eight points for effective communication:

- helping employees understand the business;
- providing employees with financial information and objectives;
- exhibiting strong leadership by management;
- aligning employees' actions with customer needs;
- educating employees about organisational culture and values;
- explaining new programmes and policies;
- integrating new employees;
- providing employees with information on their rewards programmes.

READING POINT

Ingenium (2009) emphasises that 'the pivot point for transformative employee communications is culture', and that this may need attention before any internal communications strategy is designed. Johnson and Scholes suggest a cultural web to examine the culture of an organisation. They pose questions around six areas:

- Stories: What core beliefs are reflected? Who are the heroes and villains? What norms do mavericks deviate from?
- Rituals and routines: Which are emphasised? What behaviour do routines encourage?
- Control systems: What is monitored? Is there an emphasis on reward or punishment?
- Organisational structures: How flat or hierarchical are the structures? Do they encourage collaboration or competition?
- Power structures: How is power distributed?
- Symbols: What status symbols are there? Do particular symbols represent the organisation?
- Overall: What is the dominant culture? How easy is this to change? (Johnson and Scholes 2005: 201–3)

It is no good trying to introduce two-way communication methods if the company is very formal with a rigid hierarchy. If only compliant behaviour is rewarded, then employees will not be willing to become visible by suggesting innovative ideas.

Using Johnson and Scholes' headings, can you define the culture of the organisation that you work in? Does it encourage participation? Are employees' opinions valued? How involved are the staff in the success of the company? Do the communication methods used match the needs of employees? How does the language used reflect the attitude of management to employees? What are the elements of 'the way we do things around here'?

SKILLS NEEDED IN INTERNAL COMMUNICATIONS

Dewhurst and FitzPatrick (2012) set out 12 categories of competencies for internal communicators (see Table 19.1). Their framework can then be used in personal career planning and development, or in devising specifications for specific roles. Several qualifications have also been developed which have addressed IC as a specialism.

READING POINT

Liam FitzPatrick's chapter in the *Public Relations Handbook* (ed. Theaker, 2016: 296–335) contains more insights from his work in internal communications around the world.

TABLE 19.1 The 12 core competencies of an internal communicator

Competency	Definition
Building effective relationships	Developing and maintaining relationships that inspire trust and respect. Building a network and being able to influence others to make things happen.
Business focus	Having a clear understanding of the business issues and using communication to help solve organisational problems and achieve organisational objectives.
Consulting and coaching	Recommending appropriate solutions to customers; helping others to make informed decisions; building people's communications competence.
Craft (writing and design)	Using and developing the right mix of practical communication abilities (e.g. writing and design management) to hold the confidence of peers and colleagues.
Cross-functional awareness	Understanding the different contributions from other disciplines and working with colleagues from across the organisation to achieve better results.
Developing other communicators	Helping other communicators build their communications competence and develop their careers.
Innovation and creativity	Looking for new ways of working, exploring best practice and delivering original and imaginative approaches to communication problems.
Listening	Conducting research and managing mechanisms for gathering feedback and employee reaction.
Making it happen (including persuasion)	Turning plans into successfully implemented actions.
Planning	Planning communication programmes and operations, evaluating results.
Specialist	Having specific subject matter expertise in a specialist area.
Vision and standards	Defining or applying a consistent approach to communication and maintaining professional and ethical standards.

Source: Used by permission of Sue Dewhurst and Liam FitzPatrick

DEVELOPMENTS IN EMPLOYEE ENGAGEMENT

Smythe (2004) defines engagement as 'the degree to which participants identify with the need or opportunity behind a decision'. He lists four conditions for successful engagement:

- The right people must be involved in any project
- Leaders and employees must be invited to participate
- Self-discovery should be encouraged rather than just telling people what to do
- There must be value for the organisation and its members.

Organisations have various motives to try and increase engagement. Employees need to feel they are taking an active part. Smythe sets out four approaches:

1 Telling the many what has been decided by the few. This can result in employees becoming spectators. Methods include cascade briefings and newsletters.

2 Selling to the many what has been decided by the few. Employees may become compliant collaborators. This approach would involve more entertainment and some attempts to collect ideas and create a sense of involvement. Employees could participate in workshops to understand the reasons behind the change.

3 Involving people as individuals. Giving them time to apply change to their own work. The aim is for employees to become willing collaborators. Web-based consultation and learning could be used, local task groups and councils might encourage employees to see the gaps between their workplace performance and the desired change and a corporate 'university' could equip people with the skills they will need.

4 Co-creation. Working with those who will add value in the decision-making, resulting in personally committed reformers. Business simulation games could set real challenges, employee involvement must be seen to influence the agenda and workshops could be used to identify priority areas to change or develop.

Smythe proposes that any of the four methods may be appropriate, depending on the circumstances.

Melcrum's engagement survey (2005) showed that, whilst 48 per cent of organisations had carried out an engagement survey, more than a quarter had no way of evaluating the degree of engagement within their organisations. Moynihan and Hathi (2015) found that 70 per cent of communicators stated that their communication strategy was aligned with their business strategy but only 16 per cent were satisfied with their ability to measure its effectiveness. Whilst the most used metrics were content popularity, opens and clicks, only half used them. Cox (2015) felt that measurement would be one of the most important trends for internal communications: 'Getting our hands on metrics, such as page views, opens, comments to make a cohesive view across the organization.' Practitioners should aim to be able to demonstrate total engagement results by location, channel, department, audience, device, business unit.

Babaee (2016) reported that Engage for Success, the government-sponsored industry-led movement, had published an update to its 2012 *The Evidence* report. Maplin reported £1 million more growth in year-on-year sales in the 50 per cent of stores that managed engagement better while The Co-operative Group described an average £14,000 sales difference between stores in the top and bottom quartiles of engagement. There was a 4 per cent increase in customer satisfaction where staff were highly engaged, as well as a 20 per cent fall in employee turnover and a 25 per cent reduction in absence. However, only around a third of employees were highly engaged and productivity was lower in the UK than in other G7 countries.

TALKING POINT

DO YOU LOVE WHERE YOU WORK?

Great Place to Work (2016) published the results of its Best Workplaces survey. They found that in the best workplaces, 84 per cent of people looked forward to coming to work, compared with 42 per cent in average workplaces. This was connected to whether management delivered on their promises (82 per cent), if management's actions matched their words (82 per cent) and trust in the leadership (82%).

The best ways to reward staff were by recognition, monetary reward and good talent management. The top drivers of engagement were teamwork, career and development opportunities, the values and ethics of the organisation, concern for well-being and CSR.

The survey suggested that engagement needed senior-level buy-in and that it was the role of the human resources function to ensure that directors committed to this. In order to become a great employer, they recommended communicating the vision for the future to build and maintain trust. 'Employee opinion and involvement, and action, should be central to your improvement strategy.' A virtuous cycle of survey/feedback/action/resurvey was suggested to identify what could be done to make the greatest impact.

What makes a great place to work in your opinion? How can the public relations internal communications practitioner contribute to improving engagement? What examples of good internal communications have you experienced in your career?

USING NEW TECHNOLOGY

More organisations are developing their own intranet. Instead of publishing newsletters, information can be made available on an internal website, accessed by password. It can be particularly useful for multinational companies, as everyone can receive information simultaneously. It also means that information can be disseminated rapidly, rather than producing it in printed form. However, shift workers on a production line may not have dedicated computers and managers may have to be persuaded to allow them the time off from their workstations to check the intranet on a communal computer. Moynihan and Hathi (2015) found that the three most used channels were intranet (93%), email (90%) and leadership communications (84%), and the least used was the print newsletter (46%).

Working in a large organisation, I found that so many staff announcements were posted on the intranet that there was a constant tension to try and keep information on the front page. Even though all announcements were listed in the archive, employees were unwilling to scroll down to access them. Mass emails were regularly abused by senior management, with non-essential information being sent to all staff, leading to a kind of 'cry wolf' effect.

Public relations practitioners have to adjust too, as every employee can be a communicator. Communication must constantly be updated. The PR function has to work with human resources and information technology departments to make sure that the intranet works for everyone and that conflicting information is not posted. Holtz (2014) warned that organisations have to be willing to let go of control. He found that only 38 per cent of companies had centralised ownership of social media, while 48 per cent said they have a 'matrixed', or shared ownership, model.

Social and collaboration tools are becoming an integral part of modern intranets. Employees have always talked among themselves and worked together in teams or business units. Social tools now have the potential to supercharge these discussions and connect people in new ways. People can 'like' and 'follow' news and use an 'activity stream' to keep track of what's happening across the organisation. Staff expertise can be highlighted and help others find the right expert when they need one. Social tools are a natural platform for generating ideas and solving problems. Intranets can help improve customer service as customer-facing employees rely heavily on having the right information, regardless of whether they are in government, banks or supermarkets (Robertson, 2014).

Crystal Interactive (2006) found that many companies host corporate blogs, where the CEO posts an online diary and employees can add comments. Melcrum's survey of internal communication (2006) found that 23 per cent of companies were planning to introduce blogs as part of their strategy. For this to be successful, the CEO must write it themselves and not simply rely on anodyne comments, otherwise it becomes seen as a 'clog' (corporate blog) or worse, a 'flog' (fake blog). But Melcrum also found that only half of employees were able to feed back ideas to the CEO. Of these, 5 per cent found that the CEO never responded. Thus the upward communication ability of new technologies was not being exploited.

Hurd (2010) maintains that a good social media policy can be beneficial. By auditing which employees are already using these tools, they can be encouraged to adapt their skills to create business results. 'If you can enable 5 per cent of your employee base to effectively use social media for the good of the company – you have captured an enormous company asset.' Being willing to let go and utilise these tools can have real business benefits. McKinsey & Co. (2012, cited in Robertson, 2014) found a 20 to 25 per cent productivity gain when these tools were used to support interaction among workers. Social tools provide employees with a voice.

Quirke (2001) warned against getting the balance between 'high tech and high touch' wrong. He set out three things that businesses were trying to do with their communication:

- provide information and make it accessible;
- demonstrate leadership and give people direction;
- build a sense of community, belonging and collaboration.

He felt that an intranet can only achieve the first of these, and that 'Face-to-face communication . . . is vital for retaining staff.' Gray (2004) found that what was most likely to increase satisfaction was communication from senior management and the CEO. The human touch is still the most effective when it comes to engagement and motivation. Tyler (2011) gives an account of successful communication at LOFT, where the fact that managers asked their store team the simple question 'How are you?' at the start of every shift made employees feel that they mattered and were valued as a person. Tyler quotes a manager at Ann Taylor as saying, 'They say business isn't personal, but it is.'

Social tools don't compete with or replace existing platforms and practices. Content and news will always have an important role, but now they are sitting alongside rich social interaction. With tools becoming ever cheaper and more sophisticated, now is the time to harness them for real business value (Robertson, 2014).

BEST PRACTICE

There is no shortage of advice available suggesting best practice in internal communication. As we have seen, any programme must have demonstrable buy-in from top management and be adequately resourced.

The following case studies show how organisations have developed their internal communcations based on clear objectives both for the company and for their employees and illustrate how successful stratvegies can lead to wide-ranging business benefits.

A PIONEER FOR INTEGRATION

One of the UK coalition government's flagship policies in 2013 was to integrate health and social care services, encouraging organisations to work together more efficiently to ensure that people get the right combination of care. This was the context for the planned merger of two NHS provider organisations in South Devon: South Devon Healthcare NHS Foundation Trust, which ran Torbay Hospital, and Torbay and Southern Devon Health and Care NHS Trust, which ran community services (including nine community hospitals) and adult social care. Both organisations had reputations for being innovative and high-performing and were already working together and sharing services in many areas – including communications. Merging the two trusts to create a single integrated care organisation (ICO) was the next obvious step to take. This would give greater flexibility and control over people's care pathways at home, in their local communities and in hospital. Crucially, in an environment of public sector austerity funding, it would also drive further efficiencies and savings, maximising the amount of money available for frontline care.

Whilst sounding relatively simple and straightforward, the merger process would be long and complicated, with the ICO finally coming into existence on 1 October 2015, more than two years after the formal process began. Legislatively, the process was a takeover of the community trust by the hospital trust, involving the (then) Competition Commission, local and regional commissioners and health regulators, Monitor and the Trust Development Agency. Creating the new ICO was the first step in ambitious plans to revolutionise health and social care in Torbay and South Devon – changing the emphasis from asking people 'what's the matter with you?' to asking 'what matters to you?' Both trusts were thus embarking on whole-scale organisational change that would last several years into the life of the new ICO. There was one final complication: whilst plans were under way to merge, the two trusts found themselves on opposite sides of an employment tribunal, in a damaging whistleblowing case. Relationships were strained and time and effort had to be invested in rebuilding a culture of shared trust.

A comprehensive stakeholder communications and engagement plan was developed, and one of the primary publics was internal: success of the ICO required the full commitment and engagement of staff across both predecessor organisations. Key objectives were to ensure that staff felt well-briefed about the case for change and able to engage in shaping services and culture. A range of traditional communication techniques were used to keep staff briefed, including: executive presentations at manage-ment meetings; updates and 'FAQs' on the staff intranets; leaflets distributed with payslips; executive and non-executive 'open-door drop-in sessions' and articles in staff magazines. There was also an online 'rumours board', where, throughout the merger process, staff could anonymously post questions, concerns and rumours that they may have heard. The rumours board was administered by the PR team, but comments and questions were passed to executives to answer, and responses were posted online. The forum proved so successful that it was continued as 'Just Ask', once the ICO was up and running.

The primary activity stream was one of engagement as staff needed to own the values and brand DNA of the new organisation. An early commitment was given to 'no compulsory redundancies' so that staff would have some assurance about their future and feel better able to engage with the change process.

A series of workshops was held in different workplaces, across the ICO's whole geography, with all staff from both organisations invited to attend. Each workshop was led by executive directors who gave a brief presentation before staff engaged in focused discussions about the culture and values of their new, shared organisation. Staff were also able to request a tailored session in their own workplace and two groups took up this offer.

An open invitation was issued for staff to volunteer as ICO champions. More than 40 people from all parts of the organisation and at all levels volunteered. These individuals met as a group every two or three weeks, led by the Director of HR and with the chief executive often in attendance. Crucially the champions had a range of views as to whether or not the merger was going to be positive. This meant they represented the views and feelings of many other staff, ideally positioning them to act as a sounding board for executives developing the ICO's vision, purpose and values. They also provided feedback from their teams about any current issues and concerns. Action taken as a result of their feedback was reported back to staff via the intranet FAQs, e-bulletins and in regular team meetings. The ICO champions also decided on a longlist of potential organisational straplines from hundreds of suggestions from the wider staff body. Executive directors then selected a shortlist which was put to staff for an open vote. The strapline had to sum up the direction of the new ICO and the eventual winner was 'Working with you, for you'. It was felt this best indicated the new emphasis on health promotion, illness prevention, empowerment through working in partnership with the individual and the importance of partnership working with other agencies (including the voluntary and community sector) to support people to live well. The ICO champions proved to be a very important group and the group continues to be important in developing staff communications and engagement in the ICO.

On 1 October 2015, the chief executive welcomed staff to their new organisation (Figure 19.1). Rebranding costs had been kept to a minimum, with vinyl overlays produced for key signage, but all other printed material (including uniforms) was to be replaced once old stock had been used. The exception to this was ID badges: staff were asked to update their badges within the first month, for security purposes, and lanyards bearing the ICO's new name were produced for all staff. The speed with which these were claimed indicated the sense of pride staff felt in their new organisation.

FIGURE 19.1 Torbay IC launch day

Pride was the unifying factor in bringing the two organisations together: at every workshop it was clear that staff were fiercely proud of their work and their colleagues and wanted to bring the best from their existing trust into the new ICO. The PR team developed a project to illustrate the breadth of services provided by the ICO in a video. PR staff and their colleagues from the Education team filmed staff in various roles and asked them what was important to them and what motivated them to come to work each day. Phrases from their responses were used as captions to the video. That video is now available to view on vimeo as 'Proud to be working with you, for you' (https://vimeo.com/155106331).

Was the communications and engagement plan a success in helping staff to make the transition into the new ICO? There are some metrics, such as how many staff attended workshops or took part in polls, but the first real test of opinion was the annual NHS staff survey. Results were published in February 2016. Nearly 3,000 staff responded to the survey and rated the Trust highly as a place to work and receive treatment. In 28 out of the 32 areas surveyed, the ICO was rated as higher or on a par with other NHS organisations. This included opportunities to work flexibly, health and well-being of staff and the relatively low number of staff suffering with work-related stress. This bodes well for the new organisation, which is in the early phase of an exciting five-year plan to integrate health and social care and achieve a change that improves the health and well-being of the population of Torbay and South Devon.

With thanks to Corinne Farrell, Head of Communications at Torbay and South Devon NHS Foundation Trust.

ACTION POINT

DOING THE RIGHT THING

The Severn Trent Way: case study

Severn Trent Plc is a leading FTSE 100 company that focuses on the provision, removal and treatment of water in the UK and internationally. The Company refreshed its code of conduct in 2011, in partnership with Radley Yeldar, one of Europe's leading communications consultancies and experts in ethical business practice. The updated code needed to continue to provide a common and consistent framework for responsible business practices and set out the standards employees need to follow in their day-to-day activities. As part of the refresh, a strategy was developed for engaging over 8,000 employees internationally with the new code, as the Company wanted to make sure it did not just become a booklet that ended up at the bottom of employees' drawers.

Bringing it to life

The new code was given an approachable title: 'Doing the right thing the Severn Trent way' (Figure 19.2). It was then brought to life with engaging, inclusive language, for example 'Standing up for what's right' was the title of the whistleblowing section. Translatability had to be considered throughout as several language versions had to be published for the Company's global internal audience. Each section was concise and maximised white space as well as imagery to make the pages inviting.

FIGURE 19.2 Doing the right thing

Making it real

The code featured photographs of employees from across the business to help all employees identify with it. Each section opened with an example of a real employee dilemma to give it authenticity and to help employees feel joint ownership of the issues being addressed. This was followed by Severn Trent's position on the issue, an outline of the Company's principles and a list of relevant Company policies.

Engaging key influencers early

The Severn Trent board was involved throughout the development of the code, which ensured management buy-in at the very top, right from the outset. Each director assigned a senior manager in a position of influence in his or her team to be a champion for the code during the roll out.

Embedding it in the business

A pilot was carried out with representatives across the business to test the effectiveness of the code and the engagement activities surrounding it. Appropriate adjustments were then made prior to launch to maximise impact. Face-to-face communication between managers and their teams formed a core part of the engagement strategy when it launched. Managers knew how best to reach their teams, whether co-located in a single office or based out in the field. They were also able to address issues on the spot. Other tools were then used to reinforce the message:

- **Phase 1 – Getting managers on board:** The champions were used to get managers on board as it was crucial that they understood and bought into the messages they were communicating. Managers were given an advance copy of the code and an implementation guide to help them prepare to engage their teams.
- **Phase 2 – Creating employee awareness:** Managers were given an awareness presentation to deliver, to ensure consistent messages were delivered across the business. Copies of the new code were also handed out. A DVD was also shown, to help bring employees' ethical dilemmas to life. Managers were also given activities and a deck of 'dilemma cards', again based on real employee scenarios, to help stimulate discussion, with worksheets to encourage teams to actively participate. Finally, to wrap up each session, teams filled out 'commitment forms' to help cement learning.
- **Phase 3 – Training to embed behaviours:** Soon after the awareness sessions, employees were given access to a digital e-learning tool, designed to help reinforce the principles and enable them to understand the outcomes and consequences of different ethical choices.
- **Phase 4 – Keeping it alive:** A regular slot for the code was introduced to the Company's monthly Team Talk to enable managers to continue discussing pre-set, relevant topics face-to-face with their teams, in order to keep the door to dialogue open. New starters will also be introduced to the code in their inductions so that the principles are instilled from their first day. The code was made available in the governance area of the corporate website so it would remain accessible to employees, with or without intranet access, such as field workers. Finally, managers and

employees were provided with a channel to feed their views on the code or the communication surrounding it back to the Company, to enable engagement to be continually optimised. The code is also being used as a springboard for other communication campaigns and to form employee award categories.

With thanks to Loretta Smith (Deputy Head of Internal Communication) and Helen Davies (Head of Internal Communication) at Severn Trent Water and Radley Yeldar.

ACTION POINT

FRESHFIELDS BRUCKHAUS DERINGER LLP – OLYMPIC INSPIRATION

The HR and communications team at City law firm Freshfields was tasked with generating pride in the firm and inspiring a sense of excitement and international patriotism around its involvement with the London 2012 Olympic and Paralympic Games as the official legal services provider. As well as a once-in-a-lifetime event, the firm wanted to provide employees with an interesting and engaging way to speak about the scope and scale of the services offered by Freshfields.

The relationship with the Games was seen as a chance to achieve a common sense of purpose throughout the business and to leave a lasting legacy within the firm. Three major milestone events were held:

- Lord Sebastian Coe announced the sponsorship in 2009.
- In 2010, a lunch was attended by Cultural Olympiad director Ruth Mackenzie, and a trapeze artist gave a breathtaking performance that inspired staff.
- At 500 days to go, a 'Question Time'-style panel event included Karren Brady and James Cracknell, offering their thoughts on the true legacy of the Games.

In addition, regular Olympic Park tours gave employees the chance to see how work was progressing on the site. A new London 2012 visual identity, including motivational imagery and messaging, was introduced. Online internal communications on the London 2012 social networking intranet, Gateway London 2012, encouraged discussions and information sharing about the office-wide sports and cultural programme. London 2010 and 2011 Marathon training was arranged with Richard Whitehead, one of three ambassador athletes. The London 2012 mascots came to the office for a staff children's party. The annual internal London festival featured 'A Question of Sport' and a fascinating Q&A session with Phil Lane, chief executive of ParalympicsGB. In May 2011, Freshfields hosted the London 2012 Partners Sitting Volleyball tournament, encouraging staff members to engage with Paralympic sport (Figure 19.3). A summer carnival was held for all London employees in July 2011 where employees had the chance to meet past and present Olympians and try out unusual Olympic and Paralympic sports, as well as enjoy an evening of music, dancing and food in a carnival atmosphere

FIGURE 19.3 Freshfields staff training with Paralympic athlete

(Figure 19.4). Over 700 staff attended, representing almost 40 per cent of staff in the London office. From August 2011, staff had the chance to attend various test events as London prepared to host the Games as team-bonding exercises.

'London 2012 has helped us engage with more than 75 per cent of London employees', says Programme Manager Phillippa Piper. In January 2011, Freshfields undertook the first independent employee engagement survey to track the success of the London 2012 project. The results were:

- 90 per cent of staff intended to get involved in the Games to some extent;
- 76 per cent were advocates (talking positively to clients, friends and family about it);
- 72 per cent felt more positive about the firm as a result of the sponsorship; and
- 81 per cent were proud of Freshfields' involvement.

Similar surveys were held every six months until September 2012 to fine-tune the campaign and track progress.

Other factors demonstrating the success of the programme:

- 1,300 people out of a total population of 1,700 registered with, and regularly used, Gateway London 2012.

FIGURE 19.4 Trapeze artist at Freshfields' launch of their 2012 internal communications programme

- Milestone events attracted between 500 and 600 attendees, compared with an average attendance of 300 at previous internal events. More than 100 staff children attended the mascot party.

- There was a 21 per cent increase in hours volunteered in the community in 2009/2010, and this increased further in 2011/2012.

Employees were actively engaged in the project and the legacy of the project will affect how people work together and how the firm is viewed (both internally and externally) for a long time into the future.

The London 2012 'story' was incorporated in the wider communications strategy and client-facing and recruitment materials – such as the annual review, external website and UK graduate recruitment.

END POINT

The key point for a successful internal communications strategy is to make sure that any cultural issues are taken into account before new internal communications initiatives are introduced. In addition, the methods used must be led by the requirements of the employees themselves. The examples provided show that as well as having beneficial effects on staff commitment to the organisation, good internal communications can have wide-ranging effects on relationships with other stakeholders.

CHAPTER 20

Inter-organisational relationships

Heather Yaxley

This chapter provides an understanding of communicating with, and for, organisations where there is a focus on engaging other organisations as the primary public. In addition to examining public relations within the business to business (B2B) sector, the chapter considers inter-organisational communications (IOC) in relation to the public and not-for-profit sectors. The effect of technological developments on inter-organisational relationships (IORs) is a key thread throughout the chapter.

CHECK POINT

At the end of this chapter, you should be able to:

- Understand the role of public relations in the business to business (B2B) sector
- Appreciate the scope of inter-organisational relationships (IOR)
- Identify the characteristics of inter-organisational communications (IOC)
- Select appropriate tools and techniques for building inter-organisational relations (IORs).

Collaboration between organisations involves communicative activities that seek to build effective working relationships. These require that PR practitioners understand varying inter-organisational needs and devise appropriate plans. Many individuals and functions potentially have a role in identifying and building relationships between organisations. However, inter-organisational communication generally involves a defined number of contacts (sometimes identified individually), for example as potential customers or existing suppliers.

ROLE OF PUBLIC RELATIONS IN THE B2B SECTOR

In-house PR practitioners may be employed to undertake B2B communications, and the sector is the primary client base for many consultancies and independent practitioners. Fill (2002: 376–7) states that 'the effectiveness of public relations in a B2B context should not be underestimated' and stresses its role in providing 'credibility and richness to an organisation's communications'.

Purpose of inter-organisational communications in the B2B sector

Within the B2B sector, motives for inter-organisational communication relate typically to procurement processes. Three main buying motives can be identified:

1 General consumption – goods and services used in the organisation's general operations. For example: office furniture, stationery, insurance, technology, public relations and other professional services.

2 Resourcing production – goods and services used by the organisation in producing its own products and services. For example: raw materials, components, manufacturing equipment.

3 Resale/retail – goods and services that are sold on to other businesses or consumers as part of a marketing channel. For example: franchise, online or through retail outlets.

Traditionally public relations in the B2B sector is viewed as supporting sales and marketing functions. Beyond this narrow perspective, PR practitioners can help to attain organisational goals such as client development, reputation building, thought leadership, securing financial support, participation in industry bodies, crisis management and enacting social responsibility strategies.

TALKING POINT

In November 2016, BMW, Daimler, Ford and the Volkswagen group announced a joint venture project to build a network of fast-charging sites for electric vehicles throughout Europe. The intention is to ensure an industry standard system that enables convenient charging stations and encourages greater e-mobility.

What are the main purposes (organisational goals) of this initiative? Which of these can PR practitioners help to attain? How might they do this to reach relevant inter-organisational (B2B) stakeholders?

B2B sector considerations

The commercial private sector is dominated by small and medium enterprises (SMEs). Small businesses employ between 0 and 49 people, with medium-sized organisations defined as those with 50–249 employees. UK government statistics (Business Population Estimates, 2016) show that SMEs accounted for 99.9 per cent of the record 5.5 million private sector businesses in the UK at the start of 2016. They represent 60 per cent of the 26 million people employed in the private sector and have a combined annual turnover of £1.8 trillion.

Yet research by Moss *et al.* (2003: 207) suggested that SMEs 'may have a rather limited, and at times, naïve understanding of the concept of public relations'. Indeed, this study found that communications activities (including PR) tend to be undertaken by non-specialist personnel as part of their other duties in smaller organisations. A minority of SMEs were said to employ external agency support.

Surprisingly, there has been limited further research into public relations within SMEs. Atanassova and Clark (2015: 164) report that such organisations 'rely on personal networking, relationship building and word-of-mouth, which can be costly and resource intensive'. Social media are seen as offering an inexpensive means for SMEs to enhance stakeholder relationships. In particular, Atanassova and Clark note the geographical advantages and opportunities for knowledge sharing of online technologies. However, they observe a lack of skills and knowledge within SMEs regarding digital communications.

Some industries are dominated by SMEs (specifically those within the service sector) whilst others (notably those in the financial and insurance sector) feature a greater number of large organisations (defined as having more than 250 employees). Construction is the largest industry sector accounting for 20 per cent of UK private enterprises, with 15 per cent involved in professional, scientific and technical activities and 10 per cent operating in the wholesale/retail trade and repair sector.

ACTION POINT

Specialist fields have developed in respect of B2B communications, for example within professional service firms (PSFs). Beke (2014) discusses the growing area of litigation PR that involves practitioners working in law firms. Their role may be to draw on crisis management competencies to help protect the reputation of clients in respect of legal matters. Further, public relations is helpful in representing the interests of legal firms, for example, in building their reputation, managing issues (e.g. with regulators) and promoting services to prospective and existing clients, influencers and other organisations.

PSFs offer their clients highly skilled services such as accountancy, management consultancy, architecture, real estate, environmental management, insurance, actuarial, recruitment, marketing, advertising and public relations. These types of organisation depend on the quality and expertise of their employees who need to have, or attain, professional qualifications.

Empson *et al*. (2015: 1) note that PSFs comprise 'one of the most rapidly growing, profitable and significant sectors of the global economy'. PricewaterhouseCooper (PwC) is the second largest PSF in the world with more than 223,000 employees and operations in 157 countries. In 2016, 422 companies in the Fortune Global 500 list used the services of PwC firms.

Historically PSFs operated in specific local areas. The majority retain this small firm focus, although an increasing number have expanded their scope and scale to operate regionally, nationally or internationally. These may specialise in particular industries or sectors. Other PSFs form or join networks (such as IR Global) to extend their offering across a large geographical area or to provide clients with a wider range of services.

The largest PSFs operate on a worldwide basis with an international client base. For example, DLA Piper was formed in 2005 from a merger of two US and one UK-based law firms. It employs 4,200 lawyers located in over 30 countries. In addition, it has multidisciplinary teams comprising those with experience of political office, lawyers, lobbyists, and public relations, marketing and polling experts. Their B2B work provides clients with services that encompass strategic counsel, risk assessment, public policy, legislative, regulatory, legal and communications.

Maister *et al*. (2000: ix) argue that 'the ability to work with clients in such a way as to earn their trust and gain their confidence' is key in professional service firms. Consequently they recommend that those working in PSFs develop a role as a 'trusted advisor' (p. ix). This is important as it emphasises a strategic partnership approach for inter-organisational relationships within the B2B sector that goes beyond simply providing expert services.

Expertise is an intangible product and public relations can help to build and enhance this strategic asset through management of reputational capital, organisational culture, corporate identity, thought leadership and other approaches as discussed elsewhere in this chapter. Whilst PR practitioners may decide to specialise in the PSF sector (e.g. within financial services), there has been limited academic research in this area.

There are two key dimensions of inter-organisational PR practice within or for PSFs. The first involves provision of communicative activities and support for inter-organisational relationship development on behalf of the employing firm either as a consultancy or in-house function. The second sees public relations as a professional service offered to clients of the firm. As such, public relations itself may be positioned as one among many multidisciplinary professional services provided by a PSF.

SCOPE OF INTER-ORGANISATIONAL RELATIONSHIPS

Communications and relationship building between organisations is not restricted to business enterprises, but includes entities in the public and not-for-profit sectors. As already discussed, the focus of inter-organisational public relations may be on forming new relationships or managing existing ones. These might be developed with external entities or involve working with those within a wider organisational structure. Examples of this latter type of intra-organisational relationship include:

- Communications between government departments
- Joint projects involving a network of public service providers
- Policy development across companies belonging to a larger corporate group.

Organisations increasingly establish alliances, networks and partnerships. For example, they form joint ventures, develop cross-sector initiatives, address issues as members of collaborative bodies or combine into single virtual organisations. Entities involved in such concerns will need to plan integrated or coordinated PR activities.

Inter-organisational relationships between business organisations and public sector bodies include Public–Private Partnerships (PPPs) that involve outsourcing the provision of public services, assets or infrastructure projects by the state to private sector organisations. Large-scale initiatives may involve a private consortium comprising a number of organisations. Alternatively, a public sector body may employ an expert intermediary or project manager to oversee PPPs or other inter-organisational services.

TALKING POINT

The Crown Commercial Service (CCS) executive agency has a remit to develop policy, advice and direct buying services in the UK to ensure effective and efficient procurement of goods and services by government departments. CCS is directly responsible for buying some £2.5 billion of goods and services for central government departments. However, the National Audit Office (2016) reports that this centralised approach has run into difficulties, with poor inter-organisational communications among the noted criticisms.

On a smaller scale, communications and relationship building takes place at a local level between businesses and other types of organisations. Beyond the type of exchange relationship involved in procurement, IOC/IOR may relate to enactment of policies, securing licence to operate, development of CSR programmes and so on.

Not-for-profit organisations also build relationships and communicate with similar organisations as well as those in the public and private sectors. Figures published by the Charity Commission (September 2016) indicate that there are 166,311 registered charities in the UK. These have an annual combined income of over £72 billion. Four out of ten have an annual income of under £10,000, whilst 1.3 per cent generate over £5 million each year. This illustrates the enormous variation in sizes and type of charitable concerns that may potentially engage with public sector and/or private sector organisations.

TALKING POINT

In 2015, the merger of Breast Cancer Campaign and Breakthrough Breast Cancer created Breast Cancer Now as the UK's largest breast cancer charity. According to the charity's chief executive, Baroness Delyth Morgan, developing the new brand involved 'looking to build on existing collaborations with corporate partners and other charities and institutions'.

Inter-organisational communications may be deployed within tactical fundraising and campaigning initiatives in addition to establishing and developing mutually beneficial strategic partnerships.

Research organisations are involved with Breast Cancer Now. In what way do they help the charity to achieve its aims? How might these organisations communicate their relationship with Breast Cancer Now to their stakeholders, including employees?

Inter-organisational public relations is important for trade/employer associations, which concentrate on matters of interest for specific industries and predominantly have organisations as members. In contrast, professional bodies and trade unions tend to represent particular occupations and have individual members (although some offer subscriptions to organisations with multiple individual members).

Public relations practitioners working for such entities will undertake inter-organisational communications in support of membership and other operational or reputational matters. They will also be involved in communications with stakeholders and engaging influencers, including politicians, regulators, and specialist media.

A hybrid form of organisation is the social enterprise. These organisations use trade to address social issues, benefit communities and improve the environment. Examples of such organisations with a social purpose in the UK include: The Big Issue, the Eden Project, and Fair Trade companies such Divine Chocolate and Cafedirect (see www.socialenterprise.org.uk/). They need to build relationships with other organisations, including those which offer social finance.

CHARACTERISTICS OF INTER-ORGANISATIONAL COMMUNICATIONS

There are many motivations for inter-organisational engagement including resource procurement, supply chain management, collaborative service provision and financial arrangements. The following discussion highlights three main characteristics of inter-organisational public relations:

1 Engagement with stakeholders and publics on the basis of their **occupation**

2 Communications that **support** relationship building between employees of the client and target organisations

3 Importance of inter-organisational **influencers and communication channels** (including trade media).

Occupational considerations

Inter-organisational communications may involve exchange relationships within which specific roles are adopted. In the case of buyers and sellers, a formal procurement process will involve information transfer and relationship building between functions including sales, account management, purchasing and finance.

Individuals working within these functions establish inter-organisational relationships. These may operate at a personal as well as a professional/occupational level. Indeed, Grunig *et al.* (2002: 552) note that 'relationships often begin as exchanges and then develop into communal relationships as they mature. At other times, public relations professionals may need to build a communal relationship with a public before an exchange can occur.' This latter point relates to the subjective added-value of human relationships, such as mutual respect.

Blyth (2006) reports that individuals employed by organisations act both rationally and emotionally when making decisions. He notes that organisations are generally risk-averse and rely on procedures and hierarchical responsibilities to reduce risk, particularly for costly purchases. This means that senior executives are likely to be involved with major decisions, whereas junior personnel will have responsibility for more routine or repetitive purchases.

Hierarchical responsibilities may also reflect organisational or national cultural differences. The tradition with Japanese companies has been to develop long-term inter-organisational relationships. Other cultural circumstances may stipulate that organisations typically undertake annual renegotiation of accounts or are happy to agree informal trust-based arrangements.

Individuals operating within inter-organisational relationships reflect their occupational roles. For example, a fleet manager has responsibility for an organisation's company vehicle operations and needs to maintain expert knowledge of the latest models, legislative and political developments, financing options and so forth. This is achieved through contact with representatives of vehicle manufacturers, trade media, attending exhibitions, etc. In this example, politicians will also be key influencers as they determine tax rates and other economic constraints which impact on the choice of vehicle offered to employees. Consequently, public affairs may be employed by individual organisations or collectively through trade bodies (such as the Society of Motor Manufacturers & Traders in the case of the automotive industry) with relevant political stakeholders.

Supporting communications and relationship building

Gregory and Willis (2013) propose that stakeholders who have a close relationship with an organisation are part of a value-chain. They list delivery partners, suppliers, distributors and regulators in this category. This is an important aspect as such level stakeholder relationships help organisations to put into practice their 'societal and corporate intentions' (2013: 38–9).

Modern 24/7 global environments have resulted in ever more complex arrangements and interactions between organisations as well as with other stakeholders. Where connections are of strategic importance, they require personal communications to build long-term, close relationships (e.g. between key account managers and corporate clients).

According to Gregory and Willis (2013) PR practitioners plays a role in supporting value-chain relationships. They may need to communicate with other organisations that have the potential to impact negatively, such as activist groups (as discussed in Chapter 18). PR functions may also look to represent the views and interests of value-chain stakeholders – including critics – to senior management.

Tactically, PR practitioners develop communication materials and support attendance at events to enhance inter-organisational relationship building. There are hundreds of conferences and exhibitions held in the UK and overseas each year, with other events (such as visits to premises or launch activities) organised for a specific purpose, possibly by the organisation itself to establish new, or enhance existing, relationships.

Techniques such as use of live webinars, video broadcasting and social media activities can extend the reach of exhibitions, conferences and events. In addition, practitioners may engage directly with other organisations. This may include liaising with their PR functions to develop mutually beneficial opportunities. For example, a case study of the organisation's services being employed by a customer may be produced. This could be used as part of a thought leadership programme, as a flyer, in a speech or conference presentation, on websites, in trade media materials, or as a direct mail piece, for example.

CeBIT is the largest digital business show in the world. It takes place over five days in March each year at the Hanover Messe in Germany, with conferences alongside exhibition stands. High-profile speakers are attracted to present trends and innovations as well as to consider the societal impact of the digital industry. In 2016, CeBIT attracted 200,000 visitors and 3,000 exhibitors. CeBIT is attended by businesses, customers, media, politicians and other industry influencers. It offers a media centre for accredited journalists and exhibitors' public relations teams.

Consider the tactics that public relations would provide at such an exhibition. Look at Part II, 'Public relations planning', and reflect on the steps required to put together a programme, including objectives and evaluation of presence at a trade exhibition.

It is important to have a clear brief from the relevant function (e.g. sales and marketing) in order to determine the most appropriate way in which PR can provide assistance for inter-organisational relationships. This ensures that plans contribute towards strategic as well as tactical objectives.

As discussed earlier, PR practitioners should take opportunities to build relationships with their counterparts in other organisations. Sector expertise can be particularly helpful as relationships can be established and maintained over time. These may be developed through networking within professional bodies, attending conferences and events, and general relationship building approaches.

There are potential ethical issues concerning relationships developed between PR practitioners working in different organisations. Compliance with competition legislation is intended to ensure that organisations are operating fairly. This may include aspects of communication where discussions may be considered as breaching competition law. PR practitioners need to be familiar with legislative constraints and ensure that they do not discuss any inappropriate matters when meeting with other practitioners, including at trade or professional bodies events.

Inter-organisational influencers and communications channels

Securing media coverage is traditionally important in inter-organisational PR. Within particular occupations and industries, this will involve working with specialist publications or broadcasters. Smith (2012: 373) confirms that 'effective targeting is essential', necessitating that appropriate trade titles, exhibitions or other channels are identified as influential for inter-organisational PR campaigns.

Three Rs apply to inter-organisational media planning: reach, relevance and reputation. A publication may be chosen because it reaches 100 per cent of the target audience (e.g. the *Veterinary Times* is distributed by name to all veterinary surgeons and nurses in the UK). It is also important to establish the relevance and reputation of a publication with the target audience. Too often, trade publications or emailed digital magazines are received but not read. A checklist of factors to consider in media planning is included in the Appendices.

Social media and digital communications are increasingly important for inter-organisational communications. Many trade publications have become digital-only. Indeed, the renowned EMAP brand has been retired with its print publications being replaced by online-only content, including responsive websites. Building loyal user bases willing to subscribe for paid content (online or through print/broadcast media) is a challenge as a result of such a shift. This highlights the importance of ensuring that information offered to inter-organisational media is tailored, useful and designed for multiple media platforms. There may be opportunities to develop exclusive materials, although it is likely that this requires a financial budget. Such inter-organisational media can be seen as hybrid earned-paid channels.

Expert inter-organisational media remain important in breaking news stories that are subsequently picked up by more general titles. Indeed, pressures on journalism increase this likelihood and make specialist contacts useful for extending the reach and independent value of stories.

Other inter-organisational influencers include academics, industry experts, trade/professional bodies, politicians, consultants, celebrities and personal contacts (including colleagues, family and friends). Mapping techniques are useful to analyse potential influencers so PR activities can be developed to engage with, or utilise these influencers as appropriate (see Chapter 5).

Inter-organisational communications channels do not always involve a direct route. Figure 20.1 illustrates how intermediary organisations complicate what is traditionally termed a vertical communications process. Money *et al.* (2010) found that partnerships can enhance the reputation of the participants with stakeholders. However, these can also generate issues or crisis situations that can impact on reputation and require PR action.

The following Action Point demonstrates how issues affecting one organisation can lead to crisis management for its business customers and their stakeholders.

Where there are intermediaries in the inter-organisational process, public relations activities may be used to communicate direct with the end user as well as, or instead of, communicating with the intermediary. Such communications need to fulfil the need for both push and pull communications strategies (Figure 20.2).

When organisations recognise a specific need, they are likely to engage in information-seeking behaviour (pull communications) and also process information that comes (is pushed) their way. For example, attendance at an exhibition may be initiated to seek information on particular products, or a thought leadership article in a trade email newsletter may be of particular interest.

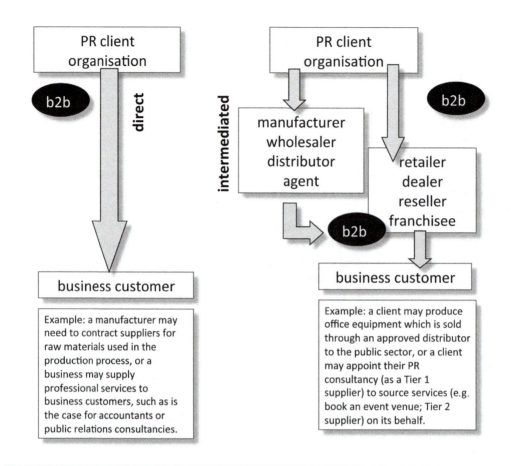

FIGURE 20.1 Comparison of direct and intermediated inter-organisational communication process

ACTION POINT

Complex supply chains present challenges for inter-organisational communications with regard to issues and crisis management. Many stake-holders have power over the organisation's ability to achieve its goals, such as government, shareholders and customers. Their concerns may be viewed as having legitimacy owing to legal or moral claims on the firm (Mitchell *et al.*, 1997). Other individuals, organisations or groups may act as influencers through their ability to highlight an issue or frame it as an urgent problem that needs to be addressed.

In order to avoid such circumstances, supply chain management involves developing standards, external benchmarking, continuous improvement initiatives and social responsibility reporting. These responses may be legally mandated or voluntary, where motivation might come from prior incidents or be value-driven.

The clothing industry is a useful example for examining ongoing challenges. It is common for brands to outsource or license manufacture and distribution of products to organisations in countries that have low costs of production. Such countries traditionally have low standards of health and safety, poor employment and working conditions, and cultural differences in what may be acceptable practices. There are often multiple intermediaries between the brand-name companies and the factories where their goods are made. Likewise, the vertical chain might include numerous distributors and wholesalers, as well as physical and online retailers.

Supply chain management and inter-organisational communications may therefore be problematic for high-profile brands that attract attention when incidents occur. This can be seen in the case of Nike that has been accused of supporting sweatshop working conditions since the 1970s. Most significantly, in June 1996 an article in *Life Magazine* revealed the use of child labour to make Nike soccer balls in factories in Pakistan. After initially denying responsibility, in 1998 the company's CEO and founder Phillip Knight announced policy changes presented as 12 promises.

Further criticism in 2001 arose when Nike published an interim report commissioned from the Global Alliance for Workers and Communities. The Global Exchange, an international human rights organisation, reported in a publication, *Still waiting for Nike to Do It,* a lack of independence, transparency, depth and scope in Nike's analysis of its corporate responsibility performance. Over the years, the issue of supplier employment conditions retained a high profile, with Nike instituting revised auditing and compliance programmes that were followed by reports from advocacy groups exposing violations, negative media reports, consumer boycotts and online activism campaigns.

This illustrates how reliance on compliance standards may not be an effective public relations approach. Today Nike has adopted a strategy of sustainable innovation that seeks to revise the manufacturing process. This includes better factory design, management training and support for labour and government bodies in the countries in which Nike operates.

The Sheffield Political Economy Research Unit (SPERI) at the University of Sheffield identifies general challenges with ethical audits and certification standards. In particular, it notes that such programmes fail to address environmental and employee issues. Further, they reduce the role of governments in regulating corporate behaviour and favour the interests of private business.

Looking forward, increasing use of industrial robots will change the nature of such issues away from worker welfare conditions towards the responsibility of organisations towards the elimination of jobs within their domestic and overseas supply chains.

Sources:

www.laborrights.org/in-the-news/six-cents-hour

https://archive.cleanclothes.org/documents/01-05NikeReport.pdf

http://about.nike.com/pages/our-ambition

http://speri.dept.shef.ac.uk/wp-content/uploads/2016/01/Global-Brief-1-Ethical-Audits-and-the-Supply-Chains-of-Global-Corporations.pdf

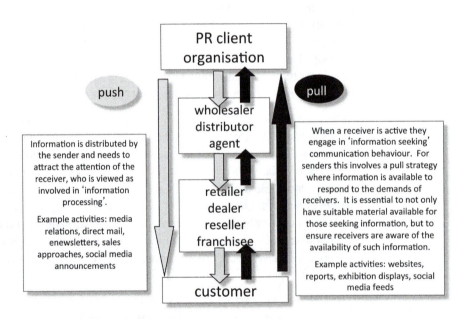

FIGURE 20.2 Push and pull communications processes

ROLE OF DECISION-MAKERS

The decision-making process that leads to establishment and development of inter-organisational relationships may involve several steps. As such it necessitates understanding of the needs of those responsible for particular roles. These may be different people or functions in larger organisations as illustrated in Figure 20.3.

Organisations may have detailed procurement procedures to manage costs, ensure consistency of approach, control order and invoicing processes or reduce

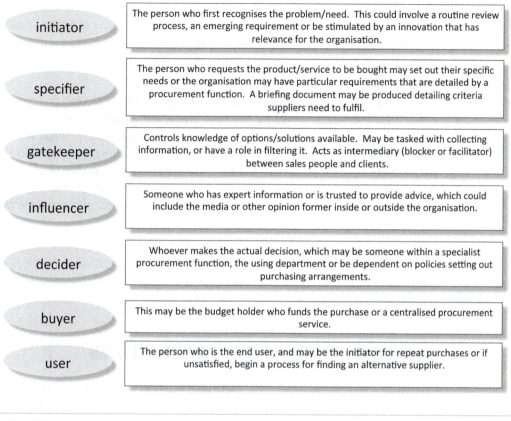

initiator	The person who first recognises the problem/need. This could involve a routine review process, an emerging requirement or be stimulated by an innovation that has relevance for the organisation.
specifier	The person who requests the product/service to be bought may set out their specific needs or the organisation may have particular requirements that are detailed by a procurement function. A briefing document may be produced detailing criteria suppliers need to fulfil.
gatekeeper	Controls knowledge of options/solutions available. May be tasked with collecting information, or have a role in filtering it. Acts as intermediary (blocker or facilitator) between sales people and clients.
influencer	Someone who has expert information or is trusted to provide advice, which could include the media or other opinion former inside or outside the organisation.
decider	Whoever makes the actual decision, which may be someone within a specialist procurement function, the using department or be dependent on policies setting out purchasing arrangements.
buyer	This may be the budget holder who funds the purchase or a centralised procurement service.
user	The person who is the end user, and may be the initiator for repeat purchases or if unsatisfied, begin a process for finding an alternative supplier.

FIGURE 20.3 Decision-making roles

risk of favouritism or unethical purchasing practices. Specific duties may be specified within the decision-making unit. When developing inter-organisational PR initiatives, it is important to be clear which stage of the decision-making process is being targeted, and the responsibilities of the people who are involved at that point.

At the heart of inter-organisational communications are personal relationships, even within the constraints of formal procurement processes. PR is able to support sales teams who proactively build relationships with prospective and existing clients, by developing a range of communications materials, initiating activities (such as attendance at exhibitions or conferences), building an opinion leadership position, generating media coverage and engaging with third-party influencers (such as experts in a particular industry).

Advice from colleagues in relevant functions is required to ensure PR communications reach the right people at the right time with the right message. They should know if there is a particular time during the year when organisations undertake procurement decisions, probably tied into a formal budget cycle.

Organisations seeking to establish new relationships require PR support to generate leads with prospective clients or partners. This may involve promotional activities (such as trade launches), pitch presentations, trade articles supported by reputational initiatives such as thought leadership, social responsibility, case studies or third-party testimonials.

Maintaining relationships is equally, if not more important. PR tactics can be used to ensure client's expertise remains top of mind or to inoculate against prospecting tactics used by competitors. Joint public relations activities may be useful in areas where organisations have shared objectives. Ongoing relationship building may involve corporate hospitality and sponsorship activities that could include sports, the arts and/or societal activities. Again knowledge of relevant legislation is vital. In the UK, this includes ensuring that adequate procedures are in place to comply with requirements of the Bribery Act 2010.

Relationships will be required with other inter-organisational stakeholders to achieve corporate objectives. These are considered elsewhere in the *PR Strategic Toolkit*, but may include managing relationships with providers of finance, professional services, trade organisations, local and national government bodies, and community groups.

INTER-ORGANISATIONAL PR STRATEGIES

The planning approaches discussed in Part II are relevant to support inter-organisational strategies. In some cases, budgets may be small in relation to the impact required and hence require practitioners to be exceptionally creative. Key activities used in inter-organisational public relations are detailed in Table 20.1.

It is likely that any inter-organisational PR campaign will need to take account of existing activities within an organisation, and *ad-hoc* opportunities that arise continuously. This emphasises the importance for developing a programme of activities in partnership with key internal parties (e.g. procurement or specific service areas).

Agile planning allows for regular reviews of activities and emerging opportunities as well as changing organisational needs. It is important to be able to demonstrate measurable benefits from specific inter-organisational PR strategies rather than spreading support too thin across a range of disparate activities.

Crisis management strategies also need to consider inter-organisational communications. In particular, existing clients and key influencers (including political and media contacts) are likely to be priorities. Consequently, relevant information needs to be prepared to be shared immediately and on an ongoing basis.

In crises and other situations, social media are a critical dimension of inter-organisational communications. A presence should be established on relevant platforms with a strategy developed for relevant materials to be shared routinely and in exceptional

TABLE 20.1 Inter-organisational PR approaches

Collateral	Publicity materials such as brochures and sales presentations need to be readily available. White papers and opinion statements can also be developed to provide ongoing opportunities for communications with existing or prospect contacts.
Online	Websites need to provide information relevant to other organisations. These may feature case studies, detailed product specification or details of services, annual reports, company histories, video and other multimedia materials (e.g. speeches), testimonials and opinion leader articles.
	Many organisations operate extranet systems where suppliers and other partners can engage in a private online environment. These may feature news and other useful materials developed by the organisation, possibly including the PR function. All sites and materials need to be optimised for mobile access through smart phones, tablets and other devices.
Interactive	Social media offer opportunities to maximise online presence and provide links to information on the organisation's website or available at other sites (existing clients, media reports and so forth). Some platforms are particularly relevant for inter-organisational communications, such as LinkedIn. The most important aspect is that social media allow for interactive inter-organisational communications. This includes opportunities for live or recorded broadcast of events.
Brand	Brand identity helps to establish a recognisable, professional impression of the organisation. Product and service brands may be developed. Logos and other aspects of the brand (such as pantone references) need to be used consistently by all functions within the organisation, and if available for use by other organisations.
	Branded materials to be used in inter-organisational communications, such as imagery and presentation templates, should be developed centrally. Detailed brand guidelines are a further way of ensuring look and feel are cohesive across the organisation.
	Merchandise (such as corporate clothing, pens and so forth) is often used with inter-organisational relationship activites.
Mailings	A wide range of materials, such as newsletters, can be developed for distribution to existing contacts and databases by post or email. They may also be available for online subscription and download.
Editorial	Knowledge of print, online and broadcast media is essential for inter-organisational communications. Therefore, it is important to build relationships with freelance and staff journalists who have specialist knowledge. Stunts and creative approaches may be required alongside more standard techniques such as industry surveys and product launches.
	Paid for media support (advertorials, sponsored online content, boosted social media posts, etc.) is normal practice in many sectors. Online influencers may include bloggers and industry specialists. These may produce well-respected editorial and news through newsletters, reports, video and so forth. Directories and yearbooks may offer sponsorship and editorial opportunities.

(continued)

TABLE 20.1 (Continued)

Events	A wide range of events and activities can be utilised for inter-organisational communications. These may include industry exhibitions, conferences and speaking opportunities. Exclusive individual or group events may be created for organisational contacts, such as facility visits. Award events are also useful for increasing profile and making contacts.
Sponsorship	Sponsorship and corporate hospitality offer opportunities for brand recognition and relationship development. Sports, arts and community programmes are available either 'off the shelf' or created specifically for the organisation.

circumstances. An online strategy needs to include proactive monitoring of review sites where opinions about the organisation may be examined as part of due diligence efforts when developing inter-organisational relationships.

Thought leadership strategy

Beddow (2015) examines the value of a thought leadership approach for professional service firms (PSFs), albeit from a business development/marketing perspective. He defines thought leadership as:

> A research based publication or campaign on a subject of current interest, produced with the aim of attracting media coverage, building a firm's brand and providing opportunities to engage a wide range of external and internal audiences including clients, prospects and colleagues.
>
> (Beddow 2015: 120)

This suggests a short-term tactical approach primarily of use within a sales development process that is akin to content marketing. In contrast, a strategic public relations approach would ensure that thought leadership reflects a value-driven commitment to enhancing inter-organisational reputation.

Given the volume of articles and white papers available on a myriad of topics online, it is increasingly important to ensure that thought leadership communications are trusted, memorable and valued by inter-organisational stakeholders.

Taking a leadership position within an industry can also be achieved by use of sponsorship and event approaches. For example, an organisation may host a workshop on a specific topic where expert speakers address matters of interest to existing and potential clients. Similarly, opportunities may be sought to speak or chair sessions at industry conferences.

A checklist on developing thought leadership can be found in the Appendix.

ACTION POINT

CASE STUDY: THE SUSTAINABLE CITIES INDEX AWARD WINNING CAMPAIGN FOR ARCADIS BY SPECIALIST B2B CONSULTANCY, MAN BITES DOG

(www.arcadis.com) (www.manbitesdog.com)

Arcadis is a leading global design and consultancy firm employing 27,000 people in over 70 countries. It identified cities as a business growth area and sought recognition as an expert, despite having little brand awareness or recognition as a credible global player in relation to urban centres.

Specific challenges to be overcome were identified by Man Bites Dog as:

- Sustainability fatigue requiring a fresh angle
- Global relevance while reflecting local challenges
- A hard to reach group of city planners, executives and policy-makers.

The strategy proposed was to benchmark urban environments and produce a Sustainable Cities Index (SCI). This would be used to stimulate debate with Arcadis positioned as driving global and regional narratives on the issue.

Research commissioned from the Centre for Economics and Business Research generated a detailed evidence-based metric. Consequently the SCI provided a unique assessment with 20 indicators of the 'triple bottom line' performance of cities worldwide. Shareable, interactive content was created, with a white paper, microsite, infographic and animated videographic materials, as well as country-specific media releases.

The key message of the first SCI, published in 2015, revealed cities prioritised Profit and Planet pillars of sustainability over those most directly concerning People. In 2016, the number of cities ranked doubled to 100. The narrative involved disparity between cities to highlight the challenge in balancing sustainability factors.

In addition to generating media coverage around the world, more than 50,000 unique users visited the website in six weeks (against a target of 1,500), with over 12,000 copies of the report being downloaded (over seven times the planned objective). More than 24,000 views of the online video were reported. The campaign was evaluated as contributing towards €20.8 million in new business wins, generating 14 thought leadership speaking opportunities and various social media metrics.

The client, Andy Rowlands, head of corporate communications at Arcadis claimed that the launch of the Sustainable Cities Index was the company's most commercially successful campaign to date.

The campaign won three awards:

- Best business communications campaign at the IBP Communication and PR Awards
- Best International Campaign Corporate Communications Magazine Awards
- Best Use of Thought Leadership at the B2B Marketing Awards.

The importance of inter-organisational public relations practice is increasingly recognised by awards such as those indicated in the above Action Point. Winning awards is a useful technique for consultancies that can use this success when pitching for new business or to demonstrate industry leadership to existing clients. Indeed, a consultancy's most important client for inter-organisational PR is itself.

END POINT

Inter-organisational communications offers considerable potential for demonstrating the strategic value of public relations where it is able to work alongside senior management to develop solutions that support the achievement of key goals. It is not restricted to commercial organisations with inter-organisational relationships of importance in the not-for-profit and government sectors.

A range of inter-organisational PR approaches can be utilised to support sales and marketing activities, as well as to achieve other relevant goals. In particular, public relations expertise contributes towards managing organisational reputation and key relationships with a variety of stakeholders.

This is critical when organisations are involved in a complex network of relationships with other organisations. Inter-organisational PR needs to ensure organisations are aware of issues that can affect credibility and trust. This means demonstrating an expert understanding of supply chain matters affecting industries, as well as inter-organisational influencers and communication channels, beyond the traditional focus on trade media.

CHAPTER 21

Community relations

Alison Theaker

CHECK POINT

Organisations want to have good relationships with the communities
they operate in. This could be dealing with people who live next to their
factory, or with school or university leavers they may want to recruit.
This chapter will:

- Define community relations (CommR)
- List the various activities that could be used in a community relations
  programme
- Compare CommR with cause-related marketing (CRM)
- Make the case for organisations to be involved with CommR
  and CSR.

Many think that any community relations programme is down to basic self-interest, to
enable the company to have an easy life. 'A corporation can gain competitive advantage by having the goodwill of local communities', suggested Werbel and Wortman
(2000: 124). Bowd (2005) suggests that benefits can include goodwill, customer and
staff loyalty. However, the Tomorrow's Company Inquiry, set up by the RSA in 1993,
found that in a competitive marketplace CommR was a necessity rather than a luxury
and that companies have to earn their 'licence to operate'.

DEFINITIONS OF COMMR

Some definitions include:

- Providing money or people, or advice, something that may be only indirectly measurable. (Graham Savage, Millennium Commission)
- Planned investment in the society in which you operate. (Ellie Gray, Corporate Development Manager at the Prince's Trust)
- The tactical approaches organisations plan in order to discharge their corporate social responsibility policy. (Tench, 2014)

READING POINT

CommR is closely related to corporate social responsibilty. You can read more about CSR in Chapter 14.

Harrison (in Kitchen, 1997: 129) feels that companies are part of the society in which they operate and need to consider what effect they have. She refers to Peach's model of the impact of business on its environment. The initial level of impact simply covers paying taxes, observing the law and dealing fairly. The second level recognises the need to minimise negative effects and act in the spirit as well as the letter of the law. At the third level the organisation 'sees itself as having a responsibility for a healthy society and accepts the job of helping to remove or alleviate problems'. The third-level company is, however, rare.

MAPPING THE COMMUNITY

So who might be part of the community? There might be a clear geographical area where the organisation is located, but not everyone in the area will have the same concerns. Some of that community are likely to also be employees. Others may be professionals or factory workers. There are also likely to be local schools, with school children, teachers and parents who will have their own particular concerns. Local media and local councillors will focus on the impact of the organisation in their patch. And then there may be activist groups who care about specific issues.

Organisations need to investigate which groups in the community are important for them to build relationships with. When opening a new store in a small Devon town where local traders had been vociferous in their opposition, Tesco ensured that it provided a platform for community groups to fundraise in the store. A common complaint was the effect on the amount of parking available, so Tesco made their own car park available for two hours free parking, enabling shoppers to visit the local traders as well as shop in the supermarket. Tesco also became involved in the town's participation in Britain in Bloom by sponsoring flower displays on a roundabout.

WHAT DO COMMR PROGRAMMES LOOK LIKE?

Cutlip *et al.* (1985: 405–6) list several kinds of activity:

- The open house: a tour of the facilities of the organisation, enabling large numbers to come onto the premises. Exhibits can give information, and using employees as guides can give them renewed pride in their workplace.
- Special events: ground-breaking for a new building or the completion of one; special seminars linked to the company's products, such as a safe driving school run by a motor manufacturer.
- Using internal newsletters: with the addition of some specific news, the internal publication can be circulated throughout the community to enable a wider knowledge of the company's activities.
- Volunteer activities: encouraging and enabling employees to perform voluntary service for local organisations, including secondment. Some schemes enable employees to do this in work time.
- Funding: sponsoring or donating money to local organisations, whether in cash or kind.

Davis (2004) adds several possible activities, such as decorating old people's homes, reading aloud to children in local schools, seconding staff to local organisations, raising funds for local causes through sponsorship and direct funding of local events. Other schemes might include providing a venue for a local organisation to hold meetings, contributing trees to landscape schemes, offering work experience to young people and creating bursaries for schools and colleges.

CommR is about improving the quality of life in the local community, so organisations may become involved in environmental clean-ups, recycling, arts programmes and children's activities.

WHAT WILL WE GET OUT OF COMMR?

This area of corporate activity used to be anecdotally referred to as the 'chairman's wife syndrome', or the support of activity according to whim or personal interest of senior management and their spouses. There are still some examples of this, such as Crealy Theme Parks in Devon and Cornwall. The MD, Angela Wright, heard about play pumps, which use a children's roundabout to pump water from bore holes. While this fits with the Crealy belief that children learn through play, no evaluation or link to visitor numbers was carried out. However, this does not mean that the programme had no value – the park raised enough for three pumps to be sent to Africa.

Wheeler and Sillanpaa (1997: 275) reported that: 'In 1993, more than 90 per cent of large companies in the US had a community involvement programme, more than two-thirds allowed time off during work for volunteering and 63 per cent had a community involvement fund.' In the UK in 1995, a survey found that only a third of large companies had a volunteer programme and only 44 per cent of those allowed time off for volunteer activities. Less than two-thirds offered financial support.

However, such schemes are now becoming more widespread. The University of Plymouth began discussions in 2010 with employees to set up a scheme where they could have paid additional leave for one or two days per year to work for a chosen charity. In addition they asked employees to vote on which local charities should benefit from institution-wide fundraising activities. Links were also made to the volunteering activities carried out by the students' union.

TALKING POINT

EVALUATING INVOLVEMENT – THE EXCELLENCE MODEL

Several merchant banks in Canary Wharf developed links with local schools (Montagu Smith, 2006). Staff from Credit Suisse volunteer to tutor children in reading, maths and IT. Heart of the City was launched in 2000 by the Bank of England, aiming to give children a working adult as a role model. Staff from Merrill Lynch mentor sixth-form students in Tower Hamlets schools. In an era when banks have been heavily criticised, such activities attempt to give them a human face.

The European Foundation for Quality Management (EFQM) Excellence Model uses a nine-point plan to understand relationships between what an organisation does and what results it achieves.

The Excellence Model has nine principles. The first five are enablers:

- *Leadership* – do the company leaders act as role models and inspire trust?
- *Policy and strategy* – does the organisation have a stakeholder-focused strategy?
- *People* – do they value and develop employees at an individual, team and organisation-wide level?
- *Partnership and resources* – does the organisation manage external partnerships to support strategy?
- *Processes* – are activities monitored to create increasing value for stakeholders?

Both an organisation and a prospective charity could use the formula to assess whether the results gained from the partnership make the relationship worthwhile.

The other side of the equation is results, and the four remaining principles are:

- *Customer results* – whether the needs of customers are being met.
- *People results* – what the organisation is achieving in relation to its own employees.
- *Society results* – what the organisation is achieving in the communities in which it operates.
- *Business results* – are the organisation's business objectives being met?

The kind of benefits that a charity could offer might include enhancing corporate reputation by association. If the company is reducing staff, affecting the local economy, the partnership can also be used to put something back into the community at the same time. Association with a cause could help influence opinion-formers, so strengthening the company's licence to operate and building customer loyalty. Product sales could be benefited through cause-related marketing, and the association may also contribute to recruitment, staff development and motivation.

If you were in the communications team of a national bank, how might you use the Excellence Model to demonstrate the benefits of engaging in a community relations programme? What charities or organisations would you suggest partnering with?

Excellence Model copyright EFQM (2013).

HOW CAN WE DO IT?

Hawn (2007) puts forward six principles for successful commuity relations. First, the organisation should set out a clear project message and commit to it, whether this is about making the community safer or providing more opportunities for young people. Next, all team members must speak with one voice, and all written materials should reflect this. A dedicated point of contact between the organisation and the community should be someone whom the community can identify with. Hawn's (2007) Risk Communication Model recommends:

- Understand your audience – identify potential issues and agendas
- Listen twice as much as you speak
- Avoid jargon
- Show empathy
- Maintain continuity of points of contact.

Multiple and regular communication methods should be used which cater to the audience and are tailored to their concerns. Finally, an exit strategy needs to be devised for the completion of the project to ensure its sustainabilty.

Tench (2014) states that CommR benefits both parties and makes a link between being a good corporate citizen and having a good reputation and improving share value, although this is debatable. Laying down a good reputational foundation may help an organisation during a crisis. Encouraging employees to become involved in their community may also improve productivity. Tench suggests that such programmes could be evaluated by assessing publicity, getting employee feedback, appreciation, opinion-former perceptions, and social media engagement and response. He goes on to say that 'community relations is not about being good or "nice to people", although this may be one of its results' (2014: 290). The programme has to be based on sound commercial principles and fulfil strategic objectives for the organisation.

Lukaszewski (2010) warns that using new media can be more of a distraction, when community relationships are 'built on spoken and written communication'. He advises that these tools should be used to provide bursts of 'positive, correct information ... crucial questions to be answered ... real insights into issues'. However, he empha-sises that local relationships may best be fostered by using 'traditional techniques and approaches'.

Good CommR programmes help to give employees a reason to be proud of the company, with all the benefits of increased engagement that brings. The following case study shows how the Environment Agency changed its way of dealing with com-munities where it was developing projects, so that opposition was reduced.

CAUSE-RELATED MARKETING (CRM)

BITC (2004) defined CRM as 'a commercial activity by which business and charities or causes form a partnership with each other to market an image, product or service for mutual benefit'. More recently, they are encourgaing organisations to practise 'sus-tainable marketing', which is about 'influencing customer behaviour to create both profit and positive societal change' (BITC, 2012).

Unlike sponsorship, which might include the donation of a one-off amount to a charity, or the provision of equipment to a special-needs school, CRM has a clear profit motive.

Why is CRM important?

- 98 per cent of consumers are aware of CRM programmes;
- 80 per cent have particpated in a CRM scheme;
- 71 per cent claimed to have been influenced in their buying decisions by CRM (Adkins, 2006).

BUILDING TRUST WITH COMMUNITIES

The Environment Agency and the Shaldon Risk Project

In the early 2000s the Environment Agency realised that its default strategy of decide–announce–defence (DAD) was not the best approach for its major construction projects. The imposition of flood defence schemes and other environmental solutions on local communities could no longer continue.

We set out to counter two widespread myths in the organisational culture, that (i) engaging with communities was expensive and time-consuming; and (ii) it was possible to choose whether or not to work with others. The plan was to shift to an inclusive way of working – engage–deliberate–decide (EDD). By engaging with our customers and building trust with communities and stakeholders right from the start of a project we would be able to agree the solution so our schemes would become less controversial and less time-consuming. Ultimately they would be less costly to the public purse.

FIGURE 21.1 Environment Agency's Shaldon project

Having already identified locations with very real tidal risk we chose Shaldon and Ringmore as our EDD pilot and brought in Lindsay Colbourne Associates to work with us. Shaldon and Ringmore are small linked villages at the mouth of the Teign Estuary in Devon. There is a 1.2 kilometre-long river frontage along the villages. Homes and businesses were in a low-lying basin behind existing, informal defences with a poor standing of flood protection. If tidal water overtopped the old flood walls houses, shops and other properties would easily flood. This tidal risk was made worse by increased waves during storms and high winds and the impact of climate change. We assessed there was a 1 in 300 chance of tidal flooding in any one year at Shaldon and Ringmore. This flooding would affect up to 418 properties with some under 2 metres of dirty river water.

As there was a lack of historical records or living memory of tidal flooding in the community, residents were initially highly sceptical of the tidal risk and potential need to be defended. Much of the income in the pretty area comes from tourism so business and home owners did not want ugly flood defences spoiling their village.

The building trust process began in October 2005 with a public exhibition setting out the facts about flood risk. We encouraged local people to tell us what they thought about the tidal risk and to let us know whether they wanted us to do anything about it. Surface water and sewer flooding caused more concern to the residents than the possibility of tidal flooding. However, at a public meeting after the exhibition the community confirmed it did understand the tidal flood risk facing the village and it did want to work with us. The next step was to agree the way of working and a local liaison group was agreed.

Twenty-eight volunteers were selected by the community to represent them on the liaison group. We held the evening meetings in the village using church halls and other rooms including group members' homes. Led by Lindsay Colbourne the group worked through the detail of the risk, the possible options to reduce the risk and this information was shared with the rest of the local people. The output from the liaison group sessions helped us address the surface water flood concerns and eventually incorporate it into the scheme design. We also brought together highway engineers and the water company to do their bit in tackling the whole flood situation.

Once we all agreed that a tidal defence scheme of flood walls and gates was required, our design engineers developed the outline design. Then members of the liaison group help to run walking tours in Shaldon and Ringmore to show to the community what was proposed to reduce their tidal flood risk.

While 83 per cent of those who made the tours were very positive about the plans and 70 per cent supported them, there was a small but growing number of people expressing concern over the height of the flood walls. We organised drop-in sessions and further walking tours to give them a further chance to discuss their concerns.

At this stage, in the light of new national data on tide levels, we decided to review and subsequently withdrew our planning application for the defences. The review of the proposals resulted in a small reduction to the height of the scheme, making it acceptable to the majority and we successfully reapplied for planning. This was a difficult time for us and we continued to ensure we were upfront and clear about the plans, coaching our staff not to become defensive or dismissive when people challenged them.

It was vital to continue our good relations with the local community during construction of the tidal defences. We appointed an on-site public liaison officer for the duration of the project, who, as a engineer himself, was able to deal with local concerns promptly and consistently. The project was completed in May 2011 and, once again, we continued to involve the locals by asking them to help us organise the official opening ceremony. The final event was a real celebration of working together, including many words of praise and thanks from the local people for their lovely flood walls and gates, and for the way we had involved them.

For our engineers and technical staff engaging in a local community in this way was initially hard work, although the benefits quickly became clear as community understanding of what we were trying to achieve developed and support grew. The time spent on building trust and relationships at the start of this project has been time very well spent. It has also helped our teams think more about the customers when designing a project that will make a real difference to people. We spent around £500,000 on community engagement on this £8.4 million project and the real value of that spend is the application of the learning across our wider business.

The Environment Agency has produced guidelines from the project so that the principles of EDD can be learned and applied by staff in future schemes and affected communities can be involved right from the start.

Bridget Beer joined the National Rivers Authority in 1991 and quickly moved into the PR team progressing into the Environment Agency. She worked across the South West specialising in holistic communications and engagement around contentious. In April 2011 she took the lead role in customer engagement at the Flood Forecasting Centre.

CUSTOMERS BECOME COMMUNICATORS WITH WESTWARD HOUSING GROUP

Taking a truly two-way symmetric approach, Westward Housing Group has a Communications Group editorial team of customers to produce their own newsletters. Whilst members receive training from the communications staff, the team decides on the content, conducts interviews and writes articles, agrees on design and proofreads the newsletters and webpages for their housing areas. Review meetings are also held for the website, and terms of reference are written with the members.

The Westward communications group has about 12 members (Figure 21.2). Westward encourages a proportional representation of age, tenancy type, needs, and location of members. Whilst membership of the team is an unpaid role, Westward funds travel and care costs.

The tone and content of the newsletter aims to be inclusive. The benefits of having publications and online material shaped by tenants are that it means we have communication both by and for residents. This means it is far more likely to result in information which is interesting to and presented for the readership in a way they would most like to see it. They know best.

As well as the experience of the group members, the readers, who may be older people living in sheltered schemes or marginalised groups, are encouraged to have broader horizons by seeing the work and activities of their peers. Features such as 'Your Story' or 'Tenant's Tale' have included moving personal achievement stories, neighbourly tales of kindness and experience of living as a disabled person, ranging through to wartime experiences and having a tattoo done in old age. A social enterprise project for marginalised people to grow and sell plants and another therapeutic enterprise run with clients who learn to reupholster furniture have also been inspirational showcases.

Residents in the communications group find their confidence to speak out and express their views flourishes as their skills and experience grow. They also interview Westward staff about changes and share the news in a clear, customer-focused way. Members say they get a lot of satisfaction from seeing their work in print and are rightly proud of their work. Melanie Crump in the Communications Group writes interviews, articles and poetry alongside her own interest as a performance poet. She is always very keen to go out and find stories from our residents.

Seeing a village pantomime celebrated in pictures, or an article about evicting anti-social neighbours has a strengthening impact on the community.

FIGURE 21.2 Westward Communication Group

A contractor who advertises an apprenticeship vacancy and appoints a resident may be interviewed, as well as the apprentice about how their new role is going. Westward works with partner organisations which have direct relevance and potential benefit for tenants. They work with the Fire Services to promote safety and liaise with the police in reporting confidence tricksters or thefts from oil tanks. Readers in the community can participate in surveys and consultations at residents' events. Staff also consult residents when producing other publications and send the drafts to the group for checking. This earns them a quality mark known as the customer approved logo.

All staff receive training at induction about the group. Staff who are out and about in the community can be a great source of possible stories to feed back to the teams. Readership and satisfaction rates are high in annual surveys with *Moor to Sea*, the Westward newsletter, being given as the main source of information for 84 per cent of general needs, 90 per cent of sheltered and 85 per cent of supported customers. Annual communication surveys through the newsletter and online establish readership and allow for feedback.

We increasingly move towards online films and Prezi presentations for customers when explaining their responsibilities and our services and staff roles, using both tenants from the communications group and staff as presenters. We invest heavily in secure online services now and our customer input to that is critical.

Vanessa Gray-Locke is Communications Manager for Westward Housing Group. She trained and worked as a journalist before moving into PR for an environmental education centre and then an organic farming research centre. Westward provides affordable housing and related services across the South West to more than 7,000 households.

Enlightened self-interest

'Like any other aspect of Lever Faberge's brand activity plans, we believe CRM programmes have to make sound commercial sense and are firmly grounded in consumer understanding', said John Ballington (2003). The company supports Comic Relief, and over three years raised more than £1 million for the cause but also raised consumer awareness of their Persil brand. In addition, after using findings from their Family Report research they found that the average infant pupil received only £1.18 arts and crafts funding per year. In 2002 they launched their Get Creative initiative which involved collecting on-pack tokens that could be redeemed for brushes or face-painting kits. Over 40,000 schools registered in the first two years of the scheme. Illustrating that such schemes must be relevant to the products of the company concerned, Persil was keen to be seen as the band that cleaned up children's paint-stained clothes!

Whilst a 2001 *Which?* report was critical of the long-running Tesco Computers for Schools scheme, claiming that parents would have to spend £250,000 on their shopping to get enough tokens to provide a computer that cost only £1,000 to buy, the programme provided more than £82 million worth of equipment in its first 12 years of operation. More than 86 per cent of UK schools registered with the scheme (Williamson, 2004). As funding is set to become even more important for schools such initiatives may become even more common. However, the NUT 2003 conference resolved to campaign against commercialisation in schools, so organisations would do well to research guidelines drawn up by ISBA, the Consumers' Association, the Department for Education and Skills and BITC on any programme that targets schools (Williamson, 2004).

A calculated strategy

CRM is a calculated strategy in which everybody wins. 'CRM isn't just about offering "buy this and 10p goes to that" – there has to be a greater marketing mix to build awareness and secure emotional engagement and loyalty' (Adkins, 2006). The CRM campaign is long-term not short-term, strategic rather than tactical.

Communication of the programme is an important element and must be handled correctly. Organisations must be upfront about the corporate motives for what they are doing. Consumers expect the company to gain from what they are doing, and if this is fudged they will be suspicious. At its best, however, Tench (2014: 283) suggests that the benefits of CRM include:

- Those needing help receive it
- The public feels good about buying/supporting the product
- The donor organisation gains reputation and sometimes sales
- It is a win–win for both parties.

Companies and charities must both assess risk when entering into CRM partnerships. Engaging in CRM can lead to a more critical examination of a company's policies. The Red Cross's decision to take £250,000 from Nestlé was reported in January 2000, and the question raised whether the charity should have taken money from a company that had been involved in unethical promotion of its baby milk products in the developing world (Wall, 2000).

The Charity Commission advises that charities should not take money from companies that perpetrate the problem the charity is trying to solve. The Red Cross responded that it had been assured by the WHO that Nestle was now complying with international law on the marketing of baby milk powder, and should that change the charity reserved the right to end the relationship. Wall (2000) quotes Stephen Lee, former head of ICFM, the professional body of fundraisers, as saying: 'It's a con. It's a mechanism dreamed up by business to promote business, with very strong rhetoric about partnership which is usually absolute rubbish.' Also see the discussion about CRM in Chapter 14.

END POINT

Community relations and cause-related marketing programmes have clear benefits for organisations who carry them out in a planned manner. Successful programmes should be based on a thorough analysis of what both organisation and community might gain; involve the community the organisation is trying to form a relationship with; empower groups within the community to participate; clearly set out any financial benefits of CRM; be communicated in an honest and transparent way.

CHAPTER 22

Consumer public relations

Alison Theaker

Public relations that deals with consumer products has to coexist and interact with marketing communications.

CHECK POINT

This chapter looks at one of the most vibrant areas of public relations. It covers:

- The relationship between PR and marketing
- A definition of consumerism
- The role of marketing communications
- Consumer buying behaviour
- Keeping customers
- Future trends.

MARKETING AND PUBLIC RELATIONS

Public relations in the field of consumer relations is often referred to as marketing communications or marketing PR (MPR). Marketing, as we have seen, is the identification of the needs of consumers and how to satisfy those needs profitably.

PR influences markets by sending persuasive messages to buyers. Moloney suggests that as much as 70 per cent of PR jobs are in the field of MPR (Moloney, 2006).

Research by Kitchen found that 15 per cent of marketing budgets was spent on brand PR in the UK and that marketing professionals spent 70 per cent of their time on marketing communications (Bacot, 2006).

Marketers tend to see PR as a subordinate part of their armoury of tools whilst public relations practitioners often see marketing as primarily concerned with selling products to consumers. Belch and Belch (2001: 576) see PR as much more about changing attitudes than promoting specific products.

Public relations and marketing should be corporate allies, working together for common goals. Cutlip *et al.* (2000: 478–9) list Harris' ten ways that PR can support marketing:

1 building excitement before advertising breaks;
2 creating news about new products;
3 creating news about a new advertising or marketing approach;
4 bringing advertising characters to life by arranging tours and public appearances;
5 extending the reach of marketing by creating links to related charities or campaigns;
6 building personal relationships with consumers;
7 sponsoring events and targeting opinion leaders;
8 communicating new product benefits of existing products;
9 building consumer trust with CSR and CRM;
10 crisis management when products may be at risk or have been sabotaged.

Increased market information results in more informed consumers, but this has resulted in a 'wall of sound'. Moloney (2006) estimates that the average American sees more than 7 million advertisements in his or her lifetime.

Davis (2004) quotes Kotler's 1991 definition of marketing public relations (MPR) as 'a variety of programmes designed to improve, maintain or protect a company or product image' (and see also the discussion of PR and marketing in Chapter 1).

Willis (2014) suggests that 'public relations should become a planned and sustained element of the wider promotional mix, working in tandem with other marketing activities'. Kitchen concluded that 'in the real world, (PR and marketing) need one another', and that MPR helped build relationships between consumers and brands (Jardine, 2006).

Swann (2010) considers that consumer relations involves:

• supporting marketing communication efforts to build consumer demand for products and services and
• maintaining mutually beneficial and lasting relationships between the organisation and consumer.

She points out that the development of the internet and related technology has had a major impact on this field. Now a disgruntled customer can use a variety of methods to get their viewpoint out to millions of web users. So paying attention to long-term relationships with consumers and activitists is imperative to try and minimise reputational damage.

Willis (2014) draws the universe of consumer PR consisting of three overlapping areas: media relations, events and sponsorship. Each of these elements help to create awareness, engagement, and third-party endorsement. Messages may be informational or entertaining. Using media relations to showcase events and sponsorship maximises their effectiveness.

CONSUMERISM

Consumerism is 'the idea that consumers should influence the design, quality, service and prices of goods and services provided by commercial enterprises' (Macmillan, in Mayer, 1989: 309). Consumerism can also be linked to overconsumption and materialism. The BBC programme *Watchdog* publicises where companies have failed to deliver a good response to complaints. The most influential organisation in this field in the UK is the Consumers' Association. Its magazine, *Which?*, also available online, carries reports on a vast range of products to enable consumers to pick the best available in their price range.

Bashford (2011) relates how Dell had to respond to consumer Jeff Jarvis in 2005 when he complained online about his computer being a 'lemon' and signed off with the words 'Dell sucks. Dell lies. Put that in your Google and smoke it.' Jarvis set out to see whether Dell was listening to social media, but it took the company over a year to really get to grips with consumer complaints. Figures on the web suggest that Dell's market share fell sharply as a result (www.ycharts.com). In 2011, however, Dell was awarded 'most social brand' by Headstream in its Social Brands 100 Report. The company gave Jarvis open access and launched a variety of social media platforms, publishing uncensored customer reviews on its website. Social media specialists were sent to business units to deal with any online issues quickly. Dell also used social media to carry out research and set up a panel of independent experts. It has recently trained over 9,000 employees worldwide to become ambassadors in the online world, responding to key word searches to find customers who may need help. Dell director of communications Stuart Handley said, 'branding today is not about how you present yourself on your website or forum; it's about how others present you'. See also Chapter 11 on brand management.

MARKETING COMMUNICATIONS AND INTEGRATED MARKETING COMMUNICATIONS (IMC)

'Marketing communications encompasses any form of communication that contributes to the conversion of a non-customer to a customer, and subsequently to the retention of such custom', says Hart (1995: 25). Ouwersloot and Duncan (2008) define IMC as 'the processes for planning, executing and monitoring the brand messages that create brand-customer relationships'. They suggest that the IMC perspective ensures that all communication activities relate to the same goals. One outcome is 'synergy . . . the interaction of individual parts in a way that makes the integrated whole greater than the sum of its parts'. Strachan and Kelley (2014) add 'IMC is a process. It is a series of intentional touch pioints that take place over time.' They emphasis the need for planning and coordination between the different elements of advertising, sponsorship, promotions, personal selling and PR.

How does PR fit here? Don Schultz coined the phrase 'integrated marketing' in 1993, promoting the value of PR alongside other marketing disciplines (Jardine, 2006). The traditional elements of the marketing mix are the four Ps – product, price, place and promotion. Price can indicate good or bad value for money; in some cases, a high price signals quality or prestige. Place means the channels of distribution and the kind of outlet where the product can be obtained – a product will be viewed differently if it is sold on a market stall rather than in a high street department store. Promotion refers to the media and messages used to influence buyer decisions. It is here that PR contributes most, bringing a range of activities which can support and supplement advertising and marketing. The selection of which medium to use to convey the messages will depend on the target market, and the combination of choices made for the most effective communication is often referred to as the 'media mix'. Davis (2004) adds on three more Ps: people (customers, employees), process (involvement of the consumer in production) and physical evidence (making the benefits of products tangible).

The size of the market affects which tactics to use. A group of people who are involved in any decision are often called the buying decision unit, or BDU. If only ten BDUs are to be approached, personal contact may be best. If there are 1,000, direct email, editorial publicity, demonstrations or telephone selling could be added. With 100,000, mass media methods and targeted use of social media can extend the reach of consumer PR messages.

The kind of message is the next consideration. A simple message could be conveyed by a poster, but a complex or technical one would need to be presented in the specialist media. Davis (2004) suggests that PR is a more cost-effective alternative to spending on advertising, as advertising alone is not persuasive enough. Moloney (2006) agrees that PR and marketing together are better able to handle promotions across a variety of channels such as media relations, events, sponsorship, exhibitions, roadshows and web-based materials.

Marketing traditionally relied on advertising to reach consumers, but this is becoming less influential with the growth of communication channels. Whilst some companies still find 'pay per click' advertising useful, most are finding that they need to use editorial methods and events to get their messages across. Traditional media also work less with younger audiences, who are digital natives. Marketing and public relations can form an effective partnership, producing both digital (website copy and social media ideas) and traditional materials (brochures, newsletters and direct mailers). Websites can now carry video, audio and text, and offer consumers games and other promotional items (Swann, 2010).

Pinsent (2011) relates how lines between functions in organisations are becoming blurred. Whether creating a TV spot, sponsoring a TV show, building a feature story for BBC *Breakfast* or defending the company on BBC *Watchdog*, it is important to ensure that they 'each help tell a consistent story'.

PUBLIC RELATIONS IN THE LAUNCH PROCESS

'Done well, a launch helps a new product rapidly establish itself amongst its target users, gain market share and enhance the company's brand position', says Joan Schneider, CEO of Schneider & Associates, a Boston-based public relations firm with more than 20 years' experience in product launches. 'Done poorly, however, it can negate all the time, money and human capital that went into developing the new product.' With this in mind, Schneider commissioned Boston University to carry out a study into how launches were conducted to identify success factors and help product managers increase their launch success rate.

The survey found that the best launches showed advance planning, with the development of the product occurring one to two years before shipping, along with selecting the advertising agency. Selection of the public relations agency took place ten to twelve months before shipping, with public relations activities starting four to six months before and continuing for at least nine months after the product was on the shelves. The most successful products had benefited from PR planning to create media coverage to build the brand. The best teams included marketing and brand managers as well as operations, manufacturing or product development. Interestingly, the less senior the overall manager of the team, the better the result. Brand or product managers had a higher success rate than senior marketing personnel or CEOs. In terms of budgets, unsurprisingly those with larger budgets were more likely to succeed, as were those that concentrated on consumer-focused activities rather than trade-focused.

Finally, it was found that the use of public relations activities, such as generating positive consumer and trade press mentions, reviews and retailer interest, was seen as having far more impact for highly successful products. 'Considering the amount of time and resources spent on new product development, new products have a surprisingly small window of opportunity during which their fates are sealed,' says Schneider. 'The keys to success are adequate planning and utilising public relations as one of the tools to create a favourable environment.'

CONSUMER BUYING BEHAVIOUR

The PR practitioner also needs to consider the consumers' buying decisions. Belch and Belch (2001) put forward a basic model of how people make choices:

- problem recognition – motivation;
- information search – perception;
- alternative evaluation – attitude formation;
- purchase decision – integration;
- post-purchase evaluation – learning.

The motivation for buying a watch – whether it is to tell the time, or to make a fashion statement – will affect whether the consumer focuses on reliability or design. Motivation is often linked to Maslow's hierarchy of needs, which suggests that it is only after basic needs such as food, shelter and sex are satisfied that people can focus on safety, then love and belonging, and finally self-esteem and self-actualisation. Marketers in the developed world assume that the basic needs are met, and may try to associate their products with one of the higher levels. Volvo concentrates on satisfying basic needs for safety in positioning its cars, while BMW focuses on the higher levels of self-esteem and status.

Kotler suggests that stimuli for buying include price, quality, availability, service, style, options and image (Williams, 1981: 156). Editorial, advertising, salespeople, friends, family and personal observation can all affect the buyer. Fisk (2004) states that consumers want to be more individualistic, so that product differentiation becomes key.

Another way to influence buying behaviour has been to associate brands with celebrities thought to appeal to the target market. Christian Aid used Ronan Keating for its

Trade Justice campaign, aimed at men and women aged 30 to 70 years old, although the majority of its supporters are over 50. Oxfam used Coldplay's Chris Martin and Kaiser Chiefs to raise awareness amongst 16 to 25 year olds. Consultancy Entertainment Media Research (EMR) rated artists' popularity by asking a cross-section of 4,500 people to rate their emotional connection to a variety of celebrities. They found that Oxfam's links worked well with their audience, while Christian Aid would have been better to use Kylie Minogue to reach their target demographic (Magee, 2007).

KEEPING CUSTOMERS

Marketing communications is not only concerned with obtaining customers, but with keeping them. Stone (1995: 141) claims that getting back a lost customer costs five times as much as keeping them happy in the first place. L.D. Young (2006) questions this and suggests that sometimes it is cheaper to attract new customers than chase existing ones.

Awareness of consumer needs means paying attention to staff relations, particularly in the retail sector. Brand and corporate reputation can be undermined by a customer's poor experience in a store. So consumer PR needs to link into human resources and internal communications so that their work is not wasted.

Hunter (2011) advises that it is not enough to simply wait until a customer complains, because by that time they may have sent their opinion out via the web to millions of others. She advises that organisations invite feedback rather than passively monitoring comments. In addition, going into the marketplace where products are sold or delivered and speaking directly to customers can help reveal 'the gap between the brand promise and the consumers' brand reality'. Hunter's consultancy, Unleashed Potential, road-tests clients' products and visits their premises to see if brands live up to their promises. At the end of the day, however, it is important to use information gathered in these ways to shape both communications and product delivery in the future.

Friend (2011) reveals that, according to YouGov, 41 per cent of people will make a complaint by phone, 63 per cent by email and 20 per cent by social media. She advises making any complaint from the latter source a private conversation as soon as possible. An apology and a willingness to solve the problem should come first.

However, Mumford (2014) quotes recent research by BA that found only 8 per cent of customer complaints were ever registered with customer services; people were far more likely to complain to the nearest employee, and the vast majority did not tell anyone at the company. Whilst they may not have mentioned it to the company, they may well have mentioned it to their friends and family, which means that the size of the problem may be far larger than shown by the level of registered complaints.

GUERRILLA PR AND VIRAL MARKETING

Different techniques have to be used to attract the consumer's attention in order to stand out from the mass of information. Guerrilla PR uses stunts and humour to obtain media coverage. Hatfield Galleria invented the protest group the Bargain Liberation Front who protested in Westminster. This linked into their advertising campaign, 'I'm a Bargain Get Me Out of Here', and to a local radio competition to find the best bargain-hunters. Sales increased by 5 per cent (Blyth, 2006). However, stunts should be carefully planned. A cartoon network placed characters on public buildings across the US, but caused widespread panic in Boston when passers-by thought they might be terrorist devices.

Buzz or 'word of mouse' can be created by viral marketing. This involves sending out a video clip and hoping it will be passed on. Three-hundred hours of video are uploaded to the YouTube website every minute, and more than 5 billion are watched each day (Donchev, 2017). T-Mobile's 'Dance' campaign produced a three-minute TV advert. Over 300 dancers were filmed breaking into a seemingly spontaneous dance routine at Liverpool Street station. Travellers' reactions were also incorporated into the film. Similar ads also show spectators filming such stunts on their phones and sending onto friends. The videos can then be posted on YouTube, creating a viral buzz and giving the ad a much greater spread than simply showing it on TV.

Mulholland (2011) warns that PR will have to demonstrate that it delivers 'measurable ROI and can genuinely make a difference to a client's business objectives'. You can read more about evaluation in Chapter 10.

FUTURE TRENDS

Lloyd (2011) advises consumer PR practitioners to anticipate future trends to be able to stay one step ahead of their competitors. She feels PR practitioners need to 'create ultimate engagement, intimacy and loyalty between brands and their consumers'. She suggests that gaming is a new way to create a more long-lasting relationship. She uses examples such as Braun's Oral B toothbrush that displays a happy face when used properly, and VW and the National Society for Road Safety in Sweden who created a speed camera lottery to reward responsible drivers. Clack (2011) also focuses on the long game, recommending the use of 'behavioural economics ... how social, cognitive and emotional factors influence economic decisions'. Clack relates how economist Richard Thaler persuaded 20–30 year olds to start saving for a pension by developing a product that only took contributions from future pay rises.

Moore (2014) reviewed a report by Weber Shandwick that marketing and PR were on course for convergence, as more complex markets and fragmented media channels required a cohesive approach between the two disciplines. One chief communicatons and marketing officer was quoted as saying, 'all stakeholders want to understand product brands and the company behind them'. Another managing director felt that 'PR has a vital role to play in the new world order, using its storytelling power and content creation to allow marketers to tailor compelling brand messages.'

Iliff (2014) and Ritter (2015) discuss the PESO model. Here Paid, Earned, Shared and Owned media channels are integrated to create influential marketing communications programmes. Paid media comprise both advertising (including social media) and paid for platforms like Hubspot which enable email marketing and testing. Earned is the more traditional PR area of pitching stories to reporters and bloggers. Shared involve crafting social media posts to involve customers and encourage them to share with their own networks. Owned media are content created and hosted on an organisation's website or blog.

The following case studies showcase several companies who take a creative approach to relating to their customers.

ACTION POINT

#LOVE MY FRIDGE

It holds just the thing we crave. Its door is always open to us. No matter what we're going through, it stays perfectly chilled. It even keeps a light on for us at night, when we need it most.

What would life be like without our refrigerators?

That was the question Bosch posed to the world in 2014. Headquartered in Germany, Bosch is an innovative worldwide leader in industrial, energy and building technology, and in the power tool, automotive and consumer appliance sectors. It traditionally enjoys high brand recognition in appliances, where the Bosch name is visible in homes throughout the world. At the influential Consumer Electronics trade show (IFA) in 2014, the company was introducing the Bosch Cool Classic refrigerator to the German market, and sought help leveraging the Bosch name, looking to connect with a younger generation of consumers still forming brand loyalties.

Bosch moved beyond storytelling and into story-doing. #lovemyfridge inspired consumers to join with the brand as content creators. They delivered amusing, touching and off-the-wall responses in an imaginative outpouring of media, including texts, photos, Instagram posts, videos and animations that they shared and reshared through their own channels, and through Bosch-branded digital media.

All that love created a 62 per cent digital share increase for Bosch over competitors and helped fuel a 23 per cent bump in year-over-year sales across the entire Bosch refrigerator line for the year.

Bosch's objectives for the campaign were:

- to increase awareness, affinity and sales for Bosch-branded refrigerators;
- to connect individuals with their refrigerators in an emotional way, and Bosch as a company that supports quality of life;
- to command the largest share of online voice and conversation;
- to engage the audience in brand-based content creation.

It's not easy to get a conversation started about household appliances. At least not a fun conversation. Most people consider them utilities and any discussion will revolve around features and benefits. PR consultancy Ketchum realised that, given the chance, people recognise how important appliances are in their everyday lives. In the case of refrigerators, the source of both sustenance and pleasure, there were often emotional connections. When the question was posed correctly, people admitted to having relationships with their refrigerators.

That was the perfect entry point for Bosch as it prepared to launch its Cool Classic refrigerator, combining nostalgic design elements with the latest in consumer technology. Thinking globally and acting digitally, key media influencers in food and consumer technology were identified across 12 targeted countries to get their followers to open up about their refrigerator relationships. In the process they became content creators and self-promoters, delivering valuable shared insights throughout the desired demographic.

Prompted by the introductory video, users were encouraged to publish their own creative #lovemyfridge entries as text, pictures or videos on the campaign microsite, or in their social network of choice, just by adding the #lovemyfridge hashtag. People were asked to share their relationship with refrigerators. Not just Bosch refrigerators. Any refrigerator.

Ketchum identified and enlisted popular food and consumer tech bloggers in 12 countries (Highfoodality – Germany, Ma P'tite cuisine – France, Chasing Delicious – USA, Finely Chopped – India, Orangenmond – Austria, The Pink Whisk – UK, Fuszer es Lelek – Hungary, Sorelle in pentola – Italy, El cocinero fiel – Spain, Instagrammer-Food, Instragrammer – Ezgi Polat). The campaign ran on the corporate website, where international food bloggers talked about their close relationships with their fridge, and shared recipes made from yesterday's leftovers. The campaign rolled out worldwide in six languages and 12 countries. Targeted media planning and placement on Facebook and Twitter along with Google AdWords and selected display networks increased public awareness of the campaign, launched shortly before the start of IFA in Berlin.

Results

More than 1,400 unique, entertaining and highly personal submissions brought the campaign to life. Users generated almost 550,000 visits to the microsite, plus total ad impressions of 340 million. On Twitter, 1,500 users posted and spread the campaign hashtag, including over 400 influencers and their thousands of followers. Six select bloggers and two Instagrammers acted as #lovemyfridge co-creators by generating their own content and spurring their communities to get involved, engaging a reach of 1,520,165 and 12,600 interactions.

Bosch dominated online conversation with a 29 per cent share, representing a 62 per cent increase over the previous quarter. During September, the month of the campaign, social and online mentions significantly peaked throughout Europe on Facebook, Twitter and Amazon – and the entire Bosch refrigerator line enjoyed a 23 per cent year-over-year sales increase. In a longer lasting development, the 'story-doing' of our content creators inspired Bosch Cool Classic advertising, demonstrating the value of making an emotional connection with the target audience.

With thanks to Stephen Waddington, Chief Engagement Officer, Ketchum.

FOCUSING ON THE PRODUCERS!

ACTION POINT

Langage Farm was originally just that. In fact it has been a working farm for over 900 years and was mentioned in the Domesday Book. In 1980, the farm started to diversify and produce clotted cream. The range of dairy products produced by Langage Farm now includes: frozen clotted cream, cream by post, pouring cream, sour cream, crème fraiche, cream cheese, cottage cheese and yogurt. They also produce a range of luxury ice creams in 45 flavours, sorbets, frozen yogurt, ice cream bombes dipped in Belgian chocolate and ice cream gateau.

Originally the aim was to utilise the milk from the farm's own Jersey and Guernsey cows. The herd had increased from 40 cows on 100 acres in

1957 to the present day 280 cows on 400 acres. The company now also support seven Channel Island farms. Langage employ over 50 local people and have over 1,000 retail customers, with expected turnover in 2016 of £3.9 million.

The company also built its own anaerobic digester plant in 2009 using food waste to produce 500–600kw to power the dairy plant and feed back into the national grid. The digester plant also incorporates an educational centre which hosts visits from local schools, as well as a demonstration kitchen which is used in partnership with local master chefs. The material used in the digester plant becomes fertiliser which is then used on the

FIGURE 22.1 Langage Farm emphasises the producers of its product

fields to improve the quality of grass and so increase the yield of the cows.

The marketing of products is distinctive in that a conscious decision was made to emphasise the real producers of the product – the cows (Figure 22.1). Packaging features named cows on the different products, and the website continues this theme. Mabel welcomes visitors to the website, and Lulu, Hyacinth and Nora feature on the clotted cream pots. Alice, Gina, Emilie and Flo introduce ice cream products. The three members of the management team all nominate their favourite cow and product on the site.

As well as conventional marketing methods, the company decided to spearhead the campaign to gain Protected Designation of Origin (PDO) status for the Devonshire Cream Tea. The application to DEFRA put forward a proposal that all components (scone, clotted cream and jam) must be produced in Devon to qualify for the name of Devonshire Cream Tea. The campaign was launched in May 2011, and gained widespread coverage from the BBC, *Daily Mail*, *Daily Telegraph*, *Daily Express* and even the *Londonderry Standard*. Paul Winterton was quoted as saying, 'It's about making sure what people are served is the genuine article. It's also good for the local economy.' The application process could take up to eight years, so the company is set to continue to milk this story.

Sales in the UK continue to be good and the company is following up exporting possibilities.

ACTION POINT

BEST IN SHOW

Falling visitor numbers to agricultural shows over the past few years highlighted a need for the Royal Bath & West Society, organisers of the long-standing annual Bath & West Show, to address the need to both maintain existing visitor levels but also future-proof the show and look to grow new visitor numbers.

JBP PR was appointed to bring a different dimension to the promotion of the Bath & West Show, specifically with a remit to address:

- How can the show attract more visitors – without being seen to dilute its agricultural foundations?
- Exploring new channels for promoting the show

- Boosting advance ticket sales
- Maintaining visitor numbers.

Following a review of all the show's assets, JBP PR set out:

- To build on the show's positioning as 'more than just an agricultural show' – creating an aspirational event that appeals to a broader audience
- To drive pre-show sales by creating reasons to buy
- To promoting advance ticket offers
- To increase the number of overall visitors (in a market where the famous Highland Show was seeing a reduction in numbers)
- To integrate PR effort across all areas of the show.

Positioning the show as more than just an agricultural show, JBP created a targeted programme of activity designed to excite regular visitors and reach out to new relevant audiences. We created exposure for the wide range of activities and features available at the show and focused predominantly on three specific target audience groups: family, food lovers and the country set.

Core to the campaign were four initiatives: a social media campaign, strategic partnership programme, Ladies' Day, Bath & West Banger – a search to find a sausage recipe to be served at the show. All initiatives challenged perceptions about the show being 'just an agricultural show' and provided rich marketing platforms to generate pre-publicity. However, recognising that media coverage alone would not sell tickets, brokering strategic partnerships with target publications and organisations was also central to JBP's strategy.

The Bath & West Banger was a competition created and launched by JBP six months in advance of the show, the theme of which was to see a new Bath & West themed sausage served at the show. Having researched and identified a regional food producer to partner with – Westaways Sausages – JBP launched a nation-wide competition asking for members of the public to create a limited edition sausage flavour that best represented the Bath & West Show. Buzz about the competition was generated through press coverage and social media channels, which resulted in 325 quality entries. JBP then used various stages of the competition process (appointing a judging panel of local media personalities, announcing the finalists, making the sausage, launching the winning flavour) to engage the media. The winning sausage was a flavour-packed Westcountry pork, Devon farmhouse Cheddar, sweet caramelised onions and dark ale from Bath Ale.

Results included live taster sessions with BBC Radio Bristol and an ITV West interview about the making of the winning sausage. This all supported pre-show awareness. Audience reach for this activity across media channels was

FIGURE 22.2 Ladies' Day at Bath and West Show

2,954,456. As an added bonus in the weeks running up to the show, the winning sausage was sold in selected South-West supermarkets. Packaging featured details promoting the show – exposing details about the show to food lovers. During the show, free samples of the Bath & West Banger were made available to visitors. This attracted footfall to the food tent during the show, along with additional media coverage.

Ladies' Day was the second campaign platform devised and implemented by JBP (Figure 22.2). To generate awareness and front the campaign, local fashion celebrity Gill Cockwell (founder of fashion label Gilly Woo Couture and star of BBC series *Turn Back Time*) was asked to judge a 'best dressed' competition on the day. JBP also identified and secured partnerships with relevant brands, including Neal's Yard, to provide exclusive goodie bags for Ladies' Day ticket holders at no extra cost to the show. JBP launched a competition on Facebook to find a team of fashion scouts who would help find the 'best dressed in Show' on Ladies' Day. In total, 120 Ladies' Day tickets were sold which generated an additional £2,000 worth of income. The Ladies' Day PR campaign reached an audience of 970,000.

JBP research highlighted that many of the target customer groups – foodies, horse lovers, parents – were engaged with Facebook and Twitter social media channels. This steered us to create a specific social media campaign which was launched four months prior to the show. When we started the campaign we had to create a new Facebook page, so started from zero followers. The

Bath & West Twitter pages had 750 followers. We contacted every show exhibitor – through their show exhibitor pack – to sign them up to supporting social media activity. This included requesting offers of incentives, prizes and news – all providing JBP with quality content. On a daily basis, JBP interacted with both Twitter and Facebook – posting news about the show's features, competitions and exhibitors' offers. We also retweeted quality content and targeted new followers. During the show, JBP encouraged exhibitors to participate in tweeting live. This resulted in significant online conversations – a first for the Bath & West Show. Campaign efforts delivered just under 1,000 new Twitter followers, 637 Facebook fans, 400 @ mentions and 30 retweets of show activity.

JBP also brokered strategic partnerships with six organisations and media groups. The most high-profile partnership was with the *Daily Telegraph*. Subscribers to the paper were offered an exclusive '2-4-1' on show tickets in return for four adverts plus a landing page on DailyTelegraph.co.uk for one month. The advertising value alone of this deal was worth £40,000, without taking into consideration the audience reach and the 600 ticket sales generated as a result. JBP arranged partnerships with niche interest/media groups including *Somerset Life*, Moneysavingexpert.com, Neal's Yard Remedies and Westaways Sausages. These partnerships involved running exclusive ticket offers via member newsletters, websites or editorial coverage.

Whilst press coverage evaluation was important to evaluating the success of the campaign, success was also measured against the objectives laid down by the client at the outset. With several County Shows reporting a decline in visitor numbers in 2010 and 2011, the results more than met the campaign objectives:

- **Boost advance ticket sales.** Early advance ticket sales were the highest in six years, 12 per cent up on 2010. The advance ticket sales showed correlation with the pre-show media coverage and activity generated by the Bath & West Banger, social media and Ladies' Day campaigns. *Daily Telegraph* partnership sold 600 tickets. Ladies' Day tickets sold 120 tickets and delivered £2,000 worth of additional ticket sales income.
- **Maintaining visitor numbers.** Overall visitor numbers to the Show were 160,300 visitors, an additional 4,500 visitors compared to the previous year (155,629).
- **Expose the Show to new audiences.** Total reach of media coverage was just under 11 million (10,753,732) with 129 items of coverage generated. Ladies' Day reached a new audience of 970,000 via lifestyle media. Bath & West Banger targeted a regional 'foodie' audience of over 2,954,456.

- **Establish a national media profile for the show.** The *Daily Telegraph* partnership was worth £40,000 in free advertising. Generated editorial coverage across national titles including in *Daily Telegraph/The Times/ Daily Mirror/*BBC online/Heart FM/*Somerset Life.*

- **Explore new channels for promoting the show.** Five strategic partnerships brokered for the show via new channels through networks and contacts: Gill Cockwell fashion couture fronted the Ladies' Day campaign free of charge but delivered significant media coverage for the show. Westaways Sausages delivered significant media coverage and exposure. They funded the sausage productions and also supported the show through their on-pack promotion across SW retail outlets. Neal's Yard sponsored Ladies' Day to the tune of £25 worth of goodies for every Ladies' Day ticket. Life Magazine Group negotiated a series of double-page spreads about food attractions at the show. This included a promotion offer which delivered 5 per cent of ticket sales. Heart FM supported the campaigns for Ladies' Day & Bath & West Banger which resulted in high levels of radio exposure and online support through their website.

In total, JBP generated 129 pieces of coverage for the Bath & West Show 2011. Having cancelled their advertising spend in favour of PR, the board of the Bath & West were more than satisfied with the result.

Lis Anderson MCIPR, Director, JBP PR & Parliamentary Affairs.

END POINT

Promoting consumer products is one of the bread and butter areas of public relations. PR needs to work with marketing and other communication disciplines to ensure that all messages are consistent and coherent. Practitioners also need to keep on top of developments in channels of communication, so that they are reaching customers in their preferred ways. Developments in new technology provide exciting ways to communicate more directly with customers, but it is important not to forget that the best communications always have a human touch.

Appendices

PR BRIEF CHECKLIST

☐ Statement of the nature of the issue/opportunity for which a proposal is required

☐ Aims and objectives to be achieved (including baseline data and success criteria)

☐ Background information on the issue, sector and organisation (historical/current)

☐ Profile of the organisation, including vision, mission, values and objectives

☐ Organisational/management structure

☐ Profile of similar/competitive organisations

☐ Operational information relating to the organisation and/or the sector, e.g. details of product/services, stakeholder/customer profiles, unique points of interest, etc.

☐ Information regarding the PR resource (in-house or consultancy, history, size, structure, reporting lines, remit, etc.)

☐ Details of existing PR personnel (responsibilities, competencies, relationships)

☐ Background on previous PR activities, including reviews and results

☐ Profile of stakeholders/publics (historical and current data, plus forecasts) and response requirements in respect of issue/opportunity being addressed

☐ Guide to organisational narrative, messages, culture, style, branding, etc.

☐ Communications audit information including channels, feedback mechanisms

☐ Identification of issues that could affect the implementation of a PR campaign

☐ Information on other communications activities (e.g. advertising) that could impact PR or be integrated with the campaign, including objectives and timings

☐ Nature of the required proposal – format, deadlines, etc.

☐ Resources available (including budget, approved suppliers, in-house resource)

☐ Timeframe for the campaign

☐ Contact details of the client

☐ Information regarding the decision-making process

☐ Details required regarding the consultancy and team members (if appropriate)

RESEARCH PROPOSAL CHECKLIST

☐ **Background:** brief description of the company, details of the main business issue or problem being addressed, explanation of why research is required and how results will be used.

☐ **Outline of any existing research** and explanation of any unusual or specific issues to be aware of when conducting the research.

☐ **Details of business and research objectives:** how the research will be used to address a key business issue or objective (and by whom), key information needs (including broad question areas), segmentation needs (audience/country/sector).

☐ **Details of research subjects:** method of defining and characteristics (e.g. of individuals, groups, companies), segmentation approaches, access (e.g. existing database or free/purchased lists), details of subjects to be excluded.

☐ **Thoughts on research approach:** need for measurable (quantitative) information, statistical considerations, sampling and analysis requirements, need for in-depth, exploratory (qualitative) information.

☐ **Required deliverables:** whether findings will be disseminated though a presentation or debrief workshop (and to whom). Requirements for interim report or executive summary, format required for feedback to support decision-making. Specific outputs (e.g. printed copies of presentations/reports, data tabulations, data files, an online portal to host data, etc.).

☐ **Timing** – key deadlines, cross-sectional vs longitudinal.

☐ **Resources** – budget, existing resources (e.g. research mechanisms), suppliers.

☐ **Requirements of the research team** – experience of similar work, qualifications and quality standards, membership of professional bodies, etc.

ANALYTICAL TOOLS CHECKLIST

Analysing the situation

☐ Content analysis of media coverage (traditional and social)

☐ Review of industry/sector: players, reports, positioning statements

☐ Feedback mechanisms

☐ Timeline and history of issue/opportunity

☐ Crisis preparedness: processes, systems, training

☐ Crisis prevention: risk scanning and analysis

☐ Case studies and previous situations: evaluation/reviews

☐ Force field analysis

☐ Scenario/trend forecasting

Analysing the organisation

☐ Internal and external data and reports (inc media reports)

☐ Reputational and performance rankings

☐ Cultural web

☐ PESTEL/SWOT analysis

☐ Organisational charts

☐ Comparative, competitor and industry reviews

☐ Core competencies

☐ Communications audit

☐ Boston Matrix, Ansoff and other marketing/positioning tools

Analysing the public

☐ Stakeholder analysis (including mapping)

☐ Influencer mapping: media, social media, opinion leaders, friends/foes

☐ Segmentation: demographics, geodemographics, life stage, psychographics and lifestyle

☐   Qualitative insight (e.g. ZMET)

☐   Identification and mapping of publics (situational model)

☐   Identification and analysis of relevant groups (including membership, leadership and influence)

☐   Media usage (information seeking or processing behaviour)

☐   Cognitive research (existing knowledge/understanding)

☐   Balance scorecard and gap analysis

☐   Attitude/opinion research (quantitative and qualitative)

☐   Co-orientation and relationship mapping research

☐   Behavioural data (including social media analytics, loyalty ladders, Rogers' diffusion of innovation, etc.)

☐   Relationship mapping of publics to issue and organisation

PESTEL CHECKLIST

Audit and analysis undertaken at national, sector, organisation, publics or issue level, covering short, medium or long-term perspectives, to identify and gain insight into issues that impact significantly on the organisation and its operations.

Political factors:

☐   Local, regional, national, international government policies and plans

☐   Statements issued by relevant institutions and individuals

☐   Incidents arising that have potential political impact

☐   Bodies and campaigns seeking change in policies

☐   Direct or indirect influences on politicians

☐   Political structure, election process, etc.

Sources: Monitoring political communications (e.g. parliament, agenda-setting media, social media). Review policy papers by key bodies (think tanks, political parties, NGOs, etc.). Analyse reports from industry bodies, academics and opinion leaders. Opinion research among political stakeholders and relevant publics on issues.

Economic factors:

☐ Economic indices (interest rates, taxation, growth data, inflation, exchange rates)

☐ Impact on key resources, e.g. labour, disposable incomes, grants/finance

☐ Trends in economic prosperity and confidence of individuals, organisations, society

☐ Controls and influences on economic environment, e.g. political decisions

☐ Internal financial position and pressures

Sources: Reports from financial bodies, institutions and analysts, financial media monitoring, announcement of financial data, statistics and indices. Surveys of confidence. Internal financial reports and contacts.

Socio-cultural:

☐ Nature and impact of demographic, cultural and social trends (e.g. gender roles, education levels, moral norms, family composition, aging community, etc.)

☐ Health, food and other human considerations

☐ Attitudes towards sector, business, corporate social responsibility, etc.

☐ Industry trends and competitor actions

☐ Statements released by think tanks, NGOs, charities, etc.

☐ Changing media usage (e.g. fragmentation, convergence)

☐ Interest in issues, civic pluralism, levels of activism, emerging campaigns

Sources: Reports from think tanks, NGOs/charities, demographic data, government research. Public opinion surveys. Internal market research data, product development research. Monitoring leading edge media and opinion leaders.

Technological:

☐ Communication technologies (including social media)

☐ Working practices and operational technologies

☐ Transport infrastructure, energy and other resources

☐ Security systems (e.g. relating to crisis management, data protection, etc.)

☐ Internal financial position and pressures

☐ Barriers and drivers of change: access, skills, efficacy, cost, ROI

Sources: Technology/news media (traditional and online), websites & forums. Research reports from think tanks, conferences/exhibitions. Contact with experts and industry leaders. Academic journals/presentations. Industry publications: newsletters, designer/engineer reports, information from suppliers and trade bodies.

Environmental:

☐ Impact on (and of) natural environment (including biodiversity)

☐ Impact of (and on) local, national, international urban environment – e.g. pollution, congestion, construction and development

☐ Migration, tourism and other human factors

☐ Health considerations, including transmission models

☐ Attitudes towards environmental technologies

☐ Consumer trends (e.g. purchase of 'green' products/services)

☐ Environmental trends, policies and expectations (including social responsibility)

☐ Drivers from legislation, economy, technology or socio-cultural factors

☐ Compliance and reporting requirements

☐ Reports from and about relevant NGOs, charities and activists

Sources: Specialist and general media (traditional and online). Research reports, sustainability, CSR and environmental reports, studies and surveys, academic journals and presentations, contact with experts, international conventions.

Legal:

☐ Regulatory framework (local, national and international)

☐ Existing and proposed legislation

☐ Influences on legislation (including campaigns)

☐ Processes and opportunity for participation in legislative process

☐ Constraints and consequences on compliance with legal framework

☐ Ethical issues

Sources: National archive of UK legislation (www.legislation.gov.uk), media coverage, consultation procedures, monitoring NGO and activist campaigns, statistics and reports, high-profile cases, contact with legal and HR personnel.

CULTURAL WEB

CULTURE – PARADIGM

☐ Paradigm provides 'worldview' evident within one or more cultures within a society, organisation, function, group, etc.

☐ Gain research data using survey/interviews with relevant population

☐ Undertake observational, content analysis or other suitable methodology

☐ Analyse data to identify taken-for-granted assumptions in following areas – outside perspective useful at this point

☐ Summarise behavioural, physical and symbolic dimensions of culture from analysis

☐ Tool can be used dynamically to determine existing and desired culture or track change over time

STORIES

☐ Narration shared with others (inside, outside, new members)

☐ Relate to history, important events, personalities

☐ Likely to concern important matters or those that deviate from the norm

☐ Identify core beliefs and norms

☐ Consider nature of stories told

SYMBOLS

☐ Aspects that have particular meaning within the culture

☐ May relate to objects, events, language, behaviours, situations, people

☐ Consider what is symbolic in communications internally/externally

☐ Look for in other elements of the web

POWER STRUCTURES

☐ Distribution of power

☐ Nature and approach of leaders

☐ Those who influence the influencers

☐ Enablers/blockers of change

ORGANISATIONAL STRUCTURES

☐ Formal vs informal, flat vs hierarchical, organic vs mechanistic, collaborative vs competitive

☐ Types of capital: political (actual/symbolic), social (relationship-based), cultural (knowledge-based)

CONTROL SYSTEMS

☐ Reward and recognition processes

☐ What is criticised and prevented

☐ What is monitored and controlled

☐ Frequency and nature of controls

RITUALS AND ROUTINES

☐ Way things are done (routines)

☐ Important events/activities (rituals)

☐ Track historical origins

☐ How easy would factors be to change

☐ What would seem odd if changed

Derived from Johnson et al. (2005)

SWOT CHECKLIST

Supports reflection on significance of results from the PESTEL audit or consideration of the internal environment in relation to a particular scenario.

FACTOR	List relevant factors, e.g. Social media
INTERNAL ANALYSIS	
Strengths	List existing competencies and other advantages
Weaknesses/ Limitations	List issues relating to potential problems
EXTERNAL ANALYSIS	
Opportunities	Identify how this factor presents opportunities
Threats	Identify how this factor presents risk or other negative outcome

Example considerations:

STRENGTHS	WEAKNESSES/LIMITATIONS
☐ Strong financial resources	☐ Conservative culture
☐ Superior market position	☐ Outdated products
☐ Industry leading products/services	☐ High staff turnover
☐ Respected leadership	☐ Reactive communications
OPPORTUNITIES	**THREATS**
☐ Emerging markets	☐ Economic instability
☐ Social changes	☐ Cultural trends
☐ Access to finance	☐ Strong competitors
☐ New legislation	☐ Technological developments

The SWOT analysis is an evaluative tool that should be based on research and reflection. It involves looking backwards as well as anticipating issues and opportunities. Alongside a risk analysis, it enables action plans to be developed to maximise opportunities and act on strengths or to address weaknesses/limitations and avoid threats.

GAP ANALYSIS

Area of inquiry	Detail relevant focus of the gap analysis, for instance, effectiveness criteria, public opinion, employee engagement
Future/optimum situation	Detail objectives, metrics, practices or outcomes that present intended or ideal situation concerning the area of inquiry
Current/existing situation	Detail current position in respect of the existing situation using same measures as considered above
Variance	Identify areas of difference between future/optimum and current/ existing situational measures. These may be analysed as specific aspects to be addressed to reach the intended situation. They should also be reviewed to ensure that the desired position is realistic or if goals need to be amended

ROOT CAUSE ANALYSIS

Approach	Implementation
Check list	Identify and analyse non-aligned factors derived from gap analysis.
Key questions	For each non-aligned factor, ask series of questions, e.g. *why* did variance occur. Consider if factors identified in answers would eliminate variance if addressed. If not, use *why* questions to further examine the contributing factors.
Antecedent-Behaviour-Consequence analysis	Look at the sequence of activities to identify what occurred immediately before any variance. Consider the consequences of this variance. Examine whether changing the antecedent would improve the outcome.
Learning loops	Reflect on efficiency and effectiveness of processes (single-loop learning), question validity and limitations of assumptions, procedures and beliefs (double-loop learning), identify patterns, structural constraints, omissions and the wider context (triple-loop learning). Consider relationship between each stage to add depth to learning about causes.
Fishbone diagrams	Visual approach plotting various contributory factors enabling an holistic examination of a situation.

COMMUNICATIONS AUDIT CHECKLIST

Step 1 – Audit Plan

☐ Objective – e.g. to gain feedback, to inform review process, to initiate improvements, to evaluate content, to compare channels

☐ Method – e.g. content analysis, interviews, focus group or survey

☐ Framework – identification of assessment criteria, e.g. usability, cost, compliance to style guidelines, recall of key messages

☐ Timetable – e.g. annual/routine process or for a specific purpose

☐ Data analysis – process to review findings and identify recommendations

☐ Outcome – e.g. use by management, to evaluate improvements

Step 2 – Identification of Communication Channels

Stakeholder/ Channel*	Internal	Local	Influencers	Trade	Political	Media	Financial	Customers	Public
Paid: marketing									
Owned: publications, websites									
Earned: media relations, advocacy									
Shared: word of mouth, social media									
Personal: conversations, correspondence, telephone									
Public: presentations, exhibitions									

*In use, this framework requires further segmentation of stakeholders/publics and also more precise identification of communication channel.

CHANNEL	DETAILS	OBJECTIVE*	AUDIT OUTCOME
For example: Thought leadership article	Monthly digital pdf, 2,000 words. Topic agreed with senior management by PR function. Written and produced by external agency.	• To increase recognition of company as industry leader • To inform key clients and influencers of areas of expertise • To generate enquiries	• Online survey identifies positive rating by 65% of respondents. • Content analysis shows 100% compliance with corporate style and expertise narrative • Enquiry tracking data

All objectives should be SMART where feasible.

CONTENT ANALYSIS CHECKLIST

TECHNIQUE

☐ Outline methodology (sample set, coding/thematic approach, etc.)

☐ Review the nature of the content with 5Ws (who, what, where, when, why)

☐ Create thematic grid to record key aspects of work (facts, stories, quotes, etc.)

☐ Create a priori coding grid to assess content against variables of interest (e.g. favourability)

☐ Use coding to evaluate positive, negative and neutral aspects of work

☐ Match content to any stimulus materials (i.e. origins), review variations

☐ Gain readership insight from those who would typically access the content (e.g. using surveys or interviews). Cover recollection, interpretation, etc.

☐ Summarise analysis visually, e.g. flow chart

☐ Create interpretive narrative overview of the content

☐ Compare analysis to objectives, benchmarks or previous analyses

☐ Develop management reports

SEGMENTATION CHECKLIST

METHOD	CRITERIA
Demographics	☐ Personal characteristics: age group, gender, education level, family size, income, occupation, religion, ethnicity, nationality
	☐ Socio-economic (A, B, C1, C2, D, E)
	☐ Life stage: newly married, full nest, empty nest, retired, solitary survivor
Geographics	☐ Residential, 'drive to work', employment, shopping, etc.
	☐ Level: society, continent, country, region, town, postcode
	☐ Environment: coastal, country, urban, suburban, etc.
	☐ Terminology: Third World, BRIC, Eurozone, EMEA (Europe, Middle East & Africa), etc.
	☐ Market: size, nature, territory (e.g. sales or retail)
	☐ Media: ITV/BBC regions, etc.
Geodemographics	☐ ACORN (www.caci.co.uk)
	☐ MOSAIC (www.experian.co.uk)
Stakeholders	☐ Bernstein: internal, local, influential groups, trade, government, media, financial, customer, general public
	☐ Intra-stakeholder, e.g. employees: occupation, department, location, grade level, union membership, length of service
	☐ External by issue: economic, socio/political, technological
Behaviour	☐ Usage: occasional, high, habitual, etc.
	☐ Technology: silver surfers, babyboomers, Gen X, Gen Y, Net Generation, Mobile Generation
	☐ Sales: prospect, customer, client, supporter, advocate, partner
	☐ Loyalty: hard-core, split, shifting, switchers
	☐ Decision roles: initiator, influencer, decider, buyer, user
	☐ Innovation: innovators, early adopter, early majority, late majority, laggards
	☐ Publics: non, latent, aware, active (single, all, hot issue)

METHOD	CRITERIA
	☐ Information seeking vs information processing
Psychographics	☐ Attitudes, opinions, beliefs, values, interests, lifestyle, motivations, self-esteem
	☐ AIO (attitudes, interests, opinions)
	☐ RISC 8 socio-cultural variables shaping European society: self-development, hedonism, plasticity, vitality, connectivity, ethics, belonging, inertia
	☐ SINUS typology: Basic orientation: Traditional (to preserve), Materialistic (to have). Changing values: Hedonism (to indulge), Post-materialism (to be), Postmodernism (to have, to be and to indulge)
	☐ VALS: innovators, thinkers, achievers, experiencers (all with high level of resources), plus believers, strivers, makers and survivors (with lower resources)
Group	☐ Demographic, geographic, etc.
	☐ Purpose (interest or pressure group), motivation for joining, relationship to organisation, etc.
	☐ Industry sector (UK standard industrial classification)
	☐ Presence: local, national, multinational, international
	☐ Number of employees
	☐ Financial criteria
	☐ Reputation
	☐ Psychographic, behavioural characteristics

STAKEHOLDER MAPPING

	LOW INTEREST	**HIGH INTEREST**
LOW POWER	Minimal effort	Keep informed
HIGH POWER	Keep satisfied	Key players: keep informed and satisfied

Groups and/or individuals can be mapped by researching or assessing levels of interest and power.

RELATIONSHIP IDENTIFICATION AND SALIENCE

Construct (Variables)	Bases		Stakeholder
POWER – transitory *(ranges from non-existent to complete)*	Coercive – *force/threat*	Independent or Combination	(1) Power = Dormant
	Utilitarian – *material/ incentives*		(2) Legitimacy = Discretionary
			(3) Urgency = Demanding
	Normative – *symbolic influences*		(4) Power + Legitimacy = Dominant
LEGITIMACY *(dynamic attribute of relationship – may not be mutually understood)*	Individual	Generalised virtue at one or more levels	(5) Power + Urgency = Dangerous
	Organisational		(6) Legitimacy + Urgency = Dependent
	Societal		
URGENCY *(may not be mutually understood)*	Time sensitivity – *degree to which managerial delay in attending to the claim or relationship is unacceptable to the stakeholder* Criticality – *importance of the claim or the relationship to the stakeholder*	Unlikely to guarantee high saliency on own	(7) All 3 variables = Definitive (8) None of the varia-bles = Non-stakeholder

Based on Mitchell *et al.* (1997) presents a dynamic (constant flux) model for considering stakeholder–organisation relationships. Indicating relevance of variables (and basis of these) for individuals and/or groups (including coalitions) assists in identifying and determining salience of each. Salience is the degree to which competing stakeholder claims are given priority.

RELATIONSHIP MAPPING

Upstream vertical relations	Industry relations (direct and indirect)	
	[1] SUPPLIERS (provide raw materials, machinery, consumables, business services, etc.)	
	Indirect relations	Direct relations
	[2] SOCIO-CULTURAL ACTORS (community groups, media, opinion leaders, etc.)	[3] ECONOMIC ACTORS (tax authorities, stock marker, finance providers, unions, employer bodies, etc.)
Horizontal relations	[4] INDUSTRY OUTSIDERS (Activists)	[5] INDUSTRY INSIDERS (Competition)
Downstream vertical relations	Industry relations (direct and indirect)	
	[6] BUYERS (product/service users or intermediaries)	
	Indirect relations	Direct relations
	[7] POLITICAL/ REGULATORY ACTORS (e.g. politicians, government, political parties, regulatory bodies, international institutions, lobbyists)	[8] TECHNOLOGICAL ACTORS (e.g. patent offices, universities, research institutes, standards bodies)

Based on DeWit and Meyer (2010: 160) identifies eight major external relational groups. Industry actors [individuals/groups: 1, 4, 5, 6] have value-added relationships with organisations. Contextual actors [individuals/groups 2, 3, 7, 8] are those who affect the context (intentionally or unintentionally) in which organisations operate. Mapping can be undertaken to set objectives and gain understanding into these relations in respect of any particular situation or issue. The relationships between the different groups of actors (or individuals within these) can also be modelled.

TOOLS, TECHNIQUES AND TACTICS CHECKLIST

ACTION COMPONENT

☐ Briefings

☐ Meetings

☐ Launch events (including openings)

☐ Product reviews and demonstrations

☐ Facility visits and open events

☐ Tours (personal appearances, media interviews, speaking engagements, presentations, roadshow events)

☐ Exhibition/conference/convention presence

☐ Educational activities (e.g. outreach programmes, school liaison, seminars, 'meet the professionals' events)

☐ Celebrity events (launches, photo-opportunities, parties, other social activities)

☐ Awards (launches, shortlist, presentation events)

☐ Festivals, shows and other community events

☐ Webinars, live video and other online events

☐ Press conferences

☐ Panel and round-table discussions

☐ Activities for/with online influencers

☐ Virtual meetings and other digital activities

☐ Stunts, pseudo-events and special opportunities (e.g. record-breaking attempts, calendar celebrations – annual, day, week, month, milestones and anniversaries)

☐ Contests, quizzes and other promotional activities

☐ Fan clubs (real world or virtual, e.g. via social networking)

☐ Sponsorship maximisation (e.g. sports, arts, community)

☐ Social responsibility activities (e.g. community, charity or fundraising events)

☐ Networking and hospitality activities (social and professional)

☐ Experiential occasions, gamification, online presence in virtual worlds, etc.

COMMUNICATION COMPONENT

☐ Corporate identity, branding, style and narrative guidelines

☐ Media information (press releases, media kits, feature articles, case studies, etc.)

☐ Multimedia resources (including audio/visual materials)

☐ Positioning statements, briefing documents, factsheets and Q&A responses

☐ Speeches and presentations

☐ White papers and opinion leader commentary (e.g. guest blog posts)

☐ Annual reports, sustainability and other corporate reports

ACTION COMPONENT

☐ Educational materials (e.g. student website materials, school resource packs, competitions)

☐ Email, letters, SMS, social media direct messaging, invitations and other correspondence

☐ Polls and surveys (traditional and online)

☐ Websites and microsites (internal and external)

☐ Apps, QR codes, games and other online/mobile interactivity

☐ Social media (blogs, forums, video, micro-blogging, social networks, photography sites)

☐ Imagery (photographs, graphics, logos)

☐ Visualisations, transmedia storytelling and infographics

☐ Online newsroom

☐ Multimedia press release

☐ Monitoring methods (RSS feeds, searches, dashboards, cuttings analysis, feedback, surveys, sales and other data)

☐ Corporate publications (printed and digital, e.g. books, newsletters, magazines, for various stakeholders, including internal)

☐ Corporate advertising

☐ Brochures, leaflets and other printed collateral

☐ Posters, exhibition materials

☐ Plans, reports, minutes and other management materials

SUPPORT SERVICES

☐ Press release (media information) distribution

☐ Media monitoring services

☐ Media directories

☐ Media training

☐ Multimedia companies

☐ Designers, printers, web designers and other visual crafts

☐ Photographers

☐ Research companies

☐ Event management and sponsorship companies

☐ Specialist PR agencies: consumer, finance, lobbying sector experts, etc.

☐ Suppliers of technology and social media services

The tools, techniques and tactics chosen need to be considered within a strategic and creative framework. They should be mapped against time and resource limitations with a rational decision-making process employed to determine cost–benefit and other reasons for selecting appropriate tools, techniques and tactics.

NARRATIVE FRAMEWORK

NARRATIVE ELEMENT		CHECKLIST
Context	Viewpoints	☐ Internal stakeholders ☐ External stakeholders ☐ Influencers
	Expectations	☐ Guidelines informing narrative ☐ Core messages and other prescriptive requirements ☐ Measures of effectiveness of narrative
Fit	Alignment	☐ Proposed communications ☐ Check against expectations ☐ Compliance or variance
	Anchoring	☐ Motives for communication ☐ Motives of stakeholders ☐ Agreement or variance
	Responsiveness	☐ Willingness to seek and respond to feedback ☐ Opportunities for stakeholder involvement ☐ Dialogic elements of communications
Resonance	Accuracy	☐ Research base for information ☐ Fact-checking process ☐ Clarity of explanation ☐ Feedback on accessibility of information
	Commonality	☐ Research into stakeholder communications ☐ Identification of shared meanings (research) ☐ Mapping of cohesion between action and communication
Destination	Outcome	☐ Purpose and function of narrative ☐ Consequences of communications ☐ Matching of organisation and stakeholder viewpoints
Narrative environment	Summary statement	☐ Factors indicating extent of common understanding (or variance) in understanding of narrative
Narrative core	Centralising idea	☐ Concept that makes sense of narrative ☐ Idea that is memorable and remarkable ☐ Overview of the issue being addressed

NARRATIVE ELEMENT	CHECKLIST
Typology	☐ Formula or genre of narrative ☐ Patterns, forms and repertoire of narrative ☐ Matching of organisation and stakeholder viewpoints
Style	☐ Repetition, episodes, themes ☐ Actors and characters ☐ Emotional elements
Approach	☐ Subject ☐ Mode ☐ Means
Talking points	☐ Metaphors ☐ Examples ☐ Events ☐ Phrases ☐ Imagery ☐ Symbols ☐ Concepts ☐ Emotional appeals ☐ Explanations ☐ Predictions
Framing	☐ Staging ☐ Structure and reference points ☐ Linkage between other elements informing the narrative core
Narrative framework	Summary statement ☐ Overview and detail from above analysis

DECISION-MAKING GUIDELINES

- ☐ Detail the problem or opportunity where a decision is required

- ☐ Determine risk/likelihood of best/worst case results occurring

- ☐ Specify factors influencing the need for decision-making (what makes this a significant matter outside routine decision-making processes)

- ☐ Identify responsibilities, deadlines and resources available in respect of planning, decision-making, solution implementation and evaluation

- ☐ Collect data on situation, publics/stakeholders and organisation

- ☐ Sort research information – analyse, prioritise, review, edit, identify key factors

- ☐ Visualise the situation and possible consequences – use diagrams (e.g. flow charts) to illustrate impact of decision

- ☐ Quantify the nature of the problem/opportunity where feasible and/or identify specific qualitative impacts (graphical representation of information is helpful)

- ☐ Identify root cause of problems or opportunity using techniques such as Ishikawa (fishbone) diagram to consider possible causes and effects. List main considerations and continuously ask 'why?' to reach back to possible causes. Use diagram to track results back through a process: i.e. this happens because …

- ☐ Determine whether additional research is required (avoid paralysis by analysis)

- ☐ Specify which causes can be addressed

- ☐ Identify possible limitations (e.g. time considerations), risks or bias and stipulate acceptable levels of tolerance

- ☐ Detail assessment criteria – cost–benefit, balanced-scorecard, impact

- ☐ Develop possible solutions or ideas to address the problem/opportunity

- ☐ Determine cost and possible consequences of actions

- ☐ Evaluate possible solutions objectively according to assessment criteria

- ☐ Test viability of preferred 2 or 3 solutions/opportunities

- ☐ Summarise chosen solution succinctly to focus on key deliverables and outcomes

- ☐ Gain agreement from key decision-makers to implement solution (subject to ongoing monitoring and evaluation)

- ☐ Assess decision-making procedures and the selected solution to ensure a continuous, adaptive, circular decision-making process

STATUS REPORTS

Where feasible, a single-page overview should be produced, using visual elements (e.g. infographic approach) to enable key metrics to be assessed immediately. More detail can be presented using tables which update status and help inform and manage resource requirements. For example:

STATUS REPORT			
Name of project/topic: Launch of product X		**Date: 1 June**	
Circulation to: JT, MS, DR, JB		Report prepared by: John Bright	
Task	**Responsibility**	**Action Date**	**Comments**
Writing project launch press release	Mandy Smith (MS)	7 June	Success criteria: complete task to required standard by deadline
• Research new product features	MS	31 May (completed)	Liaise with product development (PD)
• Draft release for approval	MS	3 June	Approval from PD and marketing
• Finalise release	MS	7 June	

SCHEDULING APPROACH

- ☐ A linear grid (Gantt chart) enables visualisation, planning and implementation of programmes of work.

- ☐ Apply critical path analysis to order tasks and determine project duration, sequencing of activities, dependencies and possible problem points.

- ☐ A PERT (Project Evaluation and Review Technique) chart can be used to illustrate flow of tasks, determine sequential and parallel activities, identify decision points and note milestones (e.g. critical deadlines, review stages).

- ☐ Visualise resource requirements by colour coding responsibilities and using a unit measurement to indicate hours or days required.

- ☐ Distinguish planning, implementation and evaluation phases.

- ☐ Determine an appropriate timeframe: year, month, week, day or hours.

- ☐ Prepare one or more grid for the project, task, individual, campaign or annual programme.

- ☐ Using technology, e.g. Microsoft Project or a spreadsheet, enables data to be represented in different forms.

- ☐ Update the grid frequently – if feasible use online (cloud) methods to enable all participants to report progress.

	Week 1 (hours)					Week 2 (hours)				
Task – producing webpage	M	T	W	T	F	M	T	W	T	F
Researching content	8									
First draft of content		8								
Approval by manager			▓							
Amend first draft				2						
Get final sign off					1					
Upload onto website					1	1				
Review web statistics								.5	.5	
Prepare report for manager										2

Workflow mapping enables processes to be examined to help improve efficiency and effectiveness. Steps may be possible to automate as chains of simple conditional statements (applets) e.g. using https://ifttt.com

MOVEMENT SCHEDULE

It is helpful to produce a schedule for the day of an activity (e.g. an event) to help everyone involved to see an overview and personal detail of implementation. An adapted Gantt chart can be used to produce documents for each person showing who is involved in which activity at what time. Another format could plot time and people with activities listed in the body of the table.

BUDGETING APPROACH

- ☐ Identify whether a specific budget has been allocated or if a budget needs to be determined based on the recommended course of action.

- ☐ Determine factors affecting budget, e.g. quality standards, time available, brand values.

- ☐ Specify key budget measures (e.g. delivery on or within budget, breakeven or profit requirements, savings on previous expenditure, income (sponsorship, attendance, etc.) figures).

- ☐ List key headings (including administration and incidental costs, e.g. postage, telephone, as well as research and evaluation) and determine which need to be included in the budget.

- ☐ Calculate the involvement of in-house resources (within the PR department and other areas) and assess against cost of sourcing externally (cost–benefit analysis).

- ☐ Identify the external resource requirements (consultancies, freelance, bought-in services). Obtain quotations to deliver the required work (to specified deadline).

- ☐ Detail and cost any skills, knowledge and training needs required to undertake activities.

- ☐ Identify additional bought costs (catering, accommodation, print, etc.).

- ☐ Distinguish between fixed and variable costs (e.g. venue hire is fixed, catering varies according to the number of attendees).

- ☐ Indicate any long-term requirements relating to the campaign which carry budget implications (cross-over of budget years, inflation considerations, opportunities to negotiate discounts, etc.).

- ☐ Ensure programme can be delivered within specified or realistic budget. If costs exceed amount, then determine optional elements that can be proposed and removed where possible (clarify benefits and impact of any decisions).

- ☐ Sanity check whether the stated outcomes can be achieved by an alternate programme at a lower cost and any implications or benefits of different options.

- ☐ Identify budget control measures and how any variance will be addressed (i.e. contingency allowance, need to eliminate aspects or renegotiation terms).

ITEM	DETAILS OF COSTING	ESTIMATED COST	ACTUAL COST
Total cost			
Difference			

Where organisations do not have an existing process for developing and reporting on budgets, a spreadsheet should be set up to enable estimated and actual costs to be recorded and managed. Budget plans must be reviewed as part of the ongoing monitoring and summative assessment of activities.

SUPPLIER BRIEFS

A number of different suppliers may be required when planning a PR campaign, e.g.

Graphic designers (including websites)

Proofreaders

Multimedia and online services

Event specialists

Printers

Research/evaluation companies

Photographers

Venue providers

Writers

Exhibition designers

Caterers

PR consultancies

All suppliers (even if internal or where there is an established relationship) should be briefed and contracts (detailing requirements and costs) put in place prior to starting a project. These should be in writing rather than verbal agreements or assuming parties are in agreement over essential details.

Purpose of brief	
Client name	
Contact details	
Dates	
Background	
Vision/target messages	
Objectives	
Target audience	
Parameters of project	
Approach	
Specific tasks	
Criteria for success	
Timeframe	
Budget	
Special considerations	
Additional information	

KEY PERFORMANCE REPORTING

Strategy statement			
Key performance indicators (list 4–10 measures) 1. 2. 3. etc.	Historic data	Current data	Forecast data

Presentation checklist	☐ Targets (SMART objectives, aims)
	☐ Scope and methodology
	☐ Data tables (including trends)
	☐ Graphic representation
	☐ Narrative explanation
	☐ Raw data
	☐ Contextualised data (previous performance, benchmarks)
	☐ Key findings (improvements, strengths, weaknesses)
	☐ Explanations for variance (limitations, learnings)
	☐ Conclusions and recommendations (priorities)
	☐ Narrative reporting accompanied by KPI data representation

RISK MANAGEMENT CHECKLIST

This process may be undertaken (adapted as necessary) at the organisational, departmental and/or campaign level by the PR function or an external consultancy.

Step 1 – Identify possible areas of risk

☐ Undertake a Risk Audit to identify areas which could reasonably be expected to cause an issue (with financial, legal or reputational consequences) in respect of the organisation's operations, the PR function's areas of responsibility and/or campaigns being planned.

☐ Identify existing organisational policies, legal requirements or societal expectations relating to the area where operations could present risk to compliance.

☐ Ask stakeholders for their input into areas of concern.

☐ Research areas of risk identified by experts (such as professional bodies) where practical guidance on action may be available.

☐ Review internal records and external reports (including media and social media) to identify issues that have occurred in the past.

☐ Take a long-term perspective to identify issues that may emerge over time as well as more immediate risks.

Step 2 – Decide who might be affected and how

☐ Undertake an audit of stakeholders and influencers (see Chapter 6) considering the psychology and requirements of various parties in relation to the identified areas of risk.

☐ Map a chain of involvement to show connections between stakeholder groups and influencers where issues could arise from their dynamic engagement.

☐ Consider others (e.g. suppliers or competitors) whose actions in relation to the issue could affect stakeholders' perceptions of the organisation.

☐ Ask different functions within the organisation to identify their stakeholders and how the area of risk could affect them.

Step 3 – Evaluate the risks and decide on precautions

☐ Produce a detailed Risk Profile for each aspect identified.

☐ Specify the probability and possible legal, financial or reputational consequences (threats and opportunities) of the identified areas of risk (using quantitative and qualitative estimates as appropriate).

☐ Highlight risk factors as presenting a high, medium or low level of threat in terms of likelihood of occurrence and potential consequence to produce a 3×3 matrix.

☐ Rank the identified risks to produce an overall record to inform development of possible precautions or control procedures.

☐ Determine (or review) the organisation's established risk criteria in order to determine acceptable levels of cost, benefit, compliance, consequential damage and so forth.

☐ Record whether the identified area presents an acceptable level of risk or requires precautionary solutions to be implemented.

☐ Determine whether any area risk could be eliminated by implementing simple precautions or controls.

☐ Identify what would be considered 'reasonably practical' precautions within the existing regulatory and compliance framework.

☐ Review sources of good practice (e.g. from existing case studies, such as those presented in the *PR Strategic Toolkit*) and compare with the organisation's precautionary measures.

☐ Assess existing precautionary or control measures in a test situation and adjust as necessary.

☐ Seek to reduce or control the level of risk by adopting different strategies, reducing exposure to the risk, implementing protective procedures.

☐ Involve stakeholders in determining the validity of proposed precautions.

☐ Review the proposed solutions to ensure they do not introduce additional areas of risk and provide benefits in reduced risk at an acceptable cost.

☐ Evaluate the solutions proposed and determine which will be implemented, assigning responsibilities where appropriate.

Step 4 – Record findings and implement them

☐ Document the risk assessment procedure and share its results (implementing training where necessary in the process and completion of documentation).

☐ Keep records simple and accessible.

☐ Ensure senior management is advised of the most significant risks identified and proposed method of addressing these to obtain their endorsement where appropriate.

☐ Demonstrate that a proper check has been undertaken which involved key stakeholders, dealt with the most significant hazards and identified reasonable precautions to reduce the level of risk.

☐ Produce a structured assessment of each risk identified covering its scope, nature, probability and significance, including details of priorities and recommended action.

☐ Produce a plan of action that prioritises the most important improvements to be made.

☐ Consider temporary solutions which can be implemented until more reliable, long-term controls are in place.

☐ Introduce a process of regular checks to ensure precautions and control measures stay in place.

☐ Assign clear responsibilities of who will lead on what action, and by when.

☐ Review the plan of action to ensure that action is completed.

☐ Identify indicators to ensure early warning for the risks identified as part of an ongoing monitoring process.

☐ Integrate the risk assessment, management and reporting process into the organisation's crisis management procedures.

☐ Produce a risk management policy which covers the key considerations used in informing the action plan which can be used as a guide for future risk assessment.

☐ Ensure risk management procedures are integrated across the organisation to identify areas where PR may be impacted or impact.

Step 5 – Review the process and update if necessary

☐ Identify required resources and secure to enable identified issues to be addressed.

☐ Establish individual responsibilities for identified risk management within the PR team.

☐ Monitor risk indicators to ensure responsiveness and effectiveness of procedures that have been implemented.

☐ Establish a process to identify and address additional and new areas of risk that may arise.

☐ Undertake a formal regular review (e.g. quarterly or annually) of risk management processes.

☐ Identify any areas of change and improvements that can be made.

☐ Consider any issues that have arisen, determine the effectiveness of procedures, identify lessons that can be learned and update risk management processes.

☐ Ensure that when change occurs or issues arise, the risk assessment and management processes are reviewed and amended as appropriate.

☐ Report systematically on the risk management process for the PR function to senior management and, where appropriate, to external stakeholders.

☐ Integrate risk management performance into governance processes such as sustainability and responsibility reports.

☐ Ensure that risk management based on an adaptive and flexible strategy rather than adherence to procedures and policies is established within the culture of the organisation.

RISK AUDIT

Used to identify areas of risk that could impact on the organisation achieving its objectives:

Risk identification techniques

Areas of risk can be identified using the following methods:

☐ Management reports

☐ Questionnaires

☐ Industry benchmarks or organisational studies

☐ Scenario forecasting

☐ Stakeholder workshops

☐ Incident investigation

☐ Observational studies

Risk analysis techniques

Data and information obtained can then be examined using:

☐ SWOT analysis (strengths, weaknesses, opportunities, threats)

☐ PESTEL analysis (political, economic, socio-cultural, technological, environmental and legal issues)

☐ Projection and trend analysis

☐ Flow diagram representation

☐ Critical path analysis

☐ Stakeholder mapping

☐ Option modelling

☐ Decision-making process

☐ Critical incident procedures – for specific situations of strategic significance

☐ Triage flow chart (steps to be followed in typical situations)

☐ Traffic light indicators (responses for red, amber or green incidents)

Bibliography

Adkins, S. (2006) 'Putting your marketing where your values are', *Market Leader*, Winter: 2–5.

Åkerström, A. and Young, P. (2013) 'Meet the digital naturals . . .', http://nemo.blogg.lu.se/meet-the-digital-naturals [Accessed 30 June 2015].

Aljandali, A. (2016) *Quantitative Analysis and IBM SPSS Statistics: A Guide for Business and Finance*. Cham, Switzerland: Springer International.

Alstiel, T. and Grow, J. (2006) *Advertising Strategy: Creative Tactics from the Outside/In*. Thousand Oaks, CA: Sage.

Altimeter (2011) 'How corporations should prioritize social business budgets', www.slideshare.net/jeremiah_owyang/how-corporations-should-prioritize-social-business-budgets [Accessed 1 Dec. 2011].

Alves, W. (2013) *Music of the Peoples of the World*, 3rd edn. Boston, MA: Schirmer.

AMEC (2011) 'Report gives welcome to Measurement Agenda – but AVEs use still high', http://amecorg.com/2011/07/report-gives-welcome-to-measurement-agenda-but-aves-use-still-high/ [Accessed 1 Dec. 2011].

Anderson, F.W., Hadley, L., Rockland, D. and Weiner, M. (1999) *Guidelines for Setting Measurable Public Relations Objectives: An Update*. Gainesville, FL: Institute for Public Relations.

Appleyard, B. (2003) 'PR: the evil art', www.bryanappleyard.com/pr-the-evil-art/ [Accessed 31 Dec. 2011].

Arrow, C. (2008) 'What is public relations?', www.catherinearrow.com [Accessed 31 Jan. 2010].

Arrow, C. (2009) 'The future practitioner', submission for *Chartered Practitioner*, Aug. www.cipr.org.uk [Accessed 31 Jan. 2010].

Atanassova, I. and Clark, L. (2015) 'Social media practices in SME marketing activities: A theoretical framework and research agenda', *Journal of Customer Behaviour*, 14(2): 163–83.

Babaee, A. (2016) 'Fresh evidence on value of employee engagement', http://headlines.uk. com/infographic-fresh-evidence-on-value-of-employee-engagement/#more-8260 [Accessed 3 May 2016].

Bacot, E. (2006) 'Which way now for PR?', *PR Business*, 13 July: 17–19.

Bailey, R. (2014) 'Media relations', in R. Tench and I. Yeomans (eds), *Exploring Public Relations*, 3rd edn. London: Pearson, pp. 235–50.

Baines, P., Egan, J. and Jefkins, F.W. (2004) *Public Relations: Contemporary Issues and Techniques*, 3rd edn. Boston, MA: Elsevier/Butterworth-Heinemann.

Baker, H., Rock, M. and Smith, R. (2016) 'Time to think different', *Influence*, Feb.: 30–7.

Ballington, J. (2003) 'Marketing society – effective CRM is built in rather than bolted on', *Media Week*, 30 Oct.

Balmer, J. (2001) 'Corporate identity, corporate branding and corporate marketing', *European Journal of Marketing*, 35(3/4): 248–91.

Balmer, J.M.T. (2013) 'Corporate brand orientation: What is it? What of it?', *Journal of Brand Management*, 20(9): 723–41.

Balmer, J.M.T. and Greyser, S.A. (2006) 'Corporate marketing', *European Journal of Marketing*, 40(7/8): 730–41.

Bandura, A. (1977) 'Self-efficacy: Toward a unifying theory of behavioral change', *Psychological Review*, 84(2): 191–215.

Baruch, Y. (2004) 'Transforming careers: From linear to multidirectional career paths: Organizational and individual perspectives', *Career Development International*, 9(1): 58–73.

Bashford, S. (2006) 'Juggling roles', *PR Week*, 6 July, www.prweek.com/uk/features/ 567711/ [Accessed 1 Dec. 2011].

Bashford, S. (2011) 'Client view: Stuart Handley, Dell – the listening revamp', *PR Week*, 12 May, www.prweek.com/uk/features/1069439/client-view-stuart-handley-dell-listening-revamp/ [Accessed 1 Dec. 2011].

Batchelor, B. (1938) *Profitable Public Relations*. New York: Harper & Brothers.

Baumgartner, F.R. (2001) 'Agendas: Political', in N.J. Smelser and P.B. Baltes (eds), *International Encyclopedia of the Social and Behavioral Sciences*. New York: Elsevier, pp. 288–91.

Beck, U. (1992) *Risk Society: Towards a New Modernity*, trans. Mark Ritter. London: Sage.

Beddow, A. (2015) 'Thought leadership transforming insights into opportunities', in N. Clark (ed.), *Professional Services Marketing Handbook: How to Build Relationships, Grow your Firm and Become a Client Champion*. London: Kogan Page, pp. 119–32.

Beke, T. (2011) 'The rise and scope of litigation public relations in England', in T. Watson (ed.), *International History of Public Relations Conference 2011*. Bournemouth: Bournemouth University, pp. 311–26.

Beke, T. (2014) *Litigation Communication: Crisis and Reputation Management in the Legal Process*. Heidelberg: Springer.

Belch, G.E. and Belch, M.A. (2001) *Advertising and Promotion*. Irwin: McGraw-Hill.

Benova, N. (2010) *A Snapshot from Bulgaria*. Research Paper. Apeiron Communication.

Bernstein, D. (1984) *Company Image and Reality*. London: Cassell.

Bettinghaus, E.P. and Cody, M.J. (1994) *Persuasive Communication*, 5th edn. Belmont, CA: Wadsworth.

Billingsley, L.G. (2002) 'Healthy choices: Reaching multicultural audiences', *Tactics*, Aug.: 19.

BITC (2004) 'Brand benefits', www.bitc.org.uk/system/files/brand_benefits_booklet.pdf [Accessed 10 June 2015].

BITC (2006) *Corporate Responsibility Index 2005*, www.bitc.org.uk/crindex, May [Accessed 31 Jan. 2010].

BITC (2012) 'How can marketers build sustainable success?', www.bitc.org.uk/our-resources/report/how-can-marketers-build-sustainable-success [Accessed 10 June 2016].

Bland, M., Theaker, A. and Wragg, D. (1996) *Effective Media Relations*. London: Kogan Page/IPR.

Blyth, A. (2006) 'Guerillas in our midst', *PR Business*, 11 May.

Blyth, A. (2011) 'Feature: Pitching a story – have I got a story for you', *PR Week*, 14 Apr., www.prweek.com/uk/features/1065337/ [Accessed 1 Dec. 2011].

Blythe, J. (2006) *Principles and Practice of Marketing*. London: Thomson Learning.

Bourland-Davis, P.G., Thompson, W. and Brooks, F.E. (2010) 'Activism in the 20th and 21st centuries', in R.L. Heath (ed.), *The Sage Handbook of Public Relations*, 2nd edn. London: Sage, pp. 409–20.

Bourne, C.D. (2016) 'Extending PR's critical conversations with advertising and marketing', in J. L'Etang, D. McKie, N. Snow and J. Xifra (eds), *The Routledge Handbook of Critical Public Relations*. Abingdon: Routledge, pp. 119–29.

Bovingdon, T. (2011) 'New crisis management standard launched', www.rmprofessional.com/rm/pas_200_launch.php [Accessed 1 Dec. 2011].

Bowd, R. (2005) 'Understanding stakeholder and management perceptions of CSR', CIPR Academic Conference, Lincoln, Mar.

Bowd, R. (2009) 'Financial public relations', in R. Tench and L. Yeomans (eds), *Exploring Public Relations*, 2nd edn. London: FT/Prentice Hall, pp. 462–80.

Bowden-Green, T. (2006) 'Public relations – a one way street?', *Profile*, Nov./Dec.: 12.

Brabbs, C. (2000) 'Is there profit in CRM tie ups?', *Marketing*, 16 Nov.

Brammer, S. and Millington, A. (2003) 'The effect of stakeholder preferences, organizational structure and industry type on corporate community involvement', *Journal of Business Ethics*, June, www.researchgate.net/profile/Stephen_Brammer2/publication/225973172_The_Effect_of_Stakeholder_Preferences_Organizational_Structure_and_Industry_Type_on_Corporate_Community_Involvement/links/548e9cf40cf225bf66a60757.pdf [Accessed 5 June 2016].

Brettschneider, F. (2008) 'The news media's use of opinion polls', in W. Donsbach and M.W. Traugott (eds), *The Sage Handbook of Public Opinion Research*. London: Sage, pp. 479–86.

Bridgen, L. (2011) 'Emotional labour and the pursuit of the personal brand: Public relations practitioners' use of social media', *Journal of Media Practice*, 12(1): 61–76.

Bright Edge (2011) 'Tracking social adoption and trends', www.brightedge.com/socialshare-November-2011-GooglePlus [Accessed 1 Dec. 2011].

Brill, P. (2011) CIPR Diploma Presentation, Bristol, Sept.

Broom, G.M. (1982) 'A comparison of sex roles in public relations', *Public Relations Review*, 8(3): 17–22.

Broom, G.M. (2009) *Cutlip and Centers Effective Public Relations*, 10th edn. Upper Saddle River, NJ: Pearson.

Broom, G.M. and Dozier, D.M. (1990) *Using Research in Public Relations*, Englewood Cliffs, NJ: Prentice Hall.

Brown, R.E. (2015) *The Ancient, Modern and Postmodern Dramatic History of an Idea*. Abingdon: Routledge.

Brunner, B.R. (2016) 'What is civic professionalism in public relations? Practitioner perspectives – a pilot study', *Public Relations Review*, 42(1): 237–9.

BSI (2011) *Crisis Management: Guidance and Good Practice*. London: British Standards Institution.

Budd, J.F. (1994) *A Pragmatic Examination of Ethical Dilemmas in Public Relations*. IPRA Gold Paper, 8.

Bureau of Investigative Journalism (2011) 'PR uncovered: What Bell Pottinger said', www. thebureauinvestigates.com/2011/12/07/pr-uncovered-what-they-said/ [Accessed 31 Dec. 2011].

Burghausen, M. (2013) 'Corporate and organizational marketing', ICIG, www.icig.org.uk/ what-is-corporate-marketing/ [Accessed 15 Mar. 2016].

Burkart, R. (2009) 'On Habermas: Understanding and public relations', in O. Ihlen, B. van Ruler and M. Fredriksson (eds), *Public Relations and Social Theory: Key Figures and Concepts*. Abingdon: Routledge, pp. 141–65.

Business Population Estimates (2016) www.gov.uk/government/statistics/business-population-estimates-2016 [Accessed 21 Mar. 2017].

Bussey, C. (2011) 'Location, location, location', *PR Week,* 28 Sept., www.prweek.com/uk/ news/1095706/Location-location-location/ [Accessed 1 Dec. 2011].

Cannon, T. (1992) *Corporate Responsibility*, 1st edn. London: Pitman Publishing.

Cartledge, P. (2009) *Ancient Greek Political Thought in Practice*. Cambridge: Cambridge University Press.

Cartmell, M. (2011a) 'Profile: Avril Lee, CEO of Ketchum Pleon', *PR Week*, 14 Apr., www. prweek.com/uk/features/1065332/Profile-Avril-Lee-CEO-Ketchum-Pleon/ [Accessed 1 Dec. 2011].

Cartmell, M. (2011b) 'PRCA calls for all members to pay interns the National Minimum Wage', *PR Week*, 17 Nov., www.prweek.com/uk/news/1104372/ [Accessed 1 Dec. 2011].

Cave, A. (2011) 'From media relations to business strategy', *CorpComms*, Sept.: 23–5.

Celsi, C. (2011) '6 alternatives to sending a press release', *PR Daily*, 5 May.

Centre for Economics and Business Research (CEBR) (2005) 'PR today: 48,000 professionals; £36.5 billion turnover. The economic significance of public relations', www.cipr.co.uk/sites/default/files/CIPR%20full%20report%20-%20November%204% 202005.pdf [Accessed 16 Dec. 2010].

Chaiken, S. (1980) 'Heuristic versus systematic information processing and source versus message cues in persuasion', *Journal of Personality and Social Psychology*, 39(5): 752–66.

Chartered Institute of Marketing (2011) www.cim.co.uk/resources/understandingmarket/ definitionmkting.aspx [Accessed 31 Dec. 2011].

Chen, N. (2013) 'Public relations in China', in H.M. Culbertson and N. Chen, *International PR: A Comparative Analysis*. Abingdon: Routledge, pp. 121–54.

Chen, S. and Chaiken, S. (1999) 'The heuristic-systematic model in its broader context', in S. Chaiken and Y. Trope (eds), *Dual-Process Theories in Social and Cognitive Psychology*. New York: Guilford Press, pp. 73–96.

Chipchase, J. (2001) 'IT sector public relations', in A. Theaker (ed.), *The Public Relations Handbook*. London: Routledge, pp. 218–38.

Chong, E. (2011) 'Managerial competencies and career advancement: A comparative study of managers in two countries', *Journal Business Research*, doi:10.1016/j.jbusres.2011. 08.015.

Christensen, L.T., Morsing, M. and Cheney, G. (2008) *Corporate Communications: Convention, Complexity and Critique*. London: Sage.

Chryssides, G.D. and Kaler, J.H. (1993) *An Introduction to Business Ethics*. London: Chapman & Hall.

CIPR (2009) *Social Media Guidelines*, www.cipr.co.uk/sites/default/files/Social%20Media%20guidelines.pdf [Accessed 31 Dec. 2010].

CIPR (2010) *State of the PR Profession Benchmarking Survey*, www.cipr.co.uk [Accessed 25 Aug. 2010].

CIPR (2011a) *Social Media Measurement Guidance*, March.

CIPR (2011b) 'CSR guide', www.cipr.co.uk/member/PRguides/CSR [Accessed 10 July 2011].

CIPR (2011c) 'Research, Planning and Measurement Toolkit', Mar., www.cipr.co.uk/content/policy-resources/for-practitioners/research-planning-and-measurement/toolkit [Accessed 1 Dec. 2011].

CIPR (2015) 'State of the profession', www.cipr.co.uk/stateofpr [Accessed 2 May 2015].

CIPR (2016) www.cipr.co.uk/content/our-organisation/professionalism-and-ethics [Accessed 9 Mar. 2016].

CISCO (2011) 'The Internet of things: How the next evolution of the Internet is changing everything', www.cisco.com/web/about/ac79/docs/innov/IoT_IBSG_0411FINAL.pdf [Accessed 30 June 2015].

Clack, A. (2011) 'Playing the long game', *PR Week*, 12 May, www.prweek.com/uk/news/1069444/Alex-Clack-Ogilvy-Playing-long-game [Accessed 1 Dec. 2011].

Clarke, A. (2000) 'Globalisation – dancing to a new tune', presentation to students at Cardiff University, 12 Oct.

Cohen, D. (2011) 'Trends in consumer PR in 2010', *PR Week*, 10 June: 25.

Cole, G.A. (2004) *Management Theory and Practice*, 6th edn. London: Thomson.

Collis, D. and Rukstad, M.G. (2008) 'Can you say what your strategy is?', *Harvard Business Review*, 86(4): 82–90.

Commission of PR Education (1999) *A Port of Entry*. London: PRSA.

Content Marketing Institute (2011) *2012 B2B Content Marketing Benchmarks, Budgets and Trends*, www.content-marketing-institute.com/2011/12/2012-b2b-content-marketing-research/ [Accessed 31 Dec. 2011].

Coombs, T. (2015) *Ongoing Crisis Communication: Planning, Managing, and Responding*, 4th edn. Thousand Oaks, CA: Sage.

Coombs, T. and Holladay, S. (2012) 'Examining the effects of mutability and framing on perceptions of human error and technical error crises: Implications for situational crisis communication theory', in T. Coombs and S. Holladay (eds), *The Handbook of Crisis Communication*. Chichester: John Wiley, pp. 181–204.

Cornelissen, J. (2008) *Corporate Communications: A Guide to Theory and Practice*. London: Sage.

Corporate Branding (2011) www.corporatebrandinginfo.com [Accessed 21 Nov. 2011].

Costa, M. (2011) 'How to extend shelf life of your campaign', *Marketing Week*, 13 Jan.: 28–30.

Covey, S.R. (1989) *The Seven Habits of Highly Effective People: Restoring the Character Ethic*. London: Simon & Schuster.

Cox, D (2015) 'Five internal communication trends to watch in 2016', www.newsweaver.com/five-internal-communication-trends-to-watch-in-2016/#.VynTkoQrLcc [Accessed 3 May 2016].

CPRS (2008) www.cprs.ca/aboutus/whatisPR.aspx [Accessed 4 May 2016].

Crush, P. (2005) 'Global PR: What does the world think?', *PR Week*, 9 Nov., www.prweek.com/uk/features/526852/ [Accessed 1 Dec. 2011].

Crystal Interactive (2006) 'The human touch', www.crystal-interactive.co.uk [Accessed 4 Apr. 2007].

Csíkszentmihalyi, M., and Rochberg-Halton, E. (1981) *The Meaning of Things: Domestic Symbols and the Self*. Cambridge: Cambridge University Press.

CSR Europe (2002) www.csreurope.org/data/files/Marketing/CSR_Europe_overview_and_service_offer.pdf [Accessed 30 June 2011].

Culbertson, H.M. and Chen, N. (2013) *International PR: A Comparative Analysis*. Abingdon: Routledge.

Curran, J. and Seaton, J. (2003) *Power without Responsibility: The Press, Broadcasting, and New Media in Britain*. Abingdon: Routledge.

Cutlip, S.M., Center, A.H. and Broom, G.M. (1985) *Effective Public Relations*, revised 6th edn. Upper Saddle River, NJ: Prentice Hall.

Cutlip, S.M., Center, A.H. and Broom, G.M. (1995) *Effective Public Relations*, 7th edn. Upper Saddle River, NJ: Prentice Hall.

Cutlip, S.M., Center, A.H. and Broom, G.M. (2000) *Effective Public Relations*, 8th edn. Upper Saddle River, NJ: Prentice Hall.

Cutlip, S.M., Center, A.H. and Broom, G.M. (2006) *Effective Public Relations*, 9th edn. Upper Saddle River, NJ: Pearson Education International.

Daily Record (2010) 'Transplant mother backs organ donor campaign', www.dailyrecord.co.uk/news/health-news/2010/02/15/transplant-mother-backs-organ-donor-campaign-86908-22044320/ [Accessed 31 Dec. 2011].

Dalton, R.J. (2014). *Citizen Politics: Public Opinion and Political Parties in Advanced Industrial Democracies*, 6th edn. Thousand Oaks, CA: Sage.

Dantz, M. (2015) 'Three crucial factors of public relations in China', www.edelman.com/post/three-crucial-factors-of-public-relations-in-china/ [Accessed 23 May 2016].

Dauncey, G. (1994) 'Shades of Green', *New Economics Foundation*, 30.

Davies, N. (2008) *Flat Earth News*. London: Chatto & Windus.

Davis, A. (2004) *Mastering Public Relations*. London: Palgrave.

Daye, D. and van Auken, B. (2008) '10 steps to successful corporate branding', www.brandingstrategyinsider.com [Accessed 21 Nov. 2011].

Daymon, C. and Holloway, I. (2011) *Qualitative Research Methods in Public Relations and Marketing Communications*, 2nd edn. Abingdon: Routledge.

Deloitte (2016) 'The future of risk', www2.deloitte.com/us/en/pages/risk/articles/future-of-risk-ten-trends.html [Accessed 21 Mar. 2017].

DeSanto, B. and Moss, D. (2004) 'Rediscovering what PR managers do: Rethinking the measurement of managerial behaviour in the public relations context', *Journal of Communication Management*, 9(2): 179–96.

Desjardins, J. (2016) 'All of the world's stock exchanges by size', http://money.visualcapitalist.com/all-of-the-worlds-stock-exchanges-by-size/ [Accessed 21 Mar. 2017].

Dewhurst, S. and FitzPatrick, L. (2007) 'Building a framework for internal communicators', *Strategic Communication Management*, 11(2), Feb./Mar.

Dewhurst, S. and FitzPatrick, L. (2016) 'What makes a competent communicator?', in Marc Wright (ed.), *Gower Handbook of Internal Communication*, 2nd edn. London: Gower Publishing, pp. 49–66.

DeWit, B. and Meyer, R. (2010) *Strategy Synthesis: Resolving Strategy Paradoxes to Create Competitive Advantage*, 3rd edn. Andover: Cengage Learning.

Dichter, E. (1986) 'Ernest Dichter: Motive Interpreter', interview with R. Banos, *Journal of Advertising Research*, Feb./Mar.: 15–20.

Dictionary of Sociology (1944) Edited by H. Fairchild. Lanham, MD: Rowman & Littlefield.

Diga, M. and Kelleher, T. (2009) 'Social media use, perceptions of decision making power, and public relations roles', *Public Relations Review*, 35: 440–2.

Digital Market Asia (2011) www.digitalmarket.asia/2011/07/the-age-of-spin-is-now-dead-says-ogilvy-pr-chief/ [Accessed 16 Apr. 2012].

Donchev, D. (2017) '36 mind blowing YouTube facts, figures and statistics – 2017', https://fortunelords.com/youtube-statistics/ [Accessed 20 Sep. 2017].

Dozier, D.M. (1992) 'The organisational roles of communicators and public relations practitioners', in J.E. Grunig (ed.), *Excellence in Public Relations and Communications Management*. Hillsdale, NJ: Lawrence Erlbaum.

Dozier, D.M. and Broom, G.M. (1995) 'Evolution of the manager role in public relations practice', *Journal of Public Relations Research*, 7(1): 3–26.

Dozier, D.M., Grunig, L.A. and Grunig, J.E. (1995) *Managers Guide to Excellence in Public Relations and Communication Management*. Hillsdale, NJ: Lawrence Erlbaum.

Duhé, S.C. (2007) 'Public relations and complexity thinking in the age of transparency', in S.C. Duhé (ed.), *New Media and Public Relations*. New York: Peter Lang, pp. 57–76.

Edmunds, H. (2000) *The Focus Group Research Handbook*. Lincolnwood, IL: NTC Business Books.

Edwards, L. (2010) *An Exploratory Study of the Experiences of BAME PR Practitioners in the UK Industry*. ESRC/Leeds Metropolitan University/CIPR.

Edwards, L. and Hodges, C.E.M. (2011) 'Introduction: Implications of a (radical) socio-cultural "turn" in public relations scholarship', in L. Edwards and C.E.M. Hodges (eds), *Public Relations, Society and Culture: Theoretical and Empirical Explorations*. Abingdon: Routledge, pp. 1–14.

EFQM (2013) 'An overview of the EFQM Excellence Model', www.efqm.org/sites/default/files/overview_efqm_2013_v1.1.pdf [Accessed 9 June 2016].

Egan, J. (2007) *Marketing Communications*. Belmont, CA: Wadsworth, Cengage Learning.

Eiró-Gomes, M. and Duarte, J. (2008) 'The case study as an evaluation tool for public relations', in B. Van Ruler and A.T. Verčič (eds), *Public Relations Metrics: Research and Evaluation*. Abingdon: Routledge, pp. 235–51.

Elkington, J. (1997) *Cannibals with Forks: The Triple Bottom Line of 21st Century Business*. Chichester: Capstone.

Elton, L. (1993) 'University teaching: A professional model for quality', in R. Ellis (ed.), *Quality Assurance for University Teaching*. Oxford: Open University Press.

Empson, L., Muzio, D., Broschak, J.P. and Hinings, B. (2015) 'Researching professional service firms: An introduction and overview', in L. Empson, D. Muzio, J.P. Broschak and B. Hinings (eds), *The Oxford Handbook of Professional Service Firms*. Oxford: Oxford University Press, pp. 1–24.

Ewen, S. (1998) *PR! A Social History of Spin*. New York: Basic Books.

Eyrich, N., Padman, M.L. and Sweetser, K.D. (2008) 'PR practitioners use of social media tools and communication technology', *Public Relations Review*, 34(4): 412–14.

Falconi, T.M. (2003) 'Europe – the PR challenge', *Profile*, May: 12–13.

Fawkes, J. (2006) 'Public relations, propaganda and the psychology of persuasion', in R. Tench and L. Yeomans (eds), *Exploring Public Relations*. Harlow: Prentice Hall.

Fawkes, J. (2007) 'Public relations models and persuasion ethics: A new approach', *Journal of Communication Management*, 11(4): 313–31.

Fawkes, J. (2012a) 'What is public relations?', in A. Theaker (ed.), *The Public Relations Handbook*, 4th edn. Abingdon: Routledge, p. 10.

Fawkes, J. (2012b) 'Public relations and communications', in A. Theaker (ed.), *The Public Relations Handbook*, 4th edn. Abingdon: Routledge, pp. 21–37.

Fawkes, J. (2015) *Public Relations Ethics and Professionalism: The Shadow of Excellence*. Abingdon: Routledge.

Fawkes, J. and Tench, R. (2004) 'Does employer resistance to theory threaten the future of public relations? A consideration of research findings, comparing UK practitioner, academic and alumni attitudes to public relations education', International Public Relations Research Symposium, Bled, Slovenia, 11 July.

Fekrat, M.A., Inclan, C. and Petroni, D. (1996) 'Corporate environmental disclosures: Competitive disclosure hypothesis using 1991 annual report data', *International Journal of Accounting*, 31(2): 175–95.

Ferrabee, D. (2010) www.ableandhow.com [Accessed 31 Oct. 2011].

Festinger, L. (1957) *A Theory of Cognitive Dissonance*. Stanford, CA: Stanford University Press.

Fields, D. and Robbins, D. (2008) *Speaking to Teenagers: How to Think about, Create, and Deliver Effective Messages*. Grand Rapids, MI: Zondervan.

Fill, C. (2002) *Marketing Communications: Contexts, Strategies and Applications*. London: FT/Prentice Hall.

Financial Times (2016) 'Financial PR spins a new global story', www.ft.com/content/e21a373e-137e-11e6-91da-096d89bd2173 [Accessed 21 Mar. 2017].

Fishbein, M. and Ajzen, I. (1980) *Predicting and Changing Behavior: The Reasoned Action Approach*. New York: Psychology Press.

Fisk, P. (2004) 'The Future of Marketing', Annual Cambridge Marketing Lecture, CMC.

FitzPatrick, K. (2006) 'Baselines for ethical advocacy in the "Marketplace of Ideas"', in K. Fitzpatrick and C. Bronstein (eds), *Ethics in Public Relations: Responsible Advocacy*. Thousand Oaks, CA: Sage, pp. 1–18.

FitzPatrick, K. and Bronstein, C. (eds) (2006) *Ethics in Public Relations: Responsible Advocacy*. Thousand Oaks, CA: Sage.

FitzPatrick, L. (2012) 'Internal communications', in A. Theaker (ed.), *The Public Relations Handbook*, 4th edn. Abingdon: Routledge, pp. 273–310.

Fleet, D. (2006) 'Think PR people don't need math? Think again', http://davefleet.com/2009/07/pr-people-math/ [Accessed 1 Dec. 2011].

Forsyth, D.R. (2009) *Group Dynamics*, 5th edition. Belmont, CA: Wadsworth, Cengage Learning.

Free Dictionary (2011) www.thefreedictionary.com/journalism [Accessed 31 Oct. 2011].

Freeman, R.E. and McVea, J. (2005) 'A stakeholder approach to strategic management', in M.A. Hitt, E. Freeman and J.S. Harrison (eds), *Handbook of Strategic Management*. Oxford: Blackwell Publishing, pp. 189–207.

Freitag, A. and Quesinberry Stokes, A. (2009) *Global Public Relations*. Abingdon: Routledge.

Friedman, M. (1993) 'The social responsibility of business is to increase its profits', in G.D. Chryssides and J.H. Kaler (eds), *An Introduction to Business Ethics*. London: Chapman & Hall.

Friend, R. (2011) 'Keep the customer satisfied', *PR Week*, 12 May, www.prweek.com/uk/features/1069448/rachel-friend-weber-shandwick-keep-customer-satisfied/ [Accessed 1 Dec. 2011].

Fritz, J. (2017) 'What every nonprofit should know about cause marketing', www.thebalance.com/what-every-nonprofit-should-know-about-cause-marketing-2502005 [Accessed 20 Sep. 2016].

Frohlich, M. (2016) 'Consumer PR', in A. Theaker (ed.), *The Public Relations Handbook*, 5th edn. Abingdon: Routledge, pp. 388–404.

Fröhlich, R. and Peters, S.B. (2007) 'PR "bunnies" caught in the agency ghetto? Gender stereotypes, organizational factors, and women's careers in PR agencies', *Journal of Public Relations Research*, 19(3): 229–54.

Fung, V.K.K., Fung, W. and Wind, Y. (2008) *Competing in a Flat World: Building Enterprises for a Borderless World*. Upper Saddle River, NJ: Prentice Hall.

Furness, P. (2008) 'Real time geodemographics: New services and business opportunities (and risks) from analyzing people in time and space', *Journal of Direct, Data and Digital Marketing Practice*, 10(2): 104–15.

Future Foundation (1998) *The Responsible Organisation*. BT.

GA (Global Alliance) (2016) www.globalalliancepr.org/website/gbok [Accessed 9 Mar. 2016].

Gangadharbatla, H. (2008) 'Facebook me: Collective self-esteem, need to belong, and internet self-efficacy as predictors of the igeneration's attitudes toward social networking sites', *Journal of Interactive Advertising*, 8(2): 5–15.

Garrick, J. and Christie, R.F. (2008) *Quantifying and Controlling Catastrophic Risks*. London: Academic Press.

Garsten, N. (2011) 'Evolution and significance of PR specialisms in contemporary Britain', History of Public Relations Conference, Bournemouth.

Garsten, N. and Howard, J. (2011) 'The evolution and significance of public relations specialisms in contemporary Britain (1985–2010)', International History of Public Relations Conference, Bournemouth University, July.

Gilpin, D.R. and Murphy, P.J. (2008) *Crisis Management in a Complex World*. Oxford: Oxford University Press.

Gladwell, M. (2000) 'The Tipping Point' website, www.gladwell.com/tippingpoint/ [Accessed 1 Dec. 2011].

Gladwell, M. (2005) *Blink: The Power of Thinking without Thinking*. London: Penguin.

Global Alliance (2009) Annual report, https://issuu.com/globalalliancepr/docs/global_alliance_annual_report_2009.

Go-Gulf (2012) 'How organizations structure social media teams', www.go-gulf.com/blog/how-organizations-structure-social-media-teams/ [Accessed 21 Mar. 2017].

Goldhaber, G.M. and Krivonos, P.D. (1977) 'The ICA communication audit: Process, status, critique', *Journal of Business Communication*, 15(1): 41–55.

Gong, B. (2014) *Understanding Institutional Shareholder Activism: A Comparative Study of the UK and China*. Abingdon: Routledge.

Goodman, G. (2010) 'Five key ingredients of lasting brands', www.entrepreneur.com [Accessed 21 Nov. 2011].

Gorkana (2011) *2011 PR Census*. London: PR Week/PRCA.

Government Office for Science (2016) *Distributed Ledger Technology: Beyond Block Chain*, www.gov.uk/government/uploads/system/uploads/attachment_data/file/492972/gs-16-1-distributed-ledger-technology.pdf [Accessed 21 Mar. 2017].

Grant, W. (2004) 'Pressure politics: The changing world of pressure groups', *Parliamentary Affairs*, 57(2): 408–19.

Gray, R. (2004) 'Finding the right direction', *Communication World*, Nov./Dec.: 26–32.

Gray, R. (2006a) 'Agencies drawn by China's riches', *PR Week*, 21 July, www.prweek.com/uk/news/570225/Feature-Agencies-drawn-Chinas-riches/ [Accessed 1 Dec. 2011].

Gray, R. (2006b) 'Feature: Time well spent?', *PR Week*, 26 Oct., www.prweek.com/uk/news/600215/Feature-Time-spent/ [Accessed 1 Dec. 2011].

Gray, R. (2007) 'Time to act on CSR', *PR Week*, 21 Feb., www.prweek.com/uk/features/634208/ [Accessed 1 Dec. 2011].

Great Place to Work (2016) Great Workplaces, Redactive Media Group.

Green, A. (2007) *Creativity in Public Relations*, 3rd edn. London: Kogan Page.

Green, A. (2010) *Creativity in Public Relations*, 4th edn. London: Kogan Page.

Greenwood, R.G. (1981) 'Management by objectives as developed by Peter Drucker, assisted by Harold Smiddy' [originally in *Academy of Management Review*, 6(2): 225–30], in J.C. Wood and M.C. Wood (eds), *Peter F. Drucker: Critical Evaluations in Business and Management*. Abingdon: Routledge, 2005, vol. 1, pp. 163–74.

Gregory, A. (2000) *Planning and Managing Public Relations Campaigns*, 2nd edn. London: Kogan Page.

Gregory, A. (2009) 'Public relations as planned communications', in R. Tench and L. Yeomans (eds), *Exploring Public Relations*. London: FT Prentice Hall, pp. 174–97.

Gregory, A. (2012) 'Public relations and management', in A. Theaker (ed.), *The Public Relations Handbook*, 4th edn. Abingdon: Routledge, pp. 60–81.

Gregory, A. (2015) *Planning and Managing Public Relations Campaigns: A Strategic Approach*, 4th edn. London: Kogan Page.

Gregory, A. and White, J. (2008) 'Introducing the Chartered Institute of Public Relations initiative: Moving on from talking about evaluation to incorporating it into better management of the practice', in B. Van Ruler and A.T. Verčič (eds), *Public Relations Metrics: Research and Evaluation*. Abingdon: Routledge, pp. 307–17.

Gregory, A. and Willis, P. (2013) *Strategic Public Relations Leadership*. Abingdon: Routledge.

Gregory, H. (2006) 'The grads are back', *PR Week*, 3 Nov.: 24–6.

Griggs, I. (2016) 'Is an ageist brain drain damaging UK agencies', *PR Week*, Feb.: 12.

Gronstedt, A. and Caywood, C.L. (2011) 'Communications research: Foundational matters', in C.L. Caywood (ed.), *The Handbook of Strategic Public Relations and Integrated Marketing Communications*, 2nd edn. New York: McGraw-Hill, pp. 13–36.

Groom, B. and Pfeifer, S. (2011) 'Privatisation defined Thatcher era', *Financial Times*, www.ft.com/cms/s/0/51ccaa1c-20c2-11e1-816d-00144feabdc0.html#axzz1hCNuwSmH [Accessed 31 Dec. 2011].

Grunig, J.E. (2001) 'Two-way symmetrical public relations: past, present and future', in R.L. Heath (ed.), *The Handbook of Public Relations*. Thousand Oaks, CA: Sage, pp. 11–30.

Grunig, J.E. (2009) 'Paradigms of global public relations in an age of digitalisation', *PRism*, 6(2), http://praxis.massev.ac.nz/prism on-line iourn.html [Accessed 31 Dec. 2010].

Grunig, J.E. (2016) 'Conventional wisdom is the principal enemy of the public relations profession', www.pr-romania.ro/dezbateri/dezbateri-actuale/reforma-reputatiei/1984-james-grunig-conventional-wisdom-is-the-principal-enemy-of-the-public-relations-profession.html [Accessed 21 Mar. 2017].

Grunig, J.E. and Grunig, L.A. (2010) 'The Third Annual Grunig Lecture Series: Public Relations Excellence 2010', PRSA International Conference, Washington, DC, 17 Oct., www.instituteforpr.org/files/uploads/Third_Grunig_Lecture_Transcript.pdf [Accessed 31 Dec. 2010].

Grunig, J.E. and Hunt, T. (1984) *Managing Public Relations*. New York: Holt, Rinehart & Winston.

Grunig, J.E. and Repper, F. (1992) 'Strategic management, publics and issues', in J. Grunig (ed.), *Excellence in Public Relations and Communications Management*. Hillsdale, NJ: Lawrence Erlbaum.

Grunig, J.E., Dozier, D.M., Ehling, W.P., Grunig, L.A., Repper, F.C. and White, J. (eds) (1992) *Excellence in Public Relations and Communication Management*. Hillsdale, NJ: Lawrence Erlbaum.

Grunig, L.A., Grunig, J.E. and Dozier, D.M. (2002) *Excellent Public Relations and Effective Organisations: A Study of Communication Management in Three Countries*. London: Routledge.

Gurău, C. (2008) 'Integrated online marketing communication: Implementation and management', *Journal of Communication Management*, 12(2): 169–84.

Hall, D.T. (2004) 'The protean career: A quarter-century journey', *Journal of Vocational Behavior*, 65(1): 1–13.

Hampden-Turner, C.M. and Trompenaars, F. (2000) *Building Cross-Cultural Competence*. New Haven, CT: Yale University Press.

Handy, C. (1989) *The Age of Unreason*. London: Random House.

Harben, J. (1998) 'The power of storytelling when cultures merge', *Journal of Communication Management*, 3(1): 80–7.

Harcup, T. (2007) *The Ethical Journalist*. London: Sage.

Harrison, C. (2011) 'Cleaning up the lobby shop', *CorpComms*, 62, Nov.: 13–17.

Hart, N. (ed.) (1995) *Strategic Public Relations*. London: Macmillan Business Press.

Harvard Business Review (2013) 'Achievers report', http://hbr.org/resources/pdfs/comm/achievers/hbr_achievers_report_sep13.pdf [Accessed 4 May 2016].

Hawn, R. (2007) 'A community relations model', www.underwatermunitions.org/idum_1/oct_10/Robin%20Hawn%20Oct10.pdf [Accessed 5 June 2016].

Hays, P.A. (2004) 'Case study research', in K. deMarrais and S.D. Lapan (eds), *Foundations for Research: Methods of Inquiry in Education and the Social Sciences*. Mahwah, NJ: Lawrence Erlbaum, pp. 217–34.

Hazlett, K. (2011a) 'Your career and you', http://kirkhazlett-aprofessorsthought.blogspot.com, 16 Jan. [Accessed 9 May 2011].

Hazlett, K. (2011b) 'Take some you time', http://kirkhazlett-aprofessorsthought.blogspot.com, 25 June [Accessed 26 June 2011].

Heath, R.L. (2001a) 'Shifting foundations: Public relations as relationship building', in R.L. Heath (ed.), *Handbook of Public Relations*. London: Sage, pp. 1–9.

Heath, R.L. (2001b) 'Globalisation – the frontier of multinationalism and cultural diversity', in R.L. Heath (ed.), *Handbook of Public Relations*. London: Sage, pp. 625–8.

Heath, R.L. (2002) 'Issues management: Its past, present and future', *Journal of Public Affairs*, 2(2): 209–14.

Hendrix, J.A. (1995) *Public Relations Cases*, 3rd edn. Belmont, CA: Wadsworth.

Hendrix, J.A. (2006) *Public Relations Cases*, 7th edn. Belmont, CA: Wadsworth.

Henry, A. (2008) *Understanding Strategic Management*. Oxford: Oxford University Press.

Hickey, S. (2015) 'The innovators: Digital nomads make office sharing a reality', *Guardian*, 4 Oct., www.theguardian.com/business/2015/oct/04/the-innovators-digital-nomads-make-office-sharing-a-reality [Accessed 22 June 2016].

Hill, N. and Alexander, J. (2006) *The Handbook of Customer Satisfaction and Loyalty Measurement*, 2nd edn. Aldershot: Gower Publishing.

Himler, P. (2011) 'PR redefined', www.forbes.com/sites/peterhimler/2011/11/21/prredefined/ [Accessed 31 Dec. 2011].

Hinchey, P.H. (2008) *Action Research Primer*. New York: Peter Lang.

Hindle, N. (2011) 'Client view – Nick Hindle, McDonald's: Managing the McFightback', *PR Week*, 7 Apr., www.prweek.com/uk/league_tables/1063766/Client-View—Nick-Hindle-McDonalds-Managing-McFightback/ [Accessed 1 Dec. 2011].

Hitchins, J. (2003) 'News from Nowhere', Current Debates in Public Relations Research and Practice, Bournemouth University, 10–12 Apr.

Holmes, P. (2007) 'A manifesto for the 21st century public relations firm', http://pr20. wordpress.com/2007/05/13/a-manifesto-for-the-21st-century-public-relations-firm/, 13 May [Accessed 31 Dec. 2010].

Holmström, S. (2004) 'Intermezzo: The reflective paradigm of public relations', in B. van Ruler and D. Verčič (eds), *Public Relations and Communication Management in Europe: A Nation-by-Nation Introduction to Public Relations Theory and Practice*. Berlin: Mouton de Gruyter, pp. 121–34.

Holtz, S. (2014) 'Socially relevant', *Communication World Online*, 8–11, http://cw.iabc.com/ [Accessed 3 May 2016].

Holtzhausen, D.R. (2002) 'Resistance from the margins: The postmodern public relations practitioner as organisational activist', *Journal of Public Relations Research*, 14(1): 57–84.

Hopkin, P. (2017) *Fundamentals of Risk Management*, 4th edn. London: Kogan Page.

Hughes, S. (2016) 'Is PR sexist?', *Influence*, Q3.

Hunt, R. (2011) 'Personality and authenticity', *PR Week*, 14 Sept., www.prweek.com/uk/league_tables/1089934/ros-hunt-cohn-wolfe-personality-authenticity/ [Accessed 1 Dec. 2011].

Hunter, S. (2011) 'It's important to listen', *PR Week*, 12 May, www.prweek.com/uk/news/1069447/Sharleen-Hunter-Unleashed-Potential-Its-important-listen/ [Accessed 1 Dec. 2011].

Hurd, B. (2010) 'Employee social media – risk and reward', http://barryhurd.com [Accessed 13 Oct. 2011].

Hutcheon, M. (2016) 'Brand Comms', *PR Week*, Feb.: 18.

Hutton, J.G. (1999) 'The definition, dimensions and domain of public relations', *Public Relations Review*, 25(2): 199–214.

Hutton, J.G. (2010) 'Defining the relationship between public relations and marketing: Public relations' most important challenge', in R.L. Heath (ed.), *The Sage Handbook of Public Relations*, 2nd edn. London: Sage, pp. 509–22.

Ihlen, O. (2009) 'On Bourdieu: Public relations in field struggles', in O. Ihlen, B. van Ruler and M. Fredriksson (eds), *Public Relations and Social Theory: Key Figures and Concepts*. Abingdon: Routledge, pp. 62–82.

Ihlen, O. (2013) 'Great day in London', https://oyvindihlen.wordpress.com/2013/07/10/great-day-in-london/ [Accessed 21 Mar. 2017].

Ihlen, O. and van Ruler, B. (2007) 'How public relations works: Theoretical roots and public relations perspectives', *Public Relations Review*, 33(3): 243–8.

Ihlen, O. and van Ruler, B. (2009) 'Introduction: Applying social theory to public relations', in O. Ihlen, B. van Ruler and M. Fredriksson (eds), *Public Relations and Social Theory: Key Figures and Concepts*. Abingdon: Routledge, pp. 1–20.

Iliff, R. (2014) 'Why PR is embracing the PESO model', http://mashable.com/2014/12/05/public-relations-industry/#cham65Y97sqS [Accessed 4 May 2016].

Ingenium (2009) 'Best practices in employee communications and engagement', Ingenium Communications, www.resultsmap.com/e/downloads/BestPractices_Employee Communications.pdf [Accessed 14 July 2011].

Ingham, F. (2015) 'Our ethics are upheld through actions, not just empty words', *PR Week*, Nov.: 86.

Ingham, F. (2016) 'Raising standards to hit the heights, not budgets', *PR Week*, Mar.: 53.

Inkson, K. (2007) *Understanding Careers: The Metaphors of Working Lives*. Thousand Oaks, CA: Sage.

Institute of Internal Communications (2005) www.ioic.org.uk/content/training/knowledgebank/741-internal-communications-makes-the-difference-to-success.html [Accessed 13 Oct. 2011].

Institute of Practitioners in Advertising (2009) 'How share of voice wins market share', Nielsen and the IPA Databank.

Institute of Risk Management (2002) 'A risk management standard', www.theirm.org/media/886059/ARMS_2002_IRM.pdf [Accessed 21 Mar. 2017].

Investor Relations Society (2016) 'Investor relations around the world', www.irs.org.uk/resources/international-ir [Accessed 21 Mar. 2017].

IPA (2010) 'Results of the Third IPA Touchpoints Survey', www.ipa.co.uk/Content/Results-of-third-IPA-TouchPoints-Survey [Accessed 28 Jan. 2011].

IPRA (1990) *Public Relations Education Recommendations and Standards.* IPRA Gold Paper, 7, Sept.

Isaacson, W. (2011) *Steve Jobs*. London: Little, Brown.

Jahansoozi, J. (2006) 'Relationships, transparency, and evaluation: The implications for public relations', in J. L'Etang and M. Pieczka (eds), *Critical Perspectives in Public Relations*. Mahwah, NJ: Lawrence Erlbaum Associates.

Janal, D. (1998) *Online Marketing Handbook*. London: John Wiley & Sons.

Jandt, F.E. (2004) *An Introduction to Intercultural Communication*, 4th edn. London: Sage.

Jandt, F.E. (2009) *An Introduction to Intercultural Communication*, 6th edn. London: Sage.

Janis, I.L. (1972) *Victims of Groupthink: A Psychological Study of Foreign-Policy Decisions and Fiascos*. Oxford: Houghton Mifflin.

Jaques, T. (2002) 'Towards a new terminology: Optimising the value of issue management', *Journal of Communication Management*, 7(2): 140–7.

Jaques, T. (2010) 'Embedding issue management: From process to policy', in R.L. Heath (ed.), *The Sage Handbook of Public Relations*, 2nd edn. London: Sage, pp. 435–46.

Jardine, A. (2006) 'MPR: The solution to the budget puzzle?', *PR Week*, 15 Mar., www.prweek.com/uk/features/547179/ [Accessed 1 Dec. 2011].

Jarvis, P. (2007) *Globalisation, Lifelong Learning and the Learning Society: Sociological Perspectives*. Abingdon: Routledge, vol. 2.

Jenkin, M. (2016) 'The 14 qualities of the kick-ass comms professional', *Influence*, Q3.

Jeston, J. and Nelis, J. (2014) *Business Process Management: Practical Guidelines to Successful Implementations*, 3rd edn. Abingdon: Routledge.

John, P., Cotteril, S., Richardson, L., Moseley, A., Stoker, G., Wales, C. and Smith, G. (2011) *Nudge, Nudge, Think, Think: Using Experiments to Change Civic Behaviour*. London: Bloomsbury.

Johns, B. (2011) 'The 9 things that matter more than GPA', *PR Daily*, 4 May, www.prdaily.com [Accessed 9 May 2011].

Johns, T. (2016) 'Prevent your media pitch falling at the first hurdle', *PR Week*, Mar.: 13.

Johnson, B. (2007) 'Blogs mark the first 10 years', *Guardian*, 7 Apr.: 31.

Johnson, J., Scholes, K. and Whittington, R. (2005) *Exploring Corporate Strategy*, 7th edn. Harlow: Pearson Education.

Johnson, J., Scholes, K. and Whittington, R. (2008) *Exploring Corporate Strategy*, 8th edn. Harlow: Pearson Education.

Johnson, K.N., Ramirez, S.A. and Shelby, C.M. (2016) 'Diversifying to mitigate risk: Can Dodd-Frank section 342 help stabilize the financial sector?', *Washington and Lee Law Review*, 73(4): 1795–1868.

Jones, B., Temperley, J. and Anderson, L. (2009) 'Corporate reputation in the era of Web 2.0: The case of Primark', 23 July, www.tandfonline.com/doi/abs/10.1362/026725709X479309.

Kaba, N. (2001) 'More is socially very appealing', *PR Week*, 24 June, www.prweek.com/uk/features/1076348/more-socially-appealing/ [Accessed 1 Dec. 2011].

Katz, E. and Lazerfield, P.F. (1995) *Personal Influence*. Glencoe, IL: Free Press.

Kayes, D.C. (2015) *Organizational Resilience: How Learning Sustains Organizations in Crisis, Disaster, and Breakdown*. Oxford: Oxford University Press.

Keller, K.L. and Aaker, D.A. (2003) 'The impact of corporate marketing on a company's brand extensions', in J. Balmer and S. Greyser (eds), *Revealing the Corporation*. London: Routledge.

Kelly, K.S. (2001) 'Stewardship: The fifth step in the public relations process', in R.L. Heath (ed.), *The Sage Handbook of Public Relations*. London: Sage, pp. 279–90.

Kelly, M. (2011) 'Judging nudging: Choice architecture and social norming in health related behaviour change', Wolfson Research Institute, Durham University, 8 Apr., www.dur.ac.uk/resources/wolfson.institute/events/WolfsonDurham080411.pdf [Accessed 1 Dec. 2011].

Kim, J.-N. and Ni, L. (2010) 'Seeing the forest through the trees: The behavioural, strategic management paradigm in public relations and its future', in R.L. Heath (ed.), *The Sage Handbook of Public Relations*, 2nd edn. London: Sage, pp. 35–57.

Kirkpatrick, J. (2007) 'The hidden power of Kirkpatrick's four levels', *Training and Development*, Aug.: 34–7.

Kitchen, P. (ed.) (1997) *Public Relations, Principles and Practice*. London: International Thomson Business Press.

Kitchen, P.J. and Panopoulos, A. (2010) 'Online public relations: The adoption process and innovation challenge, a Greek example', *Public Relations Review*, 36(3): 222–9.

Klein, N. (2000) 'Tyranny of the brands', *New Statesman*, 24 Jan.: 25–8.

Knapton, S. (2016) 'High street shops secretly track customers using smartphones', *Daily Telegraph*, 27 Dec., www.telegraph.co.uk/science/2016/12/27/high-street-shops-secretly-track-customers-using-smartphones/ [Accessed 21 Mar. 2017].

Kneebone, R.L. (2009) 'Practice, rehearsal, and performance: An approach for simulation-based surgical and procedure training', *JAMA*, 302(12): 1336–8.

Knox, S. and Bickerton, D. (2003) 'Six conventions of corporate brand management', *European Journal of Marketing*, 37(7/8): 998–1016.

Koch, C. (2016) 'The fraught culture of always-on (& burnt out)', *Influence*, Q3.

Koenig, D.T. (2003) *The Engineer Entrepreneur*. New York: ASME Press.

Koerber, A. (2000) 'Toward a feminist rhetoric of technology', *Journal of Business and Technical Communication*, 14(1): 58–73.

Kotler, P. and Mindak, W. (1978) 'Marketing and public relations', *Journal of Marketing*, 42(10): 13–20.

La Due Lake, R., and Huckfeldt, R. (1998) 'Social capital, social networks, and political participation', *Political Psychology*, 19(3): 567–84.

Lambert, C. (2015) *Shadow Work: The Unpaid, Unseen Jobs that Fill your Day*. Berkeley, CA: Counterpoint.

Lansons Communications (2011) 'UK social media census', www.lansonsconversations. com/financial-services/infographic-the-uk-social-media-census-2011/ [Accessed 1 Dec. 2011].

Larson, C.U. (2004) *Persuasion: Reception and Responsibility*, 10th edn. Belmont, CA: Wadsworth.

Lawrence, F. (2011) 'Fat profits: Health hangover as big brands woo world's poorest shoppers', *Guardian*, 24 Nov.: 29.

Lazare, A. (2005) *On Apology*. New York: Oxford University Press.

Lees-Marshment, J. (2014) *Political Marketing: Principles and Applications*, 2nd edn. Abingdon: Routledge.

Lerbinger, O. (2001) 'Diversity and global communication require social interactive approach', *Purview*, 8 Jan.

L'Etang, J. (1996) 'Public relations and corporate responsibility', in J. L'Etang and M. Pieczka (eds), *Critical Perspectives in Public Relations*. London: International Thomson Business Press, pp. 82–105.

L'Etang, J. (2003) 'The myth of the "ethical guardian": An examination of its origins, potency and illusions', *Journal of Communication Management*, 8(1): 53–67.

L'Etang, J. (2004) *Public Relations in Britain: A History of the Professional Practice in the 20th Century*. Mahwah, NJ: Lawrence Erlbaum.

L'Etang, J. (2006a) 'Corporate responsibility and public relations ethics', in J. L'Etang and M. Pieczka (eds), *Critical Perspectives in Public Relations*. London: International Thomson Business Press.

L'Etang, J. (2006b) 'Public relations as diplomacy', in J. L'Etang and M. Pieczka (eds), *Critical Perspectives in Public Relations*. London: International Thomson Business Press.

L'Etang, J. (2006c) 'Public relations and rhetoric', in J. L'Etang and M. Pieczka (eds), *Critical Perspectives in Public Relations*. London: International Thomson Business Press.

L'Etang, J. (2008) *Public Relations: Concepts, Practice and Critique*. London: Sage.

L'Etang, J. (2009) 'Radical PR – catalyst for change or an aporia?', *Ethical Space*, 6(2): 13–18.

L'Etang, J. and Pieczka, M. (eds) (2006a) *Critical Perspectives in Public Relations*. London: International Thomson Business Press.

L'Etang, J. and Pieczka, M. (eds) (2006b) *Public Relations, Critical Debates and Contemporary Practice*. Mahwah, NJ: Lawrence Erlbaum.

Levco, J. (2001) 'The key to catching a reporter's eye? Pitch like one', 14 July, www.prdaily. com (members only).

Levine, R., Locke, C., Searls, D. and Weinberger D. (2009) *The Cluetrain Manifesto: 10th Anniversary Edition*. New York: Basic Books.

Lilleker, D.G. and Jackson, N. (2011) 'Political public relations and political marketing'. In J. Strömbäck and S. Kiousis (eds), *Political Public Relations: Principles and Applications*. Abingdon: Routledge, pp. 157–76.

Lilleker, D., Thorsen, E., Jackson, D. and Veneti, A. (2016) *US Election Analysis 2016: Media, Voters and the Campaign*, www.electionanalysis2016.US [Accessed 1 Dec. 2016].

Lindenmann, W.K. (2003) *Guidelines for Measuring the Effectiveness of PR Programs and Activities*. Gainesville, FL: Institute for Public Relations.

Lindenmann, W.K. (2006) *Public Relations Research for Planning and Evaluation*. Gainesville, FL: Institute for Public Relations.

Lloyd, L. (2011) 'Stay ahead of the trend curve', *PR Week*, 12 May, www.prweek.com/uk/features/1069441/louise-lloyd-cirkle-stay-ahead-trend-curve/ [Accessed 1 Dec. 2011].

Lochbihler, P. (2009) 'The Brussels reputation story: The interplay of public affairs and reputation', in J. Klewes and R. Wreschnick (eds), *Reputation Capital: Building and Maintaining Trust in the 21st Century*. London: Springer-Verlag, pp. 101–11.

Lowe, M. (2011) 'PR must refocus', *PR Week*, 12 May, www.prweek.com/uk/features/1069446/mark-lowe-third-city-consumer-pr-refocus/ [Accessed 1 Dec. 2011].

Lukaszewski, J. (2010) 'Community relationships: Best practices for stronger relationships', http://prsay.prsa.org/2010/01/15/community-relationships-best-practices-for-stronger-relationships/ [Accessed 5 June 2016].

Ma, W. (2011) 'Ogilvy PR to abandon AVE', http://www.adnews.com.au/adnews/ogilvy-pr-to-abandon-ave.

McComas, K.A. (2010) 'Community engagement and risk management', in R.L. Heath (ed.), *The Sage Handbook of Public Relations*, 2nd edn. London: Sage, pp. 461–76.

McCusker, G. (2006a) 'Disastrous times for public relations', *Profile*, Mar./Apr.: 17.

McCusker, G. (2006b) *Public Relations Disasters: Talespin Inside Stories and Lessons Learnt*. London: Kogan Page.

McDonald, H. and Harrison, P. (1999) 'The use of marketing and public relations activities by performing arts presenters', http://smib.vuw.ac.nz:8081/www/ANZMAC1999/Site/M/McDonald.pdf [Accessed 1 Dec. 2011].

McGrath, C., Moss, D., and Harris, P. (2010) 'The evolving discipline of public affairs', *Journal of Public Affairs*, 10(4): 335–52.

McGrath, C. (2011) 'Early journalistic and parliamentary references to lobbying and lobbyists in the UK', International History of Public Relations Conference, Bournemouth.

McKeone, D.H. (1995) *Measuring your Media Profile*. Aldershot: Gower Publishing.

McLachlan, H. (2008) 'I don't know about you but I'm no killer', www.scotsman.com/news/i_don_t_know_about_you_but_i_m_no_killer_1_1083658 [Accessed 31 Dec. 2011].

MacLeod, S. (2011) 'The ABC of reputation', *PR Week*, 14 Sept., www.prweek.com/uk/league_tables/1089936/sandra-macleod-echo-research-abc-reputation/ [Accessed 1 Dec. 2011].

McNair, B. (2011) *An Introduction to Political Communication*, 5th edn. Abingdon: Routledge.

McNamara, C. (2011) *Basics in Internal Organisational Communications*, www.resultsmap.com [Accessed 13 Oct. 2010].

Macnamara, J. (1999) 'Research in public relations: A review of the use of evaluation and formative research', *Asia Pacific Public Relations Review*, 1(2): 107–33.

Macnamara, J. (2005) 'Media content analysis: Its uses, benefits and best practice methodology', *Asia Pacific Public Relations Journal*, 6(1): 1–34.

Macnamara, J. (2007) *The Fork in the Road of Media and Communication Theory and Practice*, June, www.instituteforpr.org/files/uploads/MacnamaraPaper-b.pdf [Accessed 18 Nov. 2011].

Macnamara, J. (2010) *The 21st Century Media (R)evolution: Emergent Communication Practices*. New York: Peter Lang.

Macnamara, J. (2015) 'Creating an "architecture of listening" in organizations', www.uts.edu.au/about/faculty-arts-and-social-sciences/what-we-do/research/reports/creating-architecture-listening [Accessed 21 Mar. 2017].

McNiff, J. (2013) *Action Research: Principles and Practice*, 3rd edn. Abingdon: Routledge.

Madura, J. (2016) *International Financial Management*, Abridged 12th edn. Boston, MA: Cengage Learning.

Magala, J. (2017) 'Between Davos and Porto Alegre: Democratic entrepreneurship as crowdsourcing for ideas', in M. Lewandowski and B. Kozuch (eds), *Public Sector Entrepreneurship and the Integration of Innovative Business Models*. Hershey, PA: IGI Global, pp. 1–9.

Magee, K. (2007) 'How to pick the best star for the job', *PR Week*, 11 Apr., www.prweek.com/uk/features/649853/ [Accessed 1 Dec. 2011].

Magee, K. (2010) 'Measurement: What next for measurement?', *PR Week*, 18 Aug., www.prweek.com/news/1022935/Measurement-next-measurement/ [Accessed 16 Nov. 2010].

Magee, K. (2011a) 'Top 50 consumer consultancies', *PR Week*, 10 June, http://top pragencies.prweek.co.uk/Consumer-table.aspx [Accessed 1 Dec. 2011].

Magee, K. (2011b) '5 key skills for the future', *PR Week*, 10 Aug., www.prweek.com/uk/features/1084292/5-key-skills-future/ [Accessed 1 Dec. 2011].

Magee, K. (2011c) 'Tarnished brands', *PR Week*, 14 Sept., www.prweek.com/uk/features/1091797/Tarnished-brands [Accessed 1 Dec. 2011].

Mainiero, L.A. and Sullivan, S.E. (2005) 'Kaleidoscope careers: An alternate explanation for the "opt-out" revolution', *Academy of Management Executive*, 19(1): 106–23.

Maister, D.H., Green, C.H. and Galford, R.M. (2000) *The Trusted Advisor*. New York: Free Press.

Makimoto, T. and Manners, D. (1997) *Digital Nomad*. Chichester: John Wiley.

Martin, R.L. (2002) 'The virtue matrix: Calculating the return on corporate responsibility', *Harvard Business Review*, Mar.: 69–75.

Martinelli, D.K. (2011) 'Political public relations: Remembering its roots and classics', in J. Strömbäck and S. Kiousis (eds), *Political Public Relations: Principles and Applications*. Abingdon: Routledge, pp. 33–53.

Marx, E. (2001) *Breaking through Culture Shock*. London: Nicholas Brealey Publishing.

Mayer, R.N. (1989) *The Consumer Movement: Guardians of the Marketplace*. Boston, MA: Twayne Publishers.

Melcrum Publishing (2005) *Employee Engagement*. London: Melcrum Publishing.

Miccio, M. (2015) 'Five CSR trends to watch for in 2016', http://3blmedia.com/News/Five-CSR-Trends-Watch-2016.

Miller, D. and Dinan, D. (2008) *A Century of Spin*. London: Pluto.

Mintzberg, H. (1994) *The Rise and Fall of Strategic Planning*. Harlow: Pearson Education.

Mitchell, R.K., Agle, B.R. and Wood, D.J. (1997) 'Toward a theory of stakeholder identification and salience: Defining the principle of who and what really counts', *Academy of Management Review*, 22(4): 853–86.

Mitchie, D. (1998) *The Invisible Persuaders*. London: Bantam Press.

Mittal, V., Sambandam, R. and Dholakia, U.M. (2010) 'Does media coverage of Toyota recalls reflect reality?', http://blogs.hbr.org/research/2010/03/does-media-coverage-of-toyota.html [Accessed 1 Dec. 2011].

Moffatt, G. (2008) 'Brands influence choice, so why should social marketing not?', http://radaris.co.uk/p/Giles/Moffatt/ [Accessed 1 Feb. 2011 – no longer available in full].

Molleda, J.C. (2009) 'Global public relations', www.instituteforpr.org/global-public-relations/ [Accessed 27 May 2016].

Moloney, K. (2000) *Rethinking Public Relations: The Spin and the Substance*. Abingdon: Routledge.

Moloney, K. (2006) *Rethinking Public Relations: PR Propaganda and Democracy*, 2nd edn. Abingdon: Routledge.

Moloney, K. (2009) 'Public affairs', in R. Tench and L. Yeomans (eds), *Exploring Public Relations*, 2nd edn. London: FT/Prentice Hall, pp. 441–61.

Moloney, K. (2012) 'Dissent and protest public relations', https://research.bournemouth.ac.uk/wp-content/uploads/2013/10/Dissent-and-public-relations-Bournemouth-University.pdf [Accessed 21 Mar. 2017].

Momorella, S. and Woodall, I. (2003) 'Tips for an effective online newsroom', *Public Relations Tactics*, May: 6.

Monaghan, B. (2011) '6 ways PR has changed for the better', www.inkhouse.net/six-reasonspr-has-changed-for-the-better/ [Accessed 1 Dec. 2011].

Monck, A. and Hanley, M. (2008) *Can You Trust the Media?* London: Icon.

Money, K.G., Hillenbrand, C., Day, M.B. and Magnan, G.M. (2010) 'Exploring reputation of B2B partnerships: Extending the study of reputation from the perception of single firms to the perception of inter-firm partnerships', *Industrial Marketing Management*, 39(5): 761–8.

Montagu Smith, N. (2006) 'Giving something back', *CorpComms*, May: 27–31.

Moore, L. (2014) 'One vision', *PR Week*, Oct.: 29–31.

Moore, S. (2011) 'Bawdy tittle tattle has always been part of our press – let's not lose it', *Guardian*, 16 July: 39.

Morgan, M. (2011) 'What lies ahead for consumer PR?', *PR Week*, 10 June, http://toppragencies.prweek.co.uk/Consumer-table.aspx [Accessed 1 Dec. 2011].

Moriarty, S.E. (1997) 'The Big Idea: Creativity in public relations', in C.L. Caywood (ed.), *The Handbook of Strategic Public Relations and Integrated Communications*. New York: McGraw-Hill, pp. 554–63.

Morris, T. and Goldsworthy, S. (2012) *PR Today: The Authoritative Guide to Public Relations*. Basingstoke: Palgrave Macmillan.

Morton, J. (2006) 'Internal branding and experiential marketing', www.jackmorton.com [Accessed 28 Nov. 2006].

Moss, D. and DeSanto, B. (eds) (2002) *Public Relations Cases: International Perspectives*. London: Routledge.

Moss, D. and Warnaby, G. (1997) 'A strategic perspective for public relations', in P.J. Kitchen (ed.), *Public Relations: Principles and Practice*. London: Thomson, pp. 43–73.

Moss, D., Ashford, R. and Shani, N. (2003) 'The forgotten sector: Uncovering the role of public relations in SMEs', *Journal of Communication Management*, 8(2): 197–210.

Moss, D., Newman, A. and DeSanto, B. (2004) 'Defining and refining the core elements of management in public relations/corporate communications context: What do communication managers do?', 11th International Public Relations Research Symposium, Lake Bled, Slovenia, 1–4 July.

Moss, D.A., Newman, A. and DeSanto, B. (2005) 'What do communications managers do? Refining the core elements of management in a public relations/communications context', *Journal of Mass Communication Quarterly*, 82: 873–90.

Moss, D., Powell, M. and DeSanto, B. (2010) *Public Relations Cases: International Perspectives*. London: Routledge.

Moynihan, M. and Hathi, S. (2015) 'Internal communications: Emerging trends and the use of technology', http://cdn2.hubspot.net/hub/301060/file-544707668-pdf/Whitepapers_PDF/Survey_Report_Final.pdf [Accessed 3 May 2016].

Mulholland, N. (2011) 'Market watch', *PR Week*, 10 June, http://toppragencies.prweek.co.uk/Consumer-table.aspx [Accessed 1 Dec. 2011].

Mumford, J. (2014) 'Customer complaints – they are just the tip of the iceberg!', *Market Research World*, www.marketresearchworld.net/content/view/1617/74/ [Accessed 16 June 2016].

Mumsnet (2011) 'Dear mn hq why is a government posting on mn?', www.mumsnet.com/Talk/site_stuff/1347966-dear-mn-hq-why-is-a-government-department-posting-onmn?pg=1 [Accessed 1 Dec. 2011].

Murphy, C. (1999) 'Brand values can build on charity ties', *Marketing Week*, 25 Mar.: 41–2.

Murphy, C. (2011) 'Comms director survey: Managing the chatter', *PR Week*, 30 June, www.prweek.com/uk/features/1077605/Comms-Directors-Survey-Managing-chatter [Accessed 1 Dec. 2011].

Murphy, F. (1999) 'Service with a smile', *Guardian*, 28 Oct.: 14–15.

Murray, K. (2003) 'Reputation – managing the single greatest risk facing business today', *Journal of Communication Management*, 8(2): 142–9.

Murray, K. (2006) 'Reputation 2.0', Behind the Spin Conference, College of St Mark and St John, Plymouth, Devon, 8 Sept.

Murray, K. and White, J. (2004) *CEO Views on Reputation Management: A Report on the Value of Public Relations, as Perceived by Organisational Leaders*. London: Chime Communications.

Murray, K. and White, J. (2005) 'CEO views on reputation management', *Journal of Communication Management*, 9(4): 348–58.

Murray-Leslie, N. (2007) 'Adapting to the concept of social responsibility', *Profile*, Jan./Feb.: 10.

Muthuri, J. (2008) 'Participation and accountability in corporate community involvement programmes: A research agenda', *Community Development Journal*, Apr., www.researchgate.net/publication/30934851 [Accessed 5 June 2016].

Nayan, L.M., Samsudin, K.N., Othman, S.S. and Tiung, L.K. (2012) 'The need for public relations professional competencies in Europe and Asia', *International Journal of Social Sciences*, 6(1): 45–59.

Noor Al-Deen, H.S. and Hendricks, J.A. (2011) *Social Media: Usage and Impact*. Plymouth: Lexington Books.

NSMC (2015) 'What is social marketing', www.thensmc.com/content/what-social-marketing-1 [Accessed 15 Dec. 2015].

NUJ (2011) 'Code of Practice', http://media.gn.apc.org/nujcode.html [Accessed 31 Dec. 2011].

Office of National Statistics (2016) 'Internet users in the UK: 2016', www.ons.gov.uk/businessindustryandtrade/itandinternetindustry/bulletins/internetusers/2016 [Accessed 21 Mar. 2017].

Office of National Statistics (2017) 'Population and migration', www.ons.gov.uk/peoplepopulationandcommunity/populationandmigration [Accessed 21 Mar. 2017].

Okun, B. (2011) '3 benefits of earning your accreditation in PR', www.ragan.com/Speechwriting/Articles/3_benefits_of_earning_your_Accreditation_in_PR_43396.aspx [Accessed 1 Dec. 2011].

Oliver, A. (2013) 'From nudging to budging: Using behavioural economics to inform public sector policy', *Journal of Social Policy*, 42(4): 685–700.

O'Malley, H. (1999) 'Charity begins at work', *Human Resources*, Apr.: 46–9.

ONS (2017) www.ons.gov.uk/ [Accessed 1 Dec. 2011].

Oriella (2011) 'The state of journalism in 2011', *Oriella PR Network*, www.oriellaprnetwork. com/sites/default/files/research/Oriella-Digital-Journalism-Study-2011_1.pdf [Accessed 14 July 2011].

O'Rourke, C. (2011) 'The value of reputation', *PR Week*, 14 Sept., www.prweek.com/uk/league_tables/1089931/Charlie-ORourke-AlMediaComms-value-reputation/ [Accessed 1 Dec. 2011].

O'Shaughnessy, N. (1996) 'Social propaganda and social marketing: A critical difference?', *European Journal of Marketing*, 30(10/11): 54–67.

Ouwersloot, H. and Duncan, T. (2008) *Integrated Marketing Communications*. Maidenhead: McGraw Hill.

Owyang, J. (2011) 'Data: Composition of a corporate social media team', www.webstrategist. com/blog/2011/12/22/data-composition-of-a-corporate-social-media-team/ [Accessed 31 Dec. 2011].

Paine, K.D. (2007a) *Measuring Public Relationships: The Data-Driven Communicators Guide to Success*. Berlin, NH: K.D. Paine & Partners.

Paine, K.D. (2007b) 'The Measurement Standard', *How to Measure Social Media Relations: The More Things Change, the More they Remain the Same*. Gainesville, FL: Institute for Public Relations.

Paine, K.D. (2011a) *Measure What Matters: Online Tools for Understanding Customers, Social Media, Engagement, and Key Relationships*. New York: John Wiley & Sons.

Paine, K.D. (2011b) http://kdpaine.blogs.com/themeasurementstandard [Accessed 1 Dec. 2011].

Palenchar, M.J. (2010) 'Risk communication', in R.L. Heath (ed.), *The Sage Handbook of Public Relations*, 2nd edn. London: Sage, pp. 447–61.

Palotta, D. (2011) 'A logo is not a brand', http://blogs.hbr.org/pallotta/2011/06/a-logo-is-not-a-brand.html [Accessed 1 Dec. 2011].

Papathanassopoulos, S., Negrine, R., Mancini, P., and Holtz-Bacha, C. (2007) 'Political communication in the era of professionalisation', in R. Negrine, C. Holtz-Bacha, P. Mancini and S. Papatha (eds), *The Professionalisation of Political Communication*. Bristol: Intellect Limited, pp. 9–26.

Pariser, E. (2015) 'Did Facebook's big new study kill my filter bubble thesis?', https://backchannel.com/facebook-published-a-big-new-study-on-the-filter-bubble-here-s-what-it-says-ef31a292da95#.9kl0t6q7d [Accessed 21 Mar. 2017].

Parvanta, C., Nelson, D.E., Parvanta, S.A. and Harner, R.N. (2011) *Essentials of Public Health Communication*. London: Jones & Bartlett Publishers.

Parvin, P. (2007) *Lobbying: Friend or Foe?* Hansard Society. London: Ellwood Atfield, www. ellwoodatfield.com/pdf/Lobbying_Friend_or_Foe_Report.pdf [Accessed 21 Mar. 2017].

Patterson, M. (2014) '4 ways to use social media in public relations', www.socialmediaexaminer. com/social-media-in-public-relations/ [Accessed 17 Mar. 2016].

Payne, N. (2011) 'Public relations across cultures', allaboutpublicrelations.com [Accessed 15 Nov. 2011].

Pearlfinders Index (2011) 'Q3 2011 – PR highlights', www.pearlfinders.com/ [Accessed 1 Dec. 2011].

Penn, M. (2007) *Microtrends*. London: Penguin.

Perrin, A. and Duggan, M. (2015) 'Americans' internet access: 2000–2015', www.pewinternet.org/2015/06/26/americans-internet-access-2000-2015/ [Accessed 27 May 2016].

Peter, J.P., Olson, J.C. and Grunert, K.G. (1999) *Consumer Behaviour and Marketing Strategy* (European edn). Maidenhead: McGraw-Hill.

Petty, R.E. and Cacioppo, J.T. (1986) 'The elaboration likelihood model of persuasion', in L. Berkowitz (ed.), *Advances in Experimental Social Psychology*. New York: Academic Press, pp. 123–205.

Pew Research Center (2010) 'A portrait of generation news', www.pewresearch.org/millennials [Accessed 1 Dec. 2011].

Phillimore, M. (2012) 'Financial communications', in A. Theaker (ed.), *The Public Relations Handbook*, 4th edn. Abingdon: Routledge, pp. 311–30.

Phillips, D. and Young, P. (2009) *Online Public Relations*, 2nd edn. London: Kogan Page.

Phillips, J.J. (2011) *Return on Investment in Training and Performance Improvement Programs*, 2nd edn. Abingdon: Routledge.

Pickton, D. and Broderick, A. (2005) *Integrated Marketing Communications*, 2nd edn. Harlow: FT/Prentice Hall.

Pieczka, M. (2006a) '"Chemistry" and the public relations industry: An exploration of the concept of jurisdiction and issues arising', in J. L'Etang and M. Pieczka (eds), *Public Relations: Critical Debates and Contemporary Practice*. Abingdon: Routledge, pp. 303–27.

Pieczka, M. (2006b) 'Paradigms, systems theory, and public relations', in J. L'Etang and M. Pieczka (eds), *Public Relations: Critical Debates and Contemporary Practice*. Mahwah, NJ: Lawrence Erlbaum Associates, pp. 333–57.

Pink, D.H. (1998) 'Metaphor marketing', *Fast Company*, 31 Mar., www.fastcompany.com/magazine/14/zaltman.html [Accessed 1 Dec. 2011].

Pinsent, M. (2011) 'Comms lines are blurring', *PR Week US*, 12 May, www.prweek.com/uk/features/1069445/Mark-Pinsent-Shine-Communications-Comms-lines-blurring/ [Accessed 1 Dec. 2011].

Policy Exchange (2014) 'A portrait of modern Britain', www.policyexchange.org.uk/publications/category/item/a-portrait-of-modern-britain [Accessed 16 June 2015].

Portway, S. (1995) 'Corporate social responsibility: The case for active stakeholder management', in N. A. Hart (ed.), *Strategic Public Relations*. London: Macmillan.

Powell, G., Groves, S. and Dimos, J. (2011) *ROI of Social Media: How to Improve the Return on your Social Marketing Investment*. New York: John Wiley & Sons.

PRCA (Public Relations Consultants Association) (2016a) 'PRCA announces "16 for 16": 16 recommendations for great communications in 2016', 14 Jan., http://news.prca.org.uk/prca-announces-16-for-16-16-recommendations-for-great-communications-in-2016/ [Accessed 7 Mar. 2016].

PRCA (2016b) *PR Census 2016*. London: PRCA. Available from: http://news.prca.org.uk/pr-census-2016-reveals-that-the-pr-industry-is-worth-129bn [Accessed 9 June 2016].

PRCA (2017) 'More than a third of UK PR firms still use "meaningless" AVEs for measurement', www.prweek.com/article/1424257/third-uk-pr-firms-use-meaningless-aves-measurement [Accessed 21 Mar. 2017].

PR Daily (2012) 'McDonald's sets up a Nutrition Network to change public perception about its - menu', www.prdaily.com/Awards/SpecialEdition/71.aspx [Accessed 16 Mar. 2016].

Prensky, M. (2001) 'Digital natives, digital immigrants', *On the Horizon* (MCB University Press), 9(5), Oct., www.marcprensky.com/writing/Prensky%20-%20Digital%20Natives,%20Digital %20Immigrants%20-%20Part1.pdf [Accessed 31 Dec. 2010].

Price, V. (1992) *Public Opinion*. Newbury Park, CA: Sage.

PRSA (2012) http://apps.prsa.org/AboutPRSA/publicrelationsdefined/ [Accessed 20 Sep. 2017].

Public Health Responsibility Deal (2011) www.dh.gov.uk/en/Publichealth/Publichealthres-ponsibilitydeal/index.htm [Accessed 1 Dec. 2011].

Quigley-Hicks, K. (2011) 'Being sociable on social media', http://kellyquigleyhicks.wordpress. com/2011/11/23/being-social-on-social-media/ [Accessed 1 Dec. 2011].

Quirke, B. (2001) 'Identifying the real value of communication', *Strategic Communication Management*, Feb./Mar.

Quirke, W. (1995) 'Internal communication', in N. Hart (ed.), *Strategic Public Relations*. London: Macmillan Business Press, pp. 71–94.

Rangan, V.K., Chase, L. and Karim, S. (2015) 'The truth about CSR', *Harvard Business Review*, Jan.-Feb.

Ransom, C. (2011) 'Launching a multicultural PR campaign', http://aboutpublicrelations.net [Accessed 15 Nov. 2011].

Raz, A.E. (2003) 'The slanted smile factory: Emotion management in Tokyo Disneyland', in D.A. Harper, D. Harper and H.M. Lawson (eds), *The Cultural Study of Work*. Lanham, MD: Rowman & Littlefield, pp. 210–27.

Regester Larkin (2011) *PAS 200: 2011 Crisis Management: Guidance and Good Practice. An Assessment*. London: Regester Larkin.

Riel, C.B.M. van (1995) *Principles of Corporate Communication*. London: Prentice Hall.

Riel, C.B.M. van and Balmer, J.M.T. (1997) 'Corporate identity: The concept, its measurement and management', *European Journal of Marketing*, 31(5/6): 340–55.

Riel, C.B.M. van and Fombrun, C.J. (2007) *Essentials of Corporate Communication*. London: Routledge.

Riemersma, F. (2015) 'Communicate your strategy in 3 popular ways', http://headlines.uk. com/infographic-fresh-evidence-on-value-of-employee-engagement/#more-8260 [Accessed 3 May 2016].

Ries, A. and Ries, L. (2002) *The Fall of Advertising and the Rise of PR*. New York: Harper Business.

Ritter, A. (2015) 'PESO: The new-age PR model', http://thinkpyxl.com/blog/peso-model-pr [Accessed 4 May 2016].

Robert, B. and Lajtha, C. (2002) 'A new approach to crisis management', *Journal of Contin-gencies and Crisis Management*, 10: 181–91.

Roberts, D. (2010) 'Post-truth politics', http://grist.org/article/2010-03-30-post-truth-politics/ [Accessed 21 Mar. 2017].

Robertson, J. (2014) 'Communication World Online 12–16', http://cw.iabc.com/ [Accessed 3 May 2016].

Robinson, J. and Kirkcaldy, A. (2004) *Passive Smoking Qualitative Research in Merseyside*, Research Report 99/05. University of Liverpool, www.liv.ac.uk/haccru/reports/ps_final_report.pdf [Accessed 1 Dec. 2011].

Rockland, D. (2011) 'A world without advertising value equivalents', Ketchum Pleon, www. ketchum.com/David_Rockland_Barcelona_Principles_A_World_Without_AVEs [Accessed 1 Dec. 2011].

Rodgers, S., Thorson, E. and Jin, Y. (2008) 'Social science theories of theories of traditional and internet advertising', in D.W. Stacks and M.B. Salwen (eds), *An Integrated Approach to Communication Theory and Research*, 2nd edn. Abingdon: Routledge.

Rogers, D. (2007) 'Honesty on display at ethics debate', *PR Week*, 21 Feb., www.pr week. com/uk/opinion/634571/OPINION-Honesty-display-Ethics-Debate/ [Accessed 1 Dec. 2011].

Rogers, D. (2011) 'Marketing and media focus: What keeps these guys awake at night', *PR Week*, www.prweek.com/uk/features/1081011/ [Accessed 1 Dec. 2011].

Rogers, E.M. (2003) *Diffusion of Innovations*, 5th edn. New York: New York Free Press.

Royal College of Physicians (2010) 'Passive smoking and children', www.rcplondon.ac.uk/news-media/press-releases/passive-smoking-major-health-hazard-children-says-rcp [Accessed 1 Dec. 2011].

Rozwell, C. (2010) 'Employee expression on social media – red herring or real problem?', http://blogs.gartner.com/carol_rozwell [Accessed 13 Oct. 2011].

Sanabria, J.C. and Arámburo-Lizárraga, J. (2017) 'Enhancing 21st century skills with AR: Using the gradual immersion method to develop collaborative creativity', *EURASIA Journal of Mathematics Science and Technology Education*, 13(2): 487–501.

Santi, A. (2006) 'Made to measure', *PR Business*, 25 May: 15–17.

Saunders, M., Lewis, P. and Thornhill, A. (2000) *Research Methods for Business Students*, 2nd edn. Harlow: FT/Prentice Hall.

Schein, E.H. (1991) 'What is culture?', in P. Frost, L.F. Moore, M.R. Louis, C.C. Lundberg and J. Martin (eds), *Reframing Organisational Culture*. Newbury Park, CA: Sage, pp. 243–53.

Schneider, J. (2001) *New Product Launch Report*. Boston, MA: Schneider & Associates with Boston University.

Schneider, S.C. and Barsoux, J.-L. (2003) *Managing across Cultures*, 2nd edn. London: Prentice Hall.

Sebastian, M. (2011a) '42 more signs you work in PR', *PR Daily*, 27 Apr., www.prdaily.com [Accessed 13 Oct. 2011].

Sebastian, M. (2011b) 'PRSA unveils campaign to redefine public relations', http://prdaily. com/Main/Articles/PRSA_unveils_campaign_to_redefine_public_relations_10112.aspx [Accessed 1 Dec. 2011].

Sebenius, J.K. (2002) 'The hidden challenges of cross-border negotiations', *Harvard Business Review*, Mar.: 76–85.

Seiple, P. (2016) 'How to leverage social media for public relations success', Hubspot, http://cdn2.hubspot.net/hub/53/file-13204195-pdf/docs/hubspot_social_media_pr_ebook. pdf [Accessed 17 Mar. 2016].

Seitel, F.P. (1998) *The Practice of Public Relations*, 7th edn. Upper Saddle River, NJ: Prentice Hall.

Sha, B.L. (2011) '2010 Practice analysis: Professional competencies and work categories in PR today', *Public Relations Review*, 37: 187–96.

Shah, R. (2011) 'What kind of work are clients asking for?', *PR Week*, 10 June, http://toppragencies.prweek.co.uk/Consumer-table.aspx [Accessed 1 Dec. 2011].

Shaw, T. (2016) 'Using social media for public relations', www.slideshare.net/Quorumstrategic/using-social-media-for-media-relations-3026164 [Accessed 17 Mar. 2016].

Shepherd, C. (2011) 'From classroom to boardroom: An investigation of skills required of PR practitioners', unpublished dissertation, UCLAN.

Skinner, G. and Mludzinski, T. (2011) 'Understanding society: An extraordinary year', Ipsos MORI Social Research Institute, www.ipsos-mori.com/DownloadPublication/1452_SRI_Understanding_Society_Winter_2011.pdf [Accessed 1 Dec. 2011].

Smith, B. (2015) 'How PR careers evolve', 20 Nov., www.prmoment.com/3252/how-pr-careers-evolve.aspx [Accessed 21 Nov. 2015].

Smith, L. (2012) 'Business-to-business public relations', in A. Theaker (ed.), *The Public Relations Handbook*, 4th edn. Abingdon: Routledge, pp. 370–86.

Smith, M. (2014) 'Introduction: Theories of group and movement organizing', in M. Smith (ed.), *Group Politics and Social Movements in Canada*, 2nd edn. Toronto: University of Toronto Press, pp. xi–xxxi.

Smith, R.D. (2005) *Strategic Planning for Public Relations*, 2nd edn. Mahwah, NJ: Lawrence Erlbaum Associates.

Smith, S. (2010) 'Death of internal communications', www.hillandknowlton.com/content/exaggerated-reports-death-internal-communications [Accessed 13 Oct. 2011].

Smythe, J. (2004) 'Engaging people at work to drive strategy and change', unpublished report, McKinsey, 3 Nov.

Somerville, I. and Ramsey, P. (2012) 'Public relations and politics', in A. Theaker (ed.), *The Public Relations Handbook*, 4th edn. Abingdon: Routledge, pp. 38–59.

Spangler, T. (2016) *One Step Ahead: Private Equity and Hedge Funds After the Global Financial Crisis*. London: Oneworld.

Springston, J.K. and Keyton, J. (2001) 'Public relations field dynamics', in R.L. Heath (ed.), *The Handbook of Public Relations*. London: Sage, pp. 115–26.

Sriramesh, K. and Verčič, D. (2009) *The Global Public Relations Handbook: Theory, Research, and Practice* (expanded and revised edn). London: Routledge.

Stacey, R.D. (2003) *Strategic Management and Organisational Dynamics: The Challenge of Complexity*, 4th edn. London: Pearson Education.

Stateman, A. (2003) 'A Fox reporter tells all!', *Public Relations Tactics*, May: 15.

Stauber, J. and Rampton, S. (2004) *Toxic Sludge is Good for You*. London: Robinson.

Steers, R.M., Sánchez-Runde, C.J. and Nardon, L. (2010) *Management across Cultures: Challenges and Strategies*. Cambridge: Cambridge University Press.

Stern, S. (2009) 'The hot air of CSR', *FT.Comn*, Feb.

Steyn, B. (2011) 'Integrated reporting and strategic public relations', www.prconversations.com/index.php/2011/11/integrated-reporting-and-strategic-public-relations/ [Accessed 1 Dec. 2011].

Stockholm Accords (2010) www.globalalliancepr.org/content [Accessed 19 Jan. 2011].

Stone, N. (1995) *The Management and Practice of Public Relations*. London: Macmillan Business.

Strachan, J. and Kelley, N. (2014) 'Integrated marketing communications', in R. Tench and L. Yeomans, *Exploring Public Relations*, 3rd edn. London: Pearson, pp. 395–409.

Stringer, E.T. (2014) *Action Research*, 4th edn. London: Sage.

Stringfellow, E. (2016) 'Social dialogue: An "essential dimension" of diversity management in continental Europe?', in Al Klarsfeld, E.S. Ng, L.A.E. Booys, L.C. Christiansen and B. Kuvaas (eds), *Research Handbook of International and Comparative Perspective on Diversity Management*. Cheltenham: Edward Elgar, pp. 18–44.

Strömbäck, J. and Kiousis, S. (2011) 'Political public relations: Defining and mapping an emergent field', in J. Strömbäck and S. Kiousis (eds), *Political Public Relations: Principles and Applications*. Abingdon: Routledge, pp. 1–32.

Sudhaman, A. (2010) 'Is internal communications dead?', www.holmesreport.com/featurestories-info/9687/Analysis-Is-Internal-Comms-Dead.aspx [Accessed 13 Oct. 2011].

Sullivan, S.E. and Arthur, M.B. (2006) 'The evolution of the boundaryless career concept: Examining physical and psychological mobility', *Journal of Vocational Behavior*, 69(1): 19–29.

Sung, M. (2007) 'Toward a model of scenario building from a public relations perspective', in E.L. Toth (ed.), *The Future of Excellence in Public Relations and Communication Management: Challenges for the Next Generation*. Mahwah, NJ: Lawrence Erlbaum Associates, pp. 173–98.

Surma, A. (2006) 'Challenging unreliable narrators: Writing and public relations', in J. L'Etang and M. Pieczka (eds), *Public Relations: Critical Debates and Contemporary Practice*. Abingdon: Routledge, pp. 41–60.

Sutherland, S. (1992) *Irrationality: The Enemy within*. London: Constable.

Swann, P. (2010) *Cases in Public Relations Management*. New York: Routledge.

Sweetser, K.D. (2011) 'Digital political public relations', in J. Strömbäck and S. Kiousis (eds), *Political Public Relations: Principles and Applications*. Abingdon: Routledge, pp. 293–313.

Szondi, G. (2006) 'International context of public relations', in R. Tench and L. Yeomans (eds), *Exploring Public Relations*. London: FT/Prentice Hall, pp. 113–40.

Szondi, G. (2009) 'International context of public relations', in R. Tench and L. Yeomans (eds), *Exploring Public Relations*, 2nd edn. London: FT/Prentice Hall, pp. 117–46.

Szondi, G. and Theilmann, R. (2009) 'Research and evaluation in public relations', in R. Tench and L. Yeomans (eds), *Exploring Public Relations*, 2nd edn. London: FT/Prentice Hall, pp. 198–221.

Tafara, E. (2012) 'Foreword: Observations about the crisis and reform', in El Ferran, N. Moloney, J. Hill and J.C. Coffee, Jr. (eds), *The Regulatory Aftermath of the Global Financial Crisis*. Cambridge: Cambridge University Press, pp. xi–xxvi.

Taylor Herring (2009) www.taylorherring.com/blog/index.php/2009/01/50-top-publicity-stunts/ [Accessed 1 Dec. 2011].

Tench, R (2014) 'Managing community involvement programmes', in R. Tench and L. Yeomans (eds), *Exploring Public Relations*, 3rd edn. London: Pearson, pp. 275–99.

Tench, R. and Fawkes, J. (2005) 'Mind the gap, exploring different attitudes to public relations education from employers, academics and alumni', Alan Rawel/CIPR Academic Conference, Lincoln.

Tench, R. and Yeomans, L. (eds) (2006) *Exploring Public Relations*. London: FT/Prentice Hall.

Tench, R. and Yeomans, L. (2009) 'What next? Future issues for PR', in R. Tench and L. Yeomans (eds), *Exploring Public Relations*, 2nd edn. London: FT/Prentice Hall, pp. 633–44.

Tench R. and Yeomans L. (eds) (2017) *Exploring Public Relations*, 4th edn. London: Pearson.

Thaler, R. and Sunstein, C. (2008) *Nudge: Improving Decisions about Health, Wealth and Happiness*. New Haven, CT: Yale University Press.

Theaker, A. (2001) *The Public Relations Handbook*. London: Routledge, pp. 123–6.

Theaker, A. (2004) *The Public Relations Handbook*, 2nd edn. Abingdon: Routledge.

Theaker, A. (ed.) (2007) *The Public Relations Handbook*, 3rd edn. Abingdon: Routledge.

Theaker, A. (ed.) (2012) *The Public Relations Handbook*, 4th edn. Abingdon: Routledge.

Theaker, A. (2016) 'Future challenges for PR', in A. Theaker (ed.), *The Public Relations Handbook*, 5th edn. Abingdon: Routledge, pp. 489–99.

Thomas, M.P. and McElroy, M.W. (2016) *The MultiCapital Scorecard: Rethinking Organizational Performance*. White River Junction, VT: Chelsea Green Publishing.

Thring, O. (2013) 'McDonald's: A healthier, happier meal – or just good PR?', *Guardian*, www.theguardian.com/commentisfree/2013/jan/29/mcdonalds-healthier-happier-meal-good-pr [Accessed 16 Mar. 2016].

Todorova, A. (2002) 'Technique: Inbox of tricks for sending a pitch', *PR Week US*, 22 July, www.brandrepublic.com/features/153556/ [Accessed 1 Dec. 2011].

Tyler, J. (2011) 'The value of conversations with employees', *Gallup Management Journal*, 30 June.

Van der Heijden, K. (2011) *Scenarios: The Art of Strategic Conversation*, 2nd edn. New York: John Wiley & Sons.

van Ruler, B. (2016) 'Agile strategic communication frame', http://bettekevanruler.nl/strategic-communication-frame/ [Accessed 21 Mar. 2017].

van Ruler, B., and Verčič, D. (2002) 'The Bled manifesto on public relations', 9th International Public Relations Research Symposium, Bled, Slovenia, July.

van Ruler, B. Verčič, D., Butschi, G. and Flodin, B. (2002) 'The European body of knowledge on public relations/communication management: The report of the Delphi research project 2000', European Association for Public Relations Education and Research, June.

van Ruler, B., Verčič, A.T. and Verčič, D. (2008) 'Public relations metrics measurement and evaluation – an overview', in B. van Ruler and A.T. Verčič (eds), *Public Relations Metrics: Research and Evaluation*. New York: Routledge, pp. 1–18.

Vasquez, G.M. and Taylor, M. (2001) 'Research perspectives on "the public"', in R.L. Heath (ed.), *The Handbook of Public Relations*. London: Sage, pp. 139–54.

Verčič, D. (2004) www.prstudies.com/weblog/2004/06/index.html [Accessed 31 Dec. 2011].

Verčič, D. (2014) 'Intercultural and multicultural context of public relations', in R. Tench and L. Yeomans (eds), *Exploring Public Relations*, 3rd edn. London: Pearson, pp. 70–82.

Waddington, S. (2015) 'Why China has a five year lead in social media and e-commerce', https://econsultancy.com/blog/66512-why-china-has-a-five-year-lead-in-social-media-ecommerce/ [Accessed 6 June 2016].

Wakefield, R.I. (2001) 'Effective public relations in the multinational organisation', in R.L. Heath (ed.), *The Handbook of Public Relations*. London: Sage, pp. 639–47.

Wakeman, S. (2012) 'Public sector public relations', in A. Theaker (ed.), *The Public Relations Handbook*, 4th edn. Abingdon: Routledge, pp. 331–53.

Wall, I. (2000) 'Does your charity take dirty money?', *Big Issue*, 24 Jan.: 19–20.

Walser, M.G. (2004) *Brand Strength: Building and Testing Models Based on Experiential Information*. Wiesbaden: Deutscher Universitats-Verlai.

Watson, J. (2003) *Media Communication: An Introduction to Theory and Process*, 2nd edn. London: Palgrave.

Watson, T. (2011) 'The evolution of evaluation – the accelerating march towards the measurement of public relations effectiveness', 2nd International History of Public Relations Conference, http://blogs.bournemouth.ac.uk/historyofpr/proceedings/ [Accessed 1 Dec. 2011].

Watson, T. (2015) 'PR's early response to the "information superhighway": The IPRA narrative', *Communication and Society*, 28(1): 1–12.

Watson, T. and Noble, P. (2007) *Evaluating Public Relations: A Best Practice Guide to Public Relations*. London: Kogan Page.

Watson, T. and Zerfass, A. (2011) 'Return on investment in public relations: A critique of concepts used by practitioners from communication and management sciences perspectives', *PRism*, 8(1), www.prismjournal.org/fileadmin/8_1/Watson_Zerfass.pdf [Accessed 1 Dec. 2011].

Watson Wyatt (2006) 'Effective communication: Indicators of financial performance 2005/ 2006', Communication ROI Study, www.watsonwyatt.com [Accessed 31 Dec. 2008].

Weinreich, N.K. (2006) 'What is social marketing?', www.social-marketing.com/whatis.html [Accessed 15 Dec. 2015].

Wells, T. (2006) 'Africa: A comms sector on the rise', *PR Week*, 10 Aug., www.prweek.com/ uk/analysis/576166/ [Accessed 1 Dec. 2011].

Wendt, O. and Lloyd, L.L. (2011) 'Definitions, history and legal aspects of assisted technology', in L.L. Lloyd, R.W. Quist and O. Wendt (eds), *Assistive Technology: Principles and Allocations for Communication Disorders and Special Education*. Bingley, West Yorkshire: Emerald Group, pp. 1–22.

Wenger, E.C. and Snyder, W.M. (2000) 'Communities of practice: The organisational frontier', *Harvard Business Review*, Jan.–Feb.: 139–45.

Werbel, J.D. and Wortman, M.S. (2000) 'Strategic philanthropy: Responding to negative portrayals of corporate social responsibility', *Corporate Reputation Review*, 3(2): 124–36.

Wheeler, D. and Sillanpaa, M. (1997) *The Stakeholder Corporation*. London: Pitman Publishing.

White, J. (2000) 'Psychology and public relations', in D. Moss, D, Verčič and G. Warnaby (eds), *Perspectives on Public Relations Research*. London: Routledge, pp. 145–55.

White, J. (2011) 'PR 2020: The Future of Public Relations', appendix 3, www.cipr.co.uk/ sites/ default/files/PR%202020%20Final%20Report_0.pdf [Accessed 16 Apr. 2012].

Wicks, N. (2011) 'Mixed response from agency bosses as Guardian cracks down on PR plugs', *PR Week*, 11 Aug., http://prweek.co.uk/uk/news/1084250/Mixed-response-agency- bosses-Guardian-cracks-down-PR-plugs/ [Accessed 1 Dec. 2011].

Wilcox, D.L. (2006) 'The landscape of today's global public relations', *AnÁlisi*, 34: 67–85, www.raco.cat/index.php/Analisi/article/download/55444/64576 [Accessed 27 May 2016].

Wilcox, D.L. and Cameron, G.T. (2006) *Public Relations: Strategies and Tactics*, 8th edn. Boston, MA: Allyn & Bacon.

Wilcox, D.L., Cameron, G.T., Ault, P.H. and Agee, W.K. (2003) *Public Relations, Strategies and Tactics*, 7th edn. Boston, MA: Allyn & Bacon.

Williams, K.C. (1981) *Behavioural Aspects of Marketing*. Oxford: Heinemann Professional.

Williamson, L. (2004) 'Cause-related marketing: Back to school', *PR Week*, 16 Jan., www.prweek. com/uk/news/199861/Cause-related-marketing-Back-school/ [Accessed 1 Dec. 2011].

Willis, P. (2014) 'Public relations and the consumer', in R. Tench and L. Yeomans (eds), *Exploring Public Relations*, 3rd edn. London: Pearson, pp. 329–43.

Wilson, E. (2016) 'Be afraid', *Influence* (CIPR), Q2.

Windahl, S., Signitzer, B. and Olsen, J.T. (1992) *Using Communication Theory*. London: Sage.

Wood, E. (2012) 'Public relations and corporate communications', in A. Theaker (ed.), *The Public Relations Handbook*, 4th edn. Abingdon: Routledge, pp. 107–25.

Wood, E. and Somerville, I. (2012) 'Corporate identity', in A. Theaker (ed.), *The Public Relations Handbook*, 4th edn. Abingdon: Routledge, pp. 144–71.

Wood, E. and Somerville, I. (2016) 'Corporate identity', in A. Theaker (ed.), *The Public Relations Handbook*, 5th edn. Abingdon: Routledge, pp. 144–71.

Woodward, J. (2011) 'Richard Edelman: Public relations must evolve or get left behind', *Public Relations Tactics*, 1 July.

Worcester, B. (2007) 'Internet not the be all and end all', *Profile*, May/June: 14.

Wysocki, R.K. (2011) *Effective Project Management: Traditional, Agile, Extreme*, 6th edn. Indianopolis, IN: John Wiley & Sons.

Yaxley, H. (2009) 'Societal perspectives', http://greenbanana.info/career/2011/12/05/the-social-dimension-of-csr/ [Accessed 31 Dec. 2011].

Yaxley, H. (2012a) 'Digital public relations – revolution or evolution?', in A. Theaker (ed.), *The Public Relations Handbook*, 4th edn. Abingdon: Routledge, pp. 411–22.

Yaxley, H. (2012b) 'Risk, issues and crisis management', in A. Theaker (ed.), *The Public Relations Handbook*, 4th edn. Abingdon: Routledge, pp. 154–74.

Yaxley, H. (2012c) 'Digital public relations', in A. Theaker and H. Yaxley (eds), *The Public Relations Strategic Toolkit*, 1st edn. Abingdon: Routledge, pp. 221–34.

Yaxley, H. (2015) 'Investing in sustainable professional development', in S. Hall (ed.), *Future-Proof*, pp.151–60, www.futureproofingcomms.co.uk [Accessed Mar. 2017].

Yaxley, H. (2016) 'Using new technology effectively in public relations', in A. Theaker (ed.), *The Public Relations Handbook*, 5th edn. Abingdon: Routledge, pp. 443–69.

Yeomans, L. (2009) 'Public sector communication and social marketing', in R. Tench and L. Yeomans (eds), *Exploring Public Relations*, 2nd edn. London: FT/Prentice Hall, pp. 577–99.

Yeomans, L. and Carthew, W. (2014) 'Internal communication', in R. Tench and L. Yeomans (eds), *Exploring Public Relations*, 3rd edn. London: Pearson, pp. 251–74.

Young, K., Ashby, D., Boaz, A. and Grayson, L. (2002) 'Social science and the evidence-based policy movement', *Social Policy and Society*, 1(3): 215–24.

Young, L.D. (2006) 'Urban myths and their disastrous effects on marketing', Annual Cambridge Marketing Lecture, CMC.

Young, P. (2012) 'Media relations in the social media age', in A. Theaker (ed.), *The Public Relations Handbook*, 4th edn. Abingdon: Routledge, pp. 251–72.

YouTube (2012) 'Statistics', www.youtube.com/t/press_statistics [Accessed 19 Apr. 2012].

Yu, L. (2007) *Introduction to the Semantic Web and Semantic Web Services*. Boca Raton, FL: Chapman & Hall/CRC Press.

Zack, M.H. (2002) 'Developing a knowledge strategy', in C.W. Choo and N. Bontis (eds), *The Strategic Management of Intellectual Capital and Organisational Knowledge*. New York: Oxford University Press, pp. 255–76.

Zerfass, A. (2010) 'Levels of impact and evaluation', www.communicationcontrolling.de/en/knowledge/levels-of-impact-and-evaluation.html [Accessed 9 Nov. 2010].

Zerfass, A., Tench, R., Verhoeven, P., Verčič, D. and Moreno, A. (2010) *European Communication Monitor 2010: Status Quo and Challenges for Public Relations in Europe. Results of an Empirical Survey in 46 Countries* (chart version). Brussels: EACD, EUPRERA, www.communicationmonitor.eu [Accessed 18 Nov. 2010].

Zerfass, A., Verčič, D., Verhoeven, P., Moreno, A., and Tench, R. (2015) *European Communication Monitor 2015: Creating Communication Value through Listening, Messaging and Measurement. Results of a Survey in 41 Countries*. Brussels: EACD/EUPRERA, Helios Media, www.communicationmonitor.eu/ [Accessed 30 June 2015].

Zichermann, G. and Cunningham, C. (2011) *Gamification by Design: Implementing Game Mechanics in Web and Mobile Apps*. Sebastopol, CA: O'Reilly Media.

Index

PGMO 07/24/2018